VOICES OF THE ARMY
OF THE POTOMAC

VOICES OF THE ARMY OF THE POTOMAC

Personal Reminiscences of Union Veterans

VINCENT L. BURNS

CASEMATE

Philadelphia & Oxford

Published in the United States of America and Great Britain in 2021 by
CASEMATE PUBLISHERS
1950 Lawrence Road, Havertown, PA 19083, USA
and
The Old Music Hall, 106–108 Cowley Road, Oxford OX4 1JE, UK

Hardcover Edition: ISBN 978-1-63624-072-5
Digital Edition: ISBN 978-1-63624-073-2

A CIP record for this book is available from the British Library

Printed and bound in the United States by Integrated Books International

Typeset in India by Lapiz Digital Services, Chennai.

For a complete list of Casemate titles, please contact:

CASEMATE PUBLISHERS (US)
Telephone (610) 853-9131
Fax (610) 853-9146
Email: casemate@casematepublishers.com
www.casematepublishers.com

CASEMATE PUBLISHERS (UK)
Telephone (01865) 241249
Email: casemate-uk@casematepublishers.co.uk
www.casematepublishers.co.uk

Contents

Foreword

The Civil War thrust ordinary men into extraordinary circumstances. Even those Americans who prophesied a long, deadly struggle to suppress the southern slaveholders' rebellion were altogether unprepared for the grisly scenes visited upon the nation between 1861 and 1865. In the space of four years, some 750,000, men—or nearly three percent of the population—would be killed. Many more would be maimed, diseased, or unnerved. Peach orchards became killing fields; hay mows became crowded hospital wards. In twelve brutal hours at Antietam, the war added more men to the casualty registers than had been lost in the entire U.S. War with Mexico.

Well before the muskets fell silent, drawing authority from all that they had seen, felt, and experienced, Union soldiers named themselves the rightful custodians of the Civil War's history. Soldiers supplied anxious families and civilian newspapers back home with some of the first accounts of the war. But the challenge of translating the muddle and chaos of war into clear and orderly prose proved immense. Narratives begun on patriotic stationery not infrequently lost their momentum, devolving into anguished tallies of friends and neighbors wounded and missing. In these letters, men rummaged for imperfect metaphors. Some simply attempted to catalog the war's auditory elements, believing that battle's soundscape—the crackle of musketry, the hiss of a shell, the shrill bay called the rebel yell—best conveyed its otherworldliness. Their eloquence and erudition aside, however, U.S. veterans frequently conceded their inability to render an adequate picture of combat.

Soldiers contemplated but could never completely comprehend the war's enormous scope and scale. By mounding earth into miles of entrenchments, muscling logs onto corduroy roads, and marching for miles across starkly militarized landscapes, they acquired a sense of the war's magnitude. Fighting in an army amply stocked with ethnic Germans, Irish immigrants, and old Yankees—herded into brigades that embraced Massachusetts mill workers and Pennsylvania coal miners—they looked beyond the parochial confines of their hometowns and communities (some, perhaps, for the first time) and cultivated an appreciation for the war as a national mobilization. The Army of the Potomac not only defended but embodied the Union. But again, how to reckon with all that the war had wrought in their lives? How best to preserve their personal experiences amid the proliferation of national narratives that threatened to efface their individuality? How to explain what they felt at Gettysburg, saw at Spotsylvania, and smelled at Petersburg? How to preserve the war's signal accomplishments alongside its enormous human costs?

Though most federal soldiers identified with precision what was at stake in the conflict—the fate of human slavery in the United States and the future of self-government—they yearned to understand how their performances on distant battlefields and remote picket lines wove into the war's larger tapestry. As veterans, they became the war's first, true historians—amassing large, personal libraries of personal accounts and official reports; preparing papers for regimental reunions and Grand Army campfires; consulting with former comrades to stimulate memories or confirm niggling details; collecting and displaying battlefield relics; supporting pension claims; serving on state monument commissions; and making pilgrimages back to the old killing fields. The energy and industry with which they took up this work is not merely an important index of how the war continued to occupy their minds, but a measure of their earnest desire for a complete, accurate, and honest history of the conflict. They needed to explain the war not only to future generations, but to themselves.

***

In the more than a century and a half since the war, troop movements have proved far easier to map than the war's human topography. For too long, our understanding of the Civil War as an epic, historical event has eclipsed our appreciation of it as a lived, human experience—an ordeal in which men whipsawed between hope and heartbreak, pain and pride, cynicism and conviction. For the men who suffered, sacrificed, and survived the war, its outcome was never certain; even in the months and years immediately after Appomattox, as white supremacist terrorists made a mockery of the freedom seized under fire by the formerly enslaved, the fate of Union victory remained unclear.

Quarrying the huge corpus of writing left behind by the Union's principal eastern field army, author Vincent L. Burns amplifies the voices of some men who, after battling to save the republic, joined the yet ongoing struggle to shape the war's historical memory. What emerges in the pages that follow is a multivocal account of life in the Army of the Potomac. The author asks us to read with care the words that Lincoln's legions left behind—not for what they reveal about tactics and strategy, but because they supply insight into the messy, nonlinear process by which events pass into history.

Brian Matthew Jordan

Author's Note

This is not a history of the Army of the Potomac, or any particular battle fought or campaign waged. Humbly submitted, the concern here is what these men from long ago wrote down in letters and diaries as they experienced the historic event that was the Civil War. Also, this concerns what they later remembered—or *chose* to remember—and then wrote in remembrances as the years passed and they grew older. It is in part an overview of the decades following the war as its veterans brought pen and paper together and left us their story.

As historian David W. Blight noted in *Race and Reunion: The Civil War in American Memory* (page 182), "No other historical experience in America has given rise to such a massive collection of personal narrative 'literature' written by ordinary people." This "massive collection" of memoirs, recollections, regimental histories and remembrances makes up our history of the Civil War seen through the memory of the participants. These writings contain their views on cataclysmic events, their perceptions and thinking as they lived them and later spoke of them in written form. It was important to them and whether their words align with the historical record is secondary to what they believed true and *chose* to submit as history. In an age of increased literacy, many of these men were educated, whether at West Point, Harvard or places in between. Some were not so. Some filled their pages with flowered phrases while others expressed themselves in clear, concise English. But all had something to say that, again, was important to them, as it should be with those seeking a deeper, more precise understanding of the men of that central moment in American life.

I have written of the war mostly chronologically simply to provide a frame of reference for a reader. Any conclusions or judgments expressed herein are mine and by which I'll take my stand.

I went to college in the south. Studying American History, I gravitated toward knowing particularly the past of that region I then lived in. At the time I was mildly aware of the enticing lure of the Civil War. As historian James M. McPherson noted by quoting southern writer John Bowers, "Like more than one present-day Southerner, I fought knowing more about the Civil War than I needed to know ... It was a dark abyss you might fall into and never be heard from again." Battles, campaigns and generals did not particularly interest me then. In those days my interest was centered on the South before and after the unpleasantness. After leaving school with a couple of degrees, I worked in a completely unrelated field, but always had books lying about reminding me of the research in history I didn't have time for. Then, years later and with the time, I looked at one small matter, its roots entwined in the rebellion. With notes taken and an outline, a planned paper, I figured, could be knocked out in a couple of weeks. But something happened. At first, I was unaware of the ground moving beneath me, then, suddenly, I began slipping, and as John Bowers had warned, "I myself started to slide into that deep hole of obsession from which few Civil War buffs return … I was lost."

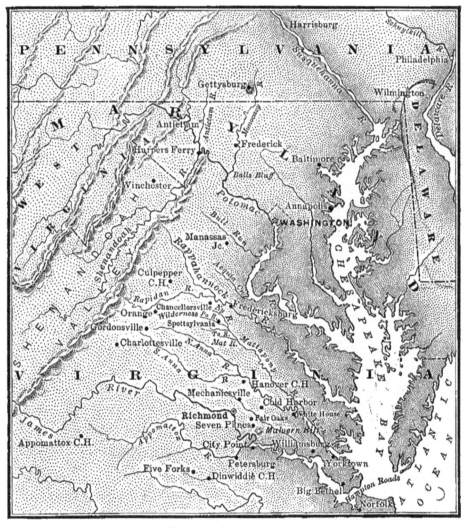

Virginia in the Civil War Era.

Preface

In Memoriam

If, looking through an old forgotten store
Of Bygone relics, you had chance to find
An old, moth-eaten cloak a soldier wore,
Would you, I wonder, with your eyes half blind
With tears, have knelt there on the oaken floor,
And cried and cried if you had chanced to find
An old moth-eaten cloak a soldier wore?

If to your eyes a picture it had brought
Of a young soldier—oh! So young and brave
Who, loving country, for that country fought,
Till at last for her his life he gave,
I think, perhaps, like me you would have caught
It to your heart—caressed it o're and o're—
That old, moth-eaten cloak a soldier wore.

Julia Fanshaw[1]

On June 23, 1864, there was a sharp action between Union and Confederate cavalry on the Virginia Peninsula. The casualties on the Union side came primarily from among the 6th New York Cavalry. The particulars of this action are not the focus here. However, the voices surrounding the event are. The day before this action Samuel Fanshaw of the 6th New York found the time to write home, having just returned from one of the war's many cavalry raids.

White House, VA
June 22, 1864

Dear Parents,
    I received your letters, Emmas of the 6th June, and fathers of the 11th. On the 20th, we were then at Dunkirk on the Mattaponi River. The next day we came to White House. We have just got back from another raid of 16 days, during which we have had some hard fighting. We left Bottoms Bridge on the 4th and got here on the 20th. The object

of the raid was to destroy the Virginia Central Railroad at Trevillians [sic] Station. Near Gordonsville we formed a large force of Cavalry and Mounted Infantry. We fought there for 2 days when the Rebs [Rebels] sent a division of infantry from Gordonsville. That night we fell back. The loss was heavy on both sides. We destroyed considerable of the road and station. We have lived on the country all through this raid. Very little rations having been furnished us, we supposed that we were coming to the White House to rest our horses and recruit up a little, for we have been on a steady go ever since we left Culpeper. There has not been three days in that time [since the beginning of the Overland Campaign] but what we have been in the saddle and a good part of the time night as well as day. But when we got to the White House we found all of Stuart's cavalry there. They shelled the place the day before, but were kept back by the gun boats and the troops that were there, composed by most of the invalid corps and darkies. The next day we put after them, we found them about three miles back, on the Bottoms Bridge and Richmond road. We had a little fighting when they retreated.

We were very short of ammunition so we did not follow them far, and as the White House is being evacuated and no more in the train, we had to be sparing of what we had. There was quite a number in the 9th N.Y. and 17th [Pennsylvania] from in our brigade wounded. The 9th lost a major, wounded in the leg. It had to be taken off above the knee yesterday. When I got about half through with my letter, we had boots and saddles again and were soon in the march. Our division took the road to Foxhall Landing. Briggs [First Sergeant Lucius C., Company K] took the road to Bottoms Bridge and I expect had some fighting last night as there was cannonading in that direction most of the night.

We are now laying in the roads near Jones Bridge, waiting for our train to come up. I expect our pickets and the rebs are popping away at each other about 1/8 of a mile from here. I think we are making for our main army to lay up a while, and draw clothing as we are pretty hard up in that line at present, having drawn nothing since we left Culpepper.

My clothes are all right yet but a few days ago my boots were almost off my feet. But I got another pair off a dead soldier. Wood is well [a friend of Samuel and the Fanshaw family], so am I. Good bye for the present. Give love to all. Your affectionate son,

Sam.[2]

Samuel Fanshaw enlisted in the 6th New York Volunteer Cavalry Regiment in New York City at the age of 22. The date was August 15, 1862, and, six days later, he was assigned to Company I. He must have learned quickly and exhibited a degree of initiative within a command that was already in the field. On November 1, just two and a half months removed from civilian life, he was promoted to corporal. Samuel rode with the regiment to Gettysburg on the last day of June 1863 and fought the next day in the war's biggest battle. His regiment then fought in the cavalry actions during Robert E. Lee's retreat from Pennsylvania as well as the maneuvering and fighting that took place in Virginia until year's end. The following spring Samuel and the 6th New York rode in Grant's Overland Campaign, fighting in the Wilderness, riding with General Philip Sheridan during his raid on Richmond and the encounter with Jeb Stuart and his cavalry at Yellow Tavern.[3] In June 1864, the regiment was in action during a strike on railroads to the northwest of Richmond. There was a serious encounter with Rebel cavalry and a long return march before they were again within Union lines. Then Samuel wrote the letter above to his family.

Two days after the cavalry action of June 23, the 6th New York was preparing to cross the James River and reunite with the Army of the Potomac that was just beginning the siege of Petersburg.

> Near Charles City C.H., Va
> June 25, 1864
>
> My Dear Friends,
>   A bitter task falls to my lot and one I scarcely know how to accomplish. May our Heavenly father in His infinite mercy prepare you, for I cannot, for the sad news it is my duty to impart to you. A gallant young soldier, a braver man whom ever breathed, the beloved of his comrades and commanding always the respect and admiration of his superiors, has given up his all for his country. In the front rank and with his noble face to the foe, Corporal Fanshaw has fallen.
>   I would fain say some words of comfort to you and your afflicted family, but time and words fail me. One of the few opportunities for mail communication has just offered itself and I avail myself of it to perform this melancholy duty in preference to writing my own family.
>   I can only say, my dear friend, that if the thought that "Sammy" was all that was noble as a soldier—never for a moment shunning duty or danger—the idol of his company, and the esteemed friend of his commanding officers—and that he died at his post can assuage in any measure the grief of his friends, this assurance and more than I can express is theirs.
>   With the assurance of the profound sympathy of this entire regiment as well as my own, I am, my dear sir,
>   Very Truly Yours,
>   Wm. H. Crocker,
>   Lt. Col. 6th N.Y. Cavalry
>   Lieutenant Colonel William H. Crocker, Commanding the 6th New York Cavalry, to the family of Corporal Samuel Fanshaw.[4]

The above letters reside today in a far corner of America's attic. Together they give us a quick glimpse at, and a faint echo from, the Civil War. For more than a century, historians have been sifting through the written record of the Civil War. In their writing the history of these years, many hundreds, indeed thousands, of excellent books have come to stand on the shelves of libraries and in the homes of those that find these years not just fascinating but profound. The vastness of the written works and their range of subjects make one almost conclude there is nothing left, an engagement or a topic, to research and then turn that research into writing. The number and range of subjects addressed in these many books are, in themselves, testimony concerning the hold this war and this era has on historians, as well as the reading public. We read these histories and sometimes wonder: What did they think? What did they hold dear in their memories? And when it came time to tell, what did they write down and leave for us to read? Given the vast number of people involved and upon whom this war touched, only a small percentage left us their thoughts, both at the time it all was happening to them and later. As the years passed, many of these men, who at the time had not recorded their thoughts and actions, wrote or contributed to regimental histories. That which remained important to them found its way into those histories. Others, when they went to war, kept diaries and all who could write mailed letters home. These contain their views, their thinking on what was happening to them and around them. From what these men put on paper is fashioned our history of this event, this Civil War, from the participant's point of view. A purpose of this book, its sketch of the war in the east, is to have some of these people speak to us, perhaps telling us what was important to them then and after.

We can never know as much about these people as we would like. The time that has elapsed since they traveled the landscape of the Civil War, along with the inadequate and missing contemporary sources, make knowing in our time only a partial knowledge. Diaries kept by individuals at the time can be enlightening only if the diarists put effort and perception into them. Memoirs, mostly written long after the fact, only leave us with what the author wants to remember, what was important to him at the time of writing, sometimes only what will be looked upon favorably later. There were no motion pictures with sound recording taken during the battles and their aftermath to aid our understanding of what it was like. There are contemporary photographs; some that can be matched to the individual who wrote something. But mostly the photographs are representative ones that to some degree show us what they looked like, what they wore and the landscape they moved over. We try to paint as accurate a picture as possible with what there is available to us. It is like putting a jigsaw puzzle together knowing in advance all the pieces aren't there.

The diaries and journals left speak to us of what was happening to their authors and those around them, of what was important. In that some speak little of a great battle, but at length about some obscure event, in itself tells us something. Perhaps it was too bloody, too horrific, to write about shortly after it happened. Of all the letters home, only a small percentage tell us something of their thoughts, feelings, impressions, or go into detail about an event of significance. We want to understand them and their times, we want to know what it was like, what they were like. Knowing the inadequacies of what we must work with, still we try.

Gilbert G. Wood, at age 21, enlisted in the 6th New York Cavalry the day before Samuel Fanshaw, on August 14, 1862, in Morrisania, New York, now a neighborhood in the south-central part of the Bronx. He was a close friend of both Samuel and the Fanshaw family. According to the regiment's roster, Gilbert was assigned to Company I on August 19. It will not hurt this history to assume the two friends conspired to join the same outfit and remain together, come what may. Samuel and Gilbert rode together for the many months that followed. Samuel's father, Samuel Raymond Fanshaw of Morrisania, was a prominent miniature portrait painter and, in July 1864, received a lengthy letter from Gilbert Wood, who had been close by when his son was killed.[5]

Headquarters, 2nd Brig. 1st Cavalry Div.
Near City Point, James River
July 5th, 1864

My dear friend,

Your letter of the 1st just reached me last night and I would have answered it immediately had I not been too busy. We are lying in camp and I am very busy with the papers of two month[s] campaign, having been in the saddle for that time (since leaving Culpepper) [sic] everything is in great disorder, consequently every moment had to be devoted to the task of straightening things for another campaign, which I fear will come soon.

Oh! Mr. Fanshaw, you cannot conceive what a relief your letter brought to me. I felt that my only friend had been carried from my side, but when I read your kind and fatherly letter, I felt and knew that another was yet left me, Aye, more than one, a family of friends.

You ask me to tell you where and how Sammie was wounded. His letter of the 22nd was written at White House, just before we advanced toward James River. We halted at night at Jones Bridge, about a mile from the Chickahominy and about three miles from Charles City C[ourt].H.[ouse]

Our regiment was sent on picket and our squadron was held on the reserve. About eight or nine o'clock next morning (23) the enemy advanced upon our pickets and the reserve was sent out to check them until the rest of the brigade could come to their assistance. They found a pretty strong and obstinate force in front of them, but yet they pushed on and drove the rebels from their strong breastworks. And there retired, the enemy having fled. At the time Sammy was hit, our company was in a field with little low pine bushes, and while advancing rapidly they ran upon the enemy's line. Sammy was a little in advance of our line and not more than ten feet from the enemy's. In fact, Mr. Fanshaw, Sammy was on one side of a bush and the rebel on the other. I was a little to the right of where he was, but as soon as I heard he was wounded, I went back, and Oh! My dear friend you cannot imagine my anguish at finding my more than brother (he whom I always looked to for advice) wounded and unconscious of my being near him. And yet I was glad it was so for he suffered no pain, but died quickly, without a struggle.

Every one who knew him mourns his loss as they would a brother. Many have said with a sigh "Poor Fanshaw! He was a man to be relied upon and he was one worthy of the name soldier!" But now he is gone.

Alas! Alas! The consequence of a cruel, cruel war.

My dear friend, I would like to write much more, but I cannot. I am nearly sick.

The day of Sammie's death I received a slight touch of sunstroke and the two have nearly prostrated me. But I hope we may be allowed to remain in camp a short time to recruit. Give my love to all the family and implore them to remember that "It was the will of God." I must stop as the light blinds me almost. I will write to Emma (tell her please) tomorrow if possible. Again, my sincere love and thanks to you and all and I will remain as ever.

Sincerely Yours, Gilbert G. Wood P.S. Please answer as soon as convenient [6]

Here at least we can share, and thus feel, something of what at least one person from this era was experiencing. Much of what is left to us from the Civil War era is similar to Gilbert Wood's letter, yellow sheets of once white paper, a note written by a soldier and read by people far from the field. Or there is a diary, with an entry that speaks of something from a particular day that was too gruesome or too tragic to fully describe, or a musty, hard-to-find book that may or may not give a modern reader some semblance of what it all had been like, what were their thoughts on what was happening. They used their words, sometimes stringing them together to form something we can recognize as a voice. It is history.

The history of any single Civil War cavalry or infantry regiment can only attempt to leave an impression of who they were, what they were doing and, hopefully, something of what they thought. By examining the writing of many from across the Army of the Potomac, perhaps we might enhance our impression. Gilbert Wood would survive the war, return home and years later contribute in his way to the record of this war and, in a small, way contribute to our knowing of it.

The tapestry of American history from its beginning and through the decades before 1860 is a rich field of study and generations of historians working that field have given us many sound reasons and causes for the bloodletting that began in 1861. Having read the sources and the interpretations, having pondered at length the material, one develops a historical construct of the times, a synthesis or consensus. But after all the study, the researching into and reading of the contemporary sources left to us from all the years before this war, it sometimes remains difficult to appreciate the ever-increasing emotional atmosphere of 1860 and 1861 when men north and south stopped talking and started killing each other.

It would be the killing and the wounding, as well as the marching, maneuvering, and fatigue, the life in camp, that would fill the remembrances through the coming years. It all would be set down on paper along with what the veterans thought of the mistakes made by generals.

Almost a year before writing his last letter, Samuel Fanshaw was in Pennsylvania riding with the 6th New York Cavalry, 2nd Brigade, 1st Cavalry Division, Army of the Potomac. There is no known record of his fighting in the great Gettysburg battle. Likewise, he recorded no known impressions the fighting made on him on July 1. If there were letters he sent home with details he witnessed or impression he formed, none are included in the slim record now residing in a museum. Many others, however, spoke of their experience with the Army of the Potomac as the events were happening and later when events could be looked at with accumulated knowledge as to their resolution. From this accumulation of contemporary writing and later remembrance is fashioned, for better or worse, history.

CHAPTER ONE

Remembrance as History

It is the duty of every soldier who served during the war, to put on record his recollections of that service where it may be referred to by the future historian.

NEWEL CHENEY, HISTORY OF THE 9TH NEW YORK CAVALRY

Perhaps someday my apology may be received, and I be wholly pardoned for putting upon the public what was originally intended for my children and neighbors. We old soldiers have flooded the country with our kind of literature, and we have been reasonably ready at all times to explain about the war; but it is not for long before our voices will be silent, our pens as rusty as our swords, and our pensions cancelled. Bear with us but a little longer, O gracious public.

THOMAS W. HYDE, MAINE VOLUNTEER, 1894

The real war will never get in the books.

WALT WHITMAN[1]

The banquet menu that night in 1889 at Boston's Revere House was impressive. It was the eighteenth reunion of the 1st Maine Volunteer Cavalry Association and the veterans and their wives feasted on Blue Point oysters, mock turtle soup *a la Anglaise,* baked chicken *a la bordelaise,* sirloin of beef with mushroom sauce, potatoes croquette, baked macaroni *a la parmesan* and, of course, the cavalryman's favorite, coffee. The printed program, decorated with cavalry yellow ribbon, listed the distinguished after-dinner speakers, one of whom was the regiment's former colonel, now General Charles H. Smith. The war of which these men were veterans was 24 years in the past, the men now in their middle or late forties, perhaps early fifties. They had traveled to Boston not only from Maine but from various corners of the country to remember, solemnly for comrades lost while with the army, but in a congenial sense with others who shared their memories, of the good as well as the bad, of being cavalrymen riding against those who would rend the Union asunder. One veteran, writing in a preface to his regiment's history, offered his thinking on gatherings such as this by the 1st Maine Cavalry:

It is not surprising that the men who had passed through the sufferings and experiences which these pages have attempted to record should feel a tenderness and sympathy for each other which did not bind them to average men.

The Boston banquet room was decorated in the national colors and those of the state of Maine. On the walls were panels inscribed with the names of the fallen of the regiment, and flowers and ferns adorned the tables set to accommodate 500 attendees and guests. The regiment's historian, former Lieutenant Edward P. Tobie, whose *History of the First Maine Cavalry, 1861–1865*, published two years previously, was in attendance. The Lieutenant Governor of Massachusetts welcomed the visiting veterans, his remarks laced with the usual platitudes. But the most appreciated guest and the most anticipated after dinner speaker was General Smith who had been a volunteer in 1861, rose to command the regiment in 1863, remained in the army after the war and was now retired. "I was not informed as to what time I was to speak to-night until four o'clock this afternoon," Smith told his former troopers, adding, "Since that time I have been devoting my whole attention to the ladies." General Smith, nevertheless, "… spoke at considerable length, reviewing old battle-fields and camp recollections, much to the delight of his hearers." At the speaker's podium prior to General Smith stood the distinguished former Major General Benjamin F. Butler. Before the war, Butler had been a leader of the Democratic Party in Massachusetts and was given a general's commission by President Lincoln because Northern Democratic commitment to the cause was deemed essential by the president and, of course, competence notwithstanding, the politician wanted it. It had been General Butler who had first contrived to categorize run-away slaves crossing into his lines on the Virginia Peninsula as "contraband of war." Such a contrivance brought many more and some would eventually fill out regiments and fight for the Union. General Butler reminded his audience that the men of Maine had answered the call in 1861, but not for glory or fame, the true fame of the common soldier being only "… to have his name misspelt in a telegraphic dispatch." You left home and families to assure "… the world that the people of this country not only could govern themselves, but they could govern themselves against the armies of the world whenever it was necessary."

It was nearing 11pm before regimental historian Edward Tobie read a poem he composed for the occasion entitled *A First Maine Cavalryman's Dream*. Then it may be assumed that the veterans slowly drifted off in one direction or another, some possibly seeking to take advantage of the previously voted resolution "… to furnish comrades with copies of the regimental history, without illustrations, for $2 each."[2] Edward Tobie's history, published by the First Maine Cavalry Association, had after the title page the following note provided by the association:

> Your Committee would call attention to the fact that this history, by Lieut. Tobie, was printed by the new firm of Emery & Hughes … the head of which is Comrade Emery, of Co. A., and formerly a member of the Band. You Committee report [sic] that they not only secured better terms, but that the history has been printed with new type, and under the personal supervision of Comrade Emery … To those who contemplate having printing done of any kind (either Book or Job) we would recommend the new firm as parties who will give good work and satisfaction in every respect.[3]

The following morning, at 8am, the veterans and wives were to take a cruise of Boston harbor, "… viewing the different points of interest and lunching at Deer Island," but "Late 'taps' necessitated a late 'reveille' and it was not until quarter past ten that the veterans marched…"[4]

Associations, loosely defined, are organized groups of individuals holding a common view, engaged in a common activity or profession, seeking a common goal, sharing a common identity or all of the above. The men that had endured the ordeal by fire that was the Civil War were quick to gather in associations, most commonly grouped by the regiment of which they were veterans. Typical was that of the First Maine Cavalry Association that had reunited in Boston in 1889. These veterans had held a common view, preservation of the Union, held a common identity, members of a singular regiment, engaged in a common activity, former cavalrymen, and a common goal: remembrance and a desire to see that what was promised was delivered. The deliverable, in the remaining decades of their century, was the promised pensions and care for infirmed and handicapped veterans and support for the widows and orphans of those taken by the war. The benefits the government had promised were to be a continuing, closely held and sensitive issue for as long as these associations survived. In the time and place these veterans held, and because of the number of veterans, it was a significant commitment for the Federal government, a national government preserved through the blood and sweat of its military veterans, providing, to a degree, a residual benefit for services rendered. Over 80 percent of northern men who turned 18 years of age in the first year of the war were now veterans, 60 percent of those born from 1837 to 1845 had served and 41 percent of those born between 1822 and 1845 became veterans.[5] At every reunion of every regiment, and in every association's communication or newsletter to or for its members, there was most often the latest relating to pensions.

A subsidiary goal, common to nearly all that made up a veterans' association was what had been its part and place in the great conflagration, its history. Starting soon after the war, and through the end of the century and beyond as the regimental veterans grew older, gatherings such as that of the 1st Maine were common throughout the nation, and nearly every regiment that made up the Union army of the Civil War and formed an association after the war, considered, in one fashion or another, the production of a regimental history. By one accounting, there are more than 700 of these histories, a good number written by regimental chaplains. Along with these volumes are individual memoirs and recollections standing now on shelves in obscure corners of university libraries. All speak of the role the regiment played in the conflict, some with extensive detail and others that lend little to our knowledge of the conflict. Some of these histories were compiled through the efforts of a committee formed by a regimental association. Others were the work of one individual veteran, such as that of Edward Tobie of the 1st Maine, trying to put into print his and his regiment's role in what all veterans considered the most profound event of their lives.

Many a Civil War soldier kept a diary, some quite detailed, while others contained cryptic notes as to the weather and places marched to and from. Some of these detailed diaries later formed the foundation for more extensive recollections. Other veterans, as the years rolled by, wrote, and had published, memoirs, sometimes labeled recollections, reminiscences or so many years in this or that army or corps or regiment. Still others published the collected letters they wrote from the army to loved ones at home, adding touches of reminiscences as links from one letter to another. Many of these memories were put into print by the major publishing houses in New York and Boston; others were produced by contracted firms and aimed at a limited audience. As reflected upon by historians, this body of writings comprises the history of the Civil War from the participant's point of view. It is a sliver of the slice of war the veteran saw from where he stood and recalled or chose to remember. The authors were keenly aware they had lived through, or survived, a significant historical event and they had something to say about it. They desired, in many cases, to inform not only their children but also future citizens of their nation of the things that had happened, their feelings about it and what they had done as a result. Newel Cheney's *History of the Ninth Regiment New York Volunteer Cavalry* "acknowledged the valuable assistance of many comrades who have given their diaries, letters and recollections" so that his regimental history, it was hoped, would be of "special interest to their children and their descendants." In his preface to the history of the 10th Massachusetts, the author notes the veterans will soon pass "leaving only their memories and the result of their services as a legacy to their descendants."[6] These veterans, writing and publishing their memories, had put down a rebellion that threatened the continued existence of the American Union and set free all those held in bondage. It all was most important to them, as it should be to us. The boys of '61 would generally remain in contact via veterans' associations. Reunions—some held annually—continued into the next century as did the production of regimental histories and the placement of unit monuments on battlefields. Perhaps it was the nature of the war itself. Not a war against a foreign foe, but one against itself.

Through the years, many regiments talked repeatedly at reunions about writing or compiling a regimental history. How to do it and who would do it? One individual or a committee? Discussion, in many cases, went on as years slipped by. For the 19th Maine Infantry, the talk covered 20 years from the start of their reunions. It was past the turn of the century before talk turned to action. In the case of the 19th Maine, a historian would be identified, but "the great difficulty has been that when members of the old Regiment who were qualified to prepare a history became interested in the project, they became sick and died." Then a former corporal in the regiment, John Day Smith, started gathering the necessary material and sent letters to others from the regiment asking for information and recollections. The answers he received, Smith noted, were "… proof … that the survivors of the Regiment are growing old. Inability to recall events that a person would suppose could never be forgotten characterized the greater part of the answers to [Smith's] letters of inquiry." Nevertheless, Smith persisted and in 1909 published the regiment's history.[7]

At these various reunions the fallen were remembered and the former soldiers, having gathered, reminisced. A New York cavalry regiment, the 6th, was not exceptional in this but, unlike the 1st Maine, left little concerning their reuniting through the end of the century. It took a few decades, but the 6th New York Cavalry finally produced its history, the result of the efforts of three of the regiment's veterans. Gilbert Wood, on the title page, was listed as historian of the *History of the Sixth New York Cavalry (Second Ira Harris Guard) Second Brigade, First Division, Cavalry Corps, Army of the Potomac, 1861–1865*. Wood, the close friend of Samuel Fanshaw, had ridden with the regiment through the remainder of 1864 and, just after the end of the war in Virginia, was promoted to sergeant on May 1, 1865, marched in the Grand Review in Washington and then was discharged in Virginia early in June. Almost certainly his friendship with Samuel Fanshaw required that he quickly returned to Morrisania.[8] Hillman A. Hall, another listed on the title page of this history, was 26 years old in 1861 when he enlisted in the 6th New York Volunteer Cavalry. This was on August 5, 15 days after the defeat of Union forces at the Battle of Bull Run in Virginia. He was made first lieutenant of Company B on September 27 and captain on April 3, 1862. In December 1862, he was made regimental quartermaster and served in that capacity until discharged for disability in February 1865.[9]

William Besley, the third member of the history committee, enlisted in Company I of the 6th New York on August 25, 1862. In October 1864, he was made regimental quartermaster sergeant and served until his discharge in June 1865. Besley eventually settled in Virginia.[10] These three veterans are responsible for the regiment's history, one that falls midway between the lesser efforts and the best of the genre.

Finally, there is Alonzo Foster of Brooklyn. The record is missing related to the date of his enlistment in the 6th New York other than he was 20 years of age at the time. In November 1862, he was promoted to sergeant, re-enlisted in December 1863 and became sergeant of Company F the same month. Foster was wounded on July 26, 1864, in the action at Deep Bottom, Virginia, and discharged from the hospital and the army in February 1865.[11] He attended reunions of the 6th New York over the years and recalled there had been talk of writing or compiling a regimental history, but years went by and nothing was done. At such reunions one can well imagine the talks about writing a history drifting late into the night as hotel waiters hovered about wishing these beyond middle-aged veterans would empty their glasses and retire to their rooms. Foster became impatient with the association's inaction on a history and took matters into his own hands. In 1892, he published, in his hometown of Brooklyn, *Reminiscences and Record of the 6th New York Veteran Volunteer Cavalry*. By way of introducing himself, Foster informed his readers that:

> When as a volunteer I joined the Sixth New York Cavalry ... among the articles of personal effects most highly prized was a copy of the New Testament presented to me by the Rev. S. H. Platt, and a pocket diary, the former I had promised to read daily, and the latter was to contain the daily events connected with my future army life, both resolutions were kept so far as the circumstances attending camp and field life would permit.[12]

Foster's daily jottings formed the core of his recollections. The same was true of a Connecticut soldier, Lawrence Van Alstyne. He kept a diary "... in a small pocket notebook, of a size convenient to carry in my pocket." When he published his diary in 1910, he recalled that keeping a record was, "... an irksome task, taking time I really needed for rest but as time went by the habit became fixed and I did not consider the day's work done until I had written in my diary of the events that came with it." Like Foster, Van Alstyne pulled his old diary from its hiding place and fashioned his *Diary of an Enlisted Man* from it.[13]

As for the 6th New York Cavalry, at the 15th reunion of the regiment's veterans' association in 1906, years after Foster's reminiscences had appeared, somehow, talk was converted into action, and the inconsequential conversations about a regimental history turned serious. Some 40 years removed from the conflict, the three veterans, Hall, Wood, and Besley, formed a committee, once again "volunteering." It took two more years with Gilbert Wood's solicitation of written remembrances from individual troopers and gathering records and documents, but in 1908 there appeared in print the *History of the Sixth New York Cavalry*. Charles L. Fitzhugh, who had briefly served as colonel of the regiment in the war's closing months, volunteered funds for the project. The regiment's former colonel had graduated from West Point but left the army after the war, married the daughter of a steel mill owner, became its president and was, by 1906, financially able to underwrite the project. The Blanchard Press of Worcester, Massachusetts, was contracted to produce the volume by the then president of the veterans' association, Furgus A. Easton, who resided in the town and put his name on the copyright. Without any apparent training, historian Gilbert Wood's work is slightly better than many of its kind, but hardly definitive and, perhaps, it wasn't meant to be. The history is a colorless chronology that relies mostly on the memory of individuals, qualified in the text as suspect, and documents out of the *Official Record*. Yet most of the recalled high points of the regiment's four years are included, recalled by those that were crossing the war's bleak landscape, a part of its story. It may be assumed each surviving member of the regiment received a copy of its history. The New York Public Library, in September 1909, was presented with a copy by the association.[14]

Even with consulting and quoting from other sources, and the written memories of its veterans, a full and complete history of an organization like the 6th New York and its place in the conflict cannot be completely spliced together. Large gaps glare at the reader of any chronology such as that produced by the regiment. Little texture or color can be provided that stems from such an organization when there is little or no direct testimony and documentation. In most cases, only generalizations from across the spectrum can be noted and those with qualifications.

However, for the modern historians and their attempted writing of an aspect of the Civil War, total reliance on unit and regimental histories from this time, such as the history of the 6th New York or the 1st Maine, is not wise. Although contemporary evidence and testimony are necessary and add to the telling of a particular aspect of the war's history, a degree of care must be taken in using these volumes. Every sentence in such volumes must be critically evaluated as to its degree of accuracy and, if possible, its tone and substance. Only after an exercise such as this can a volume of this sort be employed to amplify or correct any rendering of an event residing in the *Official Record*. Bias, predisposition, as well as many other inclusions, as well as stylistic mechanics, when quoted, are best identified as such. But remembrances, memories and such sometimes fade with the passage of time while others acquire embellishments that with added years become wedded to, or embedded in, the truth. Stephen W. Sears, a historian intimately familiar with the contemporary record of the Army of the Potomac, notes, "Civil War bookshelves, alas, are crowded with memoirs and recollections of events that never happened, retailed by old Yanks and old Johnnies seeking a little sliver of notice in what had been for them the greatest experience of their lives."[15] To advance this line of thought to include other sources as well, there is the testimony of James Kidd who, by 1864, had risen to command the 6th Michigan Cavalry. Writing in the 1880s and commenting on unit after action reports in the *Official Record*, Kidd concluded the following:

> Official reports were often but hastily and imperfectly sketched, amidst the hurry and bustle of breaking camp, or, on the eve of battle, when the mind might be preoccupied with other things of immediate and pressing importance. Moreover, they were, not seldom, written long after when it was almost as difficult to recall the exact sequence and order of events as it would be after the lapse of years. Besides, the 'youngsters' of those days, those at least who had not been trained as soldiers, failed to realize the value of their reports … [to the later writing of history].[16]

For those coming later to detail the event and movement of a particular battle from the *Official Record*, there was confusion to such a degree that "one sometimes has the feeling that the Federals and the Confederates are describing two different battles." The compilers of the early history of the 6th New York Cavalry realized this to a degree and hence qualified the remarks by individuals that contributed their memories. The authors admitted that some contributors "… found their memory grown dim and uncertain." Given the years that had passed since they had ridden with the regiment, and the scant documentation available, the committee rightly acknowledged the "… impossibility of producing a complete record of the command."[17]

For the untrained veterans, the words of a regimental history might or might not have come easily and might or might not have been of any value, but all reflected in some small degree a commitment to getting on record the contribution of his regiment in the great historical event that was the Civil War. One veteran may have a way with words that easily convey his descriptions and the events he lived while others write using 20 words when 10 will do. Some regimental historians, beyond writing their versions of the facts of a particular battle or campaign, provide their views, the thinking and feelings of the men at the time. Others simply relate the facts as known to them without adding comment or any contemporary insight that is so important to the later historian. As a result, some regimental histories, as well as some memoirs, are of more historical value than others and are frequently quoted in later histories. Some of the personal recollections or reminiscences, while stating they are authored only for the eyes of family members, go to some length in providing not only the factual detail but the reconsidered contemporary thoughts and opinions held at the time. In short, of the hundreds of unit histories and recollections, memoirs and remembrances, some are better than others. Better at providing both a vivid record of the action seen through the participant's eyes or as events unfolded. Some authors of these works gladly put down their pens at the end, saying it had all been a more tedious project than realized. Others warn the potential reader that disappointment awaits those expecting a definitive historical contribution. As the century came to a close, some regimental histories were supplemented by the inclusion of passages from the *Official Record* as those volumes became available for use and, as a result, some of these works have an underpinning of documentation that earlier ones do not. Whether weighty or not, good or bad, all these works are now our record of the Civil War as witnessed by those that did the fighting and the bleeding.

In the writing, or the reconstruction, of any particular battle, obstacles are encountered along the way to an accurate account. Any attempt to put on a page an accurate account of a Civil War action is usually hindered simply because there never seems to be enough primary, definitive, verifiable testimony to recreate the entire story in words. In many cases, there are many personal testaments, but they are, alas, devoid of historical substance. Frustrated, the historian often finds another way to use the meager results of research and, not infrequently, leans on another historian's labor, molding the telling of events around a predecessor's version of it. The recounting, or the recreation, of actions from the Civil War from the *Official Record* is, in addition, often difficult, if not nearly impossible. At times there are too few reports and communications detailing an event. At other times there are too many in the record and those are often at odds with each other. Then, too, there are the reports and communications in which its author becomes creative in explaining either why he failed to achieve the desired object of the action or did so despite the ineptitude of those either in support of him or not. As a result, many reconstructions of events from these reports and communications simply lack inherent worth. In many reports, having been written weeks or months later, the author presses to get the report finished and to get on to something else. Bare bones are jotted down, not nearly enough even for a skeleton.

In some instances, an obscure picture of a Civil War event can only emerge by employing the detail contained in recollections written by participants long after the fact. The participant spent time formulating his recollection because he was primarily concerned with accuracy, as much as a historian. In addition, his writing down the events was—and emphasis is necessary—important to him personally, he desired someone be informed of it and, again, he had something to say. Thomas Hyde was a volunteer from Maine and served mostly as a staff officer during most of the three years he was with VI Corps. Some 30 years later his recollections were published as *Following the Greek Cross or, Memoirs of the Sixth Corps*. The Greek Cross was the symbol and shape of the corps' badge. The college educated Hyde commented on the first page of his work about what he and those like him were putting on paper. "A history of those times, now hardly to be called recent, is yet to be written, and when it is written it will stand, like the line of battle, behind personal narratives, the skirmishers which precede it."[18]

What was important to these veterans as they wrote their histories and the effort they brought to the telling is illustrated by an account included in the published history of the 6th New York Cavalry. After having carefully read, considered and evaluated the various histories of the regiments comprising John Buford's cavalry division as it rode into Pennsylvania, one would think the central event in the history of the 6th New York Cavalry, the point around which the regiment's history revolves, occurred on July 1, 1863, the date of the holding action led by General John Buford and the 1st Cavalry Division at Gettysburg. Buford's action on that July morning, against overwhelming odds and before the arrival of any infantry support was, if not truly heroic, bordered on it. In the memory of the 6th New York and the committee as its history was put together, however, the focal point around which other events orbit was an action on the night of April 30, 1863, at a place referred to as Alsop's Field on a road leading to Spotsylvania Court House, Virginia. Armies were in motion and the Battle of Chancellorsville would begin in earnest the next day. As recounted in the regiment's history, "A meeting of our Association was held on Oct. 29, 1897, at the home of our former President, Lieut. Thomas B. Adams, 709 Sixth Avenue, New York city [sic]." At a point during the meeting, "Conversation of the events connected with the death of Lieut-col. Duncan McVicar disclosed the fact that there was a difference of opinion as to details." Each of those at the meeting verbalized his memory of the events of the night of April 30, 1863, and it was decided that former adjutant Fergus A. Easton would gather the memories and whatever other material relative to the action to assemble it into some coherent form. Easton started on the project, going so far as contacting former Confederate General Thomas T. Munford, who at the time commanded the 2nd Virginia Cavalry, a Rebel regiment that came in to contact with the 6th New York that night. In the overall history of the Chancellorsville battle and related events, the action involving the 6th New York on the night of April 30 remains a small and obscure event. To the regiment's veterans, however, it was not. That night the 6th New York engaged in a firefight with, and a mounted charge against, several Rebel cavalry regiments, the 2nd Virginia among them. Indeed, it turned out that General Jeb Stuart, in command of all of General Lee's cavalry, and his staff, were present as this action took place. In the desperate charge he ordered, Lieutenant Colonel McVicar, commanding the 6th at that time, was killed. McVicar, a volunteer, was well liked and had shown himself to be a capable officer and, had he lived, would likely have risen higher in the volunteer army. Former adjutant Easton produced 20 pages on this action that included a recollection contributed by Thomas Munford. The retelling of the action of July 1 under John Buford took nine pages of the regiment's history. Easton's pages eventually went into the regiment's history with the former adjutant prefacing his article by saying that on his visits "… to the South seeking information he met open arms and unbounded hospitality." His appreciation of the recollections given by Thomas Munford was recognized and at the 1898 reunion of the regiment held at Binghamton, New York, Munford was made an honorary member of the Veterans Association of the Sixth New York Cavalry, with "President Easton pinning a badge to his breast amid the plaudits of comrades and citizen." Writing in the regiment's history, Easton remarked of Munford, "We look upon him as a broad, high-minded Southern gentleman, making no excuses, but strenuous for the truth."[19]

The Civil War ended, the years quickly slipped by and the general that led the Union army to victory became president (Ulysses S. Grant). Before one realized it, a decade had passed and then another. It was then, from the lowest to the highest ranks, there began to appear in print the many hundreds of recollections and reminiscences of the war, each detailing the small role one particular individual played as the great events as four years of war went on around him. After he left the White House, even that victorious general was driven by circumstance to recall his years as a soldier, producing what is considered the most eloquent of memoirs that emerged from the conflict. On occasion, the individual veteran would pick up a pen and detail his version of the history of the unit in which he had served, a company, but more often his regiment. The generals too, the successful and the near successful, penned memoirs amplifying and, in some cases, justifying their actions in a particular battle or campaign. During the final three decades of the 19th century publishers and contracted printing firms were kept busy bringing to the public hundreds of such volumes, the remembrance as history of many a Civil War veteran and sincere histories of companies, regiments, brigades, divisions, corps and armies. As stated previously, these volumes vary widely in style, accuracy and approach to the material, but nearly all drip with sincerity and sometimes candor.

The commitment of these veterans to remembrance of both the struggle and their small role in it is illustrated by an organization, much smaller than the nation-wide Grand Army of the Republic (GAR), called the Sheridan's Veterans Association. The latter association was composed of veterans from across the army led by General Philip Sheridan in the Shenandoah Valley campaign of 1864. This force, most of it having been transferred from the Army of the Potomac, was under orders to finally subdue Confederate activity in the valley. In September 1885, the association held its second reunion at Winchester, Virginia, to which all of its members were invited. It was at Winchester that Sheridan's Army of the Shenandoah first defeated the Rebel force under General Jubal Early in September 1864. After 21 years, the former antagonists, for the most part, had at least begun to reconcile their former differences. Special trains were chartered and firms—to provide food service, camp equipage and local transportation—were put under contract. Several hundred veterans of the Valley Campaign attended some with their families. A tent camp was established outside Winchester along the Berryville Pike opposite the National Cemetery. The food service contractor was taken to task at one point in the weeklong encampment for not procuring enough Virginia ham and for not preparing coffee according to army standards (strong with plenty of sugar). In this, the on-site cook staff was given instruction by the veterans. Former Confederates were invited to attend the planned dedications of monuments and other ceremonies, and to break bread with their former foes. A rifle competition was planned with teams of "Johnnie Rebs" target shooting against teams of "Billy Yanks." The majority of Winchester's citizens were wholly in favor of the gathering and more than hospitable given the cash infusion into the local economy. There was a minority view, however, expressed in a statement placed in the local newspaper. "We, as members of the 5th Virginia Infantry, Stonewall Brigade, don't want any reunion with any 5th Yankee Regiment." Invitations to former Confederate Army veterans were mostly cordially accepted and reflected also in the local paper. "We are assured that more than nine-tenths of the members of the 5th Virginia repudiate the intimation that they still indulge in, and harbor enmity and personal hatred … but naught but good-will and friendship for their former opponents upon the battlefield."

There was some inconvenience among the former soldiers now returning to camp two decades removed from army life. The author of the reunion's report noted that, on the first night in camp, the men seamlessly divided into three "classes." The first were the "bound-to-be jolly" types with which everything was "O.K." The second, "the philosophical set," didn't expect perfection in resuming camp life. Finally, there was the "touchy-snarly group" that "wanted everything just right, and right away."

There were many speakers all with remembrances of encounters in the past and brotherly words for their former antagonists. Regimental monuments were dedicated at both the Winchester and Cedar Creek battlefields. The graves of both the Union and Confederate fallen were adorned with flowers. The ceremonies were without incident, the reconciliation of the veterans, given their words, clearly evident. Such had not been the case 19 years before on this very burial ground. In October 1866, the women of Winchester had finished the re-internment of 2,494 Confederate dead gathered from battlefield graves surrounding the town. They were now dedicating the new Confederate Stonewall Cemetery adjourning the Winchester National Cemetery containing over five thousand graves of Union dead, the result of three years of fighting around the town and in the northern Shenandoah Valley. The 1866 dedication reported, "Twenty-five hundred Confederates on one side; five thousand Yankees on the other." "The American flag flying in the adjourning National Cemetery … provided a 'good deal of rancor' from the crowd, and the members of the U.S. Burial Corps, caring for the Federal dead, were jeered and insulted." The times had indeed changed by the time Sheridan's Veterans gathered there.

Between side trips and dedications, the rifle competition was held with the Union again prevailing without gloating. This remembrance, so important to some middle-aged veterans, was commemorated in a short pamphlet detailing the event and the speeches. It was distributed to those not attending and included the instructions necessary for registering for the 1886 reunion.[20]

The 17th Pennsylvania Cavalry waited even longer than the 6th New York to begin compiling its history. This regiment had ridden with the 6th New York from the time it first joined the 2nd Brigade of the 1st Cavalry Division. At its annual reunion at Gettysburg in September 1909, a committee of seven members was formed "… to assist the historian in the compilation of a regimental history … and to make a report at the next annual reunion." The report was duly submitted the following September and said that, since having been assigned the task, some 300 pages of manuscript had been prepared from official records, recollections, remembrances, diaries and regimental rosters etc., "All of which have been carefully verified by official records, and, we believe, are sufficiently reliable to convey a reasonably authentic record …" The *History of the Seventeenth Pennsylvania Volunteer Cavalry* was published the following year. The historian had apparently started the project before the committee was formed and, although not cited as such, former bugler of Company E, Henry P. Moyer, has his picture before the title page, and probably did the actual compiling of the regiment's records and knitting the text together.[21]

> It was with many misgivings that I yielded to the demands of my comrades, and consented to undertake the preparation of a history of the 10th New York Cavalry. Fully realizing my unfitness for the work, I felt, nevertheless … actuated by a sense of duty [and] I entered upon the task.

The *History of the Tenth Regiment of Cavalry, New York State Volunteers, August, 1861 to August, 1865* was published by the Tenth New York Cavalry Association in 1892 with Noble D. Preston listed as historian. Preston was a 19-year-old corporal in 1861, rose to captain, was wounded at Trevilian Station in June 1864, and discharged later in the year for disability. His "unfitness" is not really evident in the 675 pages of text he delivered to the Association. Preston's history—introduced by General David McMurtrie Gregg, under whose command the regiment served during most of its existence—contains in its pages Preston's own writing, as well as reports, lists and contributed recollections by other members of the regiment. Preston notes in his preface that his history contains several maps and "Artistic reproductions of photographic portraits of all the prominent cavalry generals who served in the Army of the Potomac—a galaxy of leaders the peers of whom it would be difficult to find in modern times …" Preston expected there would be quibbling over details of the actions the regiment engaged in and, therefore, noted that "… not two actors in the great drama saw things from the same standpoint nor with the same eyes."[22]

The first lines written by Benjamin Crowninshield for his history of the 1st Massachusetts Cavalry notes, "This history, written after so many years have gone by, is necessarily imperfect. It is mainly the recollections of an officer of the regiment who was present with the colors continuously longer than any other." Crowninshield, writing about 30 years after the formation of the regiment, relied on the letters he wrote at the time, a journal he kept, and "a good memory." When he consulted with other members of the command, however, "Opinions as to some events have differed considerably." Overall, he maintained he strove to relate the regiment's history and not that of any one individual and, in over 700 pages, it can be said he succeeded.[23]

Every regiment that had a veterans' association also had reunions. From the record it left behind it appears the reunions of the 10th New York Cavalry were decidedly business-like affairs, complete with a stenographic record that was later converted into a pamphlet published for the membership. The 35th reunion of this command was held at the Genesee House in Buffalo in October 1896. The record of the meeting encouraged the attendees to "Bring your ladies, for they add greatly to the interest of the occasion. A trolley excursion to the Falls has been suggested for Wednesday morning, if the weather is favorable, and a trolley party without ladies would not pass muster with us." After this announcement was made the veterans settled down to business. The adjutant made his report on the financial status of the association:

> The treasury was exhausted after paying for the printing of the proceedings, and so I have made no draft on the Quartermaster, and Col. Pratt [former commander of the regiment] ordered me to send all bills to him and he would see them paid. I have *disobeyed* orders, and so they are yet unpaid, for I do not think our Colonel ought to settle these bills out of his own pocket … If I have subjected myself to court marshal [sic] for this disobeying orders, I will plead guilty and ask for charity at the hands of the court.

The unpaid bills spoken of totaled $19.50. Next the quartermaster reported that he had $212.29 cash on hand and his expenses equaled it, including the cost of the banquet ($80), the cost for the band at the banquet ($17), and the fee for the stenographer whose scribbling resulted in the record from which this information was taken ($15.48). After this report, forms for acquiring a Gettysburg Service

Medal were made available to the veterans so that each could acquire their justly earned award.[24]

It was known that the Grand Army of the Republic would hold an encampment at Buffalo that following year and it was voted that the 10th New York's next reunion would be scheduled there to coincide with it. Then, as the year 1896 was an election year, a veteran named Springsteen, now from Ohio, brought forward the following:

> As a representative of Ohio I want to say that one of our distinguished citizens is now a candidate for the Presidency of the United States, and as he is an ex-soldier, wouldn't it be well for us to send congratulations to him?

This motion was seconded, and the telegram sent.

> The Honorable William McKinley, Canton, Ohio: The surviving comrades of the 10th New York Cavalry, now in reunion, extend to you their hearty congratulations, and pledge their unanimous support.[25]

Comrade Springsteen was attending his first reunion of his old outfit and said to his fellow veterans:

> I beg you to believe me when I say that this is the most joyous time I have experienced during these long years, and my soul has been made happy by seeing you … I ponder a moment and wonder if it is not true that an honorable discharge from the old Tenth New York Cavalry is a passport to the portals of heaven.[26]

Later, a Comrade Stowits, who was a teacher, told the assembled veterans:

> … it is my privilege every day to cause the children to salute the flag, thanking God we shall never be obliged as a nation to go through the same ordeal of blood and battle you and I experienced, but that they may know at what great cost the blessings of the country were preserved.[27]

Noble Preston, who published his history of the 10th New York in 1892, sent his regrets for not attending the Buffalo reunion, adding that as the years passed the more he appreciated his association with all the 10th's veterans:

> It is fitting that the boys should assemble and renew the scenes and life that are past. To no men is it more apparent. I hope they will make the most of the occasion for their enjoyment. Tell Oliver to knock the barrel head in and use the dipper, as of old.[28]

Some of the veterans wrote they could not attend because of infirmities, "Too poor health to come," said one. Another wrote he was "… so crippled with rheumatism that he was afraid he never will be able to see his brave comrades in this world …" Ichabod Beardsley, age 81, wrote, "Am too old and feeble to undertake the journey." Another writing from Kansas said:

> My health is not good enough to make so long a journey. I had a paralytic stroke last winter. Am partially recovered, but not able to be about alone. Am anxious for the election of McKinley.[29]

"[U]pon repeated requests and letters from his comrades," wrote Joseph Ward in the third person, "and the unanimously adopted resolution of the survivors assembled in reunion at Gettysburg" in 1882, he returned to writing the *History of the One Hundred and Sixth Regiment, Pennsylvania Volunteers, 2d Brigade, 2n division, 2d corps, 1861–1865*. Ward warned in his introduction:

> … the writer makes no claims whatever for it as a work of any literary merit; but presents it as a plain statement of facts connected with the history of his regiment …[30]

Others like Ward taking up a pen while the years passed, were working against time as the number of principals grew fewer. Francis A. Walker was working on a history of II Corps and contacted all five of the corps' former commanders. All promised their cooperation in his writing. In his preface to his *History of the Second Army Corps in the Army of the Potomac*, Walker noted that he "… strained every nerve to bring my … task to completion," thinking along the way "that my task would never be done at all unless it were done all at once." Walker finished, writing the preface to his history last and saying, "as I write these closing lines, of the five [Corps Commanders] four are dead." Walker closed his brief preface saying, in essence, it was the truth and "… feeling that, in truth, the 'night cometh, when no man can work.'"[31]

Charles Davis was driven not only to present the facts of his regiment's service but also his remembrance of what the men thought at the time. In the preface to his *Three Years in the Army: The Story of the Thirteenth Massachusetts Volunteers from July 16, 1861 to August 1, 1864*, Davis wrote:

> The opinions and judgments are believed to be those shared by a majority of the regiment during its service. As we were no wiser than the rest of mankind at eighteen or twenty years of age, some of the statements may seem very crude in the light of present information. What we thought at the time, about events in which we took part, is of more value to the future historian than what we may now think about the same events or persons.

And Davis delivered his and his comrades' thinking throughout his history. As the regiment marched to Gettysburg, the young men understood what was at stake and offered their hopes, perhaps wishes, about what lay at the end of their march:

> The Army of the Potomac had fought desperately before, when success would have been achieved if the skill of its commanders had been equal to the valor of the men.

Now, as they trudged along the road into Pennsylvania, they had a new commanding general, George Meade, and the men hoped he "… would show more ability and judgment than his predecessors had shown when conducting a great battle."[32]

Reunions including both blue and gray participants increased in number during the 1880s and 1890s. The animosities caused by past issues were, over the intervening years, fading as veterans on both sides grew older and the old Confederacy ever so gradually became integrated thoroughly into the national economy and the Democratic party—its roots were never killed by the war—was once again in control in the South. One of the most significant reunions with veterans attending from both north and south was held in 1888 at Gettysburg, commemorating the 25th anniversary of the battle. The Society of the Army of the Potomac, in preparing for the three-day reunion, invited veterans of the Army of Northern Virginia to attend and approximately 300 former Confederate soldiers did so. Union veterans flooded the town in the days preceding July 1. The unofficial leader of the Confederate contingent garnered the most attention, having journeyed from Georgia to take part. The *New York Times* reported, "… the man … who is never permitted to spend a moment alone is a tall, soldierly-looking man with white hair and flowing gray whiskers." This was Lieut. Gen. James Longstreet, fondly called "Old Pete" by his own men during the rebellion. The former corps commander under Robert E. Lee attended a dedication ceremony on the afternoon of his arrival at Gettysburg. It was at the monument honoring the Iron Brigade, placed in the position the command had first occupied on July 1. Through the three days, in the orations at the dedications of monuments, the cause for which the Confederates fought might have been mentioned in an oblique manner, but certainly the men in gray were mentioned with respect, and tribute to their unflinching valor in battle was spoken of reverently in accordance with the then movement for sectional reconciliation. The oration on this particular day, reported the *Times*, "… was good, but would have given more satisfaction had there not been so much of it."

General Longstreet's principal antagonist as the battle raged on its second day, July 2, was the Army of the Potomac's III Corps then under the command of General Daniel E. Sickles, who lost a leg on the field that day. Sickles arrived at a luncheon, apparently late, but before the dedication of the Iron Brigade monument and many were "Curious to see how these old opponents on the battlefield would greet one another." The 67-year-old and somewhat infirm Longstreet:

> Pushing his chair to the rear, the Southerner reached out his right hand. It was quickly grasped by Sickles, on whose shoulder Longstreet threw his disengaged arm. They were friends in a moment and there was very little eaten at that particular table for 30 minutes as they talked about events a quarter of a century old.

Later, Longstreet was asked if General Jubal Early would be attending the ceremonies at Gettysburg that week. Longstreet stroked his whiskers and produced a small smile, saying that Early probably would not be attending because the people of Chambersburg might not care to see him. "That's so," responded one of Longstreet's listeners, "he burned the town." Actually, Chambersburg was burned by Confederate cavalry under the direct command of an officer named John McCausland. The burning was done the following year, in the summer of 1864, when a demand for tribute in gold by McCausland was not forthcoming from the city fathers. Regardless, in 1888, Jubal Early remained one of the few unreconciled Rebel veterans and would remain so. Later, after the long dedication day, Longstreet agreed to accompany former Union Colonel John B. Bachelder, the first historian of the battle, on a tour of the battlefield "in order to answer some questions." Reconciliation of the former contesting armies, its veterans, and their sections of the nation was now fully on the march. A clear example of reconciliation came four years later in the presidential election of 1892 where the Populist Party nominated Union veteran Brevet Brigadier General James E. Weaver for president and a former Confederate major from Virginia, James G. Field, for vice-president. In a campaign dominated by issues related to monetary policy, this ticket carried five states in a losing effort.

At the dedication of the battlefields at Chattanooga and Chickamauga seven years later, it can be said reconciliation had reached its zenith. At the dedication ceremonies it was estimated forty thousand veterans of both the blue and the gray were in attendance.[33]

One of the more remarkable events in the reconciliation process occurred over three years between the veterans' associations of the 9th New York Infantry and the 3rd Georgia Volunteers. As the 9th's regimental history states, these two regiments came into "contact on several occasions." About 25 years after the war, correspondence was established between the two veterans' associations culminating with the Georgians inviting the New Yorkers to their reunion in 1888. A delegation from the New York regiment was cordially welcomed when they arrived in Savannah. Speeches "flattering to both" regiments were made and reported in the local press, with Joseph Richards of the 9th speaking on one occasion "of that brotherly feeling which had taken possession of the soldier's [sic] hearts, significant of the determination that there shall be but one nation." Upon the return of the New Yorkers, the 3rd Georgia was duly invited to New York for their next reunion. It wasn't until 1891 that this could be arranged and conveniently the reunion was scheduled for the spring, 30 years after the formations of both regiments. Once in New York, the Georgians were shown the sights and provided with theater tickets. There was a banquet where the former colonel of the 9th remarked that the reunions were "a rare oasis in the great desert of the usual commonplace of modern life," and the "memories" engendered their service and by such gatherings are "our most precious possessions." The author of the 9th's history remarks when speaking of this dual reunion of former enemies:

> That a new South has risen from out of the ashes of war, more glorious, more national, and better equipped for those victories incident to the arts of peace than ever before.[34]

Curiously, the night after the 1st Maine Cavalry held its 1889 reunion banquet in Boston, the 13th New Jersey held theirs in Montclair, New Jersey. One of the guest speakers invited to this banquet was the Reverend Doctor Junkin. He was the pastor of the community's oldest church, but of greater significance was that during the war he had been a chaplain in the Army of Northern Virginia. In his speech, Reverend Junkin spoke long and fervently on the doctrine of reconciliation, admitting that the South's soldiers had fought for what they, at the time, thought to be their rights but now had reconciled and were true, loyal Unionists never again to march against the flag.[35]

Early in 1893, the New York Monuments Commission contacted each regimental association of veterans in New York State. Former III Corps commander General Daniel E. Sickles headed the commission. In July, the commission's message said, there would be a mass reunion of New York veterans at Gettysburg centered around the dedication of the state monument at the Cemetery Ridge burial ground. The state legislature was persuaded to subsidize the various railroads leading from the state to Gettysburg, allowing the veterans to travel to and from the battlefield at no cost. Seven hundred tents, 12 by 14 feet, were borrowed from the army and "set up adjacent to the cemetery for the accommodation of all veterans who desire quarters under canvas." The expected seven thousand veterans would be accommodated 10 to a tent. There would be a parade of veterans to the cemetery by each regiment that was on the field during the battle. The July reunion also included speeches, music and fireworks along with dedications of regimental monuments at various locations across the battlefield. "It is the wish of the Board that all veterans appear in the uniform usually worn on Memorial Day," the veterans were told. Each veteran that fought in the great battle would be awarded a medal of honor, struck by the United States Mint, in commemoration "…for service given by him to his country in the hour of her greatest peril."[36]

As the preparations went forward, the commission was informed that there was serious objection among some veterans to a "trolley railroad" that was under construction on the battlefield and that some veterans during the reunion planned to wreck it and stop further building, seeing it as a desecration of near-sacred ground. The commission cautioned the various regimental associations, asking them to ensure that no such plan, if it were being hatched within their memberships, go forward. The commission advised the attendees to refrain from anything physical relating to the trolley and any person connected with it, "… however obnoxious such persons may have made themselves … We ask you, veterans of New York, to let the trolley railroad alone; neither do anything to injure it, nor anything that will benefit it; do not put a penny in its treasury; *do not ride in its cars*."[37]

For the 25th anniversary of the Gettysburg battle, New Jersey's legislature funded the transportation and subsistence costs for the state's veterans attending the ceremonies that were held on those first three days of July. One Hundred and twenty-five members of Veteran Association of the Thirteenth Regiment New Jersey Volunteers took advantage of this and attended with "Joy and gladness beamed from their eyes and was proclaimed by their voices."[38] The regiment had organized itself the year before when it became known the State of New Jersey would contribute $1,000 to each regimental association planning to put a monument on the battlefield. Quickly brought together, the 13th's veterans contributed $1,700 of their own funds to the project and dedicated their monument in July 1887. The year after the 25th anniversary ceremonies, the association voted that one Thomas McAllister of Gettysburg be paid $5.00 per year "to keep the surroundings of the monument in order."[39]

The three days of ceremonies organized by the New York Monuments Commission at Gettysburg were a complete success, but, unfortunately, the U.S. Mint was only able to produce 1,000 medals in time for the July gathering. A remainder was later sent to individual regimental associations for distribution to their eligible memberships.[40]

These and hundreds of other formal reunions took place through the remaining years of the century and into the next, but there were countless others that went unrecorded, the chance meeting on the street, regimental comrades eying each other carefully, a smile of recognition crossing their faces in the seconds before the two men embraced, eyes filling with tears. The letter mailed from a far-off place, an old comrade from the regiment asking another old comrade to write down, if he could, his recollections of this or that battle so that it could be included in the regimental history then in preparation. The veterans of the same regiment, living in the same small town, donning the same blue uniform on Memorial Days, marching in the same parade down Main Street and listening to the same speeches of remembrance year after year.

Delavan Miller was 25 years removed from the 2nd New York Heavy Artillery and was working in the back of the store he owned in Watertown, New York, when, one day, two men entered, one asking the clerk if "Del" was in. Hearing the exchange, Miller approached the two men, "two rather seedy looking individuals with hats in hand …" One of the men, Miller knew, was a town resident, a veteran of the 2nd New York Heavy who bore "the scars of battle on his body." Returning from the war this veteran learned:

> … that while he was away fighting the battles for his country one of the stay-at-homes had been making love to his wife. She went west with her paramour and the veteran laid down under the load and let the battle of life go against him. He was no common bum, however, if he did try at times to drown his misery in strong drink.

He had remained a comrade of Miller's nevertheless and the shopkeeper sometimes gave him a dime or a quarter, later writing in his memoir, "I had not the heart to say no to one who blackened his coffee pail over the same campfire with me." The second man in Miller's store was at first a stranger, quick moments passing, slow recognition becoming surprise. It was "George," late of the 2nd New York Heavy. "It was the same old story," wrote Miller, "an old veteran, the war deep in the past but not in memory." Now George was with the circus, "always going somewhere and never getting anywhere." Miller and George had retreated together from the Second Battle of Bull Run in 1862, escaping capture as they did so. Just passing through town, was the way comrade George put it, with "Barnum and Bailey's greatest aggregation on earth." The circus was in town and George began a performance, uninhibited, speaking to the assembled store "clerks and customers." The circus "Something like the army. Always being under marching orders ... Plenty of fresh air. Sleeping on the ground with only a strip of canvas between him and heaven." Warming to his audience as they stepped closer to hear:

> I just close my eyes and imagine I am with the old II Corps again and Gen. Hancock is riding down the lines ... Suppose you have heard all about the general? Handsomest man and greatest fighter that ever straddled a horse. The general and the second corps never missed a fight ... Gettysburg? Sure! Rube, here, got a couple of bullet holes when we were beating back Pickett's men that afternoon. The general went down that day, too, and I can shut my eyes and see it all and hear the cheers of the Irish Brigade boys when they realize that the battle was won. Beg pardon, ladies, but I am in something of a reminiscent mood today, being as I met an old comrade. We have been holding a little reunion. Yes, we took a little something in honor of the event.

Here comrade Miller ends his remembrance of meeting an old veteran, a veteran like him, saying only:

> ... that evening the two veterans of the old second corps partook of the best that the Woodruff house could give and smoked several Nill & Jess' Pinks at the expense of one who was glad to do it, 'Just for old acquaintance sake.'[41]

When the 22nd Massachusetts Infantry published its history, it included some pages on the formation of its veterans' association. The records are sparse but noted that those officers and men that had not reenlisted as veteran volunteers were discharged at the end of their three-year enlistment and sent home in June 1864. While traveling to Boston the officers agreed to form an association that would meet each year. The Parker House in Boston was chosen as the place for the reunions. By 1870, the first year in which records were kept, the association included all that had been in the regiment during the war. At the annual reunion in 1879, a committee was created "to compile a history of the regiment." Two years later, "ladies"—taken here to mean the wives of the members—were enrolled and attended the regimental gatherings. At the same reunion of 1881, apparently in the spirit of reconciliation, former General Richard Garnett "of the rebel army" was an after-dinner speaker. Later in the 1880s, it was proposed that a 22nd Massachusetts monument be placed at Gettysburg. A design was approved and "Contracts were made with the Smith Granite Company for a monument" to be placed at the site where the regiment fought on July 2. The monument was dedicated, and the regimental history published in 1887.[42]

The veterans' associations, as the years passed, by regiment, by army, or those of General Sheridan's Valley Campaign, sought not only to remember their role in the historical event that was the Civil War and to honor the lives it took, but to almost consciously promote in their small way a form of reconciliation between the once opposing sections of the country and the individuals that had fought. In this the associations were successful to the degree that memberships, north and south, participated in many battlefield dedications and reunions. One small example of this can be seen in the 6th New York Cavalry's recognition of Thomas Munford in 1898.

As the veterans compiled their unit histories and reminiscences, the years sped by, the number published increasing as the years accelerated toward 1900 and the turning of the century. Often the better of these publications included descriptions and word pictures, whether humorous or horrific, "accentuated by time," without regard to the public's sensibilities, for the authors often remarked, in presenting their work, that the truth of what they had written was paramount. Writing to present the truth as they knew it was the reason, they were writing at all.[43] Year after year individuals contributed articles to publications aimed at veterans such as the *National Tribune* or *Confederate Veteran*. These publications sometimes detailed personal exploits or some small aspect of a battle or campaign of which the author was a participant, some containing testimonies of significance. Beginning in 1876, Volume One of the *Southern Historical Society Papers* appeared and for the next several decades put in print Civil War related documents and testaments by all levels of the war's southern participants.

In 1879, *The Philadelphia Weekly Times* published *The Annals of the War Written by the Leading Participants North and South*. The 800 pages of this volume contain more than 50 articles published by the weekly during years' previous. Many of the surviving cast of characters from the war had taken up a pen and told their story of a battle or other aspect to the Civil War. The purpose of it all, according to the editor, was to "furnish the most valuable contributions to the future historian which have yet been given to the world." This was because in the year of its publication, the editor says, "… the country is to-day without a single trustworthy history of the greatest struggle in the records of any modern civilization." Hedging just a little, he reminds the reader, the articles "… are far from perfect; but they have elicited the truth to a degree that no other means could have accomplished."[44] What the historian has in this volume is testimony and all he or she has to do is determine what the "elicited truth" might be.

Also, on a national level, the year 1884 saw the *Century Magazine* began a series that, over the next three years, brought to its pages the recollections of nearly every prominent player in the drama of the Civil War. The articles covered every major battle and campaign, but all were without the bitterness of the then contesting forces. Here was reconciliation at work before a national audience. With the series, the magazine had as its purpose to "celebrate the skill and valor of both sides," by printing "truth and not sentiment." From the perspective of a much later generation, however, the articles appear that the "veterans had forgotten their nightmares," telling "the story of the age of heroism," without hatred, without blood. As one historian remarked about the series—brought together in 1887 in a four-volume set entitled *Battles and Leaders of the Civil War*—"Not one of its varied, vivid, thrilling pages told of a war where men went mad with hatred, starved in prison camps, and invoked God's aid in damnation of the enemy." What "blood that was shed was baptismal blood, consecrating the birth of a new and greater nation."[45] Another historian noted, after studying this aspect of Civil War historiography:

> Taken together, these writings offer overwhelming testimony of the need of Union veterans to record and remember their war … [The authors] shared a genuine desire to convey a meaningful and exact record of their exploits …

Yet others, be they articles in the *National Tribune*, papers read before a state commandery of the Military Order of the Loyal Legion of the United States, or remembrances in *Battles and Leaders of the Civil War* or like publications, can speak of "a bloodless war in which little was at stake, save the reputations of cigar-chomping, whiskey-guzzling generals who moved armies around like rooks on a chessboard."[46] Yet all of these testimonials and remembrances, regardless of their style and quality, are, today, a part of the material employed by historians to underpin their telling the great—indeed, it might be argued the profound—story of the Civil War.

These materials, left to historians of a later age, became vital to their fashioning a history of this era. The historian's employment of a given source largely depends upon the writer's perception, perspective and his ability to put into words, either at the time or later, what he had seen or done. Historians of a later age consult and quote these sources to provide weight, emotion and texture to their telling of history. Although style in the telling is always a good ingredient, it is the perspective of the telling, an ability of a participant to capture accurately what happened; his ability to create a word picture clear enough for the reader to see the scene accurately, as the participant lived it. Unfortunately, the sources left to the historian of this war and the testimony left to him are often weighed down and obscured with linguistic foliage that, in extreme instances, camouflage meaning. Yet, this perceived handicap is, in itself, part of the picture, a part of the world the author traveled. All of this is the source material from which the historian constructs a history, its scope, be it large or small, dependent upon it. The continued use by historians of the words and language chosen by Civil War veterans, taken together, is the voice of the Army of the Potomac.

CHAPTER TWO

From Reunion to Revolution

Right here I wish to say that the men who fought in the first battles of the war were wedded, body and soul, to their country's cause, and that it was pure love of country that inspired them to fight and die for its sake.

CAPTAIN JACOB ROEMER, BATTERY L, 2ND NEW YORK ARTILLERY

The general result was in our favor; we gained a great deal of ground and held it ... I hope that God has given us a great success. It is all in his hands, where I am content to leave it.

GENERAL GEORGE McCLELLAN TO MRS. McCLELLAN, SEPTEMBER 18, 1862, 8AM

I have the satisfaction of knowing that God has, in His mercy, a second time made me the instrument for saving the nation, and am content with the honor that has fallen to my lot.

GENERAL GEORGE McCLELLAN TO MRS. McCLELLAN, SEPTEMBER 22, 1862, 9AM[1]

In the spring of 1861, everyone had thought it would be a short rebellion, quickly suppressed by the 75,000 volunteers President Lincoln had called for after the surrender of Fort Sumter; the Rebels would scatter on receiving the first volley of musket fire from these volunteers, their army quickly falling apart, the men just as quickly going back to their homes in the South; the wayward sister states would, somehow, ask forgiveness and return to their natural relationship within the Union while some kind of deal was made about the slaves. It did not turn out as expected. A mostly volunteer and untrained army, composed of many regiments with an enlistment commitment of just 90 days, was quickly assembled around the city of Washington, its core, supposedly, formations from the 16,000-man standing U.S. Army. Some contemporaries, both in and out of the government, hoping for a quick resolution of the situation, urged the administration to use these men quickly to stamp out the insurrection. Others, more thoughtful individuals, considered this force camped across the city little more than an armed mob. With a 90-day clock ticking, these men had to be employed quickly. Under increasing pressure, the administration gave command of this force to General Irvin McDowell, as new to a combat command as the troops he led. It was a composite army of Union volunteers, having acquired only those military skills that the weeks since the formation of the regiments in their home states could provide. General McDowell might have been new to combat command, but he had been in the army long enough to know the force under his leadership was neither ready, prepared, nor sufficiently trained to launch a serious attack. The pressure to use the troops grew to a point that the order to move had to be issued. In the middle of July, McDowell started his men on the road to Manassas, Virginia. On July 21, there was a confrontation with the Rebel force positioned behind a stream called Bull Run. McDowell attacked. The army made a direct move on the Rebel force behind the stream, while a flanking column circled to attack the enemy's left. The initial attack seemed to be going well but, later in the day, reinforcements brought in by rail from the Shenandoah Valley turned affairs in favor of the Confederates. What was to be a withdrawal for the purposes of reorganization of the Union force degenerated into a full retreat, the troops scurrying in the direction of Washington all through the evening and the next day. It was a Union defeat. General McDowell and the volunteer soldiers staggered back to the capital, disorganized and defeated. Primarily, it was the lack of coordinated control of the formations on the battlefield by McDowell and his mostly inexperienced unit commanders that resulted in the defeat.

With the defeat, a new wave of enlistment swept across the North with the recruiters having volunteers sign for three years in most cases. Hillman Hall, later to play a role in compiling the history of the 6th New York Cavalry, probably enlisted because things hadn't gone according to plan at Bull Run.

In the North, the many that had at first not chosen to volunteer now answered Lincoln's call. One of them recalled:

> The bitter discouragement [over the loss at Bull Run] was of short duration … A second uprising [of enlistments] of the north took place. Recruiting went on with vigor, and the time for which men engaged themselves was three years or during the war. In a week the north had recovered from its dejection, and girded itself anew for the conflict.[2]

Getting this new mass of men organized, trained and with proper leadership would take considerable time. The army's command structure was in disarray. As a contemporary noted, "General McDowell returned to Washington a forlorn soldier without an army. The army, if an army it might have been called, had got there before him, a disordered mob, scattered through the streets of a capital it had left at the mercy of an enemy …" After saying this, the disgust felt by this gentleman continued to bleed on to the page. Bull Run had "… taught us to distinguish between the value of a fair weather and a fighting soldier."[3]

Many knew why they had joined and its significance. In the cold of December, almost six months after Bull Run, a soldier from New Jersey could still align his thoughts and have them delivered to those at home.

We are battling, further, not merely for the present nor for ourselves, but for the future and forever, and for all the vast generations of men everywhere and through all time. The Union must not fall ... for with its fall would be extinguished all the highest and holiest hopes of mankind, the world over, and for generations to come.[4]

In this second recruitment, regiments of cavalry would be enlisted, where such formations, although offered by the Northern state governors, hadn't been at first. They had been declined by the War Department as taking much more time to train than the war would last. One of the first volunteer cavalry regiments to be mustered into Federal service, and one representative of all those cavalry regiments then in the process of being formed, was the 1st New York Cavalry, also known as the Lincoln Cavalry in honor of the President. Lincoln had been lobbied and persuaded to accept it by the German American and staunch Republican, Carl Schurz. The man targeted to lead this new mounted formation was Andrew T. McReynolds. The new colonel, "although a citizen of the United States only by adoption...." was a Mexican War veteran and had been highly recommended.[5] The formation of the regiment in 1861 was duly noted in the New York press and reflected the residual mid-19th century bias relative to immigrants and the problems of dealing with Washington. Seven companies were organized within the city, "Four of these companies are composed of wealthy, intelligent and energetic Americans," noted a New York newspaper, "the other three are composed of Germans." Additional companies were grafted on to the regiment and came from Pennsylvania, Ohio and Michigan. The problems relating to Washington's initial view concerning recruitment of volunteer cavalry were noted in the New York newspapers, not reluctant to point at the individual they thought most responsible:

> Dispatches have again been received from the Secretary of War, ordering Col. McReynolds to bring his regiment immediately to Washington. It is scarcely necessary to say that this regiment is not quite ready to move, and it is the Secretary's fault that it is not. His unwillingness to give any encouragement to those who undertook the organization of the regiment when the war first broke out is the sole cause of the delay that will now be necessary before it is ready to move. Let the department entrust Col. McReynolds with the proper authority for equipping and perfecting the regiment, and he will be ready to move with at least half his force in the course of a fortnight. Cavalry regiments, as Mr. Cameron ought to know, are things not perfected in a day.

An indeterminate period of time passed, with the colonel apparently engaged with the Washington authorities, but the papers finally reported:

> Colonel McReynolds, who is now in Washington, telegraphed to his regiment last evening that the government has agreed to furnish horses, equipments, army uniforms, and everything necessary to complete the outfit of this regiment. Orders to that effect have been issued. There is yet room for a few enterprising young men of the right stamp ... Members of the regiment are requested to report themselves at headquarters—Americans at Disbrow's riding school, and the Germans at Elm Park, tomorrow night at eight o'clock.

As the day for mustering-in approached, there was a gathering of the enlistees from the city at which Mr. D. Meldola Levi of the Young Men's Christian Association encouraged the new soldiers "… to lead a Christian life, which would be sure to make them good soldiers. The men seemed to enter heartily in the exercise …"[6] After being mustered into Federal service, the New York companies left for the south. The 1st New York:

> … got away yesterday afternoon, en route to Washington, at which place they are to hold themselves in readiness to take a prominent part in the bloody conflict about to be inaugurated for the salvation of the Union, and the perpetuation of those principles of liberty handed down to us by our forefathers. The regiment—composed of Americans, Irishmen and Germans—is one of the finest that has left the city yet. The men composing the regiment want to fight for the 'Union, the whole Union, and nothing but the Union.'[7]

The reporter writing this story did not mention, and perhaps did not know, that these recruits had before them a steep learning curve before the Lincoln cavalry, and the others like them, would be able to equal the cavalry of the Confederacy, many regiments of which were already in the field.

The situation of the Lincoln Cavalry was not an isolated occurrence. Other formations encountered similar, if not worse, organizational problems with each eventually receiving treatment in the respective regimental histories.

Taken as an example, the organization of the 6th New York Cavalry might be cited. Between July 25 and 30, 1861 the governor of New York, having received a new quota of volunteers out of Washington, called for 25,000 volunteers to be formed into 25 infantry, two cavalry and two artillery regiments. "Applications for authority to raise troops came from every quarter. The ardor of the people was beyond description …" In part, the 6th New York Cavalry and its coming into being resulted from "… a demand for mounted troops to meet the exigencies of the services that had become manifest by the operations of the famous 'Black Horse Cavalry' of the Confederate Army during the Bull Run campaign of July 1861."[8] These comments by the 6th New York's historian, Gilbert Wood, were not written in isolation. Years before, while writing the history of the 1st New Jersey Cavalry, its author formulated one near contemporary explanation for organizing volunteer cavalry. The regiment's former chaplain, Henry R. Pine, wrote:

> While the memory of Bull Run was fresh, where there was still a vivid recollection of the panic created by the mere apprehension of rebel cavalry, and a strong conviction that a few squadrons of horse might have materially changed the fortunes of the day, or at least, by covering the retreat, have prevented a rout and confusion that spread from the battle-ground into the very streets of Washington, the Secretary of War granted freely to prominent men in various sections of the country permission to raise mounted regiments for three years' service.[9]

Beyond the disaster of Bull Run and the prowess of Rebel cavalry, some men answering the call to arms still preferred riding to marching. Also, "… there hung about the cavalry service a dash and an excitement which attracted those men who had read and remembered the glorious achievements of 'Light Horse Harry' and his brigade … In short, men who had read much in history and in fiction, preferred the cavalry service."[10]

It was the army's commander-in-chief who had previously declined the offer of state governors for volunteer cavalry. In General Winfield Scott's perspective, it was going to be a brief confrontation with the South, over before trained cavalry regiments could reach the "seat of war." Besides, cavalry was expensive, each man had to have a horse that needed to be purchased and fed by the government. Feeding the animal, as well as its rider, would be a continuing expense for Washington, not to mention the special weapons needed by the troopers: sabers, revolvers and carbines. Beyond this, General Scott "knew" the state of Virginia would be where the primary confrontation was likely to occur. He and everyone else "knew" Virginia's geography precluded what was then recognized as the normal functions of cavalry. Fortunately for the Union, this thinking quickly disappeared when those beaten volunteers trudged over the Potomac bridges and back into Washington on the night of July 21.[11]

The contemporary documentation from the period does not tell us whose idea it was, but two of the cavalry regiments organized in the late summer of 1861 from New York State would acquire the name "Ira Harris Guard" along with their numerical designations. Senator Ira Harris, one of the many representatives of the people from an important and populous state, had helped to convince the War Department, under Secretary Simon Cameron, in the wake of Bull Run, that New York should furnish volunteer cavalry and was ready to do so. An officer in what became a New York Volunteer Cavalry regiment later recalled that Senator Harris and others in like positions "… whose persistent and repeated efforts, coupled with the continual requests and demands of officers of experience who were in the field, finally obtained the reluctant consent of the War Department to accept the service of Cavalry."[12] These regiments started organizing and recruiting in the last days of July, and Senator Harris, his hand lightly on the controls, became the patron of both the 5th and 6th Sixth New York Volunteer Cavalry Regiments. Othniel De Forest, previously a "broker" in New York City, and a man with apparently serious connections to the state's political machinery "… was authorized by the President to raise a regiment to form the 'Ira Harris Cavalry Brigade.'" With the authorization in hand, De Forest started at once, setting up a recruiting office at 4 Pine Street in lower Manhattan. Across the state, other offices were also signing recruits that would eventually be folded into the 12 companies of both the 5th and 6th New York Cavalry. Although approximately half of the neophyte cavalrymen came from New York City, communities beyond the city—such as Albany, Rochester, Binghamton, Poughkeepsie and places much smaller—provided men. These recruits, during September and October, were transported to Staten Island, New York, where organization of the regiments and training were to take place.

Doctor Thomas Ellis, MD, had been assigned as overseeing medical director for New York and its various recruiting camps. His impression of the facility on Staten Island was written into his diary:

> Situated in a valley and approached by a drive of three miles from the Vanderbilt Landing, along a beautiful road, which passed through the village of Clifton, the encampment named in honor of General Scott, is located … The Ira Harris Guard, or 5th and 6th New York Volunteer Cavalry Regiments (then in a state for formation), were ordered to Camp Scott. Stables had been erected, and a wooden building adjoining the old homestead, called the 'Stone-house' was used as cook-house and mess room.

What Dr. Ellis found on arrival, however, was "over one hundred men of the 6th New York Cavalry … sick with measles."

> Colonel Devin had taken command but the day before, and the total want of discipline, aggravated by the unclean condition of the camp, which recent rain had made almost impassable, increased the labor of getting the station into a healthful condition.

The doctor found the sick men still in tents throughout the camp allowing the sickness to spread and he started immediately to get things cleaned up, daily seeing to it that there was "improvement of the sanitary condition of the camp" and "enforcing habits of cleanliness among the men."[13]

In Maine, men desiring to enlist in the state's first cavalry regiment were told that only a certain sort would be accepted. The regiment's historian later wrote that only "… sound, able-bodied men in all respects between the ages of eighteen and thirty-five, of correct morals and temperate habits, active, intelligent, vigorous and hearty, weighting not less than one hundred and twenty-five or more than one hundred and sixty pounds" would be accepted. Physical attributes aside, living essentially out of doors during a Maine winter took a toll on the recruits at Augusta. The would-be regiment lost 200 men by "death and disability, on account of the cold weather and insufficient means of protection." But "… the boys of the 1st Maine Cavalry early learned to meet hardships, or, as they themselves expressed it, to 'stand grief.'"[14]

In the early history of the 6th New York, Colonel De Forest was designated as commander at Camp Scott but was destined to become the first colonel of the 5th New York Cavalry, despite having no prior military experience. However, he would learn and would later lead the regiment effectively. The dates when the recruits were deposited at Camp Scott and organized into companies, and even received some elementary training, went unrecorded by Gilbert Wood, the 6th New York's regimental historian. By early November, the 12 companies were in residence. Thus, the weeks on Staten Island were summarized:

> No incident of great importance occurred there, the time being pretty well taken up in dress, drill parade, inspection and all the other duties … attending a military organization.

Nothing concerning the imposition of the necessary military discipline was recorded. However, a member of a New York regiment training somewhat earlier recalled the initial exposure of civilians to military regime: "It took time for the free American citizen to get used to strict discipline, to learn to obey orders instead of expressing opinions."[15] By and large, the cavalry was a somewhat less disciplined force because of the nature of its operations, movement often independent of infantry formations that in many cases require a greater degree of initiative. As late as 1865, with the war over, Charles Francis Adams, a regimental commander, complained in a letter about the troopers of a new Massachusetts Cavalry regiment then being formed:

> I must confess, they are as hard a pack to manage as any I ever had to handle and a most inveterate set of stragglers and pilferers. They can only understand the sternest discipline and must be punished to enforce discipline in a way I never heard of in my old regiment. I no longer wonder slave-drivers were cruel. I am. I no longer have any bowels of mercy ...[16]

It is known from the record of the 5th New York Cavalry, in residence at Camp Scott in the fall of 1861, that some elementary cavalry training did take place, mostly dismounted, because the procurement of horses for all of the regiments forming across the Northern states took time and the procedures for which were, in large part, still being written. The initial set of officers designated to lead the two new cavalry regiments from New York were appointed from Albany, with political connections and the number of men recruited forming the basis for appointment. These "officers," as inexperienced as the men they were to lead, but receiving the benefit of after-hours schooling from regular army veterans, would prove themselves effective or not only after the command was in the field.

Some regiments being organized were lucky. New York State appointed Thomas C. Devin Colonel of the 6th New York Cavalry. Devin had been a lieutenant colonel in the state militia previously and took command of the regiment three days after his appointment in November 1861. He was 38 at the time and a product of New York City's schools. Before the fighting started, he was a partner in a paint and varnish company. It is curious that Othniel De Forest, leading the recruitment and organization of the 5th New York Cavalry, before the war lived only blocks from Devin in Manhattan (Devin at 219 East 48th Street and De Forest at 97 East 49th Street). The two men may at least have been acquainted and this may have led, somehow, to their involvement with the two consecutively numbered regiments forming on Staten Island. Indeed, both learned how to lead in combat, and both were promoted to command cavalry brigades in 1862. Devin, however, rose to divisional command in 1865 while De Forest was forced to leave the service in 1864 under charges of corruption that were never prosecuted.

Initially, Tom Devin had raised a cavalry company serving as three-month volunteers in the defense of Washington before he joined for three years and became colonel of the 6th. A regular army officer was impressed by Devin's knowledge, his quickly fitting into his role in leading cavalry. In the fall of 1861, the unnamed officer noted, "I can't teach Devin anything about cavalry, he knows more about cavalry than I do." One cavalry historian quotes a source as saying of Devin's leadership, "By early 1862, Devin's 6th New York was 'the best drilled regiment in the service.'" Devin was older than most other officers. "So reliable a subordinate was the balding, ruddy-faced Irishman that he won the sobriquets 'Old War Horse' and 'Buford's Hard-Hitter.'" He was to prove himself at Antietam and Chancellorsville. The fall of 1864 found the 6th New York in the Shenandoah Valley serving under General Philip Sheridan. Devin was wounded in one action but returned to duty in less than a month. In the closing actions of the war, Devin was made Brigadier General of Volunteers for his leadership during the Battle of Five Forks and at Saylor's Creek. After the war ended, Devin was awarded the rank of brevet brigadier general in the U.S. Army.[17]

Colonel Devin apparently arrived in command of the regiment as Doctor Ellis was making his first inspection of their camp, finding the men with measles, including the regiment's assistant surgeon and hospital orderly. The doctor related:

> Colonel Devin had taken command but the day before, and the total want of discipline, aggravated by the unclean condition of the camp, which recent rain had made almost impassable, increased the labor of getting the station into a healthful condition.

The sick were still housed in tents, "… thus spreading this contagious disease, which assumed a malignant type." Ellis's "… daily labors were exceedingly onerous; the entire duty of inspecting the recruits, vaccinating the whole regiment and treating the sick, together with the arduous sanitary inspections daily made of the tents, the appointment and instructing of the hospital-stewards, obtaining hospital supplies, devolved on the writer." Colonel Devin, once his feet were firmly on the ground had to be grateful and be among "… the officers of the regiment, before leaving the station, presented him [Ellis] with a flattering testimonial of their appreciation …" Also, they tried petitioning the surgeon-general to have Ellis assigned as the regimental medical officer. This was declined because it was said his duties across New York City were too valuable.[18]

The comment by historian Gilbert Wood that "no incident of great importance" occurred during the regiment's tenure at Camp Scott cannot be taken completely to heart because, included on the first page of the chapter in the early regimental history dealing with the camp on Staten Island, there is detailed an event, that to the rank and file, was important. Food, its quality and availability, would be a continuing concern for the average soldier over the next four years. While in the field, not much was expected, cooked bacon or salt pork, hard tack, and bitter coffee, sometimes sweetened with sugar, was typical. While in camp, however, something better was not only desired, it was expected. Camp Scott employed contractors to procure and prepare meals for the many hundreds of recruits stationed there. Meals were often served by company in a large shed with tables connected in some fashion to a "cook house." Ellis had previously looked into the preparation of meals for the men and had ordered improvements from the contractors serving Camp Scott as well as others in the New York area. He reported in his diary:

> The condition of these buildings, and the food issued to the men, I found, on my first visit of inspection, to be very bad, and I learned that the same contractors … had a monopoly of this station. Feeling that the extraordinary large number of sick in camp was, to a great extent, owing to unwholesome and badly cooked food, I issued an order that the officer of the day should at each meal be present and inspect the food. This had a twofold advantage: it obliged the contractor to furnish better rations, fearing a report being made to me on my daily inspection, and also preserved order among the men; the want of which had been urged by the mess-men as an excuse for the filthy condition of the mess-room.

The food service Ellis speaks of had apparently already made the men of the regiment disgruntled. Whether the episode related below occurred before or after Eilis's procedural revisions is not noted, but the "mess-men" had become wary of the men in uniform. On the morning of December 6, there was a disruption, or "rebellion," by troopers from the 6th New York. The regiment's quartermaster sergeant, outside the building, heard pounding as the men inside began tearing down the cookhouse. Such was the noise that it woke up Lt. Col. Duncan McVicar who asked what was happening. The sergeant told the lieutenant colonel, "I guess the boys have been given some more rotten fish for breakfast." As quoted in its early history:

> … out of bed the Colonel jumped, got quickly into his uniform, grabbed a couple of revolvers, and was off on the double quick. As he approached the cookhouse, some of the boys had got a 4 x 4 piece of timber and were about to use it as a battering ram, when one of them saw him, and, calling out, 'Oh, the Colonel!' dropped his end and ran, the others following suit. The Colonel got things settled down and then addressed the men there, two companies, telling them how foolish their action was, as now they would have no shelter to eat under, etc., and unfortunately adding, 'Now, if you had whipped the cook, it would not have been so bad, etc.' At this, a howl went up and away went a lot of the men after the cook, who had meantime fled across the field.[19]

It went unrecorded whether subsequent meals were an improvement.

This episode is contrasted with that of the 1st Maine Cavalry in recruit camp at roughly the same time in Augusta, Maine. A newly enlisted cavalryman wrote to his father about his first meal from the camp's contracted food service:

> [I]t was a good supper, too … We had cold salt beef (good), meat hash (good), hard and soft bread (good), boiled rice (can't say whether or no it was good, never having formed a friendship for the article), and some tip-top coffee, sweetened with molasses, but good. We had a merry time and ate plenty.

The next day for breakfast the 1st Maine got "… baked beans (very good), hard and soft bread, cold meat, rice, etc., milk for our coffee."[20] From a Massachusetts regiment stationed in Maryland a soldier wrote home in January 1862, "Just finished dinner, had beefsteak and rice, not cooked as mother would have done it, but nevertheless it was quite good." Then, a few days later, the same soldier wrote, "Baked beans for breakfast this Sunday morning first I have seen since leaving Boston, and the way the boys went into them ... would have astounded my Brighton cousins, I am sure."[21]

Complaints from soldiers, particularly those new to the army and about its internal operations, are as common as rumors. Once the 69th New York Infantry got into the field, the ranting via letters to the New York City's newspapers could be expected and dealt with issues beyond food service. One of the earliest, written in June 1861, came from a soldier identifying himself only as "C. G. H." and included a list of the government's considerable failings, yet:

> ... leaving out of view all the villainy practiced by contractors who have clothed our troops in uniforms that fall to pieces after a week's work, all the villainy of those other contractors who deliver food unfit for human use, in lieu of the first class provisions bargained for, putting all these matters to one side, we are brought face to face with the overwhelming danger of being led into action under Generals ... who are actually not qualified to maneuver a platoon.[22]

On December 18, the following was reported in a local New York newspaper, giving friends and family news of the regiment:

> [The 6th New York is] ... under marching orders, and will probably leave their encampment on Staten Island on Friday Next. It is understood that the destination of the regiment is York, Pennsylvania, where it will go into permanent quarters for instruction and final preparation for the field, the interest of the service permitting such a disposition of the corps. Already as much cavalry is in the field as can with advantage be employed. The regiment numbers about one thousand men, fully uniformed and armed with regulation sabers. Pistols and carbines will be furnished hereafter. Three or four hundred horses are at the camp—a few of them, however, purchased for the First regiment, now at Annapolis. The remainder of the number required will be obtained at York. The regiment is under the command of Colonel Devin (formerly Lieutenant-Colonel of the New York First state militia cavalry regiment). Lieutenant-Colonel McVicar is second in command.[23]

December 23 was a "cold, rainy day" when the 6th New York packed and left Camp Scott. The crossing to New Jersey took most of the afternoon and night, accomplished in the midst of a winter storm that resulted in making a number of men sick. Doctor Ellis noted the departure of the regiment in his diary:

> A terrible snow-storm raged on the day of their leaving Staten Island, the inhabitants of which parted with them with regret, and many ladies of the island braved the storm to witness their embarkation, which, owing to some mismanagement in the quartermaster's department, was attended with unnecessary delay and exposure that cost the lives of many of the men of this splendid regiment ...

From Elizabethport, New Jersey, the 850 men and 200 horses the command had been issued were packed on a train and sent to the town of York, Pennsylvania, arriving there on Christmas Day. At York, some companies were housed in existing buildings and others set up their tents. January arrived and of more import to the men of the 6th than the keg of beer each company received on New Year's Day was the rumor circulating through the command. Regardless of which version of the rumor one heard, the reaction by individual troopers was about the same. Either the regiment was going to be disbanded or it was going to be transferred to the infantry. The men were unanimous concerning transfer to the infantry. They "… positively declined to serve as such." In other cavalry regiments then forming, the same rumor circulated and engendered the same reaction, essentially, "if we wanted to be in the infantry, we would have joined the infantry." Cavalry training went forward, however, and in early February General George Stoneman, the Chief of Cavalry, inspected the regiment. According to the unit's early history, Stoneman saw the 6th as an "… efficient and disciplined regiment," although without a full complement of horses and "… it refused to go as infantry."[24] Basically, horses, or the lack thereof, were at the root of the rumors about disbanding or transferring to the infantry. Because it had been thought, prior to Bull Run, a heavy force of cavalry would not be needed in suppressing the rebellion, little had been done by the army to acquire anywhere near the number required to mount the many state volunteer cavalry regiments now forming across the North. A competition naturally arose between state and federal agents seeking to purchase horses and prices escalated accordingly. Also, a cavalry force would also need saddles and all the various other equipment associated with a mounted command. This, also, had not been contracted. Although the 6th New York had been issued sabers, they still did not have the pistols and carbines a cavalry trooper needed to fight. The slow wheels of military procurement were turning beyond the vision of the men in the 6th New York, but it would take time for the rumors to dissipate.

On the positive side of the ledger, however, by February, everyone in the regiment was fully aware of who was in charge. It was Thomas Devin. Although written many years later and with the acquired knowledge of having served under him for four years, the compilers of the 6th's history depicted Devin in early 1862 as follows:

> The more the men saw of their Colonel (Devin) the better they liked him. He was a man of great military skill; he possessed all the qualifications necessary to fit him for his position; he was very sociable, but his commands must be obeyed to the very letter—the men knew there were but few as well, and none better, drilled than he.[25]

This regiment had been lucky in the assignment of Thomas Devin as commander. It had the right command structure in place, some horses and equipment, and each day they were learning a little more about being cavalry.

An unidentified trooper from the 8th New York cavalry, being under the command of a regular army colonel, was so grateful he wrote a letter to the Governor of New York in appreciation:

> To His Excellency Gov. Morgan … I thought of you and intrude upon your time so fully occupied, just to express to you our sense of obligation for the commission of Col. [Benjamin] Davis, of the Regular Cavalry, nominated by Gen. Stoneman upon the unanimous petition of our officers—to him, for an experienced and competent cavalry officer to take up and make

something of us … The bearing of our colonel among us has given us a lofty example of the hard-working soldier and of the man of honor, at home in his work, quiet, thoughtful, cheerful, of few words, and, like the weight and pendulum of a clock, a ceaseless and noiseless influence on all the wheels … That he means to do his duty is evident, and no one is left in doubt that he expects the rest of us to do our.[26]

Over the next couple of years many more than this one soldier would be grateful that Benjamin Davis was their leader. A soldier writing long after the war remembered that, for the average American citizen, "It takes a raw recruit some time to learn that he is not to think or suggest but obey. Some never do learn."[27]

For cavalry regiments accepting recruits from northern cities, their populations saturated with European immigrants, familiarity with horses was rare. In addition to training a recruit in the ways of the army and all that entailed, the would-be cavalryman most often had to be taught how to ride a horse as well as how to care for the animal. This process no doubt extended the time it took to field mounted regiments and was one of the reasons Secretary of War Simon Cameron and General Scott had initially declined accepting volunteers for mounted service. As a contemporary that had been unsuccessfully trying to form a volunteer cavalry regiment, Secretary Cameron held that "young men would no doubt like to ride to the war at the country's expense; but to open a great riding school for the accommodation of the young gentlemen was a question requiring very serious consideration." However, needing large numbers of men as quickly as possible, city recruits were not asked whether they had ever ridden a horse. The War Department's view of volunteer cavalry evolved as one new recruit put it when speaking of this period:

It must be remembered that I am writing of what occurred before the Government made the greatest of military discoveries, that it is not necessary a man first learn to ride before you entrust him with a horse and equipments, and send him, disable with carbine, sabre and pistols, into the field to fight the enemy.[28]

A trooper from another regiment forming at this time later recalled:

Few, especially in cities, were accustomed to riding, and the great majority of men who would enlist in the cavalry must learn to ride and to use arms on horseback, as well as learn drill, discipline, camp duties, and the duties of the service generally.

This contemporary described the initial marriage of recruit and horse as:

With green men and green horses, there were lively times in the first lessons of mounted drill. The horses reared and kicked … with annoying want of regard for the rides, whose frantic efforts to ride the animal often only made matters worse.

Beyond merely riding the creature, the trooper had to learn how to care for his mode of transportation. The animal had to be groomed twice a day, in the morning and at day's end, fed grain and water morning and evening, and hay for "lunch." One consequence, concluded one historian, was the poor performance of the Federal cavalry in the first year after it arrived on the battlefield. A memoirist writing after the war remembered the experience of the 2nd New York Cavalry:

> We find, however, that the trouble is not only with the horses, but frequently with the men, many of whom have never bridled a horse or touched a saddle. And then, too, these curbed bits in the mouths of animals that had been trained with the common bridle, produce a most rebellious temper, causing many of them to pitch up into the air as though they had suddenly been transformed into monstrous kangaroos, while the riders showed signs of having taken lessons in somersaults.

Slowly, horses, as new to the service as the men who were to ride and care for them, were trained. "Several of our wildest and seemingly incorrigible ones we have been compelled to run up the steepest hill in the vicinity, under the wholesome discipline of sharp spurs, until the evil has been sweated out of them."[29]

Along with the purchase of horses for the cavalrymen, the other major expense was providing them with weapons. What distinguished cavalry from infantry was that the men on horseback carried a saber, a pistol and a carbine rather than a rifle. Just as horses had to be purchased and distributed to the regiments, so had the weapons. Aware of General Scott's thinking that a large force of cavalry would not be required, the War Department made few purchases of cavalry weapons as the war began. After Bull Run, orders were placed, but it would take considerable time to fill them and get the weapons into the hands of the troopers.

Getting the soldiers paid was one of the continuing problems during the Civil War and a cause of much annoyance within the ranks that found its way into their letters and occasionally the press. Revenue flowing into the Treasury often did not meet the obligations incurred by the Government. Suppliers and contractors required payment in a prompt and timely manner and payment to the soldiers in the field was necessarily delayed so the flow of those things needed by the army would not be interrupted. As early as October 1861, men were complaining about not being paid and a group of soldiers from the 73rd New York, apparently having gone without pay since being mustered into Federal service, notified a New York newspaper of that annoyance:

> We would wish to state unanimously … we have not as yet received one cent of the payment due to us by the United States Government, and, as far as we can hear, we are far from it yet. Our families now (a good many of them) are bordering on destitution … There is a good deal of dissatisfaction manifesting itself among the men on account of it.[30]

President Lincoln, in the wake of Bull Run, called on General George B. McClellan who had been leading troops and doing some fighting in western Virginia. He was given command of all the troops accumulated about the capital and the others that were on their way; organize, equip, and train the various elements, making it an army and present a plan that would defeat the Rebel forces in the field and, therefore, suppress the rebellion. These were essentially the orders given to General McClellan and he set about fulfilling the president's wishes. What this new commanding general

General George McClellan and his wife Ellen. His letters to her reveal much about the general. (Library of Congress)

did was create the Army of the Potomac that, in the next four years, would suffer humiliating defeats and epic victories. It would eventually defeat the Rebel army standing before it and in doing so essentially end the Civil War.

Organizing such a force was hardly a simple task but McClellan did have a cadre of experienced, professional army officers to accomplish the mission. Company officers early in the war were usually elected by the men they recruited while those ranking higher, field officer majors and lieutenant colonels, as well as the regiment's commander, a colonel, were appointed by state governors. During the war's first year, many were, in one way or another, encouraged to resign for a variety of reasons, not least among them, incompetence. If the light of reason shone not among these individuals, they were simply dismissed and sent home. William Averell, a regular army officer, when put in command of the 3rd Pennsylvania Cavalry, disposed of 21 officers as well as the surgeon and his assistant shortly after taking command. Between April and November 1862, thirteen more "resigned" while three lieutenants were "dismissed."[31]

During the first year of the war, and as General McClellan molded the volunteers of what was to become the Army of the Potomac into something capable of fighting the Rebels, examination boards composed of regular officers were instituted to further weed out officers not sufficiently versed in the drills and tactics those new to the military were required to fully digest and be able to put into practice. Even with the benefit of after hours' study and coaching, some officers preferred to resign rather than face an examining board. Some officers, who had volunteered in the heat generated by the defeat at Bull Run, were simply too old and they came to realize it once in camp and resigned. Some of those that faced examination and failed but had the proper political connections in their home state, were occasionally reinstated. Overall, the examining boards helped improve the volunteer officer corps and, beginning in the fall of 1861 and through the first half of 1862, many junior and field grade officers, as well as some regimental colonels, felt it their duty to contribute to the war effort from the civilian sector.[32]

Resignations came in all forms and circumstances, and some were unrelated to competence. As late as 1863, as the northward movement of the Army of Northern Virginia was first being noticed, Captain David Bennett, on June 5, commanding Company F of the 1st New York Cavalry, had "forwarded to Washington his resignation, which to the surprise of everybody, was accepted. But Capt. B.'s love for the service would not permit him to leave it; he purchased a wagon and became 'a cheese and cake peddler' to soldiers. In military phraseology, 'he's gone as a Sutler.'" In his place, Lt. Charles Woodruff took over command of Company F "in accordance with the wishes of the boys; for we value and respect an officer that is on hand and in fighting trim …"

Even at this advanced stage of the war, with new regiments still being recruited, little attention was being paid to the qualifications of potential leaders. Major J. W. Dickinson, formerly of the 8th New York Cavalry, received authorization to organize a new regiment to be called the Seymour Guards in honor of the New York governor. The newspaper articles announcing the recruitment included the following: "Men of sterling character, and of influence in their respective towns, desirous of being commissioned as captains, lieutenants, or non-commissioned officers should address the Major at Rochester."[33]

In some cases, officers raising significant numbers of troops often got significant rank. Lemuel B. Platt was 50 years old and a well-to-do farmer from Colchester, Vermont. The governor had turned down his request to raise and equip a cavalry regiment, so Lemuel approached Secretary of War Simon Cameron. Platt was "… of tall and powerful frame, of marked energy, and of considerable prominence in local politics." However, "He was wholly without military training, and frankly told the Secretary, when he inquired concerning his military experience, that it … consisted of three days spent at a militia muster when he was a young man, two of which he passed in the guard house."[34] Platt became Colonel Platt of the 1st Vermont Volunteer Cavalry Regiment. He got the regiment mounted on sturdy Vermont horses and into camp at Annapolis, Maryland, by the end of 1861. He then had the good sense to resign and, having done his duty, return to Vermont. The regiment was turned over to a West Point regular and veteran cavalry officer, Jonas P. Holliday, age 33, from New York. Colonel Holliday, in the spring of 1862, led the regiment on its first deployment in the Shenandoah Valley. In a post-war sketch of the regiment, Holliday was described as "… tall, slender, grave, a thorough disciplinarian and a spirited and sensitive gentleman." Once in the valley, however, the colonel appeared over several weeks:

> … in an unsound condition of both mind and body. He brooded over the fact that his command was not in what he considered a proper condition to take the field, and his depression deepened as the days went on.

On April 5, as the regiment marched between Strasburg and Fisher's Hill, Holliday rode off by himself toward the Shenandoah River. After a time, an adjutant followed and found Holliday "…close by the water … A pistol ball, fired by his own hand, had pierced the center of his forehead, and his face and beard dripping with blood."[35]

Beyond the success General McClellan had in western Virginia, another reason for Lincoln calling him to command in Washington was the age of the General in Chief of the Army, Winfield Scott. Because of his age, General Scott was confined to commanding the army from behind a desk. The masses of troops around the capital, it was now understood, needed time and training so the quotation marks surrounding the "army" could be removed. Someone new had to be seen, by the troops as well, to take it in hand, organize it and oversee the training, taking its potential and employing it correctly. George McClellan was West Point trained but had left the army in the 1850s to become a railroad executive. At the outbreak of hostilities, he had quickly returned and had been given command in Ohio facing secessionist Virginia. Of significance in the president's calculations when he called McClellan to Washington was his knowledge that, before he had left the army, McClellan had been marked as one of the country's next generation of senior military leaders. He had served in Mexico, been sent to Europe as an observer during the Crimean War and had studied at close range the various continental armies and reported on them to the War Department. With the knowledge of the defeat at Bull Run and what he had seen and heard while he traveled to Washington, McClellan probably didn't need to be told, but the president told him anyway; take in hand this force then standing around the capital, get it trained and equipped, have it officered by professionals, or at least competent volunteers, and get it into the field, defeat the Rebels and win the war. The new army commander spent the rest of 1861 taking what some knowledgeable contemporaries considered but a conglomeration of civilians, most of whom one would not care to be associated with under other circumstances, and turned it into the Army of the Potomac. As he stood before the president and got his orders, it may be safely assumed Abraham Lincoln could not possibly conceive that this 34-year-old man would become so controversial and so opposed to his policies that the political opposition would offer him up as his replacement in the election of 1864.

George McClellan is not only the foremost among the cast of unappealing characters of the Civil War Era; he is quite possibly the foremost unappealing commander in all of the history of the American army. Words used in describing the general from his assumption of command in Washington in July 1861, through to his final relief in November of 1862, range from egotistical to messianic, self-deceiving to delusional, hesitant to detached, opinionated to insolent, arrogant, haughty and on and on. Yet whenever he rode among the troops of "his army" the men cheered him. One needs only to read the letters written to his wife, Ellen, whether from the capital or from the field, to quickly acquire an aversion to this individual. In the first six or seven months of his tenure, though, he created the Army of the Potomac. McClellan had the ability to take a composite crowd of militia and hastily recruited volunteers, close to one hundred thousand when he was done, and make it an army. Then the question became what to do with it and when and where, the questions the impatient and worried politicians in Washington, including the president and his cabinet, were asking as 1861 turned to 1862. Added to this were the editors of the large circulation newspapers, the molders of public opinion, that, as the weeks turned to months, kept inquiring when the Army of the Potomac would get on to Richmond.

Brought to Washington as the potential savior of the nation's military fortunes, one studying McClellan's words and actions is in awe of the speed with which the general turned most the nation's political class and most of the newspaper editors into disgruntled critics of "Young Napoleon," as the general came to be called. Perhaps unfairly, certainly during the autumn and winter of 1861 and into 1862, as McClellan and the many West Point officers under him went about creating the new army, this happened. All knew that spring would eventually come to Virginia and with it the army must have a plan, must move, must fight and defeat the Rebels. There was arrogance, even a degree of contempt, in McClellan's ignoring the inquiries concerning when and where the army would win the war.

Volunteers continued arriving in the capital and one individual left his impression. Private Warren Goss, after surviving the war, wrote his memoir like so many others. His writing was deemed good enough to be included in the highly successful 1880s collection of Civil War recollections entitled *Battles and Leaders of the Civil War*. Of Washington at this time he says:

> The Capitol, with its unfinished dome … and other public buildings, were in marked and classic contrast with the dilapidated, tumble-down, shabby look of the average homes, stores, groceries, and groggeries, which increased in shabbiness and dirty depilation as they approached the suburbs.

In most of his writing of this period, Goss included an undercurrent of humor:

> The climate in Washington was gentle, but in the winter months the mud was fearful. I have drilled in it, marched in it, and ran from the provost guard in it.

Pennsylvania Avenue was to be avoided in that there were so many officers about that an enlisted man's arm quickly grew weary saluting:

> Brigadier-generals were more numerous there than I ever knew them to be at the front. These officers, many of whom won their positions by political wire pulling in Washington, we privates thought the great bane of the war.[36]

From his headquarters, General McClellan directed the training of the recruits streaming into Washington, seeing that it was done by mostly West Point trained regular army officers. In addition, he designed, and had built, the fortifications that were to become the defensive perimeter of the capital. When not in his office, McClellan was on horseback, visiting the training camp or conducting reviews of regiments and brigades. All through the autumn and winter months Lincoln waited for the general to tell him of his plans for the new army, hopefully one for quelling the rebellion. As his patience grew thin, Lincoln went so far as to issue an order that the army was to take the field to subdue the rebellion on February 22, Washington's birthday. The birthday came and went with McClellan still training and reviewing the new army. The continual waiting for something to happen surfaced in the national press, its editorial writers wondering out loud when the army would take to the road and be "on to Richmond," or at least marching beyond the outskirts of Washington. There was now a new Secretary of War, Edwin Stanton; he replaced Simon Cameron who was deemed not up to the critical and dire situation confronting the War Department. Early on in his tenure at the War Department, Stanton wrote a confidential letter to Charles A. Dana, editor of the influential *New York Tribune*. In his way, he was telling Dana he needed time to gain control of the department, to set it on the right track and get McClellan and his men moving. In apparent confidence, Stanton, in writing to the newspaper, was apparently trying to apply some pressure on the general. With his words to Dana, the secretary allowed some of his frustration to drip on to the writing paper:

> This army has to fight or run away and while men are striving nobly in the west, the champagne and oysters on the Potomac must be stopped. Be patient for a short while only is all I ask.[37]

Stanton's problem was his personality—called, among other things, abrasive—and that of McClellan could not mix. McClellan, a product of the conservative institution that was the U.S. Army, had his view of the war and of himself that did not appeal to the secretary. In the letters he wrote to Ellen, the real George McClellan comes through, revealing himself to be such a person that many a historian has perspired mightily in gathering the appropriate words to describe him, his personality and the psychology driving both.

That General McClellan could organize and train an army, getting it all fit and ready to fight, all agree. Unfortunately, it is at the completion of this effort that the positives relating to the general end. In the months after arriving in the capital and taking the army in hand, the general, if he hadn't already been in possession of it, developed "… an imperious arrogance toward anyone he considered in his way … Those who questioned his judgments were without redeeming merit … cabinet members were geese; Washington's politicians were wretches and despicable triflers …" In his letters, the general reveals himself in possession of a nascent "messianic vision," of his role in the war. Finally, his plan developed and approved, McClellan had gone to the Virginia Peninsula with the army, been defeated there by Robert E. Lee, he and his men recalled to the capital, relieved of command, and quickly reinstated after the defeat of the Army of Virginia under the command of General John Pope at the Second Battle of Bull Run in August 1862. Washington and Commander-in-Chief Lincoln were then faced with a Rebel surge into Maryland that would culminate with the Battle of Antietam. General Pope's army was merged into the Army of the Potomac and, after a quick reorganization, marched to counter General Lee somewhere above the Potomac River. It was now September 1862, after all that had happened, the recall and relief, and as he is about to leave the capital to meet General Lee again, McClellan wrote to Ellen, "The case is desperate but with God's help I will try unselfishly to do my best, and, if He wills it, accomplish the salvation of the nation." Then, a couple of days later, and again to his wife, he wrote, "I have now the entire confidence of the Govt & the love of the army—my enemies are silent & disarmed—if I defeat the rebels I shall be master of the situation." The general was of the belief, one had to assume, that the best place for a commander was at headquarters.[38] McClellan was not the kind of general to lead from the front, or close to it, as noted by historian Stephen W. Sears:

> It was not his habit to lead or observe from the front, leaving that to his lieutenants—indeed, he had never been on the field when his army went into a major action …[39]

By March 1862, this new army was equipped, trained, organized and officered. The Army of the Potomac, in the field and in the presence of the enemy, and only there, would prove one way or another the competence of this army's leaders, from the commanding general down to the hundreds of second lieutenants. This army had a confidence oozing from it and it wasn't a false or assumed confidence put on to impress the president and politicians. The Army of the Potomac, 100,000 strong, was ready to march, the men eager to confront the Rebels, and the nation's press and public eager for them to do so, encouraging them with the slogan "On to Richmond." When McClellan gave the order, it did march, all the way to Manassas, Virginia. It had been learned the Confederate army that had stood at Centerville and Manassas had withdrawn, moving south behind the Rappahannock River. McClellan moved on Manassas and found only the smoking ashes of the supplies the Rebels had burned, and logs painted black to look like cannons. Quaker guns they were called. The Manassas excursion forced McClellan to revise his plan. Instead of the amphibious operation he had planned to land at the town of Urbanna at the mouth of the Rappahannock River, and still within the confines of the Chesapeake Bay, McClellan would now have to take the army to the Virginia Peninsula. There he would land his force, march up the peninsula with the York and James Rivers on his flanks and take the city of Richmond, cutting the head off the rebellion. Because McClellan's intelligence sources were telling him the Rebel army that had stood, primarily at Manassas, was much greater than his, the general believed a frontal attack on it too much of a risk. Hence that amphibious flanking maneuver. This flanking approach to Richmond might achieve its goal before the supposed superior numbers of the Rebels could be brought to bear. In fact, the Virginia force that had occupied Manassas numbered only about 45,000.

Lincoln, acknowledging McClellan's military judgment, approved the plan, but with one caveat; the general was to leave enough of a force in or near Washington to protect it from any counterstrike or raid by Confederate forces while he and his force were on the peninsula. McClellan reluctantly left the troops and put his plan in motion.

Landing at the tip of the Virginia Peninsula and moving on to Yorktown took General McClellan weeks, weeks spent during a still lingering wet season improving roads so that siege guns could be brought to the front. Meanwhile, the scratch Rebel force defending the peninsula masqueraded as an army. When McClellan was finally ready to move on Yorktown, the Rebels were gone, retiring to Williamsburg to repeat their army in effigy performance.

There was fighting at Williamsburg and more time was spent, but the Confederate force, by a combination of pushing by McClellan and voluntary retirement, moved to defensive positions close to Richmond. The army that had been positioned along the Rappahannock River had arrived and was now standing before the capital. The number of Rebel soldiers defending their capital, according to the intelligence sources reporting to McClellan, and he in turn reported to Washington, were sometimes twice the number of soldiers in the Army of the Potomac. This would be the case all the while the general commanded the army; there were always more of them and, therefore, he always needed more and asked for them in dispatch after dispatch. These overestimates were labeled "fairly incredible hallucinations," by one memoirist suspicious even as the campaign was in progress. McClellan's army always outnumbered that of his adversary. It would, if necessary, be an excuse for any defeat he suffered, however illusionary.[40]

The commanding general of the Confederate forces defending Richmond at this time was Lieutenant General Joseph E. Johnston. On the last day of May, in action before the city, Johnston was wounded. President Jefferson Davis moved quickly to place another general in command of the defense of the Confederacy's capital. This individual had been previously called to the capital to be a military advisor to the Confederate president, but surely the president knew General Winfield Scott in Washington, the year before, had offered this former colonel command of the Union Army. He declined the offer from General Scott, resigned from the national army and offered his services to his native state of Virginia. The Army of the Potomac could hear the church bells of Richmond ring from where it stood, and now, on to the innumerable pages of history that would be written of this time, came Lieutenant General Robert E. Lee.

Days passed, plans made, troop maneuvered into position, until all was ready for a strike to be made. General Lee could see that a static defense of the city could only lead to a siege that in turn would lead to either abandonment of the capital or surrender. Lee would defend Richmond by attacking the army standing before it. Historians would later call it the "Seven Days," the number of days Lee would fight that ended McClellan's "on to Richmond" campaign. These seven days were bloody; some of the actions ordered by Lee caused casualties within his force greater than was necessary and the inevitable mistakes by subordinates resulted in more casualties. After the seven days, however, George McClellan's army was compressed into an enclave called Harrison's Landing on the James River under the protection of the navy's guns. Richmond's church bells could not be heard from there. In these seven days, Robert E. Lee took the first steps that soon led to legendary status among the men he commanded and the people of the South, as well as those reading of his campaigns down the years.

During these seven days, McClellan's subordinate generals executed a fighting withdrawal from before Richmond, across the peninsula, to the James River. It was a skillful operation if in reverse. The casualties were enormous compared to those inflicted thus far in the war; for the Army of the Potomac, approximately 15,800. There were casualties in other places as well. A Massachusetts regiment had been marching about northern Virginia and had several exchanges with rebels along its path. The 13th Massachusetts had been organized the previous year:

> [when it] … left Boston, eleven month since they numbered 1,011 men; now we have not more than 500 fighting men, a great many are sick, some have been discharged, but few have been killed in skirmishes that we have had with the rebels. At this rate, how many original members

of the Thirteenth will return home when our three years are up? It must be apparent to every one, I think, that we have been in the hands of incompetent generals.[41]

What is left unsaid by anyone in the Potomac army at this time was that McClellan's "change of base" was, essentially, acknowledgment of his defeat. It wasn't the amphibious operation to the Virginia Peninsula that was a problem, but primarily McClellan's deliberately slow crawl toward Richmond in the face of well-executed delaying tactics by relatively weak Rebel forces that had consumed so many weeks. This allowed the Confederate force in and around Manassas, and then behind the Rappahannock, to re-deploy before Richmond. It enabled Stonewall Jackson's corps to be brought from the Shenandoah Valley to augment the Confederate force defending Richmond and add weight to the eventual attack on McClellan, and, of course, what else could be expected, McClellan implied; he had been vastly outnumbered the entire time, or so he continually said.

In the days, and then weeks, following McClellan's installation at Harrison's Landing, the general engaged in a protracted exchange of messages with Washington. The telegrams generally centered on what he would do next to defeat the Rebels and how many more troops he would require to do it. The most revealing of McClellan's thoughts at this time are those contained in the letters written to his wife Ellen at their home in Trenton, New Jersey. No one in Washington, in his view, one he repeated often, would support him as his army faced "vastly superior numbers." President Lincoln had to see the situation for himself and took a steamer from Washington to visit Harrison's Landing in early July. On the deck of the steamer the president, "head and shoulders" taller than the general, conferred. From another craft in the river, they could be seen in conference by one of the staff of the Sanitary Commission. "They sat down together, apparently with a map between them, to which McClellan pointed from time to time with the end of his cigar."[42] On July 8, the general told Ellen, "I have written a strong, frank letter to the President … If he acts upon it the country will be saved." Then, after some hours had passed, he added to the letter, "The terrible moments I have undergone of late I regard as a part of the cross I have to bear…." The letter to Lincoln is dated July 7 and most likely given to the president the next day. Then, in a letter to Ellen dated July 9, McClellan wrote:

> His excellency was here yesterday and left this morning. He found the army anything but demoralized and dispirited; in excellent spirits. I do not know to what extent he has profited from his visit; not much, I fear.[43]

The general sent a copy of the July 7 letter to his wife. On July 17, apparently speaking of his wife's reaction at reading the letter, McClellan said:

> So you like my letter to the President? I feel that I did my duty in writing it, though I apprehend it will do no good whatever; but it clears my conscience.[44]

McClellan's Harrison's Landing letter to the president is extraordinary. It is a soldier telling his elected national executive what the war aims of the nation should be and what actions the government should do, and most particularly, not do to achieve victory. "These views," the general began, "amount to convictions, and deeply impressed upon my mind and heart." After this, the general advances into his lecture on "national affairs" for the benefit of the chief executive. These affairs "… must now be assumed and exercised by you, or our cause will be lost." This is followed by a list for the president's benefit. "Neither confiscation of property, political execution of persons, territorial organization of States, or forcible abolition of slavery should be contemplated for a moment." In stating these points, McClellan advocates "policies thus constitutional and conservative, and pervaded by the influences of Christianity and freedom" would be supported by the public and army. McClellan feared "radical views" about slavery would "Disintegrate our present armies."[45] It is recorded that Lincoln read the letter with McClellan present. He then apparently folded it and slipped it into his pocket without comment.

It is interesting, but speculative, regarding any editing done to the letters the general wrote to his wife before they appeared in the memoir *McClellan's Own Story*, published in 1887. Historian Stephen W. Sears, editor of McClellan's papers, maintained the letters to his wife were "never intended for publication." This is understandable in that they reveal so much of the general's thinking and character, most all of which reflect negatively on him. The memoir is attributed to the general alone, but Ellen M. McClellan held the copyright after the general's death in 1885. In a note added at the bottom of the page containing the text of McClellan's letter to Lincoln, the original editor added a note saying the general wrote the letter without any consultation with others. Also, the editor adds, Lincoln must have shown the letter to the cabinet, a group of men already not favorably disposed toward the general, it only adding to their eagerness to be rid of him. The editorial note contains the following as it relates to the general *vis-a vis* the cabinet, "Pure devotion to duty, without thought of self, is incomprehensible to the average politician."[46]

***

With McClellan penned up in the Harrison's Landing enclave, Lee, in military terms, delivered a final, contemptuous blow to the general and the Army of the Potomac. General Lee and his army turned their backs on McClellan and marched north, intent on dealing with the force commanded by General John Pope, the Army of Virginia. Lee at this time considered a move against Pope's army the most favorable option open to him, but it is hard not to look at this as a military rebuke. The resulting campaign would lead to the Second Battle of Bull Run and from there to Maryland and to a small village named Sharpsburg.

Leading the way north from Richmond as August opened was the Confederate corps led by General Thomas "Stonewall" Jackson. As a brigade commander at Bull Run the year before, Jackson had earned his nickname by standing with his brigade, firing volley after volley into Union regiments attempting to drive his men from their position. Now commanding one of the two corps making up Lee's army, Jackson was marching north near a place called Cedar Mountain where elements of a defensive force, part of the Army of Virginia, were emplaced. A battle would be fought, and Jackson's advance would continue its march, followed at a distance by General Lee and an army corps commanded by General James Longstreet.

Jacob Roemer was a German immigrant living in Flushing, New York, in 1861. He had been instrumental in recruiting a volunteer artillery battery in Flushing and became its captain. In his reminiscence, Roemer speaks at length of the first action his command saw in the Civil War. It was against Jackson at Cedar Mountain in August. When it was over, Roemer remembered:

> … the dead and wounded lay thick around us, yet we could pay no attention to them. They had been our comrades and we felt for them, but we were fighting to save our country and that had to be our first care.[47]

Roemer's Battery L of the New York Artillery fought well in its first engagement and suffered no casualties that day. This would not be the case as the war continued. One of the incidents of that day's battle remained with him for the more than 30 years before he wrote his reminiscences. It is an example of the things men are likely to remember as the world around them is set on fire. Early on the morning of August 9, Roemer had his battery ready to move and, while waiting for orders, the captain walked some distance away from his camp to get a better view of the landscape.

> A group of officers were standing a little distance away, and they called to me to come over. I went and Gen. Crawford, our Brigade commander, saluted me as I approached with, 'Good morning, Captain: have you had your breakfast?' 'Not this morning, General,' I replied. Thereupon he called out to his cook, 'Bring the captain a chop.' The cook brought it … The general at the same time handed me a musket cartridge, saying, 'Captain Roemer, we have no salt this morning, and as you will have to smell powder today, you may as well eat some this morning. They say it is very encouraging before a battle, even better than whiskey; it fires the blood, but doesn't stupefy as whiskey does.' I had several of these chops, broiled over hot coals and eaten on the spot with the seasoning given me by Gen. Crawford. I defy an epicure to prepare anything finer.[48]

With McClellan and his army showing no signs of advancing out of their enclave at Harrison's Landing and with a new army, General Pope's Army of Virginia, created from new recruits and elements of Washington's defensive force, advancing from the north, Generals Lee and Stonewall Jackson knew what had to be done. The result after the engagement at Cedar Mountain was a sweeping flanking that brought Jackson to the huge Union supply base at Manassas Junction. General Lee followed, hoping to eliminate the force under

General Pope before McClellan began to stir from his place on the James River. The always-hungry Confederate troops of Jackson's command, while at Manassas, feasted on Union supplies and took as much as they could carry before setting fire to everything else. Jackson then retired a few miles to the west and waited for the arrival of Lee and Longstreet. On August 28, Jackson was located and attacked. The next day, August 29, Pope and his army arrived. Longstreet arrives with Lee riding with him and, on August 30, using artillery to good effect against Pope, launched a counterattack that pushed the Army of Virginia back some distance. After dark, Pope retired in the direction of Washington with only a small portion of the troops McClellan had been ordered to bring to Washington from the James River seeing any action in support of the Virginia army. McClellan had been ordered out of his river enclave but did not comply fully until it was too late to fully unite the Armies of the Potomac and Virginia to overwhelm Lee and perhaps end the Confederate military threat in the eastern United States.

The Seven Days, the maneuvering and then the Second Battle of Bull Run cemented Robert E. Lee's reputation as an aggressive army commander and brilliant tactician. Audacious would be a word applied to his generalship by historians during this part of the Civil War. It was a descriptive word used with some frequency in memoirs of Confederate veterans. Speaking of Lee's conduct in directing the Second Battle of Bull Run, historian James M. McPherson said:

> [Lee] … determined on what was becoming a typical Lee stratagem: he divided his army and sent Jackson's corps on a long clockwise flanking march to cut Union rail communications deep in Pope's rear. This maneuver defied military maxims about keeping an army concentrated in the presence of an enemy of equal or greater size. But Lee believed that the South could never win by following maxims. His well-bred Episcopalian demeanor concealed the audacity of a skillful gambler ready to stake all on the turn of a card. The dour Presbyterian [Jackson] who similarly concealed a heart of a gambler was the man to carry out Lee's strategy.[49]

It would be this type of maneuver, performed with skill and courage that would characterize Lee's extraordinary command of the newly named Army of Northern Virginia. Of course, General Lee had the soldiers, committed both to him and the cause. Isaac Rathbun, of the 86th New York, was among the Union walking wounded retiring from the Second Bull Run battlefield when he came upon and talked with some Rebel prisoners. Rathbun noted in his diary his speaking to some of them:

> They were all sick of the war and wished it could be settled but they were determined to fight as long as they lived before they would be ruled by the Yankees. They seemed to think that we were fighting for negroes [sic] or something else while they were fighting for their homes. They acknowledged that our troops were brave … but they would fight until they died.[50]

On September 4, Lee and his army waded the Potomac River, beginning his campaigning in Maryland.

As with all Civil War campaigns there was a lot of hard marching before the soldiers were told to form a line of battle and load their rifles. Captain Charles Walcott of the 21st Massachusetts recalled the march as it neared Frederick, Maryland:

> We saw a terrible example of the discipline then enforced in the rebel army; two corpses in ragged gray uniforms were hanging on a tree beside the road, and we were told by citizens that they were two of Jackson's men, whom he had ordered to be hung for stealing. Although the rebel army (ragged and half-fed) had just passed over the road by which we were moving, the ripe apples were left hanging untouched on the trees that lined the road; but, in sad contrast with rebel discipline, the straggling plunders for our well provided delivering army left few apples, chickens, or young pigs behind them on the march.

Jerome Wheeler of the 6th New York Cavalry did not see the men hanging from the tree, or at least didn't mention it in a remembrance he wrote for his regiment's history. Wheeler did remember, however, seeing the valley where Frederick is located for the first time.

> As we gained the crest of the hill and secured an unobstructed view of the valley, with fields of golden grain and verdant pastures stretching far to the west, ever to the base of the Blue Ridge Mountains, the roar of the heavy guns and the rattle of musketry were unheeded for the moment in the contemplation of this magnificent panorama.[51]

The Army of the Potomac, by September 13, was in the vicinity of Frederick, Maryland. As they strolled near the field assigned for their regiment's bivouac outside the town, two soldiers from the 27th Indiana noticed something laying on the ground. Inspection revealed it to be a document folded around three cigars. The paper, when it found its way to General George McClellan soon after, revealed the orders Lee had given his commanders as of September 9 and his army's dispositions for several days thereafter. In the hours that followed, the Union general could plan and then move to defeat the Confederate army in Maryland. Lee's Special Order 191 was discovered and read by McClellan close to noon on September 13. It said that Lee's army was scattered over the western Maryland landscape, not within easy supporting distance of each other. A quick and aggressive movement to take advantage of the order's contents was called for. The elements of Lee's army could be engaged separately and defeated in detail. Typical of McClellan, though, it took another 18 hours for the Army of the Potomac to advance. From the area surrounding Frederick, what lay between McClellan and the forces under Lee was South Mountain to the west. The general needed to move, cross the mountain via the roads through the gaps and advance to confrontations with Lee's separated commands. As on the Peninsula, McClellan was slow to react and slow to advance. It wasn't until the next day, September 14, that McClellan's army moved to cross over South Mountain via the National Road that ran through Turner's Gap and on to Boonsboro and Hagerstown. It remains a lingering, unresolved footnote of Civil War history concerning the final disposition of the three cigars. All historians are of the opinion the soldiers that found the order should have received at least two of them.

When he had crossed into Maryland, Lee detached the corps under Stonewall Jackson's command to strike Harper's Ferry and eliminate the Union force stationed there, preventing it from interfering with his movement while above the Potomac. A byproduct of its capture was a large haul of supplies, equipment and weapons. Meanwhile, James Longstreet was to advance with his I Corps to Hagerstown, Maryland, with a division commanded by General D. H. Hill covering the rear of this force at Boonsboro, the small town on the western side of South Mountain and on the National Road leading from Turner's Gap.

The advance to the battlefield to be called Antietam began with McClellan's army moving on the gaps in South Mountain, Turner's Gap leading to Boonsboro and Crompton's Gap, five or six miles to the south, that would take a portion of McClellan's force to Harper's Ferry. "In front of us loomed up almost against the sky the long ridge called South Mountain," an officer noted later as his regiment marched from the vicinity of Frederick on the road leading to Turner's Gap.[52] General D. H. Hill stood in Turner's Gap watching the Union advance along the National Road. He deployed his command, hoping to stall the advance until support he had asked for from General Lee arrived. Near Turner's Gap, about a mile to the south, is a second cut in the mountain with a road running through it. It is called Fox's Gap and it was here that contact was first made with the approaching Union force. Ohio troops advanced and found the Rebels behind a stone wall. The fighting on the bright September Sunday to clear the gaps would last all day. Casualties were heavy on both sides. Union troops, when confronted by the Rebels moved by the flanks to gain an advantage. The Union force at Fox's Gap was two Ohio regiments. The troops of the 23rd Ohio were ordered to charge the stone wall. The regiment's commander, Lt. Col. Rutherford B. Hayes, yelled at his men as they advanced, "Give 'em hell! Give the sons of bitches hell!" Hayes, who would be elected president 14 years later, was wounded in the left arm in this action and, while later recovering, admitted in his diary that during the charge, "I feared confusion" among his men as they advanced, so he "… exhorted, swore, and threatened. The men did pretty well." Hayes also noted in his diary that, as he lay on the ground "… I had a considerable talk with a wounded [Confederate] soldier lying near me. We were right jolly and friendly; it was by no means an unpleasant experience."[53] In the record of this action, there is no note concerning the participation of another future president serving with the same regiment, supply Sergeant William McKinley.[54]

As for clearing the way over South Mountain, there followed a lull until mid to late afternoon as troops went into position to flank Turner's Gap from the north while others advanced up the National Road. Although reinforced during the day by General Lee, with the coming of night the Confederate blocking force in each of the gaps was withdrawn, allowing the Union force to cross over to the western side of the mountain the next day. An infantryman from IX Corps, David L. Thompson, later recalled the part of the fight in which he participated, the passage of years softening his point of view somewhat. His regiment was supporting an artillery battery and a short distance in its front was a wooded area. From among the trees charged Rebel infantry that the artillery cut down easily with canister and a regiment adjoining Thompson's was, because of its position, able to fire on the charge at extremely close range. In his recollection, Thompson spoke of the brief aftermath of the action. "All about us grew pennyroyal, bruised by the trampling of a hundred feet, and the smell of it has always been associated in my memory with that battle." Later, when it was known that Thompson's regiment would remain in place through the night, he recalled,

> Before the sunlight faded, I walked over the narrow field. All around lay Confederate dead, undersized men mostly… with sallow, hatchet faces, and clad in 'butternut'—a color running all the way from a deep, coffee brown up to the whitish brown of ordinary dust. As I looked down on the poor, pinched faces, worn with marching and scant fare, all enmity died out. There was no 'secession' in their rigid forms, nor in those fixed eyes staring blankly at the sky.[55]

Tradition has it that McClellan, having at least heard the sound of the fighting by one of the I Corps' brigades and its severity, then and there, anointed the brigade with a nickname that would define the command throughout the remainder of the war. Thereafter the 2nd, 6th, and 7th Wisconsin and the 17th Indiana infantry regiments, would be known as the "Iron Brigade." The command wore high crowned black hats with the brim on one side turned up, and was the 1st Brigade of the 1st Division of I Corps. Its black hats, when recognized during engagements thereafter, would quickly draw the attention, and the fire, of their Confederate opponents. The brigade would emerge from the war vastly depleted but with a reputation as one of the elite formations in the Union army.

Further to the south, at Crampton's Gap, a small Rebel force held a formidable defensive position. A conference of the Union generals moving on the gap was called. They sat in a field, smoking cigars after lunch, discussing an attack. Half of those gathered wanted to attack in one way and half in another. Colonel Joseph Bartlett, commanding a brigade, was called over to the casual council and asked for his opinion. When he gave it, the tie was broken and the attack went forward. By then it was 4pm and the commanding general thought it wise to dictate a note to McClellan saying the gap might not be cleared before dark, but the troops doing the fighting pushed the enemy and drove them from the gap. Shortly thereafter, Colonel Bartlett was promoted to brigadier general.[56]

With the Rebels gone from the gaps, early on September 15, the Union infantry started west, through Boonsboro and along the road leading to Sharpsburg, Maryland. That morning, General McClellan and some staff crossed through Turner's Gap. Staff officer David Strother rode with the general:

At the summit we came upon their dead lying scattered through the woods and on the summit a stone fence lane entering the road at right angles. The dead lay so thick that the lane was choked with them. Here [General] Sturgis had them thrown aside to move his artillery forward.

This battlefield atop South Mountain, the overture to Antietam, was visited a couple of days later by the 9th Massachusetts Infantry. In their regimental history, published in 1867, its author's memory remains relatively fresh, and he wrote,

One of the most revolting scenes we have ever witnessed actually came under our notice … We came to a field enclosed on every side by stone walls, literally covered by dead men, in indescribable confusion … There they lay in all attitudes of death; some stiff and cold, in the act of firing; some calmly lay, as if in sleep, others appeared like living men resting against trees which were there; again there were masses of men, many maimed, bruised, and so mangled by shot and shell as scarcely to retain the appearance of human beings.[57]

As they started their march that day, a soldier in the 12th Massachusetts later recalled:

… early Monday morning we move down the west side of [South] Mountain; and it has a strange look to us, tired, ragged, and dirty as we are, to see Gen. Hooker in the saddle taking his brandy and water, looking as clean and trim as though he had just made his morning toilet at Willard's.[58]

The campaign that began with the march from the vicinity of Washington and over South Mountain would acquire the name Antietam and two days after the men of the 12th Massachusetts watched General Hooker by the roadside, his corps would be the first to make contact with Lee's army at the start of the bloodiest single day of the war.

When the Army of the Potomac began its march in pursuit of General Lee, it added a new regiment as it was leaving Washington, assigning it to the 2nd Division of II Corps. It was a regiment that had been recruited quickly in July and August and had gotten itself to the training camp outside Washington only two weeks before McClellan called it into service for this campaign. The command was the 132nd Pennsylvania Volunteer Infantry Regiment. It would see its first combat at Antietam. The volunteer adjutant of the 132nd was Frederick Hitchcock, his commission from the governor of Pennsylvania dated August 22. Hitchcock was a friend of the regiment's colonel, Richard Oakford, and it can be assumed politics on some level secured the adjutant's appointment, and it was good that it was so. It took 40 years, but Frederick Hitchcock appears to have expended considerable time and effort fashioning a memoir from the notes written into a diary he kept while with the regiment. *War from the Inside or, Personal Experiences, Impressions, and Reminiscences of one of the "Boys" in the War of Rebellion*, is one of the best of its type, detailed and rich in description of events as they occurred both on and off the battlefield. Hitchcock, writing for the most part in unadorned English, said he had received much encouragement in writing the memoir and was attempting to provide the reader with "... the inner life of the soldier as we experienced it."[59]

After fighting its way over South Mountain, the army advanced following the Rebel army. On September 16, the army's advance stopped. Across a creek called Antietam, arrayed on higher ground and waiting, was the army of Robert E. Lee. A simple glance at the landscape told the infantry that there would be battle the next day, September 17. "Never did day open more beautiful ..." Hitchcock noted. There had only been small campfires allowed for boiling coffee and no reveille had been sounded. None was needed. "The absence of all joking and play and the almost painful sobriety of action, where jollity had been the rule, was particularly noticeable." The night before "Letters were written home—many of them 'last words'—and quiet talks were had, and promises made between comrades. Promises ... 'If the worst happens, Jack!'"

For the evening of September 16, Hitchcock recalled:

> I shall never forget the quiet words of Colonel Oakford as he inquired very particularly if my roster of officers and men of the regiment was complete, for, said he, with a smile, 'We shall not all be here to-morrow night.'[60]

Hitchcock's regiment marched into position early the next morning, and off somewhere in the distance the firing had already begun. He describes the firing as "dreadful," and notes "... fatalities by musketry at close quarters, as the two armies fought at Antietam and all through the Civil War, as compared with those by artillery, are at least 100 to 1, probably more than that." The firing sounded "... like the tearing of heavy canvas ..." Once in position for a short time the regiment counter marched and as they did so some "... few temporarily fell out, unable to endure the nervous strain, which was simply awful [sic]." "The compressed lip and set teeth showed that nerve and resolution had been summoned to the discharge of duty."[61]

The 132nd gave a good account of itself on this day but suffered greatly. It had been one of the regiments advancing on the position the Rebels had established in the sunken road; the famous sunken road as Hitchcock phrased it in his memoir. The regiment had been only able to crest a knoll in front of a portion of the sunken road before a volley of fire drove them back. All that could be done was for the men to lay on the ground, crawl to the knoll crest, fire and crawl back to reload. This they did for upward of three hours by Hitchcock's watch. Colonel Oakford was killed almost at the outset of the firing:

> Except that my mind was so absorbed in my duties, I do not know how I could have endured the strain. Yet out of this pandemonium memory brings several incredible incidents. They came and went with the rapidity of a quickly revolving kaleidoscope.

There was a major trying to rally his men:

> … swing his hat and cheering his men forward, when a solid shot decapitated him. His poor body went down as though some giant had picked it up and furiously slammed it on the ground …

The firing by Hitchcock's regiment on the Rebels in the sunken road apparently killed or wounded all that were in the regiment's immediate front. Some of the Pennsylvanians went forward:

> They brought back the lieutenant-colonel, a fine-looking man, who was mortally wounded. I shook his hand, and he said, 'God bless you, boys, you are very kind.' He asked to be laid down in some sheltered place, for, said he, 'I have but a few moments to live.' I well remember his refined, gentlemanly appearance, and how profoundly sorry I felt for him. He was young, lithely built, of sandy complexion, and wore a comparatively new uniform of Confederate gray.[62]

According to Hitchcock, the 132nd, being comparatively new to the army, had 798 men active that morning. Less than 300 were left at the end of the fighting on September 17, representative of the Civil War's worst single day.

Rufus Dawes led the 6th Wisconsin to the attack early on the morning of September 17 along the Hagerstown Turnpike, his regiment and brigade trying to advance on the church of the German Baptist Brethren. Because the brethren practiced full immersion baptism, outsiders called them "Dunkers," their church ever since being called the "Dunker Church." In his recounting of Antietam, Dawes spoke with some emotion of what he witnessed:

> There is in my mind as I write, the spectacle of a young officer, with uplifted sword, shouting in a loud imperative voice the order I had given him, 'Company E on the right by file into line!' A bullet passes into his open mouth, and the voice is forever silent.

Dawes, some pages on, then wrote of his passage along the same ground a day later:

> My horse, as I rode through the narrow lane [Hagerstown Pike] made by piling the bodies beside the turnpike fences, trembled in every limb with fright and was wet with perspiration. Friend and foe were indiscriminately mingled.

Dawes rode a little further:

> In front of the haystacks where Battery B, 4th U.S. Artillery, had been planted was seen a horse, apparently in the act of rising from the ground. Its head was held proudly aloft, and its fore legs set firmly forward. Nothing could be more vigorous of life-like than the pose of this animal. But like all surrounding it on that horrid aceldama, this horse was dead.

Benjamin Cook, an officer in the 12th Massachusetts, fought on this same portion of the battlefield and later included in his regiment's history:

> The smoke and fog lifted; and almost at our feet, concealed in a hollow behind a demolished fence, lies a rebel brigade pouring into our ranks the most deadly fire. What was left of us open

The horse on the battlefield at Antietam spoken of by Rufus Dawes. (Library of Congress)

on them with a cheer; and the next day the burial-parties put up a board immediately in front of the position held by the Twelfth with the following inscription: 'In this trench be buried the colonel, major, six line officers, and one hundred and forty men of the _____ Georgia Regiment.'[63]

Also, in this fought over area was the 2nd Massachusetts Infantry. It had advanced to the attack and saw considerable action on this September morning. The Lieutenant-Colonel of the regiment, Wilder Dwight, was wounded. As the action went on around him, some of the regiment's soldiers tried carrying Dwight to the rear but he had them stop because of the pain it was causing him. Later, the 2nd Massachusetts was forced to retreat some distance and Dwight was left alone between the two battle lines. While there, he took a pencil and some paper from his pocket and scribbled a note, its legibility was later noted as reflecting the pain he was in:

> Dearest Mother,
> —I am wounded so as to be helpless. Good by [sic], if so it must be. I think I die in victory. God defend our country. I trust in God, and love you all to the last. Dearest love to father and all my dear brothers. Our troops have left the part of the field where I lay.
> Mother, yours Wilder.[64]

As the fighting later spread to another part of the field, some of the 2nd's troops returned and carried Dwight from the field to a house in the rear where he later died.

McClellan's staff officer, David Strother, had a look at part of the field the next day and recorded in a diary:

> In front of the woods was the bloody cornfield where lay two or three hundred festering bodies, nearly all Rebels, the most hideous exhibition I had yet seen.

Strother later looked at the sunken lane, noting:

> In front of this lane was a long double line of dead showing where they fell in line of battle. The line was a quarter of a mile in length and they were close enough to touch each other.

A captain in the 9th Massachusetts recalled shortly after the war that many of the dead were "piled in stagnant ditches" by the roads and that on "Some of the bodies of the dead rebels we noticed papers attached, giving names of the unfortunate men, and requesting that their graves might be marked, as a means of future identification."[65]

When the accounting was done and then checked through the decades that followed, Antietam, it was determined, was the single bloodiest day not only in the Civil War but in all American history. There were about 6,000 dead on the field and 17,000 more wounded. Considering just the dead, Antietam was almost three times deadlier than the initial Normandy landing and twice as many died that day in Maryland than in the War of 1812, the Mexican War and the Spanish-American War combined. The battle was called then, first by General McClellan, and then others, a Union victory. This, it can be argued, is because after standing in position all through September 18, waiting for another Union assault that didn't happen, Lee slipped away and crossed the Potomac that night, leaving McClellan on the field. Probably in his heart McClellan knew the contest had been a drawn one. At Antietam, McClellan was not defeated, which was almost as important, and Lee was not defeated in a battle he could not win simply because of the numbers. Yet, Lee had stood at Sharpsburg and dared McClellan to attack on September 16. The Union general had to attack simply because of the defiant stance of Lee and his army; Lee's daring allowed no alternative. There was no excuse McClellan could use for not attacking that would be believed by his men and those in Washington. He fought General Lee the next day, but without a "conviction that he could win this battle, only that he could not lose it." The best he could say, and this was at 8am the next morning in a letter to his wife, "The general result was in our favor; we gained a great deal of ground and held it." On the morning of September 18, McClellan had upwards of 30,000 fresh men on the field with which to renew the fight and these alone were more troops than Lee had within his lines. The general did not attack or even maneuver, a victim of his continual gross overestimating of Lee's strength. The casualties from the day before were a gross reality, however. Later, there would be a truce for collecting the wounded left on the field and for grave digging. Perhaps unwittingly, McClellan left us a clue about the day after the battle in that early morning letter: "I hope that God has given us a great success. It is all in his hands, where I am content to leave it."[66]

Of course, after Lee's withdrawal, McClellan did not really make an effort at pursuit. Lee had to get supplies and ammunition obtainable in Virginia, so he moved. Looking back on the summer of 1862, Lee and his troops had fought impressively, major victories resulting from the Seven Days and the Second Bull Run, minor victories at Cedar Mountain, Chantilly, and a successful delaying action at South Mountain. Some in Washington or in the North might refer to the Antietam battle as a victory, but if they read the *New York Tribune* on Friday September 19, the paper's reporter, who witnessed the battle and left the field at 9pm that night to file his story, spoke of it as "partly a success, not a victory, but an advantage has been gained." Then "Every thing was favorable for a renewal of the fight in the morning. If the plan of the battle is sound, there is every reason why McClellan should win it." In that Lee and his army left the field on the night of September 18, the Union called it a victory but, outnumbered significantly, the Army of Northern Virginia had, in reality, fought the Army of the Potomac to a draw on September 17 and was standing, ready to fight the next day if it came to that.[67] After leaving the outcome of Antietam in other hands, McClellan reported to his wife, in the letter of September 18, what was probably the reflex impression of the acolytes of the headquarters staff. "Those in whose judgment I rely tell me that I fought the battle splendidly and that it was a masterpiece of art."[68] David Strother of the headquarters staff was of a slightly different opinion as he recorded his sense of the battle on September 19 with Lee gone from the field. "Everybody looks pleased but I feel as if an indecisive victory was in our circumstances equivalent to a defeat."[69]

Advertised as a victory, the Antietam battle put to rest the thought of European intervention in favor of the Confederacy. However, there was success of a kind for the Union cause resulting from Antietam. If Antietam was a victory, or not so much of a victory, President Lincoln seized upon it. He quickly retrieved from his desk drawer and announced the preliminary Emancipation Proclamation that he had been writing and proof reading through the summer. General McClellan's real victory was in the White House and when he learned of it, he also learned his letter from Harrison's Landing to Lincoln, recommending what to do and not do, had been ignored. The war for the Union, or the war for Reunion had become revolution, slavery would not outlast the war, but the general believed he had his consolation. Writing to his wife on September 22:

> I have the satisfaction of knowing that God has, in His mercy, a second time made me the instrument for saving the nation, and I am content with the honor that has fallen to my lot.[70]

During the Antietam battle, one artillery battery had fired all of its ammunition except for some powder bags and when General Burnside was told this he ordered the battery commanded by an officer named Benjamin to fire blanks in order to keep the Rebels at least intimidated. Staff officer Strother, a Virginian, reacting to the announced proclamation, wrote on September 23, "I fear the Father Abraham's paper wads won't do as much service as Benjamin's blank cartridges." Then the next day:

> The war is going against us heavily. The revolution is raging at all points while the folly, weakness, and criminality of our heads is becoming more decidedly manifest. Abraham Lincoln has neither sense or principle. McClellan is a capital soldier but has no capacity to take political lead. The people are strong and willing but 'there is no king in Israel.' The man of the day has not yet come.

At this point the editor of Strother's diary adds a note that from this date on the "journal begins to reflect the frustration of a man who knows the gigantic power of a country unable to use it effectively"[71] and the next day, September 25, again Strother wrote, again in frustration:

> Another proclamation from Lincoln suspending the writ of *habeas corpus*. These wild blows show that the revolution is progressing to its grand denouement.[72]

Still McClellan was railing against Washington, in particular his superiors, the Secretary of War Edwin Stanton and General Halleck, a general called from the west to at least administer the army if he could not run it. On September 20, McClellan wrote to Ellen, "I am tired of fighting against such disadvantages," he said, "and feel that it is now time for the country to come to my help and remove those difficulties from my path." The difficulties as McClellan saw them were the secretary and the general and it is not difficult to see a political agenda of some sort being advocated here by McClellan. Then later in the letter he added, "I feel that I have done all that can be asked in twice saving the country."[73] Five days later with his supposed wounds dripping with self-pity, he told his Ellen, "the President's late proclamation, the continuation of Stanton and Halleck in office, render it almost impossible for me to retain my commission and self-respect at the same time."[74]

A young James Wilson, later to serve on General Grant's staff and then become a cavalry general, was briefly on McClellan's staff at the time of the Battle of Antietam. In his memoirs published 50 years later, Wilson tells an interesting story relative to the coming change of command for the Army of the Potomac. Wilson recounts that, after the battle, while in Washington, he had been told by a general from his native state of Illinois that Lincoln was going to relieve McClellan of command of the Army of the Potomac and the delay in this happening was that the president had yet to settle on a successor. Wilson was advised to tell this to McClellan when he returned to the army's headquarters. This Wilson did, the army at the time still in Maryland and not in pursuit of Lee who by this time was slowly withdrawing in Virginia. McClellan, Wilson says, was not at all surprised. However, the general's staff, who was also suspecting his relief had grown angry, if not seditious, their talk around the headquarters campfire, fueled by whiskey, of the politics and prosecution of the war. Some opined about a move on Washington by the army with the general assuming both civil and full military control. Some said resignation and a return home would be enough for them if the rumor turned to reality. One staff officer from Kentucky seemed to remain loyal to the cause and told off his comrades, citing what was probably the truth of the matter as far as McClellan's staff was concerned. "I am tired of such senseless talk," the Kentucky officer said as he pulled his wallet out of his pocket. "I'll bet fifty dollars, and here's the money, that not a d—d one of you ever resigns so long as Uncle Abraham's greenback mill keeps grinding. Now put up or shut up!" With this statement echoing over the staff officers, Wilson says, "that was the end of the sedition talk that night."[75] This kind of talk extended beyond those close to army headquarters as remembered by Mason Tyler of the 37th Massachusetts Infantry. Tyler was the son of a professor of Greek at Amherst College. He left after him a reminiscence and letters written while with VI Corps. Writing at a distance, Tyler remembered many in the army:

> … felt that he [McClellan] was a much wronged man … and many of them verged on mutiny in expressing their sympathy with him, and devotion to him. But the sober second thought and sound sense even of those who were his strongest friends raised loyalty to the country far above personal devotion to their leaders.[76]

When William Pickerill published his *History of the Third Indiana Cavalry* in the early 20th century, he included his evaluation of George McClellan at this time as commander of the Army of the Potomac, an evaluation that still retains its substance after another century has passed. This regimental historian, writing when he did, acknowledged that the effects of the proclaimed victory in the battle at Antietam and the announced Preliminary Emancipation Proclamation had changed the character of the war. From merely suppressing the rebellion and bring the seceded states back into the Union, the war moved to permanently eliminating the root cause of secession and the war. This could be achieved only by destroying slavery and Lee's army and the others in the field, something General McClellan would not or could not do. Pickerill said that, during his time in army command, McClellan welcomed the coverage by the Northern press that habitually hung around his headquarters, cultivating through them the favorable opinion of both the public and his troops "… by the diplomacy which flatterers always employ." In any case, in the fall of 1862 and possible relief from command of the army, some were apt to think the army McClellan led would mutiny as a result, possibly marching on Washington to set things right. Pickerill, who was there with the army at the time, said, "The fact was that no such felling existed." The simple fact by the time of Pickerill's writing was that "… the impartial verdict of history is that McClellan, and not the war, was a failure."[77] A soldier in the 13th Vermont Infantry, a nine-month regiment called into the defense of Washington in the fall of 1862, commented in a brigade history written while the war still raged:

Who has done so much as McClellan? Who but he drove the enemy from Yorktown to Richmond? The hellish intrigues of demagogues, prevented its Capture? It was though the majority felt: "None done so much as he! When he left the foe where he found them? None so brave on the field! When he was never under fire ... So deaf to faction! When his political friends are crying 'Peace'? so true to his country! When his country lavished everything upon him, and he had done nothing in return.' This author concludes that at this time the army felt it ... not so much who leads them, as that he, who does, shall lead them to victory![78]

A near contemporary assessment of General McClellan comes from his former aide-de-camp, Philippe Comte de Paris. His assessment, written with the knowledge of the Antietam campaign as well as the Peninsula, he summarized in one sentence. After forming and training the Potomac army and then leading it ineffectually in battle, the French aide says of his general, "Unfortunately for himself, McClellan succeeded too quickly and too soon to the command of the principle [sic] army of the Republic."[79]

As for the bloodiest single day of the war, the battle called Sharpsburg in the South, and Antietam in the North, one soldier, James Madison Stone of the 21st Massachusetts Infantry, took a note from the diary he kept and detailed it in his later reminiscence, a memory he'd rather recall than the fighting that day. Stone was in IX Corps and his regiment was part of the brigade that stormed the bridge over Antietam Creek that was later named for corps commander, Ambrose Burnside. After the shooting stopped and it was dark, a nurse that had been attending the wounded to the rear came up to Stone's advance position and asked for the help of some men to accompany her into no man's land between the armies and collect some of the wounded. A detail was put together and went with the nurse, named Clara Barton, and gathered in some of those still alive. When the detail returned, Ms. Barton asked where the men that helped her were from. All were from Worcester County, Massachusetts, and this brought a big smile to Clara's face for she was from the town of Oxford in the same county. As Stone recalled, introductions were made and Barton "vowed eternal friendship" with the men. Some time later, while the regiment was still in Maryland, Ms. Barton again called on the men that had helped her and "She was made a daughter of the regiment." "After the war," as Stone tells it, Clara Barton, instrumental in founding the American Red Cross and its president for many years, "became a member of the regimental association, was a regular attendant at the annual reunions, and ever declared herself a comrade of the boys of the regiment."[80]

What did the men of the Potomac army think of the president's action on emancipation? The root cause of the political divide between north and south, the fundamental reason for the formation of the Republican party, the cause for a split in the Democratic party that allowed the election of Lincoln in 1860, the cause behind the secession crisis, the cause of all the killing and the president's action after Antietam that turned the war into revolution, was slavery. As early as July 1862, President Lincoln had talked of emancipation of slaves. His offer of gradual emancipations and compensation for the owners residing in the border states had gone nowhere with the authorities. This led to his consideration of emancipation cloaked as a war measure issued by the commander-in-chief, thus denying the rebellion of a constituent element of its economy. Some in the cabinet, when told, advised against it. From the outside, it would look like the government grasping at straws while it was under siege and with Lee's army on the move against it. The officer corps of the U.S. Army, the regular army, was a politically and socially conservative body that had been infused with a huge mass of volunteers, officers and enlisted men that had come to the colors to put down the rebellion and restore the Union and only that. How would the conservative regulars and the volunteers react? The President already knew what the general in charge of the army nearest the capital thought of emancipation. As noted by historian James M. McPherson, the Northern volunteers of 1861 "… had no love for slavery, most of them had no love for slaves either." One volunteer at this time noted, "I did not come out here to shed my blood for the sake of rising the niggers on an equal footing with the whites."[81] Now, with the Battle of Antietam announced as a northern victory, Lincoln issued the Preliminary Emancipation Proclamation, a war measure freeing slaves in areas in rebellion and not under the control of the Federal Government as of January 1, 1863. As for the officers serving under McClellan, if they were opposed to the president's action, they may have muttered about it among themselves, but didn't do much more than that. Most ordinary 19th century Americans that comprised the Army of the Potomac harbored deeply prejudiced views of African Americans to such a degree that today they would be looked upon as virulent in the extreme. Therefore, the troops in the field, having no liking for slaves, nevertheless initially looked upon the proclamation unfavorably, having joined for Constitution and Union, but then seeing it as a war measure they could see the point of depriving the enemy a resource. Gradually, most of the rank and file grew to accept the measure if it helped the cause and shortened the war. A Vermont soldier writing within a year of the proclamation's announcement noted:

> The President's proclamation causes little discussion. Many are glad that it is issued, thinking it is wise and just, wise, that by as much as you reduce the number of slaves laboring at home, so much you reduce the number of our enemies in the field; just, that all men should be free. Some think it impolitic, however just; that it will serve to distract the North; now and then, one portends to regard it as unconstitutional.

An officer from Pennsylvania, many years in the future, mentioned the announcement of the proclamation in his regimental history but included no mention of the soldier's reaction to it, merely saying the war would be fought for "preservation of the Union," a "preservation on the basis of justice and humanity."[82]

There were exceptions, of course. Matters were different in the 19th Maine Infantry. Lieutenant Joseph Nichols was a competent and well-liked officer. Before the war he had been quite active in Democratic politics in Maine and when he volunteered, his political friends "… laughed at him for going into the army to fight for the d——d nigger." At some point after the proclamation's announcement, Nichols submitted his resignation, citing the president's proclamation and his disapproval. Nichols expected merely a reprimand from his superiors and his resignation's disapproval. With that out of the way, Nichols could continue his service for the cause while appeasing his political friends at home. His resignation was disapproved at the division and corps level as Nichols expected; the lieutenant was not reprimanded but arrested, brought up on unspecified charges. He was then court-martialed and cashiered in February 1863.[83] A short while after the announcement of the proclamation a brigade commander in the XII Corps, George H. Gordon, encountered the brother of the famous pre-war anti-slavery clergyman, Henry Ward Beecher. The brother, a chaplain in a New York regiment, had a conversation with Gordon who described him as a "Democrat of the old school." Apparently, the subject of the proclamation came up and Gordon relates the chaplain's reaction to it. "He even now, with the proclamation of freedom ringing in his ears, did not hesitate to declare that the negro [sic] girl in a log-house near my tent did not belong to the same human family with himself."[84] With some, as 1862 came to a close and with all the fighting and marching that was their lives, the spirit of 1861 and continuance of the American Union still prevailed. In his diary for November 4, Thaddeus Keith of the 12th Massachusetts wrote:

> … the only comfort that I can get from the knowledge [of spending another winter in the field] is, that we are here to protect our country from the hands of those who seek to destroy it. And may God give us strength, even if thousands of America's best sons, nay, and if I too, have to fall, to restore it whole and untarnished.[85]

Thaddeus Keith was killed in the Wilderness in 1864.

Before November was far along, George McClellan was relieved from command of the Army of the Potomac. As early as August 10, before the fighting in August and September, a general in McClellan's army wrote, "would that this army was in Washington to rid us of incumbents ruining our country."[86] It is probable such a statement would not have been put on paper if it wasn't, at least tacitly, agreed with by one general officer above him. For McClellan's relief, the reasons were many, among them the rumors of his behind the scenes dabbling in, and correspondence with, Democratic politicians, his views on the purpose of the war and its persecution, his slowness to come to grips with the enemy in the field and his continual blaming superiors for his failures, or potential failures, but primarily it was his idleness as Lee's army went back to Virginia unmolested after Antietam. At the time it was felt if he had vigorously pursued Lee when he retreated from Antietam, and caught him, the war might have been ended. That General George Meade did not dabble in army politics did not mean he was unaware of it as rumors were a common pastime around the evening's campfires. As the army stood in Maryland and Lee withdrew and replenished, Meade predicted what would happen. Writing to his wife, he said if McClellan "does not advance soon & [sic] do something brilliant, he will be superseded" by General Hooker. And if McClellan wanted to replace General Halleck as general-in chief, Meade thought it unlikely because Secretary Stanton "& [sic] the ultra Republicans or abolitionists have the influence they are known to have with the Presdt [sic]."[87]

Lincoln, shortly after Antietam, had written a letter to McClellan urging him to advance and catch up with Lee's army in Virginia. It was, said Lincoln, not an order, but it was a test and the general did not pass for he remained motionless for weeks to follow. It was during this period that the president decided to relieve McClellan, but he did not issue the order until after the mid-term congressional elections early in November. Once the elections were passed, an officer was sent on November 7 to General Burnside's headquarters, now in Virginia, with the order for him to assume command of the army. If he refused, the alternative was General Joe Hooker. Burnside, reluctantly, agreed and accompanied the officer to McClellan headquarters. As the general was writing a letter to Ellen, there was an interruption by Burnside and the officer from Washington. The order was given to McClellan and command passed to Ambrose Burnside. The two left and McClellan continued his letter to Ellen. It was 11:30pm. "They have made a great mistake," he wrote. "Alas for my poor country." Later in the letter, he wrote, "Our consolation must be that we have tried to do what was right, if we have failed it was not our fault."[88]

David Strother of McClellan's staff waited until November 14 to pen his evaluation of the general and those, by his observation, around him:

> My opinion of McClellan is that he is the most capable man we have in military affairs. His head is clear and his knowledge complete. He wants force of character and is swayed by those around him.

Here Strother is referring to General Fitz John Porter, who embodies "a total want of judgment [and] has been the evil genius, and has ruined him [McClellan]." And further, "The people about McClellan ... were the most ungallant, good-for-nothing set of martinets that I have yet met with ... Not a man among them was worth a damn as a military advisor—or had any show of fire or boldness." The general's "... mildness of manner, voice, and deportment show him unfitted by character to weld successfully a great power ..."[89]

With the proclamation and with the assent of Congress, during the coming year, regiments of African American soldiers were formed, armed and put into the field. Many were detailed for rear area guard duty or assigned other peripheral duties, but those regiments that served at the front generally did so effectively, some with distinction, through the remainder of the war. Freedom and equality were, and remained, two vastly different things.

Nevertheless, the war went on. General Burnside gradually moved the army south to the Rappahannock River as the weather turned, a cold and wet winter on the horizon. Cavalry officer Charles Francis Adams wrote in mid-November of the army's inability to move wagons with supplies and ammunition, keeping up with the marching men, the Virginia mud confounding all efforts by the quartermasters:

> But Lord! How it vexes and amuses us to think how easy it is, after a full dinner, to sip your wine in the gaslight, and look severely into a fine fire across the table, and criticize and find fault with us poor devils, at the very time preparing to lie down before our fires, mud to the middle, wet through, after a fine meal of hard bread and water, and with nothing between us and the sky but the November clouds. I don't complain of these little incidents of our life myself, and only I do wish they found less fault at home.[90]

CHAPTER THREE

An Incident on the Road to Spotsylvania Court House

Thursday, April 30, 1863

This morning the whole country is covered with a mantel of snow fully a foot deep. It was nearly up to my knees as I stepped out this morning … No cars from Richmond yesterday. I fear our short rations for men and horse will have to be curtailed … I owe Mr. F. J. Hooker no thanks for keeping me here. He ought to have made up his mind long ago what to do.

GENERAL R. E. LEE TO MRS. LEE, FEBRUARY 23, 1863

Woke up this morning with my blanket covered with snow that had drifted in under my tent, and altogether felt rather blue …

MAJOR JAMES F. RUSLING, II CORPS, ARMY OF THE POTOMAC, FEBRUARY 23, 1863[1]

The Irish Brigade sponsored a St. Patrick's Day celebration on March 17, 1863, to which all the officers of II Corps, Army of the Potomac, along with the generals from the army's other commands, were invited. It was to be a celebration "observed with all the exhaustless spirit and enthusiasm of the Irish nature." Brigadier General Thomas Francis Meagher, the brigade's commander, had his headquarters decorated with green boughs and Irish flags. Well in advance, the brigade's quartermaster had been detailed to Washington. His orders were to procure the essentials for the sustenance of the various invited officers of the corps and Army of the Potomac. This included 35 hams, a half-roasted ox, a pig stuffed with boiled turkeys and uncounted chickens. In addition, the quartermaster returned with eight baskets of champagne, 10 gallons of rum and 22 gallons of whiskey, refreshments for the guests during the day and evening. A "punch" was concocted the night before the event using some of the acquired beverages. Two captains from the brigade were selected to supervise the creation of the "punch" and "… labored so diligently that before the mixture was complete both felt over-powered by the labor and had to be relieved from duty."[2]

The day began with a military mass celebrated by the brigade's chaplain, Father William Corby, in a church hastily built for the occasion and decorated with evergreens. As Father Corby later recalled:

General Joseph Hooker commander of the Army of the Potomac at Chancellorsville. (Library of Congress)

> This day's celebration was devoutly opened … and perhaps few congregations on that day assisted at divine services with greater piety, many saying to themselves 'It may be'—as it really was for many—'the last St, Patrick's Day we shall live to see.'[3]

A racecourse had been laid out for a steeplechase and at 11am Major General Joseph Hooker, newly installed commander of the Army of the Potomac, and the other notables arrived at a specially built grandstand to witness the racing. An officer looking on later noted in his diary, "Hooker looked superb, followed by a great crowd of staff officers and a retinue of mounted ladies" who were said to be visitors. General Meagher arrived in a topless ambulance accompanied by several "ladies" who were visiting the camp. The general was "deep-chested, muscular, gay, witty, sporting a trim mustache … entirely looking the part of the dashing Irish soldier." An exiled Irish revolutionary, Meagher was a late resident of what passed for Australia's 19th century version of

Botany Bay and most recently a community organizer of sorts among the growing Irish population of New York City. The general had initially been reported killed at Antietam leading the brigade he had recruited in battle. This was an error common to any confused battlefield shrouded in gun smoke allowing for only the briefest of glances by witnesses. The heat and noise of battle, a skittish horse and an infusion of Irish whiskey had combined at the wrong moment and the general had fallen from his mount and thought shot. Another account had the general's horse being shot and collapsing with Meagher and "… being stunned by the fall he had to be carried to the rear." Either version of the incident has the necessary elements for believability.

As estimated by Father Corby, 20,000 spectators joined the esteemed guests for the races. Cash prizes for winners in several categories were awarded. At 1pm there followed a lunch for 1,500 guests. General Meagher had two tents pitched in front of his headquarters and the guests enjoyed "Mountains of sandwiches" while "pop, pop went the explosions that preceded copious draughts of rich wines." In the afternoon there were foot races and other competitions followed by a banquet that evening. One of the steeplechase contestants later recalled:

> There were thousands in the field … and the scene was a gay one. Every one who could muster a horse, from the general on his splendid charger to the private of cavalry on his worn-down steed, appeared mounted, and not unnaturally officers and soldiers appeared in as good-looking a garb as they could.

Unfortunately, as the contests proceeded that afternoon, the rumble of cannon fire from the west, up along the Rappahannock River, required some of the attending generals to excuse themselves to inquire if they or their commands were needed. After the day of racing and competitions there was the banquet of which there is no mention of the delicacies served save for the note that a captain served the spiced whiskey "punch" … ladled from "an enormous bowl, holding not much less than thirty gallons." Although no comment is in the record of what General Hooker thought of the celebration, other contemporary testimony affirms that a good time was had by all in attendance.[4]

The month of March was succeeded by April springtime in Virginia, the land blooming and promising to dry out. During the wet and cold weather of this winter past, General Joseph Hooker had taken command of the Army of the Potomac from General Ambrose Burnside. Hooker was West Point, a professional and, as a division and corps commander, had shown himself to be competent and aggressive, so much so that the newspapers—their reporters always welcome at his headquarters—inadvertently referred to him as "Fighting Joe." The general was held in some quarters as not quite a gentleman, though, given a supposed taste for strong drink and his affinity for ladies of dubious reputation. The opinionated Massachusetts patrician, Charles Francis Adams, of the distinguished Adams line and an officer in a Bay State cavalry regiment, some 50 years later still retained a prejudicial view of

Charles Francis Adams, second from the right, the opinionated cavalry officer and the grandson and great grandson of presidents. (Library of Congress)

his former commander. In his autobiography, Adams expounds at length about the general then commanding the Army of the Potomac:

> But here I would like to refer to a matter which has for years been to me a constant annoyance. Ever since it was placed there I passed by the front of the State House without feeling a sense of wrong and insult at the presence, opposite the head of Park Street, of an equestrian statue of Hooker. The statue I look upon as an opprobrium cast on every genuine Massachusetts man who served in the Civil War. Hooker in no way and in no degree represents the typical soldiery of the Commonwealth … he was in 1861 and from that time forward little better than a drunken, West Point military adventurer … I can say from personal knowledge and experience, that the Headquarters of the Army of the Potomac was a place to which no self-respecting man liked to go, and no decent woman could go. It was a combination of barroom and brothel.[5]

Joe Hooker was as opinionated as Lieutenant Adams, and seriously ambitious, one who had all along thought himself quite capable of successfully commanding the Army of the Potomac and bringing it victory. The would-be victor over Robert E. Lee had left the army during the 1850s to be a farmer in California. When the war started, he quickly returned east and sought reappointment in Washington. Although not immediately welcomed back into the army he was not rejected either. By some contrivance he had observed the Battle of Bull Run in July 1861 and sometime later was introduced to President Lincoln. Apparently without hesitation, Hooker related to the commander-in-chief, "I was at Bull Run the other day, Mr. President, and it is no vanity in me to say that I am a damn sight better general than any you had on that field." Lincoln's response to this statement went unrecorded, but with lightning speed in military terms, Joseph Hooker was made a brigadier general of volunteers.[6] As a fighting general in the actions that followed, he was recognized while he related his negative assessment of the performance of superiors in subtle ways to friendly Washington politicians while allowing the performance of "Fighting Joe" to fill out the picture. The general's opinions were not limited to fellow generals but included musings about some in the civilian leadership in Washington and the conduct of the war thus far. It was reported of Hooker—gossip that swam up stream and into the capital—that the country might require a dictator to ensure victory. Other officers also had their opinions at this time, such as General George Meade, then commanding V Corps. Although Meade did not actively dabble in army politics, he was not above offering his views confidentially to his wife, Margaret. While McClellan and the army stood motionless in October 1862 after the battle at Antietam, and rumors of a change in command surfaced, Meade offered his wife a view of Joe Hooker:

> Hooker is a Democrat and an anti-abolitionist ... that is to say, he was. What he will be, when the command of the army is held out to him, is more than anyone can tell, because I fear he is open to temptation and liable to be seduced by flattery.

Now, however, in the wake of General Burnside's performance in command— performance that might easily be labeled a disaster—from Lincoln came the appointment he wanted, along with a note containing the not-so-subtle reminder that only successful generals became dictators. Ambrose Burnside was sent to Ohio. A soldier in the 3rd Michigan Infantry left his thinking on the matter as he no doubt heard it elsewhere:

> Now, we felt that General Hooker will be like the poor man that won the elephant at the raffle. After he got the animal he did not know what to do with him. So with fighting Joseph. He is now in command of a mighty large elephant.[7]

The army Hooker had been given to command was discouraged, its morale at a low point. The immediate cause was General Burnside allowing a large portion of it to be mowed down at close range in a futile assault on the high ground behind the town of Fredericksburg, Virginia, on December 13. The Army of the Potomac had crossed the Rappahannock River with Robert E. Lee and his army arrayed on the heights behind the town in as strong a defensive position as a 19th century army could ask for. The whole idea should have been more closely and carefully considered, particularly when the pontoons for bridging the river were many days late in arriving thus allowing Lee and his army to mass behind the town to meet the Union force. The result was not so much a battle in the conventional sense, but the inexcusable murder of men dressed in blue. John Day Smith, when he compiled the history of the 19th Maine Infantry 47 years later, referred to the Fredericksburg battle saying:

> It would be unprofitable to describe the sickening details of the unprecedented and criminal slaughter of our troops as they charged hopelessly against the impregnable Confederate works along Marye's Heights.

James Madison Stone, in the 21st Massachusetts Infantry, had lived with his memory of Fredericksburg and his small role after the assault upon Lee's position for over 50 years. Stone was part of the burial detail some days after the assault. It was, he wrote:

> ... the most ghastly, the most shocking, the most humiliating scene possible. The field was covered with dead men. Dead men everywhere, some black in the face, most of them had the characteristic pallor of death; nearly all had been stripped of every article of clothing. All were frozen, some with their heads off, some with their arms off, some with their legs off, dismembered, torn to pieces, and they lay there single, in rows and in piles.

Stone and the detail he was part of buried 987 bodies. The work "... was enough to upset one's mind if anything could upset it." The observance by James Stone was also noted by a Confederate soldier. Randolph Shotwell had left Princeton when the war began and joined the first regiment he encountered upon reaching Virginia. It was 8th Virginia Infantry. Writing of Fredericksburg, Shotwell recalled:

> ...fully eleven hundred dead bodies—perfectly naked—swollen to twice the natural size—black as negroes [sic] in most cases—lying in every conceivable posture—some on their backs with gaping jaws—some with eyes large as walnuts, protruding with glassy stare—some doubled up like a contortionist—here one without head—there one without legs—yonder a head and legs without a trunk—everywhere horrible expressions—fear, rage, agony, madness, torture—lying in pools of blood—lying with hands half buried in mud—with fragments of shell sticking from oozing brain—with bullet holes all over the puffed limbs ... Indeed, it is well established fact that many of the more cowardly Yankees actually sought safety by crouching behind piles of their own slain ... Our skirmishers were astonished to have some of the supposed corpus jump up and surrender themselves ... I noticed one peculiarity of the slain—that the majority were foreigners. Scarcely an English face was to be seen on the field, unless of an officer. Most of the bodies had the unmistakable Irish cast of features, and this gave the impression among our men the 'Meagher's Irish Brigade' had been annihilated— which turned out not to be the case.[8]

Those away from the battlefield, on duty outside the capital could see the defeat at Fredericksburg with a somewhat wider perspective. From the 13th Vermont Infantry came the comment of December 15:

The skies are dark this morning; and if Burnside is beaten, darker still our national affairs; not from the blow received from the rebels; but the traitors in the North will seize on this, and cry 'Peace.'[9]

The numbers at Fredericksburg speak for themselves. It is estimated that between 35,000 and 40,000 men were available for the advance on Marye's Heights outside Fredericksburg where Robert E. Lee had set part of his defensive line. It was up hill with the Confederate infantry positioned on the heights with plenty of artillery and in a sunken road protected by a stonewall below the guns. The Federals were organized into 85 regiments, in 18 brigades, in six divisions, with elements of other commands available. The attacking force had little artillery support. The "Noonday was turned to dusk by the smoke and storm of battle." An officer in the 116th Pennsylvania of the Irish Brigade later recalled that as his regiment moved up to cross the Rappahannock on a pontoon bridge, there was the tension of approaching battle, but also:

> … not so pleasant was the reception by the professional embalmers who, alive to business, thrust their cards into the hands of the men as they went along. The cards were suggestive of an early trip home, nicely boxed up and delivered to loving friends by quick express, sweet as a nut and in perfect preservation, etc., etc.[10]

The advance of the Irish Brigade against the Rebel position "was actually impeded by the bodies piled upon one another." "It was not a battle—it was a wholesale slaughter of human beings—sacrificed to the blind ambition and incapacity of some parties." While the advance on Marye's Heights went forward, there was to be a flanking attack by a Union force that crossed the river below the town. Confusion, or a misreading of orders, turned this thrust into nothing more than a peripheral engagement. When it was over, when the Army of the Potomac was again on the other side of the river, the results were added up. There were 1,284 Union dead, 9,600 wounded and 1,769 missing. Burial parties like that of James Stone later noted that of those dead soldiers that fell closest to the stonewall all were from the Irish Brigade.[11]

The numbers cited in the early history of the Irish Brigade when it was published may not be reliable, but it was thought that as many as 1,867 Union dead were left on the field. As for the brigade, composed of five regiments, but numbering not over 1,200 men for the assault, only 273 returned. "Never since the war began have the Union forces met with such a disaster as that we have just suffered," wrote an officer from the Irish Brigade just after the battle. "As for the Brigade, may the Lord pity and protect the widows and orphans of nearly all those belonging to it. It will be a sad, sad Christmas by many an Irish hearthstone in New York, Pennsylvania, and Massachusetts."[12] The following month a Requiem Mass was celebrated at St. Patrick's Cathedral in New York for the dead of the brigade in the war thus far. General Meagher led the mourners followed by the city's political leaders. The ceremony produced

Sketch of the mass at St Patrick's Cathedral for those killed from the Irish Brigade after Fredericksburg. (Library of Congress)

"a sensation of awe and devotion to which no heart susceptible of the finer emotions of our nature could be indifferent."[13]

As for the rest of the army, a cavalryman commented later:

> The Army of the Potomac was, indeed, in a bad way. It had not been paid in six months. It had lost heavily in killed and wounded at Fredericksburg, with no adequate results.[14]

In January, Burnside had attempted another crossing of the Rappahannock but in the advance only some leading elements got even close to the river. It had started raining as the army moved and the rain did not stop. What had been dry roads became bottomless troughs of mud unique to Virginia, a combination of clay, rainwater and soil that swallowed artillery pieces up to their axles and wagons to their floor beds. Horses died trying to pull vehicles from this substance. "One half of the army," it was noted, "had to be employed to dig the other half out of the mud."[15] After a couple of days of this "mud march," Burnside ordered a return to the army's camps. Now with two defeats on his record as army commander, one by Robert E. Lee and the other by Mother Nature, as well as a near revolt by subordinate generals that no longer had faith in his leadership and desired the recall of George McClellan to the army, a change was necessary. This noise reached the ear of the president directly from two generals, representative of others, that sought the removal of Burnside. When the commanding general became aware of this conspiracy of sorts, he demanded the dismissal of a number of individuals or he himself would resign. Lincoln, after a time, allowed Burnside to depart for another assignment and appointed Hooker with the knowledge that he would certainly reshuffle the generalship in the army below him. The morale issues went deeper than this, though. The Army of the Potomac, since acquiring its name, had only been able to achieve a draw at Antietam the previous September and had been ordered off the Virginia Peninsula after its "change of base" caused primarily by Robert E. Lee. Fredericksburg was, in reality, the latest in a run of what some might call bad luck while others, standing closer to it, might call it mismanagement at best, incompetence at worse. A historian in the future, looking at this army, as it had stood around Washington in late August 1862, as General John Pope's Army of Virginia and elements of the Potomac Army were thrashed by General Lee at the Second Battle of Bull Run, coldly spoke of the force created by George B. McClellan, the Army of the Potomac:

> In the end it would become an army of legend, with a great name that still clangs when you touch it. The orators, the brass bands and the faded flags of innumerable Decoration Day observances, waiting for it in the years ahead, would at last create a haze of romance, deepening spring by spring until the regiments and brigades became unreal—colored-lithograph figures out of a picture-book war, with dignified graybeards bemused by their own fogged memories of a great day when all the world was young and all the comrades were valiant.[16]

That was a future unknown, undreamed of by the Irishmen celebrating St. Patrick's Day or the rank and file soldiers waiting for the inevitable next campaign that was to start sometime in the spring.

For now, the army Hooker took over, discouraged by defeats, desertions and the damn Virginia winter weather, waited for spring. All of this was known in Washington and Hooker had more or less a free hand in setting things straight. The general opinion, current within the middle echelons, was captured in a letter home by Major Rufus Dawes of the 6th Wisconsin Infantry of the Iron Brigade, one of the army's elite units. What had become clear during this winter and noted by Major Dawes was that:

[the] … army seems to be overburdened with second-rate men in high positions, from General Burnside down. Common place and whisky are too much in power for the most beautiful of future. This winter is, indeed, the Valley Forge of the war.

Another soldier, lower in echelon, would not stop there, writing with obvious sarcasm, he looked to the horizon for change. "Alas, my poor country!" he mourned before the anger surfaced, "… but the brains, the brains—have we no brains to use … Perhaps Old Abe has some funny story to tell, appropriate to the occasion." Then some days passed, and he was again writing, "Mother do not wonder that my loyalty is growing weak … I am sick and tired of disaster and the fools that bring disaster upon us." Reading these contemporary sources, it can be appreciated that the army was, to a degree, demoralized. But beyond that, and coming from those that did the fighting and the bleeding, there was anger. These soldiers had pride, believed they were better, and fighting for a cause more worthy, than those opposing them. They deserved better than they had received. They deserved better leadership.[17] These words, originally employed by Bruce Catton in his work *Gory Road*, are simply too illustrative of the Potomac army at this time to go unspoken here. The new commanding general, if he didn't appreciate the depth and degree of the demoralization that was symptomatic of this anger, nevertheless knew he wanted new men in command positions below him. Generals left the Potomac army and others were promoted and assumed the vacancies. Time and the coming campaign would prove General Hooker's personnel moves beneficial or not.

The chaplain of the 15th New Jersey remembered and spoke at length of the issues prevalent in the December days after the Fredericksburg battle in the regiment's later history:

> A settled gloom pervaded the camps of the Army of the Potomac, and increased as the weary days wore away. Fuel became scarce, and the water was poor and muddy, and not fit to use without boiling. The ground was wet and spongy … Most of the men were in sad need of clothing … Their shoes were completely worn out. The food was without variety, mostly army crackers and pork, with occasionally an issue of poor beef, and no vegetables. For a time we compared ourselves to Washington's army at Valley Forge. … Typhoid fever prevailed, and made fearful havoc among our ranks … There seemed to be a race in mortality between the Fifteenth and Thirty-third Regiments … It was sad to have a brave man fall in battle, but it was sadder to see our most promising youth expire, lying on the cold ground, with only a single blanket under them.[18]

Upon assuming command from Burnside, orders began flying from Hooker's headquarters at a rate and degree of detail not seen before and aimed at fixing some of the army's problems. One of the army's chaplains, assigned to the 102nd Pennsylvania, noted in a letter composed in April:

> The army, when he [Hooker] took it, was defeated, discouraged, querulous, and, to some degree demoralized … One sensible order after another has been quietly issued and enforced, until a very high degree of efficiency, in order, drill and promptness, has been attained. Not only this,

but the soldiers seem universally to have the fullest confidence in Gen. Hooker, and, also, in themselves ... What will result will be, in time and coming events will unfold.[19]

Foremost among the issues to be addressed by the new commander, one that could not be put off, was desertion. Civil War combat was horrific, but to fight a battle like Fredericksburg was beyond being merely an unfortunate occurrence, the fortune of war; it illustrated to many of the volunteers, comprising the overwhelming bulk of the Union army, that they were being led in many instances by incompetents. Hence, many were driven to reconsider their role in suppressing the rebellion and then walking away from a situation that, if not addressed in a significant manner, was sure to kill them. James Stone of the 21st Massachusetts remembered and later wrote:

> ... the conviction was general that the men in the ranks were superior in intelligence to the southerners and just as brave, the army was better disciplined, and much better supplied, that what we lacked was leaders, the men were not tired of fighting, but they were tired of being sent to slaughter by incompetent generals.[20]

To relieve the desertion situation, Hooker granted a number of furloughs to soldiers during the winter and, with the aid of the administration in Washington, those that had deserted were given a window of time in which to return without facing punishment. Some wayward soldiers took advantage of this. Food, often marginal in quality and just as often as absent as some of the soldiers, was improved. Soft bread, fresh meat and vegetables became available in the winter camps that dotted the countryside surrounding Falmouth, Virginia. The effect on morale was immediate, but also the improvement of the army's diet helped to a great degree in improving the army's general health. The sickness rate among the soldiers declined, reducing the numbers of hospital patients suffering from afflictions stemming from an inadequate diet. As for the hospitals themselves, they were ordered cleaned and the staffs ordered to attend to duties precisely. A miracle of sorts occurred within the army bureaucracy with the appearance of paymasters from Washington with the army's back pay. General Hooker approved the creation of corps badges, pieces of cloth, elementary in design, that were sown on the soldier's hats or uniform sleeve. "This idea had great practical value," a Massachusetts officer later explained. "It excited enthusiasm, checked straggling, and identified wounded and dead partially."[21]

The cavalry, until now often ordered around by infantry division and corps commanders, was consolidated into a corps with a corps commander to lead it, General George Stoneman. This organizational change prompted the historian of the 1st New Jersey Cavalry to later judge Hooker's move a success, concluding that "For the first time the cavalry found themselves made useful by their general, and treated as something better than military watchmen of the army."[22] Shortly thereafter, the Union cavalry became not only an independent strike force, but a formation that could fight and win against, what had been during the war's initial two years, a superior Rebel mounted force under General Jeb Stuart. Indeed, on the very day the Irish Brigade was entertaining most of the army, the rumbling of artillery heard by the celebrants was the 2nd Cavalry Division in action against a Rebel mounted force up stream along the Rappahannock at a place, given the day, appropriately named Kelly's Ford. Also, to acquire the best knowledge of the enemy's dispositions and strength, Hooker established the Bureau of Military Information. The Bureau with its spies, and by interrogation of prisoners, along with other intelligence techniques, eventually provided the commanding general with a fairly accurate order of battle for the Army of Northern Virginia. In all of these innovations and in the improved morale of the army, Hooker had shown himself to be an adept administrator and conscientious officer. But there was a negative side, supported with the aid of hindsight that found its way into the retelling of this piece of the war's history. John Bigelow in *The Campaign of Chancellorsville*, published in 1910, summarized the contemporary view of General Hooker at the time. "Up to a certain point of responsibility which he had not yet reached, he was capable of brilliant achievement, but at that point, if he reached it, he would break down." General Hooker, "… among the higher officers who had grown up in the service with him and judged him critically, he was not generally admired."[23] Coupled with the negative contemporary view of such personalities as Charles Francis Adams, Joseph Hooker to this day generally retains his tarnished reputation in the history of this war.

In early April, President Lincoln traveled to Falmouth to assess the army for himself, to talk with Hooker and his senior subordinates and, generally, to be seen by the troops. Hooker ordered a review; the majority of the army marching passed the commander-in-chief. According to one that marched that day, the president "… wore a high silk hat and a plain frock coat. His face wore that peculiar somber expression … But it lighted up into a half-smile as he occasionally lifted his hat in acknowledgment of the cheering of the men." An officer in the 111th Pennsylvania Infantry, after the passage of three decades, recalled seeing the president on this occasion and, with years of accumulated hindsight, pronounced Abraham Lincoln as he remembered this day, "the greatest man of the nineteenth century." There were other witnesses to the review that day. The "enemy … were intently interested spectators … for the review was held in full view of the whole of their army … We could see them swarming over Marye's Heights … intently gazing upon us." "It was an occasion not to be forgotten," recalled a cavalry trooper, "the sight being one of the most magnificent many of us ever saw." An officer that survived through to the end of the war judged the Army of the Potomac at this moment to be "… composed of better material than ever before or after."[24]

The army was ready to move and fight. An officer from New Jersey in letters written in March and April forcefully reminded those at home why he was camped on the bank of the Rappahannock River in Virginia and came as close as he ever did to cursing those of dissimilar views:

Am here to fight for your safety and your liberties; and see to it, that you duly appreciate them. If you turn Copperhead, or forget the flag that has so long flapped defiance to the enemies of mankind, may your right hands forget their cunning, and your tongues cleave the roofs of your mouths.

In April, he said:

The *Advocate* is a sterling sheet and I prize it highly. Am proud of it, as a periodical; and I honor you New Jersey Methodists for the unqualified manner in which they have 'spoken out' on the great question of the times. It is not so bad to be known as a Methodist, when the Church takes such a high and patriotic ground, even in a Copperhead State.[25]

Morale had been improved with the coming of better food, some new clothing, better weather and a renewed emphasis on training and drill, but there had been that hard core of the army that hadn't succumbed to despondency and desertion. An Irish immigrant from the Irish Brigade no less spoke of what it all meant to him. Sergeant Peter Welsh of the 28th Massachusetts expressed it best for himself and probably for others like him. This country is, Welch wrote, "my country as much as the man born on the soil …" and "the maintenance of the government and laws and the integrity of the nation [are his] as any other man." The war had meaning beyond just America too:

This war with all its evils with all its error and mismanagement is a war in which the people of all nations have a vital interest. [T]his is the first test of a modern free government in the act of sustaining itself against internal enemys [sic] and matured rebellion, all men who love free government and equal laws are watching this crisis to see if a republic can sustain itself in such a case. [I]f it fails then the hopes of millions fall and the desighns [sic] and wishes of all tyrants will succeed.[26]

As the weather improved, the men became more active and animated as the army waited for the inevitable orders to march. With the ground dry near their winter huts, "ball-playing" became "a mania in the camp." According to the historian of the 10th Massachusetts, "the game is the fashionable 'New York Game,' played by nine on a side, and nine innings making a game. An undecided game is now pending between the 10th Massachusetts and 36th New York Regiments." The regiment's history failed to record the outcome of the game, probably because the same day there was a regimental inspection and issuing of eight days' rations to the men, a sure indication of an imminent movement.[27]

While morale and conditions had improved, and the season slowly changed, General Hooker pondered his campaign, put together a plan to fight and defeat the Army of Northern Virginia, after which, some thought, the war might be ended. With the experience of Fredericksburg to draw on, Hooker knew another direct lunge at General Lee on the opposite side of the river was out of the question. The river had to be crossed but not at a place where the Rebel army could watch. Delayed from starting in April by heavy rains, the plan Hooker finally settled on involved sending a force downstream from Lee's position at Fredericksburg, putting pontoon bridges across the river and crossing enough strength to demonstrate convincingly, threatening the Rebel army and holding it in place. While this movement went forward, Hooker, with his main striking force, would move up stream, cross the river and turn back to the east and quickly move on Fredericksburg, forcing Lee and his army out of their entrenchments or be taken from the rear. Hooker surmised the Rebels would have to retreat or confront the Army of the Potomac in open country where Union firepower and numbers would prevail. Simultaneous with these moves, the Cavalry Corps was to move to the west, cross the river and raid deep behind Lee's position, severing supply lines and communications with Richmond, as well as intercepting Lee's army if he retreated. The only mounted force that would be retained with the army while the cavalry raid went forward was a brigade led by Col. Thomas Devin, the former commander of the 6th New York. The brigade included Devin's own New Yorkers and the 8th and 17th Pennsylvania, in all about 1,500 troopers. During the coming days, however, Brigadier General Alfred Pleasonton, commander of the 1st Cavalry Division, would command the three regiments. Cavalry corps commander General Stoneman had ridden south but without Pleasonton, an unusual occurrence. In a regimental history published in 1868 by the surgeon of the 8th Illinois Cavalry, the doctor commented that:

> This arrangement was very displeasing to General Pleasonton; as an opportunity to gain military renown would thus be afforded to those who accompanied the great raid, where as none was in prospect for those left behind[28]

General Pleasonton later remedied the opportunity for renown when the reports were written of the coming battle.

When Hooker's strike force of three corps began its movement upstream, each was preceded by a cavalry regiment. The regiments left camp on April 27 at 10am, getting to Kelly's Ford at 4pm. Pontoons were brought up and a bridge put across the Rappahannock. The next morning, the 6th New York Cavalry led XII Corps across, advancing to Germanna Ford on the Rapidan River. There it met a Rebel force in rifle pits on the far side. The early history of the 6th New York states that:

> Lieutenant-colonel McVicar ordered fifty men to dismount and advance as skirmishers to the ford, and hold it if possible ... The firing was very brisk for about an hour, when some infantry (2nd Massachusetts and 73td Pennsylvania) came up and, all combined, soon forced the enemy to fall back, leaving sixty prisoners in our hands. During the fight Colonel McVicar took the carbine of J. N. Crawford of Troop C and fired several shots. Corporal Samuel A. Fanshaw of Troop I was wounded in the left knee."

The next day, April 29, the three infantry corps moved to and occupied the area around the Chancellorsville crossroads. Chancellorsville was a large, columned, roadside inn with several outbuildings. It was surrounded by a large open area where wagons and artillery could be parked and troops could mass. The battle fought in the surrounding

Germanna Ford on the Rapidan River. (Library of Congress)

area would take its name from the building standing in this clearing. Locally, the countryside for several miles around was known as the Wilderness, an expanse of dense woodland of second growth trees, scrub oak and pine, with thick, tangled undergrowth covering terrain laced with small and sometimes stagnant streams.[29]

With the holding force established in a lodgment downstream from Fredericksburg and the strike force at Chancellorsville, Hooker's plan for defeating the Army of Northern Virginia seemed to be proceeding as planned. To Hooker, General Lee and his army were now, or soon to be, his property. The strike force was in position to advance on Fredericksburg and the Cavalry Corps was in Lee's rear, ripping up railroad tracks and burning anything that could be of use to the Rebel army. But by sending practically all his cavalry to the south, Hooker, now trying to maneuver for an advantageous position and for battle with the enemy, had retained with his army a cavalry force—only three regiments—that was insufficient given his plan. There were simply too few horsemen to provide proper flank protection, movement screening and adequate reconnaissance, even if the army remained stationary.

Lee's cavalry quickly became aware of the river crossing to the west and notified General Lee who then had a decision to make. Which of the forces now over the river was the main threat? It was the western force, he decided, and immediately started the greater part of his army to the west to confront it, leaving only a small force to contend with the demonstration. Thomas Jackson's corps and another two infantry divisions moved to the west to confront Hooker's force that, for the moment, was standing at Chancellorsville and not attempting to free itself from the woods and heavy undergrowth that surrounded it.

Given the ground cover of thick, tangling brush and briars and the thick stand of trees, visibility any distance was severely restricted, not to mention movement. Indeed, as for movement, men could easily lose orientation and be found traveling in a completely different direction than intended. An officer who was there remembered "the woods and under growth each side of the road was so dense that we could not see into it a half-dozen steps." Therefore, when regiment-size formations were introduced into this terrain, they easily became partially blind and just as easily disoriented, the ability to maneuver limited.

On April 30, Hooker had ordered the troops that had reached Chancellorsville to stop their advance. In the time granted to him by this halt, Lee was able to rush his opposing force into position to contest the advance by Hooker to the east. The next day, May 1, a resumption of the advance was halted by Hooker only hours after it began and after the Union advance had made contact with Lee's force that had arrived from the Fredericksburg area. Hooker's troops returned to the positions they held the previous night. The general, it was said, had received erroneous information that Longstreet's Corps was advancing to re-join Lee. Hooker, rather than attacking and overpowering his enemy, consolidated his position to receive an attack. The fighting on May 1 had spread out on either side of the principal roads bisecting the Wilderness to the east of Chancellorsville, the Orange Turnpike and the Orange Plank Road, both of which led to Fredericksburg. The fighting had been confused as well as ferocious, a struggle in which unit cohesion and command and control were luxuries. Gun smoke drifted through the Wilderness, enhanced by fires started by rifle bullets striking the dry brush and igniting it.

Despite the difficulties and long odds facing the Army of Northern Virginia, Hooker's halting of his advance was a gift to Lee, allowing him during the waning hours of May 1 the time he needed to formulate a response to the threat his army faced.

***

It is now 34 years later. A meeting had been called of the Veteran Association of the Sixth New York Cavalry, the attendees just those available from within New York City. It was October 29, 1897, and among those attending were former Lieutenant Colonel G. M. Van Buren, Captain W. L. Herrmance, Adjutant F. A. Easton, and Alonzo Foster. As previously noted, in speaking from their individual memories about the events of April 30, 1863, discrepancies were apparent. There began the compiling of the events by the former regiment's adjutant that would eventually be incorporated into the history of the 6th New York Cavalry. Adjutant Easton gathered the facts, the memories and at least one document written by the cavalry's adversary and wrote "Engagement Near Todd's Tavern, April 30, 1863."

This engagement, of all those in the history of the regiment, generated the most ink as various survivors scoured their memories in later years for facts concerning it and the words to describe it. The knitting together of what are considered the facts of this one action, from the few contemporary written sources, remembrances and the like is a classic example of the conflicting nature of Civil War documentation that the historian confronts in attempting to detail this period and this war. At its best, a recounting of the events and the motivations driving them can only be, in many cases, an educated guess, a reconstruction of events in their most probable order of occurrence, the chances for full accuracy slightly better than 60/40. This one incident involved just one Union regiment contending with four of the Rebels. Consider the task of piecing together a battle in which a hundred different commands of both antagonists were involved, some leaving behind detailed action reports and some none at all. It can be a daunting exercise.

It was April 30, 1863, and on this Thursday afternoon Lt. Col. Duncan McVicar, commanding the 6th New York Cavalry, was ordered to the XII Corps headquarters of General Henry Slocum near Chancellorsville. As with many such episodes from this war, the events recorded at the time or remembered later, if not at variance with one another, are, nevertheless, quite confusing, but here Adjutant Easton was employing his own memory for he had accompanied McVicar that afternoon and remembered Slocum's orders:

> You will proceed with your command to Spotsylvania Court-house, where you will be joined by other of our troops. Should you meet the enemy in force and offering resistance, you will gradually fall back and report to me by courier. Meeting no resistance, you will continue the march.[30]

McVicar took the orders and with Easton began riding to join the regiment. Along the way, Easton remembers McVicar saying, "I wish for more definite information as to the troops we shall meet at Spotsylvania, and to whom I shall report." This said, McVicar stopped, turned around and returned to Slocum's headquarters. To the general McVicar, "… began his request. He was interrupted by General Slocum, who said, 'You have your orders, sir, go.'" Easton recalled that after this rebuff from Slocum, McVicar "appeared saddened and serious."[31] It might be said here that in any reading of any history of the Chancellorsville campaign there was no plan for Union forces to be in the Spotsylvania area, located approximately eight miles southeast of the Chancellorsville crossroads where the army stood at that time. Hooker's plan was to move directly east, toward Fredericksburg to confront Lee.

When they got to the regiment, the command mounted and started on a road supposedly leading to Spotsylvania. After riding only about half a mile McVicar halted the regiment, ordering the men to close in on him as best they could. Then McVicar spoke to the men "admonishing them to a full performance of their duty as soldiers and Christians." Closing his remarks, he said, "to-morrow we shall meet in Fredericksburg or heaven." The mention of Fredericksburg, miles to the east as opposed to Spotsylvania, located to the southeast of McVicar's starting point, cannot be reconciled from the record. Easton then continues, "The speech, as a whole, had a bad effect, for we felt impressed with coming disaster. The ranks became silent … It was not with our usual gaiety and dash that the march was resumed." The regiment, in column of fours, continued in the direction of Spotsylvania Court House.[32]

Brigadier General Alfred Pleasonton, who had remained with Tom Devin's 2nd Brigade as General Stoneman went on his raid, years later wrote his account of the Chancellorsville Campaign that was included in the 1880s in the popular and successful compilation *Battles and Leaders of the Civil War*. In the article, Pleasonton provides his evaluation of the cavalry as well as the generals in this campaign, but, as part of the article, he gives the reason for the movement of the 6th New York at this moment. At a point during the day, after Hooker had arrived at Chancellorsville, Pleasonton had suggested to the general that infantry advance out of the Wilderness into open country in the direction of Spotsylvania so that the right flank of the army not be taken by surprise, given the smothering woodland and undergrowth surrounding the army in its present position. In that the left flank of the army was covered by the Rappahannock, Pleasonton's suggestion appears logical. Hooker, however, rejected the proposal. Pleasonton then writes that "… I then asked permission to send some cavalry to Spotsylvania, to find out what was going on in the open country beyond the woods." This Hooker agreed to, and Pleasonton says.

> … I ordered the 6th New York Cavalry, under Lieutenant-Colonel McVicar, to proceed down the road from Chancellorsville to Spotsylvania, ascertain if the enemy were anywhere in that vicinity, and, having done so, return before daybreak. This could easily be done, as the distance was not more than eight miles … McVicar went to Spotsylvania, saw no enemy, but on his return, it being moonlight, he found a body of cavalry in his front, barring his passage to Chancellorsville. He immediately deployed his regiment, some three or four hundred strong, and after a murderous fire from the saddle he charged the enemy with sabers and completely routed them. This force was the 5th Virginia Regiment, and with it were General Stuart and staff. They scattered in every direction and were pursued by the 6th New York Cavalry until the 2d Virginia Regiment, coming to their assistance, stopped the pursuit. The 6th New York Cavalry, unmolested, returned to Chancellorsville …
>
> The 6th New York Cavalry were only able to report that they had to cut their way through a heavy body of cavalry, and this by moonlight; they were unable to say whether any infantry were in that direction.[33]

According to this recollection, then, the movement by the 6th New York was a reconnaissance and not one designed to link with another Union army command, as Adjutant Easton wrote were the orders coming from General Slocum to which Easton says he had heard issued to McVicar in person.

But Pleasonton's recollection, written in later years, is at variance with what he wrote in his report on the campaign while, supposedly, memory was still fresh. In his report written on May 18, 1863, the general said:

> The Sixth New York Cavalry ... was ordered to move down the road leading to Spotsylvania Court-house, to take post in front of our infantry, and send strong detachments out on the road to feel the enemy in that direction ... the Sixth New York advanced beyond where it was proposed for it to go, and the enemy placed himself in force in its rear. On seeing this, the brave McVicar immediately charged them ... yet such was the dash and spirit of the affair that comparatively few were lost or captured, and the movement, as has since been ascertained from the enemy, perplexed them not a little.[34]

This recounting of events, if actually valid, describes not a rendezvous with friendly troops but picket and/or flank protection duty with a reconnaissance component thrown in.

Pleasonton's reputation both during and after the Civil War, summarized by one cavalry historian, was of an officer that had climbed the "... ladder of rank with speed disproportional to his ability ... He was not adept at reconnaissance; his dispatches ... were full of sound and fury, signifying nothing. His penchant for hearsay, speculation, and fancy would prompt postwar writers to dub him 'the Knight of Romance.'" Uninhibited with his opinions, Charles Francis Adams, in a letter written near this time, commented on General Pleasonton from his position in a regiment under his command. On May 12, Adams writes, "... Pleasonton ... is pure and simple a newspaper humbug ... He does nothing save with a view to a newspaper paragraph."[35]

There exists a recounting of events on April 30 written by a correspondent for *The New York Times*. Civil War newspaper accounts of actions, when compared to actual and verified facts, are often found to be wide of the mark, prejudiced in favor of one side or the other and often composed from material provided by participants interviewed after that fact rather than a reporter's eyewitness recording. Therefore, the historian must be judicious in quoting them. In this instance, however, the correspondent, identifying himself merely by the initials "Z. W. B.," explained his presence with the 6th that day in his dispatch to his paper penned on May 1:

> As there was nothing more interesting on hand I determined to see what a reconnaissance might be like. I accordingly dashed across the country and overtook the expedition about two miles beyond our outer pickets. I found Col. McVicar proceeding slowly along the road to Spotsylvania Court-house, stopping at every crossroad, and sending men to right and left, to see what might be on his flanks, and searching every house.[36]

According to the regiment's early history, the command moved forward after McVicar spoke to the men and then halted again after some distance, the men standing to horse, waiting for the moon to rise. Lieutenant J. Hamilton Bell with a few men then scouted the road ahead and returned saying that there were Rebels blocking the road.

The *Times* man reported:

> Mile after mile we passed, and yet we saw no sign of any great force of the rebels. Citizens that we picked up told us there had been a hundred troopers along a short time before; but they were not to be found.[37]

According to Adjutant Easton, McVicar was to meet Union troops at Spotsylvania, but this recalling had to be the result of faulty memory induced by the passage of years, for there were no Union forces in that area. Mostly likely, Slocum's orders were to scout in the Spotsylvania direction to learn if any Rebel troops were deployed in the area or were approaching from that direction, something similar to what Pleasonton wrote in his 1863 report. The *Times* correspondent, in his next paragraph, wrote:

> The Colonel was mistaken in his orders, which he supposed directed him to keep on until he should meet some large force of the enemy. A courier, with a modification of the orders, had been sent, but never reached him.

This understanding was, most likely, obtained after the reporter was again within Union lines. He then says that by now McVicar:

> … was becoming a little disturbed about his position, knowing that he was a long way from any support, and in a country where the rebels were likely to come down upon him at any moment. But he would not disobey orders.
>
> At length a halt was called, at a fork in the road leading to Spotsylvania. The roads here form a Y, with woods on both sides and an open field in the fork, bounded by a ravine some three hundred yards back. Rear and advance guards were posted, and the main body dismounted. A consultation was held, and it was determined to make a raid upon the next farmhouse, and, if possible, obtain some forage for our horses and some food for ourselves. This was just at dusk.
>
> Just as the order to mount was given, the rear guard discovered some men stealing up through the bushes. The sharp crack of their carbines hurried us into the saddle. At the first discharge the enemy charged out with an unearthly yell, which seemed to be their battle-cry, and succeeded in capturing three or four of our men. They then fell back and stood in the road, yelling defiance. Springing to our saddles, we rushed into the field and instantly formed in line of battle in three squadrons, awaiting the onset of the enemy. Meantime we opened a deadly carbine fire upon them …[38]

Trooper Alonzo Foster of Company F was there and later recorded his memory of the event:

> About dark, after marching through the woods, we reached a small clearing; the order to halt and dismount was given; a mounted guard was thrown out to the rear, and Captain Bell, with a few men, was sent towards the Court-house … Captain Bell soon returned and reported that there was a heavy force at the Court-house; about the same time the rear guard was fired upon and driven in … It was now very dark, and there was some fear that some of our own troops had come up and, by mistake, had fired upon the rear guard. Colonel McVicar sent Captain Goler back to ascertain the true state of affairs. Going back to the junction of the roads … he

was challenged and on answering, 'The Sixth New York Cavalry,' was fired upon and driven back to the main body. As the enemy came down the road, which was only wide enough for a column of fours, our men formed a line, fired upon them and checked their advance.[39]

The man from *the New York Times* continued:

> Finding that they would not meet us in a fair field the bugle was sounded, and the brave boys charged with drawn sabers. The Colonel and Lieut. Bell led the advance guard of twenty men. The rest followed in good order, except the second squadron was in advance of the first. Capt. Beardslee was ordered to the rear to close up the column, and see that the wounded were cared for. For a few moments the zip, zip, z—z—s of the Minie balls and the sharp ring of the sabers were heard above the noise of the shooting.
>
> Among the first to fall was Col. McVicar, who was killed instantly, while attacking an officer with his sabre. The rebels were driven back ... and the second squadron, led by Capt. Geo. A. Crocker, swept on in pursuit. The first squadron, being without officers, halted where they were. The enemy from the woods formed in behind the second squadron. Capt. Van Buren, of the third squadron, rode up, and ordering the first to follow him, charged upon the rebels. Before the first could do this, the Captain and Sergt. Sanders, of Company I, were through the rebels and with the second. Capt. Van Buren, being the senior officer present, took command.
>
> Lieut. Phillips and Lieut. Blunt took command of the third squadron, charging at the head of it. They cut through the lines, and joined the second, the first squadron followed them. They passed down the road until they crossed the creek, where they formed on the opposite bank and held the ford. Capt. Beardslee, with the rear guard and the wounded, were cut off by the closing in of the rebels. Taking with him a number of prisoners who he had captured, he retreated to the fork in the road, where the Surgeon was at work. Questioning the prisoners separately, they said that Fitzhugh Lee, with four regiments of cavalry, had surrounded us ... We had charged upon and driven the regiments in front, and a portion of our number has escaped, a number were wounded, some taken prisoner. Eighty men were left behind, and upon those the two regiments charged. We dashed into the woods, and galloped through them at a headlong rate ... the rascals thundering at our heels ...
>
> The column became separated. Capt. Beardslee, with twenty-two men, reached the party who were guarding the ford, and led them to our lines, while Lieut. O'Neil and myself led fifty-eight along way through the woods, and came safely in.[40]

Trooper Foster's account, as he remembered it, said:

> The Colonel McVicar ordered the command to draw sabre, break by fours to the right, and cut our way through. As our bugle sounded the charge, it was at the same moment sounded by the Fifth Virginia, and the notes rang out clear and full in defiance of each other, as we rode down to where they waited for us. In the darkness it seemed as though a sheet of fire belched forth from their carbines, and at the first fire the brave McVicar fell, and the rest of the command were mixed up with the Confederates, as we rode through them. Besides Colonel McVicar, who was killed, three officers were wounded and about twenty men killed and wounded. These were left behind, and the survivors drove the enemy until the cross-roads were reached, where the Confederates took the one to Todd's Tavern, and our men went on to our own lines at Chancellorsville. The wounded were taken to a house near where they fell, and after a few days sent to Libby Prison.[41]

The best estimate of the location at which these events took place is at the fork in the road to the west of a farm owned by one Hugh Alsop.

Jeb Stuart had been at a place called Todd's Tavern, about two miles to the west along Brock Road, and that night he and his staff were riding in the direction of Fredericksburg and Lee's headquarters. While riding, Stuart was reported as saying, "Things are not quite right up front." An aide went forward and was soon galloping back, chased by some troopers from the 6th New York. Stuart retreated in the direction of Todd's Tavern and located and then advanced the brigade of Fitz Lee. Alert to the enemy's presence in his front and knowing that the road he was on was too narrow to fight on, McVicar led the command through a gate and into a field on Alsop's farm. The regiment, now in the field was suddenly fired upon from three directions. For some reason it was thought the fire was from some Union command and Lieutenant Bell rode forward shouting, "Who are you anyway?" The answer he received was "Third Virginia." The Rebels then charged and, as Adjutant Easton recalled, "… and clear above the clatter of hoofs and arms could be heard the terror-striking 'rebel yell.'" Up to the gate to the field came the Rebels but they were driven back by heavy fire from the 6th. A second charge was also repulsed. There appeared to be many more Rebels than Yankees in this area and for a reason that was never explained, McVicar, knowing he was outnumbered, decided on a charge to get his command out of the enemy's presence. He drew his saber and "… raising in his saddle, at the top of his voice," shouted to the command 'Sixth New York, follow me, charge!'" The troopers charged to the gate they had passed through, McVicar in the lead. Approaching the gate McVicar was shot off his horse, killed instantly. The troopers got through the gate and on to the road, charging down the road back to Chancellorsville, but some of the troopers still in the field were captured. According to Easton, the charge down the road was in the direction of Todd's Tavern, but the 6th stopped when it came to a crossroad. Now, according to Thomas Munford, Colonel of the 2nd Virginia, he attacked the rear of this contingent at the crossroad. But as Easton wrote in his account there was great confusion and "Just all that occurred at this time may never be known." In the dark, men became separated, some not getting within Union lines until the next day.[42]

In 1910, John Bigelow published his *The Campaign of Chancellorsville* and in it uses the 6th New York's regimental history and letters from then Colonel T. T. Munford's 2nd Virginia Cavalry and two of his troopers to recount the regiment's situation while gathered in Alsop's field:

> Colonel McVicar, perceiving that he was heavily outnumbered, concluded that he was in danger of being surrounded and captured with his whole force. So, forming a column of fours with sabers drawn, and rising in his stirrups, he called out: 'Sixth New York follow me, *Charge!*'

Bigelow then says that McVicar fell about 70 feet from the gate leading into the field.[43]

There were losses but the 6th managed to escape via its desperate charge and get back to Chancellorsville. As reported, the loss to the 6th was 51 including 36 that became prisoners. As later remembered by Captain William L. Herrmance, one of the officers wounded that night, in addition to McVicar, three officers were wounded, and 20 troopers killed or wounded at Alsop's farm.[44]

Later, probably in the pre-dawn hours, Fitz Lee learned that the lieutenant-colonel of the regiment he had engaged had been killed. Lee ordered the body recovered. McVicar's ... body was conveyed to a house near by and tenderly cared for. General Lee sent the Rev. Dabney Ball, chaplain of the First Virginia Cavalry, who prayed over the remains of our gallant McVicar.[45]

Alonzo Foster included in his rendering of the confrontation with Stuart an excerpt from the Scottish publication, *Blackwood's Magazine,* published in 1866 that included an account by Major Heros von Borcke, a member of Stuart's staff. The major wrote soon after the war that:

> General Stuart and his staff were trotting along at the head of the column, when, at the moment of emergency out of the dark forest, we suddenly discovered in the open field before us and at a distance of not more than one hundred and sixty yards, a line of hostile cavalry, who received us with a severe fire which concentrated on the narrow road. Fully conscious of our critical position, Stuart drew his sword, and with his clear ringing voice, gave the order to attack, taking the lead himself. For once our horsemen refused to follow their gallant commander; they wavered under the thick storm of bullets; soon all discipline ceased, and in a few minutes the great part of this splendid regiment, which had distinguished itself in so many battlefields, broke to the rear in utter confusion. At this moment the enemy's bugle sounded the charge, and in a few seconds after we blunted the shock of the attack which broke upon us like a thunder cloud, and bore our little band along with its vehement rush, as if driven by a mighty wave, sweeping us along with it in the darkness of the forest.[46]

This engagement with Stuart and Lee's cavalry became, in subsequent years, a prominent and often spoken of episode in the history of the 6th New York at its many reunions. In all likelihood, this was because the regiment lost its well-liked and respected leader. William L. Herrmance recalled years later the saber fight with the Rebels:

> I was with one on my right, before I could turn my horse to give the 'left cut' to one who had a pistol that I could feel pressed against me, he fired, the ball going through my left arm and making a wound in my stomach; at the same time a blow on my head knocked me from my horse, and I was left behind to be taken to Libby Prison.

Herrmance said that years later he met one Benjamin F. Median, a former captain in the 5th Virginia Cavalry. The two men had fought one another in the action of April 30, with Medina receiving a saber wound from Herrmance. The morning after the engagement, while waiting to be removed to Libby Prison in Richmond, Herrmance was told that when Fitz Lee learned that the regiment's commander had been killed and lay dead on the field, he ordered the body removed and appropriately buried. In speaking with Fitz Lee after the war, Captain Herrmance was told by the former general that in regard to the charge "… he never had seen one equal to it in his service."[47]

After the Chancellorsville campaign, and upon returning to their camps on the north side of the river, Thomas Devin penned a letter to McVicar's widow:

> Camp of Second Brigade, Pleasonton's Cavalry Division
> May 9, 1863
>
> My dear Madam:
>   It has become my grievous duty to inform you, by letter, of the sad and painful bereavement yourself and family have sustained in the loss of a husband and father. The news must have already reached you through the columns of the press, and I am spared the painful task of breaking it to you for the first time. He was endeared to us all by his many virtues, his earnest simplicity of his character, and by his honesty of purpose and by his soldierly contempt for danger, which alas, in the end hurried him to a soldier's grave.
>   He fell as he would have chosen, gloriously fighting at the head of his noble regiment— fighting to maintain the institution of his adopted country, and setting an illustrious example that many of her degenerate sons would do well to follow. His brave antagonist, General Fitzhugh Lee, showed every respect to his remains, sending his own chaplain to perform the funeral rites. He is buried near the spot where he fell, on the farm of Mr. Alsop, in Spotsylvania County, Virginia.
>   As soon as possible and military necessity admit, we shall recover all that remains of our lamented brother officer, in order that he may sleep in the land he loved best, "our own free north."
>   Allow me, on the part of myself and brother officers, to tender our sincere and heartfelt condolence in your affliction, and I fervently trust the nation for whom husband so bravely fought and nobly fell, although it cannot restore him to those who mourn his loss, will at least hold in grateful remembrance the service he had rendered, the great sacrifice he made, and the helpless one he had left to that nation's care.
>   Believe me, my dear madam, with the sincerest sympathy,
>   Yours very respectfully,
>   Thomas C. Devin
>   Col. 6th N. Y. V. Cavalry, 2d Brigade.[48]

At a point in time after this letter was sent, a contingent from the 6th New York, under a flag of truce, crossed the Rappahannock, rode to Alsop's farm and recovered McVicar's body. The "… body was embalmed at Falmouth. Appeared quite natural." It was then sent to the family in Rochester, New York.[49]

W. A. Morgan of the 1st Virginia Cavalry was riding over Alsop's Field the morning after the fight and among the refuse of the engagement were two guidons from the 6th New York Cavalry. Morgan dismounted and picked them up. At some point later, he mailed the small flags to his home, a souvenir. Thirty-five years passed, and a friend of former regimental adjutant, F. A. Easton, had made the acquaintance of the now former colonel Morgan who lived in West Virginia and noted that, hanging on a wall of his home, were the two guidons from the 6th New York. The friend and Morgan spoke about the guidons and his friendship with Easton of the 6th New York. Morgan said he would like to return the mementos to the regiment's veterans' association and arrangements were eventually made. Easton and some others from the 6th New York met Morgan, accompanied by his son, daughter and grandchild at the National Cemetery at Antietam in June 1898. "We met at the entrance to the cemetery, and as we clasped hands and looked into each other's eyes," Easton later wrote, "I thanked God for a reunited country." Morgan, now "a fine old man, seventy-one years of age, but still robust," in returning the guidons said, "I address you as friends and fellow countrymen, and in the capacity of an old Confederate veteran I warmly welcome you here to-day, and offer you the right hand of good fellowship"[50] To the reconciled former foes this action was only one of the innumerable others that took place across the country during the closing years of the century.

***

At about noon on May 1, the Union force had advanced some three miles to the east of the Chancellorsville clearing. There they met Lee and the formations he had marched from Fredericksburg. The fighting was inconclusive in that Hooker did not press the advance but ordered his troops back to Chancellorsville into the positions held the day before. In the late afternoon, with some of Jackson's Corps placed along Lee's line of resistance and other elements still arriving, the firing gradually waned. Stonewall went to where General Lee and his staff had dismounted. Jackson's arrival brought Lee's force east of Chancellorsville to about 45,000 troops against Hooker's 80,000. That Fighting Joe had halted his army's advance that day would later provide Lee and Jackson with the opportunity that would lead them to victory.

As the twilight faded, Lee and Jackson sat before a campfire, away from the scattered rifle shots of nervous pickets and the smoke of the burning bushes. Quietly they ruminated on the next day's action against the Yankees. That Lee faced a force at least twice the size of his did not seem to give Stonewall pause. While the two generals talked, cavalry leader Jeb Stuart rode up with news gathered by scouting. He reported to Lee and Jackson that the Union right flank some miles to the west was open or in the air, covered by a mere couple of regiments. It was open to attack, there being insufficient cavalry with the Federals for screening in that direction. Stuart's report was quickly digested, the two generals seeing the opportunity as well as the risk. An attempt could be made to maneuver a force to the west, get within striking distance of the exposed flank unseen and, once aligned, attack. If there were roads to use that were hidden from Yankee eyes, this semblance of a plan might work to their advantage. This was left to be determined as the generals slept for a few hours on the ground among the pines. In the darkness before dawn, the local knowledge of a former resident of the Wilderness was employed, the roads located that were mostly unobserved from the positions Union forces then occupied. The roads would get Jackson to where he needed to be. The maneuver was laden with more risk than any Lee had ordered before in this war. In the decades to come, the maneuver and the attack launched on this day would again write in the lengthy ledger of military history the names of both generals. To consider such a plan involving such risk was one thing, for a commander to accept and consent to it and then have it succeed would advance Robert E. Lee and Thomas Jackson to a status among generals exceeded only by their fellow Virginian from the previous century. As evaluated by one historian, the plan consented to by Lee and executed by Jackson "…was the distilled and concentrated essence of extreme daring."[51]

That morning and afternoon of May 2, Jackson circled around the battlefield and got his command into position to attack the flank of the Union's XI Corps. Without Jackson's corps as it marched to the west, the numbers facing Lee were overwhelming. Lee was essentially alone, in a position to be crushed if Fighting Joe chose to continue his eastward advance. Lee had weighed the chances and given his approval and Jackson marched. In the day's early hours, as the sky brightened, Jackson encountered Lee as his troops waited for the order to move. Lee asked, "General, what do you propose to make this movement with?" The grim faced Stonewall must have momentarily wondered why he was being asked such a question at such a time. He answered, "Why my whole corps." "What will you leave me?" inquired Lee. Stonewall said, "The divisions of Anderson and McLaws." Lee had already known the answer to his question but still one can picture the gray bearded general simply nodding his consent again with a half-smile crossing his face. "Well, go on," he said.

Jackson was leaving Lee with a mere 15,000 troops with which to maintain his line of battle of the previous day. If Hooker pushed, decided to continue his advance through the Wilderness, could that line hold? Would it hold? Without Jackson's corps, Lee was facing odds that had gone from something like two to one the day before to at least five to one.[52] This was audacity as only General Lee could stage.

It was just past 5pm and in an open area to the two west-facing Union regiments that constituted XI Corps' right flank, as well as that of the Army of the Potomac, the Yankee soldiers were preparing dinner, cooking fires stoked, rifles stacked. The remainder of the corps was aligned facing south in prepared positions, something the two regiments facing west had not done. The terrain to the west was like all the rest of the Wilderness, a tangle near the ground and fully leaved or in blossom trees above. Lieutenant William Wheeler of the 13th New York Battery, in a letter written soon after the battle remarked XI Corps expected the enemy to attack from the front that was facing roughly south, "and a heavy flank attack not dreamed of." Stonewall Jackson, in Wheeler's opinion maneuvered his force "… with such perfect secrecy and skill that the miserable scouts we sent out reported three or four hundred dismounted cavalry and nothing more."[53] Without warning, noiseless, a deer bounded out of the trees to the west and flashed through the soldier's camp. Then another deer, headed the same way, was running through the Yankee camp, then another.

The soldiers standing over their cook fires looked on, curious. One or two rabbits scurried past, following the deer. A moment passed and while the Yankees were still wondering what the deer and rabbits were up to, a line of Confederate infantry came running out of the Wilderness, bayonets fixed. The first Rebel line was quickly followed by another gray wave. The gray and butternut troops would stop only to raise their rifles and fire into the shocked blue mass before them. Those not hit with the first volley simply turned and ran to the east. The troops facing to the south were now taken in the rear or, if they had a chance, they ran too. Jackson's infantry was driving everything dressed in blue before them. Soon one Union division was running to the east to be followed within moments by the next in line. Whenever a group of soldiers turned to make something of a stand, they were soon out flanked and had to continue running or be surrounded. By 7pm, Jackson had pushed the Union force back somewhat more than a mile while Lee, as he had most of the day, had occupied the Federals before his position with probing attacks using portions of his two divisions.[54]

A staff officer in V Corps, Captain Richard Auchmuty, was back at the Chancellorsville House, writing a letter:

> Saturday, May 2nd, 5 P.M. My Dear Mother,—I have been interrupted once or twice; it is now near sundown; the men are cooking their suppers and becoming more desirous for the rebels to attack as the chances vanish. Our loss in the division yesterday was one killed and four wounded.
> 10 P.M. A terrible battle has taken place; our division not engaged. [General] Sykes sent to re-enforce … I write by moonlight. I cannot see.

It wasn't until May 4 that Captain Auchmuty could elaborate:

> My Dear Mother,—I wrote you on Saturday, 10 P.M …
> At 5:30 a really tremendous battle commenced. Three lines were formed, we, with Sykes, being the third. Towards eight o'clock the two outer lines were gone, and we stood face to face with Stonewall Jackson; but in the two hours we had thrown up earthworks, and, except with artillery, no attack was made … Both armies suffered heavily. The result was, we 'contracted our lines.' The Southerners fought more furiously than ever before … To add to the other horrors, the woods filled with wounded, caught fire.[55]

In the gathering darkness, and as the pace of the attack slowed, Jackson decided to ride forward and check on the position of his troops and possibly scout the terrain ahead for a further advance. Riding with some of his staff, the general and his group were mistaken for Yankees and fired upon by Confederate troops. Jackson was hit in the arm and carried from the field. The arm was amputated but complications set in and the general died a few days later. Thomas Jackson, with his movement and attack on May 2 had given Lee his victory at Chancellorsville. There would still be fighting over the next few days, but the move by Jackson and the subsequent irresolution of General Hooker would decide the battle's outcome. Irresolution is a strong word, and it cannot be known whether Hooker would have acted differently if he had not been knocked unconscious and probably suffered a concussion when a pillar of the Chancellorsville Mansion was hit by a solid shot. Jackson's maneuver, and possibly that solid shot, essentially, decided the battle's outcome. One of the many historians reflecting on this battle, and Stonewall's contribution to it, summarized that "Jackson had the one great virtue of an aggressive soldier: he believed that no victory was complete as long as a single enemy was on his feet and breathing." An epitaph of sorts later penned by historian Emory Thomas aptly covers Stonewall Jackson's life as a soldier and his death: "Alive, Jackson was an eccentric genius, part Southern Calvinist and part killer. Dead, this Cromwell reincarnate took first place in the pantheon of heroes in a nation of cavaliers."[56] His loss to the Southern cause, to Robert E. Lee and the Army of Northern Virginia, would not, could not, be made up.

XI Corps was running from Jackson's sudden attack, all in an easterly direction. Under the command of General Daniel Sickles, III Corps had established itself earlier in the vicinity of a clearing known as Hazel Grove. According to the commander of the 8th Pennsylvania, Colonel Pennock Huey, it was about 4pm when the brigade was ordered from the open area around Chancellorsville to Hazel Grove, reporting to Sickles. General Pleasonton and Colonel Devin were with the column and met with Sickles near the firing line. Huey recalled:

> Almost immediately after General Pleasonton had reported to General Sickles with his brigade, the 6th New York Cavalry was ordered to the front to report to the officer in command there, and the other two regiments and Martin's battery were ordered back to Hazel Grove, with instructions to dismount and stand to horse till further orders …

Accounts differ radically concerning the events that followed. Some accounts tell of General Howard asking for a cavalry regiment to help him restore order among his panicked troops, others say that Rebel troops were following closely behind XI Corps fugitives and Pleasonton ordered the 8th Pennsylvania stop them and restore a semblance of order. Huey and his regiments were called from Hazel Grove and started up a narrow-wooded path as it was becoming dark. The trail led in some fashion back to Chancellorsville. Riding in a compacted column along the narrow path, the regiment was ambushed by an element of Jackson's corps that had advanced following the retreating XI Corps. The Pennsylvania troopers tried to escape in one direction and then, at a crossroad, in another. Finally, Huey had to order a charge, a desperate move in a confined space like the Wilderness. When the order to charge was received by the rest of the command, one of Huey's officers was reported as saying, "I think this is the last of the 8th Pennsylvania Cavalry." The 8th Pennsylvania charged, sabers and pistols in hand, and by the time it reached safety, had lost three officers and 30 men.[57]

While this was taking place a force of about 200 soldiers from Jackson's corps arrived out of the woods and into Hazel Grove. This open area had in it at that moment, supply wagons, ambulances and stragglers. There were batteries placed on high ground and some infantry units standing nearby and these 200 Rebels were quickly driven back into the woods by those with rifles and an array of cannon parked in the grove. In fact, the Rebels had been ordered back just as they became involved with the Union force in the grove. Pleasonton, however, reported that in the crisis, he placed the guns, aimed them, and ordered them fired to repulse the Rebel horde and managed to "stop the stampede & [sic] check Jackson," thus saving the day. Pleasonton also credited himself with ordering Huey's desperate charge to escape from the Rebels he had encountered, despite this taking place some distance removed from Hazel Grove. Cavalry historian Edward G. Longacre has committed the true facts to paper concerning this episode. "The facts are these," says Longacre. "The attack on Hazel Grove was made in less than regimental strength; the Confederate themselves halted it; and Pleasonton directed the fire of only one battery, Martin's. Any connection he had with the 8th Pennsylvania occurred after its bloodletting in the woods."[58] The reports written after the campaign and the remembrances written after the war were still sore spots with Colonel Huey in 1888 when he published *A True History of the Charge of the Eighth Pennsylvania Cavalry at Chancellorsville.* In it he had nothing good to say concerning his formed division commander, the "Knight of Romance," Alfred Pleasonton. Huey maintains that Pleasonton "… gained his promotion to command of the Cavalry Corps solely through the reckless misstatement and deceptions perpetrated by him in … his reports of the battle of Chancellorsville." Of Pleasonton's saving the day by deploying and firing the guns at Hazel Grove, it "is an absolute falsehood made of whole cloth," while another officer from the 8th Pennsylvania characterized the general's role at Hazel Grove as "impudent and unfounded." Huey quotes J. F. Huntington of the 1st Ohio Light Artillery as saying, "The falsity of [Pleasonton's] statement is shown by the fact that the guns …" were in position long before the enemy appeared in the grove. That he ordered the charge of the 8th "is grossly untrue, and he knows it."[59] Such emphatic denials by so many participants' calls into question any report written by Pleasonton during, or any article he wrote after, the war. His contemporaries, some of them at least, took his stories as gospel, among them Generals Sickles and Hooker. Later, Hooker even introduced Pleasonton to President Lincoln with the words, "Mr. President, this is General Pleasonton, who saved the Army of the Potomac the other night."[60]

Because many in XI Corps, perhaps a majority, were of German extraction or newly arrived German immigrants, the corps was often referred to as the "Flying Dutchmen" after it had run from Jackson's attack. The running stopped when they reached the general area surrounding the Chancellorsville Mansion. The soldiers were exhausted, confused as to what had happened, and hungry. The fighting along the line subsided and full darkness descended on the Wilderness. The men needed rest for everyone knew the battle would be resumed in the morning. Adjutant Hitchcock of the 132nd Pennsylvania relates one of those stories, occurring in the dark hours between May 2 and 3, the truth of which, because of its weirdness, might just have happened as he relates in his memoir. Before the stampeded XI Corps reached the vicinity of the Chancellorsville clearing, several beef cows had been driven up to be butchered, the meat to be issued to the troops in the immediate area. No sooner had this happened than XI Corps overran the area and somehow to cows were, at first, neglected and then became casualties of the battle. In the dark, with the fighting at an end, it was discovered that a beef carcass was between the contending lines. During the night, a few Union troops crawled out in an attempt to bring back some of the beef. They were working on one side of a cow when they heard activity on the other. One of the Union men whispered, "Hello, Johnny, are ye there?" "Yes, Yank, too bad to let this 'fresh' spoil. I say, Yank, lend me your knife, mine's a poor one. We 'uns and you 'uns is all right here. Yank, I'll help you if you'll help me, and we'll get all we want."

Hitchcock relates, "the knife was passed over, and these two foes helped each other in that friendly darkness. How much actual truth there is in this story, I do not know, but I do know there was considerable fresh beef among the men in the morning …"[61]

By 10am on May 3, Jackson's Corps, now under the temporary command of Jeb Stuart, and Lee's force had attacked and Hooker had yielded territory, contracting his line but allowing Confederate artillery to deploy in higher ground and then pound the area around the Chancellorsville house almost at will. It was in this artillery action that Hooker was possibly knocked unconscious. While he was being attended, subordinates directed the fighting. The fighting continued all day and into the next, casualties mounting by the hour. At midnight, in the first hour of May 5, General Hooker, seemingly recovered in the view of some, not so in the opinion of others, met with the corps commanders. The generals voted to remain and fight it out with Lee, but Hooker overruled them and ordered a withdrawal to the north side of the Rappahannock. The withdrawal started that night and by the morning of May 6 all of the Union troops, including those that had crossed the river below Fredericksburg, were again on the north side of the Rappahannock. The Potomac army had suffered 17,000 casualties.

With its many German immigrants, XI Corps got the blame for the defeat at Chancellorsville, at least among the rank-and-file soldiers that did the fighting and were near at hand as they tried getting out of Jackson's way. Others, further away from the stampede of May 2, thought simply that General Lee had outgeneraled Fighting Joe. Lieutenant Wheeler, who was fighting with XI Corps, wrote home after the battle and provided his estimate of the events of May 2:

> I have heard some say that they [XI Corps] would not fight because they did not have Sigel [the former corps commander]; this is absurd, and yet allowance must be made for

the great influence on the men, produced by their losing the man on whom they leaned unreservedly, and who they would follow to the death, and getting in his place a person unknown, peculiarly uncongenial to the German mind, and considered by them as a parson in uniform.

General O. O. Howard, the XI's commander, was noted throughout the army for his deeply held religious view and was not averse to letting his men know it. Howard may also have had some residual mid-19th century prejudice toward immigrants with different customs, language and outlook, but Wheeler again added that the position of May 2 taken by the corps "could not have failed to be overwhelmed." Hooker had allowed General Howard, the man that replaced the beloved General Sigel, to "scatter the corps" and when it was driven, allowed the blame to remain with XI Corps, but Howard had already "… made himself conspicuous by his zeal in promoting religious observances … to say nothing of a somewhat ostentatious display of personal piety, and now his religious character has to bear the burden of his military errors …"[62] The Chancellorsville defeat made Lieutenant Wheeler take a long view of the Union's struggle as he then saw it. Wheeler wrote soon after the battle:

> …every defeat of ours puts the end further off, but make our work more sure and thorough, and the final peace more deep and noble; the longer we work upon laying our foundation stones, the more pains we take with the selection of our site and the nature of the ground we build on, the more beautiful and lasting will be our edifice, which we can entrust to the religion of coming centuries to complete …[63]

General Hooker's operational plan for defeating Robert E. Lee had begun and went forward according to the way it had been put on paper up until he had ordered his infantry to halt at the Chancellorsville positions. With an aggressive drive on May 1 or May 2, when Lee had only had two divisions facing the Potomac army, Hooker might have been able to exit the Wilderness, getting to more open ground where he could maneuver all his forces and employ his artillery against the greatly outnumbered Lee. The cavalry raid by General Stoneman to the south did succeed in cutting communications and supply lines with Richmond for a time, but in doing so Hooker had left the army with so little cavalry that there was no flank coverage for the routed XI Corps and no troopers scouting out in front of the lines that might have observed and reported Jackson's flanking movement long before it could be deployed for an attack. By the time it got dark on May 2, General Hooker was facing defeat and by darkness the day after that, he essentially was defeated. Mister F. J. Hooker ordered his army to the north side of the Rappahannock.

General Lee was being celebrated throughout the South and Stonewall Jackson deeply mourned. Lee, however, realized the 13,000 casualties he had sustained would be difficult to make up from the South's shrinking manpower pool and Stonewall was irreplaceable. No material advantage had been gained for the South by its victory at Chancellorsville. The Army of the Potomac was still intact and still dangerous, still just on the other side of the river. Two months would go by and perhaps Lee, hoping to finish what he had not been able to do in the Virginia springtime, looked to the Pennsylvania countryside in July. Perhaps this, in the background of his thinking, would lead him to say, "The enemy is there, and I am going to attack him there." He did attack, smashing a significant portion of his army against a stonewall at Gettysburg on July 3.

The Federal soldiers crossed the Rappahannock and returned to their camps around Falmouth. Morale would be low but not because the men believed they had failed against the soldiers of the Army of Northern Virginia. The blame rested not with them but with Fighting Joe. An officer in a Massachusetts infantry regiment later noted, "the sentiment generally expressed was that Hooker had been beaten—not the army."[64] In a letter home, an officer in III Corps spoke of the defeat with a wider view:

> I still believed in General Hooker. At any rate I cannot forsake him, because he has failed once. He never failed before; and McClellan always failed.

And of the battle itself, this officer knew who was to blame. "The army did well, except for the Eleventh Corps. They broke and ran, discreditably. '*I fights mit Sigel*' is played out. Tell S—— that his Dutchmen can't begin to stand up against the fury and rush of Americans, even if they are Rebels." After saying that General Howard's conduct in command of the XI Corps had been "negligent," and the performance of the corps "disgraceful," a staff officer, writing to his father volunteered, "I am sorry to say that the army have very little confidence in General Hooker." This sentiment wasn't limited to junior officers. George Meade had a lot to tell his wife and began writing her as soon as he got back to the camp on the north side of the Rappahannock. On May 8, he told her, "He [Hooker] was more cautious and took to digging quicker ever than McClellan, thus proving that a man may talk very big when he had no responsibility." Then later Meade relates what might have been more than common camp talk, usually generated by light from campfires and warmth of whiskey:

> I have been a good deal flattered by the expressions of opinion on the part of many officers, that they thought and wished I should be placed in command, and poor Hooker himself, after he had determined to withdraw, said to me, in the most desponding manner, that he was ready to turn over to me the Army of the Potomac.

General Meade, again writing to his wife two days later said:

> ...the last operations have shaken the confidence of the army in Hooker's judgment, particularly among the superior officers. I have been much gratified at the frequent expressions of opinion that I ought to be placed in command."

Historians agree that George Meade did not actively pursue or intrigue for the army's command, but he could not ignore the talk of others, or pretend to be unaware that talk by senior officers nearly always found its way to Lincoln.

As far back a January, before General Hooker had taken command of the army, a common soldier from Vermont put his thoughts on paper when he had heard of the Fredericksburg defeat. It may be confidently said that, in the eyes of Private E. F. Palmer, standing in the defenses of Washington and soon to be swallowed into the Gettysburg Campaign, still believed:

> If there is anything more important than that the American soldier should be fed well, clothed well, and paid well, (as they are) it is, that they should know to a certainty, as long as there is a single dollar or man that is able to bear arms, left in the North, that the war shall never be abandoned till every armed foe of the Republic is subdued.

Long after the fighting had passed, and the veterans of the Chancellorsville campaign were either elderly or approaching it, John R. Boyle, a Methodist minister in later years, and former captain in the 111th Pennsylvania Infantry, published the regiment's history, *Soldiers True*, in 1903. The work, Boyle said, was entered into "at the earnest and unanimous request of the survivors of the command." "Its preparations," Boyle noted in his preface, "has been a labor of love, and such patience and care have attended it as the author could command amid the daily exactions of an important city pastorate." By the time of his gathering the material for his history, many works by others had been published, and Boyle acknowledged his reliance on such works as the *Rebellion Record,* Bates's *History of Pennsylvania Volunteers*, Pennypacker's *Life of General Meade*, and the memoirs of Grant and Longstreet. Boyle and his regiment, part of XII Corps, after a detailed account of the Chancellorsville battle of May 2 and 3, concluded that Hooker's force outnumbered Lee's army two to one and "could have and should have overwhelmed it." With the passage of years and with a wealth of both published material and hindsight, Boyle, without apology, offered his judgment: "The results cannot be excused."

In the wake of Chancellorsville, and unexpectedly, General Thomas Meagher of the Irish Brigade resigned on May 19 and returned to New York City. The general would remain close to the regiments he had recruited through the war's end and after. As noted by a former captain under his command, W. L. D. O'Grady:

> [that] ... while not excellent as a tactician, General Meagher was most thoughtful of his men, and his magnetism in recruiting not only our brigade, but inducing the Irish to flock to the defense of the Union, was worth a thousand men. He was a victim of jealously; and his men suffered too by coldness and lack of promotion instead of receiving the recognition they had earned.

By way of explanation, the captain said only two Medals of Honor were awarded in the brigade's 88th New York Infantry, one to "The late Captain Ford who was allowed to die in poverty without a pension, though most grievously wounded, and on whose breast Lincoln himself had pinned the coveted decoration."

There is one additional note written by General Pleasonton in early June 1863. It was not acted upon then but would be many months later. In his report on Chancellorsville, one of suspect value, Pleasonton did note something that can be taken as truth:

> I would respectfully recommend to the favorable notice of the major-general commanding Col. T. C. Devin, 6th New York Cavalry, commanding the Second Cavalry Brigade, as an officer worthy of promotion for his gallant conduct near Chancellorsville.

CHAPTER FOUR

One Vast Field of Intense, Earnest Action

Brandy Station, Tuesday, June 9, 1863

> I reviewed the cavalry in this section yesterday. It was a splendid sight. The men and horses looked well. They have recuperated since last fall. Stuart was in all his glory. Your sons and nephews were well and flourishing. The country here looks very green and pretty, notwithstanding the ravages of war.
>
> R. E. LEE TO MRS. LEE, PROBABLY WRITTEN JUNE 9, 1863

> How little did we then think that on this very ground a few days later just such a charge would be made in reality in the greatest cavalry action of modern times.
>
> W. W. BLACKFORD RECALLING THE CAVALRY REVIEW OF JUNE 5, 1863[1]

The trains arriving at Culpeper, Virginia, on June 4 brought the invited guests. The ladies and gentlemen from as far off as Richmond were invited by Confederate cavalry commander General Jeb Stuart and his officers. The invitees were to witness a grand review of the cavalry of the Army of Northern Virginia the next day. "[W]e all assembled at the station to receive them, and forward them to their destination by ambulances and wagons we had got prepared for that purpose," recalled an observer. "In the evening there was a ball at the Town Hall … and when the moon rose, we were glad to avail ourselves of her services by adjourning to the spacious verandah."[2] The guests assembled the next day in a large field at nearby Brandy Station, along the route of the Orange and Alexandria Railroad, to witness the review. General Jeb Stuart with his officers were "… resplendent in new uniforms." A trooper remembered:

> About 10 o'clock the whole column, which was about two miles long, was ready … Stuart and staff rode along the front of the line from one end to the other … a long black ostrich feather plume waved gracefully from a black slouch hat cocked up on one side, and was held with a golden clasp which also stayed the plume.

Another witness that day recalled:

> General Stuart had taken up his position on a slight eminence, wither many hundreds of spectators, mostly ladies, had gathered, in ambulances and on horseback, anxiously awaiting the approach of the troops.

When all spectators and the cavalry commander were in place "eight thousand cavalry passed under the eye of their commander, in columns of squadrons, first at a walk, and then at the charge. While the guns of the artillery battalion, on the hill opposite the stand, gave forth fire and smoke … It was a brilliant day, and the thirst for the 'pomp and circumstance' of war was fully satisfied."[3] The galloping charge across the field with sabers flashing, the horse artillery firing blanks, was later recalled by one of Stuart's staff watching from the stands. "The effect was thrilling … while the ladies clasped their hands and sank into the arms, sometimes, of their escorts in a swoon, if the escorts were handy, but if not they did not." Another observer remembered, "… a shrill yell was uttered and sabers brandished."[4]

The flamboyant General Stuart must have been quite pleased. At his headquarters at nearby Fleetwood Hill that evening Stuart hosted another entertainment. "That night we gave a ball at headquarters on the turf by moonlight, assisted by huge wood fires, firelight to dance by and moonlight for the strolls," a staff member remembered. A foreign observer with the army recalled "… we danced in the open air … by the light of enormous woodfires, the ruddy glare of which upon the animated groups of our assembly gave to the whole scene a wild and romantic effect." This indeed was the Civil War of romance, of storybooks and later of Hollywood. Cavaliers and ladies under the springtime moon, without a care, all as if the war and killing was happening on another planet. But later, in remembrance, that night was recalled as "… the last of our frolics for a long time."[5]

Of course, General Lee had been invited to the review, but was unable to attend. He was busy overseeing the movement of the newly reorganized Army of Northern Virginia, a realignment necessitated by the death of Stonewall Jackson the month before at Chancellorsville. However, he was available of June 8 and Stuart staged the entire affair again, but without the thundering saber charge, the firing artillery and the ball. Lee had ordered it to save on powder and horse flesh, and the ladies had returned home. "The troops to-day were reviewed by the great master of war and the famous chieftain of the Confederate Army, General Robert E. Lee." Nevertheless, the general was impressed. And General Fitz Lee and his brigade marched again that day and, knowing that his friend General John B. Hood was now at Culpeper, the cavalryman invited him to attend, adding, "Bring any of your people." General Hood arrived at the review with his "people"—his entire infantry division.[6]

Stuart had never had so much cavalry to command, five brigades numbering, by one informed estimate, 10,292 troopers.[7] With General Lee's plan for a forward movement across the Potomac approved by Richmond, Stuart's command was scheduled to start the summer's campaign the next morning.

On the northern side of the Rappahannock, in the aftermath of the Chancellorsville battle, a head or two had to roll, started on its way by the commanding general when he was certain his head was to be held in place. An infantry corps commander asked to be relieved. His reason was that he could no longer serve under Hooker, given the recent battle and his decision to break contact with Lee and return to the north side of the Rappahannock. Hooker, after surveying the surviving generals, focused his gaze on General George Stoneman of the Cavalry Corps. In Hooker's estimation, the cavalry raid had not accomplished much, if anything, and therefore the leader was to blame. This was an unfair assessment but, suspecting what was coming, Stoneman requested medical leave for hemorrhoids and it was granted. The general retreated to Washington. Into the breech rode Brigadier General Alfred Pleasonton, put there by Hooker as a temporary replacement. Hooker would have preferred to put Brigadier General John Buford in corps command but Pleasonton's commission as a brigadier general predated that of Buford. Rank, and the date of it being acquired, was almost as important to Civil War generals as defeating the Rebels.

In early June, General Hooker was aware of movement by Lee below the Rappahannock. Hooker ordered John Buford to investigate. Buford reported on June 5:

> I have just received information, which I consider reliable, that all of the available cavalry of the Confederacy is in Culpeper County. Stuart, the two Lees, Robertson, Jenkins, and Jones are all there. Robertson came from North Carolina, Jenkins from Kanawha, and Jones from the Valley. Jones arrived at Culpeper on the 4d [sic], after the others.

The numbers provided to headquarters by Buford were exaggerated and the brigade commanded by Jenkins was not there, but this remained good information, something that could be acted upon.[8] Hooker then order Pleasonton to cross the river and to "disperse and destroy" Stuart's command when found. Whether the cavalry's crossing of the river was also a reconnaissance in force or a spoiling attack has remained conjecture. An officer in the 1st Pennsylvania Cavalry later explained the mission as "merely to see what was up, and at the same time to take some of the conceit out of the rebel cavalry." The object of destroying Stuart and his force went unfulfilled, however, although the Rebels lost over 400 men in the resulting Battle of Brandy Station. However, the "conceit" inherent in Stuart's cavalry, if it ever existed, would no longer be as brash. Not counting two infantry brigades, numbering 1,500 men each, to march with Pleasonton to provide additional combat power to the strike, the corps commander had 7,981 horsemen, in three divisions, with which to cross the river, plus four horse artillery batteries.[9]

A cavalryman in the 6th Pennsylvania remembered that on the morning of June 8, "ammunition, forage, and rations are distributed, and orders issued to be ready to move at a minute's notice." Then the cavalry moved toward the Rappahannock and a trooper from the 1st Maine remembered:

> All the afternoon could be seen immense clouds of dust across the river, indicating that large forces of the enemy's troops were also in motion, and the boys felt there was hot work in store for them.

The dust was probably that kicked up the Stuart's horsemen parading for General Lee. After dark on June 8, the Union cavalry was in place, close to the river they would cross at dawn. Because there would be no fires in the bivouac that night, there would be no coffee and the cavalryman recalled, "we made our supper on cold ham and hard tack." And after "messages are committed to friends to be transmitted to distant loved ones, 'in case anything should occur.' After a solemn and earnest prayer we are all sleeping soundly."[10]

> Scarcely had the golden sunlight cast its rays upon the silver clouds that skirted the eastern horizon, when 'boots and saddles' were sounded and the bury bustle of camp betokened work for the cavaliers.

This was how an officer of the 8th Illinois Cavalry recalled the dawn of June 9, not many years later and providing the reader with no warning of the blood that would be spilled over the next several hours.[11] Within the 10th New York, an officer later recalled:

> I never witnessed, before or after, more enthusiasm and confidence that the men exhibited on this occasion. There was a positive eagerness for the meeting.[12]

John Buford would lead the 1st Division and cross at Beverly Ford. General David Gregg with the 3rd Division and Alfred Duffie with the 2nd Division would cross at Kelly's Ford some miles downstream. Gregg's and Buford's divisions were to rendezvous at Brandy Station and march to Culpeper with Duffie on the left flank. They would attack Stuart wherever he was found. Unknown to Pleasonton, Stuart had remained at the Brandy Station and Fleetwood Hill—his headquarters—location after the review for General Lee the day before.

With the Union force in place on the north side of the river, strict silence was to be maintained throughout the night. At 4am, Buford's men were awake and prepared to move. At dawn they were ready to cross at the ford:

> The ford was deep and the banks abrupt, and two could only cross abreast. A staff officer of Colonel Davis of the 8th New York was stationed at the river and as each company officer came through the stream, he received the order to 'draw sabers,' which was obeyed.[13]

The Rebel pickets were soon in action on the southern riverbank, firing while couriers rode back to Fleetwood Hill to alert Stuart and the brigades bivouacked in the surround area. Buford's men advanced on the road leading from the ford to the south with the pickets firing as they withdrew in the direction of St. James Church about a mile distant. The 8th New York and Colonel Benjamin Davis, commanding the 1st Division's 1st Brigade, were leading on the road to the church, with woods on either side. Suddenly they were charged by about 100 Rebel cavalrymen that had been alerted and had rushed from their camps. There was confusion and the 8th New York were forced back and, as Davis was trying to rally the regiment and continue along the road, he was shot and later died.[14] An unidentified New York newspaper, when reporting on the death of Colonel Davis, said that:

> He was shot through the head while charging at the head of his regiment … While raising his sabre to cut down an officer, a rebel turned upon him and shot him with his revolver. His death was immediately avenged by one of his aids. Seeing his Colonel fall, he leaped his horse to his adversary's side, and felled the officer to the ground with a sabre blow, which clove his skull and killed him instantly.

Another paper reported the Davis was avenged by a Lieutenant Parsons, the brigade's Assistant Adjutant General who "… raising in his stirrups, with one well directed blow of his sabre, he laid his head open midway between eyes and chin, and the wretch fell dead in the dust at his horse's feet."[15] Colonel Davis was as well thought of by the men of his regiment as Duncan McVicar had been by the 6th New York.

The Rebels, now fully aware of their enemy's approach quickly formed a defensive line at St. James Church and it was here that Buford's troopers met the first stalwart resistance, mounted and dismounted cavalrymen and artillery that had rushed from their camp area close by when they heard the firing at the ford. Buford's drive to Fleetwood Hill and Brandy Station had stalled. The Rebel defensive line extending on both sides of the church, with some artillery able to sweep the half-mile open ground around the church. Dismounted cavalrymen used a stonewall near St. James as cover. The fire from the now organized resistance forced Buford to order the command back into the woods.[16] General Stuart, after sending a brigade to cover the approach from Kelly's Ford, rode to St. James to direct the fight.

General Pleasonton sent the following message from Beverly Ford to army headquarters at 6am:

> Enemy has opened with Artillery, and shows some force of cavalry. Had a sharp skirmish. Colonel Davis, commanding the 2d Brigade, 1st Division, led his column across, and is badly wounded.[17]

Then, at 7:40am, June 9, Pleasonton said:

> The enemy is in strong force here. We have had a severe fight. They were aware of our movement, and were prepared.[18]

There was a fight, certainly, but as to being aware that the Union cavalry was coming, Pleasonton changes some of the facts the next day. On June 10, at 4:30pm in a follow up report, Pleasonton informs headquarters that his command captured a contraband, an officer's servant.

> …he thinks the attack yesterday on their cavalry has set them back for some time, as their horses, being grass-fed, were broken down by their hard work … He states… that we killed more than we wounded … He states that if our advance had not stopped when Colonel Davis fell, we would have captured all their artillery, as the camp was in bed asleep, and no support rearer [sic] than a mile.[19]

That the entire brigade would stop when Colonel Davis fell seems unlikely as Colonel Tom Devin of the 6th New York immediately assumed command.

As for Pleasonton's order to withdraw later that afternoon, permission had already been given to him at 12:10pm from Hooker's chief of staff:

> If you cannot make head against the force in front of you, return and take your position on the north bank of the river, and defend it. At this distance it is impossible for the general to understand all of your circumstances. Exercise your best judgment, and the general will be satisfied.[20]

Twenty minutes later, at 12:30pm, Pleasonton, from "Near Beverly Ford," reported:

> General Gregg has joined me, and I will now attack the enemy with my whole force … We have had a sharp fight, and have lost heavily, as we had the whole force in front of one-half of my command … Buford and Ames [leading an infantry brigade] have driven their whole force out of their strongest position.
>
> It would be well to send a good forces of the Fifth Corps toward Brandy Station, if it can be spared.[21]

General Gregg, because of a delay in the movement of Duffie's division, didn't get across the river at Kelly's Ford until sometime after 8, possibly 9am. When he did, the 2nd Division peeled off and marched six miles to Stevensburg, the flank protection maneuver designed to protect Gregg and Buford as they advanced. This move essentially took the 2nd Division out of the day's action, when it was found that Stuart was concentrated around Brandy Station and adjourning Fleetwood Hill and not at Culpeper. By not taking the direct road to the Station, but a more obscure path, Gregg essentially avoided the picket force that Stuart had posted on the shorter route to the station.[22] But Gregg, by noon, was closing in on the Station. Stuart, now aware of Gregg's force in his rear, directed some of the regiments fighting Buford to ride back to Fleetwood Hill and engage the approaching enemy. The two forces collided at and around Fleetwood Hill soon after. The action by the two Union generals quickly evolved into the largest cavalry battle of the Civil War. A Rebel trooper remembered the confrontation at Fleetwood Hill:

> [it] … was a great and imposing spectacle of squadrons charging in every portion of the field—men falling, cut out of the saddle with the saber, artillery roaring, carbines cracking—a perfect hurly-burly of combat.

A 1st Pennsylvania cavalryman of Gregg's division recalled, "At the time the dust was so thick that we could not tell friend from foe."[23] David Gregg later remembered Fleetwood Hill as:

> Charges and counter charges, guns captured and recaptured, the roar of sound made by the hurrahs and shouts of the contestants, all contributed to an excitement not heretofore experienced.[24]

It went on through the afternoon hours, with Buford making gains, advancing from St. James Church and approaching Fleetwood Hill. But just as he was seeing progress on his front, Pleasonton sent word for the engaged force to withdraw to the fords and cross. The same orders went to Gregg, who had been pushed back from Fleetwood Hill to the area south of Brandy Station in the most severe fighting of the battle. Gregg then moved, with Duffie and his command having now ridden into the area, to the northeast, to cross the river at Beverly Ford.

Leading one of Gregg's brigades was a then 22-year-old colonel from New Jersey, Judson Kilpatrick. He had risen quickly in the volunteer ranks since graduating from West Point and would become one of the more flamboyant and controversial cavalry leaders of the war. This day, Kilpatrick led a small brigade consisting of the 2nd and 10th New York and the 1st Maine to battle at Brandy Station. Both New York regiments, in charging the Rebels had been thrown back and in at least this portion of the battle, the Federal cavalry appeared to be losing. Kilpatrick called out to the 1st Maine to charge and to "save the day." It was later recorded in the history of the 1st Maine that:

> … at the right of a large open field of undulating ground, with woods at their right, at the left, as far as the eye could reach, were to be seen bodies of Union cavalry [Gregg's Division] advancing with quick movements toward the enemy's cavalry, who were also in full sight, and apparently active … The whole plain was one vast field of intense, earnest action. It was a scene to be witnessed but once in a lifetime, and one well worth the risks of battle to witness.

This was done and soon after Gregg was able to withdraw under Pleasonton's orders and cross the Rappahannock. In 1880, at a reunion of the 1st Maine, the now former General Judson Kilpatrick, an invited guest of the regiment, was called upon for his memory of the Brandy Station battle. His eloquent recapitulation of events closely resembles that included in the regiment's later written history. That evening, Kilpatrick, noted for the purple of his prose and its inherent insincerity, ended his reminiscences with the note: "And I say here tonight, before all this goodly company, to the 1st Maine Cavalry I owe the silver star I won that day upon the field of battle."[25]

Walter Newhall of the 3rd Pennsylvania, part of Duffie's division, later reported the action his command saw at Brandy Station somewhat differently. Newhall's division had not been inactive after it crossed the Rappahannock River at Kelly's Ford and took the road to Stevensburg. There the command skirmished with the Rebels, driving them about two miles, but were then ordered to go to the support of General Gregg's division, in action at Brandy Station:

> We came up just in time to save the Third Division pushing through the rebels right, and joined the Regulars, &c., at Beverly Ford, just as our cavalry was recrossing the river.

In the action Newhall's division lost about 25 men killed and wounded, but none were missing, "except the reporter." In summary, Newhall reported in his diary, that they captured over 60 prisoners, "saved Gregg, and not so much as mentioned in the papers, because our correspondent undertook to get to the rear during an important movement, an account of which he 'was anxious to furnish by the day's mail.'" The newspaper man, likely would not be appreciated again riding with this regiment, for Newhall said:

> Of course, it was known by telegraph that there was hot work again on the Rappahannock, and all who had friends in the cavalry were in a fever of anxiety, while the Associated Press was vainly asking *ubi est ille reporter?*[26]

The new Cavalry Corps commander had satisfied himself that his mission was accomplished. This is especially so in that Daniel Butterfield, General Hooker's chief of staff, had already given permission to withdraw. However, Pleasonton had not dispersed or destroyed Stuart's cavalry force as Hooker had ordered. But then his real purpose in crossing the river, Pleasonton later maintained, was really a reconnaissance, finding Stuart and his command. This had been done when he ordered the withdrawal, and besides, Rebel infantry was observed approaching. David Gregg, fighting in front of Brandy Station some distance from Pleasonton remembered "it was reported to me that cars ladened with infantry from Culpepper [sic] were approaching."[27] Confederate infantry did arrive from Culpeper while the battle raged, but they were not engaged as the order to withdraw had been given when they were detected arriving. Henry Meyer, a clerk reporting to the 2nd New York Cavalry's adjutant-general, later remembered that, when the Rebel infantry were seen arriving, the orders to withdraw were issued and Gregg's division withdrew "without molestation by the enemy."[28]

In a message to headquarters from Rappahannock Station timed at 8pm June 9, Pleasonton informed headquarters:

> A short time after my last dispatch to you, General Gregg, with his infantry and cavalry, joined me about 2 miles from the river, to which point I had driven the enemy. He reported that he had encountered a much superior number of the enemy's cavalry and had a severe fight. Also, that a train of cars had been run up to Brandy Station filled with infantry, who opened on his men. I also received information from letters and official reports captured in the enemy's camp, as well as from prisoners that the enemy had upward of 12,000 cavalry (which was double my own force of cavalry) and twenty-five pieces of artillery. I also learned from contrabands and prisoners that a large force of infantry had been sent from Culpeper as well as Longstreet's command from Ellis' Ford and having crippled the enemy by desperate fighting so that he could not follow me, I returned with my command to the north side of the Rappahannock.
>
> Tomorrow morning Stuart was to have started on a raid into Maryland, so captured papers state. You may rest assured he will not attempt it.

Buford's cavalry had a long and desperate encounter, hand to hand, with the enemy in which he drove them handsomely before him ... Over 200 prisoners were captured and one battle flag. [29]

David Gregg had moved to the Rappahannock and made contact with Pleasonton as he said in his message, "and, at about sunset crossed the river at Rappahannock Station Ford" accompanying eight Rebel officers, 107 enlisted men and two Confederate battle flags, but leaving 376 of his men behind as casualties. "[T] he enemy had been met on a fair field with the odds in his favor, and yet we had maintained our own against him, and conscious of our strength, were eager for further trails with him."[30]

At 5:30am on June 10, Pleasonton sent another dispatch to headquarters with much of the same information he sent the night before. But in this June 10 message he added:

> We [Buford's division] drove them over 2 miles before Gregg came up. It must be assumed it was two miles from Beverly Ford that the Rebels were driven. ... when I found out he had as hard a time as ourselves, no fresh troops to call on, I returned to the north bank of the Rappahannock ...
>
> Buford's loss is 250 wounded. Killed not yet known ... Gregg lost two guns before he joined me, but they were lost with honor, all his people engaged, and his battery was without support. The battery men fought their pieces until cut down at their side. One gun in the same battery burst—Sixth New York. [Battery][31]

The next evening, Pleasonton sent Hooker's headquarters another piece of intelligence. The cavalry had taken another contraband, another officer's servant and he told his interrogators that orders had come down "... to issue rations for three days, after that they were to ration themselves up in Pennsylvania (this was said to the cavalry). These rations were to be issued the day we went over there. There seems to be truth in this information." Chief of Staff Butterfield, at the same time was inquiring of Pleasonton about Rebel infantry: "Did you encounter any yesterday?"[32] About an hour later Pleasonton answered:

> We did encounter infantry yesterday, both mounted and on foot. Those mounted are armed with rifles made at Fayetteville, and marked C. S. A. Some were captured. Infantry at Brandy Station jumped from cars, and attacked Gregg's people ... I am satisfied their cavalry was crippled yesterday, while mine was not.[33]

After the war, all of its many battles were re-fought by participants with paper and ink substituting for small arms and artillery. One Frederick C. Newhall, who ended the war with the rank of colonel and not shy in providing his opinions, submitted an article about the engagement at Brandy Station that referred to it as a reconnaissance in force. The mission may have been intended to be that, but the battle resulted in "ruining [Stuart's] plans, which had soared high; it enabled General Pleasonton to anticipate him on the east flank of the Blue Ridge as he marched toward to Potomac, and to hold him in check by the well fought battle of

Aldie, Middleburg and Upperville ..." Nor was this all, Newhall maintained that the papers collected on the battlefield at Brandy Station by Pleasonton "... provided information which enabled General Hooker to move in good time to keep pace with Lee's army of invasion ..." Stephen Weld, a staff officer not involved in the raid, heard of the papers back with the army in camp and on June 10 mentioned them in a letter to his father:

> Yesterday our cavalry had a real hand-to-hand fight with the rebels near Kelly's Ford ... We captured all of Stuart's private papers, and found that he was to have started this morning ... to make his raid into Pennsylvania.

Additional corroboration of the intelligence gathered from Stuart comes from a member of General Gregg's staff at the time, Pvt. Henry Meyer, who reported years later that in the action "Kilpatrick's men soon reached the house [on Fleetwood Hill, Stuart's headquarters] capturing Stuart's adjutant-general and his papers."[34] The conclusions derived by Newhall from what was obtained at Brandy Station are exaggerated. Whatever was in the papers, their influencing of events that followed has never been detailed in that the papers themselves and the information therein have not come to light and, therefore, cannot be compared with the known actions of Pleasonton and the Cavalry Corps in the weeks that followed. It all might be a case of memory somewhat awry finding its way into later reminiscences.

In subsequent days, as Stuart moved along the eastern slope of the Blue Ridge, he was screening Lee's army from observation as part of it moved toward the Potomac. Federal cavalry, handled properly and aggressively, would not need orders from headquarters to try to gather all intelligence on what was behind the screen. The subsequent cavalry engagements on the roads leading to the Blue Ridge gaps all went in General Stuart's favor. No significant intelligence was gathered by the Cavalry Corps concerning Lee's plans or destination other than he was headed for the Potomac River and, therefore, the territory north of it, Maryland and Pennsylvania. Brandy Station was an inconclusive engagement resulting in heavy casualties for both sides while enhancing both the combat capability and overall morale of the Army of the Potomac's Cavalry Corps.

What had been three cavalry divisions under General Pleasonton were consolidated on June 11 and 12 into two with the approval of Hooker. Buford and Gregg would lead the first and second divisions respectively.[35] In the near-term, Corps Commander Pleasonton would shuffle component commanders also with an eye to ridding the corps of officers of foreign birth. Soon after Brandy Station, Pleasonton had privately recorded his feelings concerning foreign-born officers he had inherited:

> I conscientiously believe that Americans only should rule in this matter & [sic] settle this rebellion—& that in every instance foreigners have injured our cause.[36]

Before confronting General Lee in Pennsylvania, Pleasonton would dispose of the former division commander Alfred Duffie, French, and brigade commanders Luigi Palma di Cesnola, Italian, and Sir Percy Wyndham, English. Later, when Julius Stahel's cavalry division was absorbed into the Cavalry Corps from the Defenses of Washington, the Hungarian Stahel was immediately disposed of. Curiously, Pleasonton seemed not to have a problem with Irish-born William Gamble taking command of the 1st Brigade of Buford's division, replacing the fallen Benjamin Davis, probably because Gamble had been a sergeant major in the 1st Dragoons before the war and, unlike the others, could not really be considered a volunteer.[37]

The death at Beverly Ford of Colonel Benjamin Davis was a blow to the 1st Division. The West Point graduate was highly thought of and would probably have attained higher rank had he lived. A newspaper account of his death reported that he was:

> ... a native of Mississippi, which State he left after the passage of the ordnance of secession, to engage in the Union cause, and his devotion to which he has sealed with his life ... Colonel Davis was to be married to a young lady in Baltimore, to whom he had been engaged from some months. His body was embalmed today, and will be forwarded to West Point for interment. The gallant Col. Benj. F. Davis ... was the same officer who, when Harper's Ferry was invested by Stonewall Jackson, withdrew his troops without loss, capturing a valuable ammunition train of the enemy's ... Faithful among the faithless, he stood by the Government without flinching, though his state seceded, and his most intimate friends proved disloyal.

Lieutenant Parsons of the 8th New York, who had avenged Davis's killing, accompanied the remains to New York before spending a few days at home prior to returning to the regiment.[38]

Meanwhile, at army headquarters, the question that needed an answer was what were Lee's intentions once he reached the Potomac? Headquarters admonished Pleasonton as he moved in the shadow of the Rebel cavalry. At 3:20pm on June 12, he was sent this message:

> Look sharply to your right. By no means allow the enemy to turn it. Though he [Stuart's cavalry] may be crippled by your gallant attack of the 9th, he will use the more exertion to get you or us at a disadvantage. Be watchful, vigilant, and let nothing escape you.[39]

It was still early in June, days after the action at Brandy Station and, along the northern bank of the Rappahannock, soldiers started to move, all in response to those southern formations that, under Lee's orders, were also moving. The marching and the fighting for these Union soldiers would not end until they were again along this river's banks about a month and a half in the future, their ranks thinned by the loss of over 20,000 of their comrades. From army headquarters, the orders filtered down until the lowest private got the word: Get ready to move. The Army of the Potomac had at this time about 15 months of history recorded in action reports, in the newspapers, in the letters home of its soldiers, and from notes and fragments scribbled into the diaries that many carried with them. This army's past would be brought into focus and placed alongside the record it would inscribe in new reports, letters and diary entries during the coming weeks. Some would be dimly aware of it at the time. A soldier in the 63rd New York Infantry, writing to a newspaper, after the campaign was over and he was back along the Rappahannock, on July 30, 1863:

> It is with feelings of pride that the soldiers belonging to the Army of the Potomac can point to their brilliant campaign of the last six or seven weeks, and although when marching orders arrived for them to leave their beautiful ground on the bank of the Rappahannock, they were still harboring the most bitter feelings over the two disastrous retreats they had made when they crossed that fated river to attack the great Rebel works in December under Gen. Burnside, and in May under Gen. Hooker, yet with alacrity with which they obeyed the order, has only been equalled [sic] by the bravery and endurace [sic] they have since shown in their recent engagements with the enemy ...[40]

On June 17, Union cavalry was attempting to ride to a gap in the Blue Ridge to see into the Shenandoah Valley and spot Lee's movement toward the Potomac. As they approached the town of Aldie, a small place below the gap, a brigade of Gregg's cavalry division encountered Stuart's screening force. A fight quickly started, the Union troops were under the command of Judson Kilpatrick, or Kill-cavalry as his troopers called him. From the early history of another regiment not engaged in the fight it was noted that Kilpatrick's men "suffered severely in killed and wounded." Kilpatrick had ordered the 1st Maine and the 1st Massachusetts to charge the Rebels that were arrayed behind a stonewall. "[A]s a consequence the dear Union soldiers lay strewn along the road by scores, presenting a terrible spectacle. Colonel Doughtery [sic], of the 1st Maine, and forty men were left dead upon the field." Years later, the former cavalry leader, Judson Kilpatrick, was invited to speak at one of reunions held by the 1st Maine Cavalry. Of the fight at Aldie, he remarked:

> I looked back in despair: there I saw old Colonel Douty with the First Maine, I said: 'Men of Maine, you saved the day at Brandy Station, save it again at Aldie:' and upon the run you went, and I had the honor to ride side by side with your gallant old colonel Douty, and, sad to say, saw him go down in a soldier's death upon the bloody field.[41]

When the fight was over it was noted in the early history of the 8th Illinois, that Kilpatrick remarked to a Captain Hynes of the 1st Maine on the "gallant manner in which his men had driven the enemy." Captain Hynes, not noticing Kilpatrick's rank quickly replied, "asking where the dead rebels were. 'I can see plenty of your dead but few rebels.'"[42]

***

Army rumors were in flight all through Virginia, beginning when it was known that General Lee was on the move, the weight of his army shifting from place to place with no one certain where the bulk of it was or what the general's intentions were. The Union command occupying Winchester, Virginia, had been driven out of the valley by part of Lee's army. Jeb Stuart was screening the gaps in the Blue Ridge in an aggressive manner and the people in Pennsylvania, and in the North generally, were speaking of what was happening, or about to happen, as an invasion. As late as June 23, a Vermont soldier, E. F. Palmer, was telling his family:

> Such is Tuesday evening, with many rumors about the invasion of the North ... Lee is thought to be in Maryland and intending an attack on Washington or Baltimore ... An orderly has just come from headquarters to tell us that the whole brigade is to march in the morning.[43]

Five day later, the soldiers of this brigade had marched from Washington to near the Pennsylvania state line and reported to I Corps as it too moved north. It was Sunday, June 28:

> My Dear Father:—I have just time to tell you that I am well, and feeling well. We have been marching for three days, and are now somewhere in Maryland ... There are thousands of rumors, and if any of them are true, we shall have a brush with the rebels before night. Don't worry about me; for I shall come out all right, and do my duty the best I can.
> Your affectionate Son.

Palmer also kept a pocket diary, occasionally jotting down a note or a thought or a description. He described the soldier that marched next to him that Sunday. "His face is fiery red, and sweat running down it like rain on window panes; but still we push on ..." And then, the next morning, camped along the roadside:

> Beeves were shot and dressed last night, so we have fresh meat with hard tack for breakfast this morning ... We in the ranks actually know nothing at all where we are going.

They had passed through Emmitsburg, Maryland, and, on July 1, were marching north, "... when, suddenly, at four [p.m.], the smoke, like a vast, dark, snow-drifting cloud, rolls up before us from the field of Gettysburgh [sic], five or six miles away."[44]

Palmer, his Vermont regiment and the corps it was part of were marching into a 19th century battle, the largest of this war. Gilbert Wood and the 6th New York Cavalry were already there. Every man in the Army of the Potomac, either already in Pennsylvania or marching toward it, knew the reason for his going there. They spoke of it as an invasion. To turn it back, to defeat it they knew would require a great effusion of blood. Where it would all lead, they could not then imagine. And the cost of it all: unthinkable.

CHAPTER FIVE

If There is No Objection—
None in the World

Tuesday, June 30, 1863

I pray that our merciful Father in Heaven may protect and direct us! In that case I fear no odds and no numbers.

ROBERT E. LEE TO MRS. LEE, MAY 31, 1863[1]

We have found the Johnnies. They are just above and to the left of us, and the woods are full of 'em.

UNIDENTIFIED TROOPER, SIXTH NEW YORK CAVALRY, JUNE 30, 1863[2]

Years later he remembered. He thought of it for a time before picking up a pen for it was important to him that we should know. James Kidd, of Michigan, was one of many of his kind who, with pen and paper, left us his story. For that we are grateful and indebted to all these men, with no ability to repay other than by retelling their stories. It is not known when James Kidd began his remembrance, but it was put in book form in 1908. Kidd remembered:

Before we reached the town it was apparent that something unusual was going on. It was a gala day. The people were out in force, and in their Sunday attire to welcome the troopers in blue. The church bells rang out a joyous peal, and dense masses of beaming faces filled the street, as the narrow column of fours threaded its way through their midst. Lines of men stood on either side, with pails of water or apple-butter, and passed a 'sandwich' to each soldier as he passed.

Another Michigan man riding in the same column recalled, "… a young lady standing in the door singing the 'Star Spangled Banner' as loud as she could sing. We hailed her with hearty cheers."[3]

The church bells and the attire were appropriate for this was a Sunday, the last one in June 1863. The faces lining the streets of the town were reflecting relief, the departure of anxiety, if not fear, as the blue uniformed men rode among them.

It was early summer, a time that the men riding their horses in the long column would remember for the remainder of their lives. Many, after it was all over, would write of it in the manner of James Kidd, in their way telling us, or trying to, what it had been like. One cavalryman noted that the day before "… the people were enthusiastic in their greetings and expressions of satisfaction at the approach of the Union army … One old man stood beside the road near Monterey Springs, with his hat off and tears streaming down his face. As the column passed the men cheered him heartily."[4]

Early summer in the northeastern United States that year was a succession of sunny, hot, and humid days interspersed with some that were rainy and sometimes stormy, thunder and lightning, and wind. Overall, there were more wet days than dry. In the daylight they were moving. This day and tomorrow, they would remember. Because of them we, now, generations later, remember it also. The roads they traveled either choked them with dust when dry or splattered them with mud when wet. The people watching them pass were pleased to see them, generally, for moving about their prosperous countryside there were others, not friendly, taking what they cared to, invaders, ill clothed, dirty, plainly speaking English, but making it sound different.

North of the Potomac River the landscape in western Maryland and southern Pennsylvania was pleasing to the eye and remains so to this day. One of the riders in the column remembered, "We passed through the pretty town of Frederick, which is situated in one of the most beautiful valley's [sic] I ever saw."[5] Why would these riders remember this, the countryside, the weather, the citizens standing by the side of the road? Because of subsequent events, their memories of these days are indelibly marked and held close. One rider in the column had no trouble recalling a Tuesday morning, June 30. After the passage of many years, he spoke of it using a pen, leaving his words for us to read. He was young then, a soldier, and the next 24 hours would be one of the historic landmarks of his four years riding with a Union cavalry regiment. It was 11a.m. and this was how it began:

> The citizens, already in a state of terror and excitement over the great invasion, gazed with interest and satisfaction as the long column of veteran troopers, with trampling horses and fluttering guidons, moved through their streets. The troops were highly welcomed; such enthusiasm and loyalty were seldom witnessed. Hundreds of women and children line the walks and cheered the men with the 'Red, White and Blue,' which they sang most loyally and charmingly, while handkerchiefs and banners waved most earnestly and gracefully from *stalwart arms* and delicate hands. The rebels had but just disappeared over the hills, and no wonder that the people should manifest gladness and joy at our coming. A supper was ready for any of the "boys" who desired to eat, and much was done in that line, of course, by the cavaliers.[6]

These men had gotten to the place they had been ordered to. Perhaps they could rest for a time after sampling the offerings of these citizens.

This scene had been repeated in every town the column had passed through since leaving Virginia days earlier. The day before the troopers heard the "Red, White and Blue" being sung, they had ridden over South Mountain to Boonsboro, Maryland, and then north through Cavetown and Smithburg before traversing South Mountain again via Monterey Pass, camping at Fountaindale and along the mountain's eastern slope. A trooper in the 8th Illinois Cavalry remembered:

> ...the day was perfect, the roads were good. We passed over the mountain twice and had charming views. We marched through a rich, highly cultivated country, and by the homes of our own people.

The column stopped that evening, east of the mountain's crest, bivouacked, boiled coffee, and gnawed on hard tack crackers while some officers rode back to the Monterey Springs Hotel for a dinner of "... beard, butter, ham, apple-butter and coffee."[7] It was reported in the early history of one regiment of this command, the 17th Pennsylvania Cavalry, that many members of Company G were from Waynesboro, a town about eight miles from the camp occupied that night. The captain of the company asked the 17th's colonel for permission for those men to make a quick visit home that night. The colonel obliged on "... condition that every member of the company must report for duty again at sunrise the following morning; and that, to the credit of Company G, it could be faithfully said that every member of the company answered roll call the next morning."[8]

The leader of the column was Brigadier General John Buford, commanding the 1st Cavalry Division, Army of the Potomac. At that time, and since, the 37-year-old Buford was considered the most capable cavalry leader then serving. On the morning of June 30, he had ridden into this town at the head of two brigades. He already knew the enemy was close. In the twilight the evening before, as his division bivouacked, Buford may have ridden to a high point on the South Mountain near Monterey Pass that overlooked the town of Fairfield, Pennsylvania. As the darkness approach he may have "... perceived in the distance, along the Fairfield road, the bivouac-fires of a hostile body of troops ..."[9] Then, early on this Tuesday morning, as his cavalry column neared the town of Fairfield, eight miles south and west of the community now hosting he and his men, there had been skirmishing with Rebel infantry. Abner Hard of the 8th Illinois remembered:

> ...moving on the Hagerstown ... road, we reached Fairfield, where we found the enemy in possession. The atmosphere was so foggy that our skirmishers came upon them unexpectedly. Shots were rapidly exchanged.[10]

Buford's orders were to scout the country ahead of the infantry advancing on the eastern side of South Mountain and get to this place. So, rather than turn the exchange of shots into a serious fight, he disengaged, leaving the 6th New York to cover his withdrawal. "The Sixth New York advanced upon the town," says the regiment's early history, "and commenced skirmishing with the enemy, while the division marched by another route to Emmitsburg."[11] From Emmitsburg it would be about an 11-mile march to this place, its streets now lined with anxious men, women, and children waving and singing, refreshments eagerly offered. This place was Gettysburg,

General John Buford commander of the First Cavalry Division which confronted the Rebel advance on Gettysburg on July 1. (Library of Congress)

Pennsylvania, today hallowed ground. In its environs would be fought a 19th century battle, the largest of this war. It will begin tomorrow.

John Buford was born in Kentucky in 1826. He spent the majority of his early years in Illinois before entering the West Point class of 1848. Most of the 1850s was spent on the frontier, with the then 2nd Dragoons, protecting settlers and fighting Indians. Buford and his regiment were part of the expedition to Utah in 1857 to restore order and "to assert federal authority over" the territory then controlled by Brigham Young and the Church of Latter-Day Saints.[12] When the Civil War started, Buford returned to the east and was initially assigned to the defenses of the capital and then given command of a brigade under General John Pope. He was wounded in the Second Battle of Bull Run and, after recovering, was assigned by General George McClellan as chief of cavalry for the Army of the Potomac. This was merely a staff position and not a field command. A command in the field came in 1863 with his assignment to the 1st Cavalry Division.[13]

Of his early morning run-in with Rebels, near the small community of Fairfield, Buford later reported:

> The inhabitants knew of my arrival and the position of the enemy's camp, yet not one of them gave me a particle of information, nor even mentioned the fact of the enemy's presence. The whole community seemed stampeded, and afraid to speak or to act, often offering as excuses for not showing some little enterprise, 'The rebels will destroy our houses if we tell anything.' Had any one given me timely information, and acted as a guide that night, I could have surprised and captured or destroyed this force, which proved next day to be two Mississippi regiments of infantry and two guns.[14]

As a result of the detour Buford took through Emmitsburg that morning, he almost certainly encountered Major General John Reynolds, normally the commander of I Corps. This body of troops was the first of three corps that composed the left wing of the Army of the Potomac with Reynolds in overall command. This morning Reynolds was on the road that passed through Emmitsburg and led to Gettysburg.

Before heading out on Emmitsburg Road and moving on Gettysburg, Buford and Reynolds must have talked. Buford certainly would have informed Reynolds of his earlier encounter with Rebels. Anything else they may have talked of or decided was not recorded, but it must be assumed that the two generals considered that contact with the Rebels was likely the further toward Gettysburg they advanced. Contact would mean a fight. If Buford did not already know it, Reynolds may have mentioned that for part of the previous year he had been stationed at Carlisle Barracks, Pennsylvania, a town some miles north of Gettysburg. Reynolds, therefore, might have had a passing familiarity with the town and surrounding terrain. This one unrecorded conversation on the morning of June 30 might have set the course for both the coming battle and the campaign as a whole.[15]

The leading element of I Corps was its 1st Division, commanded by Brigadier General James Wadsworth. One of his artillerymen, Augustus Buell, heard comments by Buford's boys as they rode passed on the road headed for Gettysburg. "They had plenty of news for us," Buell later remembered, "and it was of an exciting character. They would sing out as they rode by, 'We have found the Johnnies; they are just above and to the left of us, and the woods are full of 'em.'" This was exciting news indeed. Then Buford's column stopped for a time and the troopers told the curious and anxious artillerymen more. Buell recalled:

> … some of the 6th New York men told us that they had tried to go to Gettysburg early in the morning by a shorter route, and had encountered a large force of Confederate infantry, which had compelled them to turn back and come round Emmittsburg [sic]. The Colonel of the 6th New York told [Battery Captain James] Stewart that there was no doubt but that Lee's whole army was in front of us, and that they—the cavalry—were advancing to bring on an engagement.

Years later, when writing his memoir, Augustus Buell added a note that almost every written remembrance of the days just prior to the battle includes in one fashion or another:

> The known proximity of the enemy in great force, and the certainty of an immediate battle, which every one said was bound to be the greatest and most desperate yet fought began to have a perceptible effect on the men.[16]

The captain of an artillery battery parked along Emmitsburg Road that day was one James Stewart and 30 years later he recalled this Tuesday, the last day of June. It was the end of the month and the battery's returns for men, equipment and ordnance had to be submitted not later than the next morning. Stewart remembered:

> I was extremely anxious to have the returns off my hands, having been informed by an aide to General Buford's that the cavalry had met a part of A. P. Hill's infantry, and that more than likely a battle would take place the following day (July 1).[17]

On this summer morning, Colonel William S. Christian of the Army of Northern Virginia was closer to Gettysburg than John Buford and his troopers. Colonel

Christian and his command, the 55th Virginia Infantry, were part of his army's III Corps, commanded by General A. P. Hill. His regiment was doing picket duty in advance of General Henry Heth's infantry division near Cashtown, Pennsylvania, on the road leading to Gettysburg. Mindful of what had gone before, and sensing the significance of being out of Virginia, marching toward another battle, Christian had written to his wife two days before:

> Camp near Greenwood, PA., June 28, 1863,
>
> My own dear wife ... As you can see by the date of this that we are now in Pennsylvania. We crossed the line day before yesterday, and are resting to-day near a little one-horse town on the road to Gettysburgh [sic], which we will reach; settled tomorrow. We are paying back these people for some of the damage they have done us. We are getting up all the horses, etc., and feeding our army with their beef and flour, etc., but there are strict orders about the interruption of any private property by individual soldiers.
>
> Though with these orders, fowls and pigs and eatables don't stand much of a chance. I felt when I first came here, that I would like to revenge myself upon these people for the desolation they have brought upon our once beautiful home; that home where we could have lived so happily, and that we have loved so much, from which their vandalism has driven you and my helpless little ones. But though I had such severe wrongs and grievances to redress ... yet when I got among these people I could not find it in my heart to molest them. They looked so dreadfully scared and talked so humble that I invariably endeavored to protect their property, and have prevented soldiers from taking chickens, even in the main road ... No houses were searched and robbed like our houses were done by the Yankees. Pigs, chickens, geese, etc are finding their way into our camp; it can't be prevented, and I can't think it ought to be. We must show them something of war.
>
> The country that we have passed through is beautiful and everything in the greatest abundance. You never saw such a land of plenty. We could live here mighty well for the next twelve months, but I suppose old Hooker [General Joseph Hooker, commanding the Army of the Potomac] will try to put a stop to us pretty soon. Of course, we will have to fight here, and when it comes it will be the biggest on record. Our men feel that there is to be no back-out. A defeat here would be ruinous. This army has never done such fighting as it will do now ... We must conquer a peace ... We will show the Yankees this time how we can fight.
>
> Be of good cheer, and write often to your fondly attached husband, Wm. S. Christian.[18]

Colonel Christian's wife never received this letter. It was found on the battlefield some days later. General Dorsey Pender, a division commander in Robert E. Lee's Army of Northern Virginia, was equally impressed with the country, but that was all. In a letter to his wife, he said. "This is the most magnificent country to look at; but the most miserable people. I have yet to see a nice-looking lady ... And the barns I never dreamed of." A soldier in the Rebel column left his impression of Pennsylvania with his sister. The people impressed him the most "... nothing but Dutch and Irish and the dirty ... meanest looking creatures that I ever saw for to call themselves white girls."[19] Other southerners noticed this also. Moxley Sorrel, a staff officer wrote, "The women of the country were a hard-featured lot. The population principally Pennsylvania Dutch, are an ignorant offshoot of a certain class of Germans long settled there ... Many can speak no English."[20] This was at variance with a trooper in a horse artillery unit riding through Pennsylvania with the army. This soldier recalled:

> I saw some beautiful, rosy-cheeked, bonny lassies on the street in Greencastle, but they looked as sour as a crab apple, frowns an inch wide and warranted pure vinegar playing over their lovely faces, like the shadow of the cloud that flits across the blushes of an opening rose. I wonder what made them look so frownful. We did not come here to harm nor molest the charming creatures, but we may hurt some of their relatives if they get after us with guns.[21]

James H. Hodam remembered the movement in Pennsylvania and later wrote:

> The country through which we passed toward Gettysburg seemed to abound chiefly in Dutch women who could not speak English, sweet cherries, and apple butter. As we marched along, the women and children would stand at the front gate with large loaves of bread and a crock of apple butter, and effectively prevent an entrance of the premises by the gray invaders.[22]

Passing through a town on the way to Gettysburg, a cavalry trooper noticed not the women but the men. Luther Hopkins of the 6th Virginia Cavalry observed

> … a great number of young men between the ages of 18 and 45 in citizen's clothes. This had a rather depressing effect upon us, because it showed us that the North had reserves to draw from, while our men, within the age limit, were all in the army.[23]

For a week, the citizens of this portion of Pennsylvania had columns of Rebels moving among them, most helping themselves to whatever food and livestock happened to be within reach. In some cases, anything else that could be useful was appropriated. Officially, this was not looting. Those things or commodities required were to be paid for with Confederate cash—worthless paper in the North—or with promissory notes, signed by an officer to be redeemed by the bearer from the Confederate Treasury upon independence. Arriving at Chambersburg, Pennsylvania, a cavalry brigade under General Albert Jenkins needed some supplies. A German-speaking lieutenant, Herman Shiericht of the 14th Virginia, noted in his diary:

> General Jenkins ordered the shopkeepers to open their establishments, and we purchased what we needed, paying in Confederate money. The inhabitants had to provide rations for the troops and we fared very well, but their feelings toward us were very adverse.

Others were not so adverse. Those with political leanings supporting the "peace-party" were well disposed to the lieutenant, "… especially were the Germans in favor of peace."[24] On Friday June 26, a division of Lieutenant General Richard Ewell's Second Corp, Army of Northern Virginia, commanded by Brigadier General Jubal Early, had passed through Gettysburg marching toward the Susquehanna River. Tillie Pierce, a young Gettysburg resident, remembered "Rushing to the door, and standing in the front portico we beheld … a dark, dense mass, moving toward town." Another Gettysburg resident noted, "The advance guard of the enemy, consisting of 180 to

200 men, rode into Gettysburg at 3 ½ p.m., shouting and yelling like so many savages from the Rocky Mountains ..." Soon after there followed "... 5,000 infantry ... Most of the men were exceedingly dirty, some ragged, some without shoes, and some surmounted by the skeleton of what was once an entire hat, affording unmistakable evidence that they stood in great need of having their wardrobe replenished ..."[25] While these Rebels briefly lingered in the town, they appropriated any horses from the inhabitants that had not been hidden away and any clothing, particularly shoes, inventoried by Gettysburg's retailers. In some instances, the Confederate units had no money with which to make their "purchases" and neglected to issue promissory notes for what they required. The pickings from the retailers, however, were meager, most merchants having spirited away their goods on hearing of the approach of the Rebels. "They wanted horses, clothing, anything and almost everything they could conveniently carry away," Ms. Pierce recalled, "Nor were they particular about asking." In addition, that evening, they "... divested the taverns and liquor stores of the liquors."[26] The next morning, to the relief of the town's citizens, Early's troops marched on. Were there more and would they be coming to their town? This appropriation or confiscation, or whatever name was applied to the actions of Lee's army in Pennsylvania, did have a more sinister aspect to it, one that went to the core of the conflict. An officer in the 3rd Pennsylvania Cavalry made note of it as his regiment moved north of the Potomac, searching for Robert E. Lee and his army:

> The banks sent their specie to New York, a few people buried their plate, a few others fled across the Delaware. But the only class with whom the terror was universal were the poor negroes [sic], not the contrabands alone, but the free black, born and brought up on Northern soil, who, on a sudden, saw slavery yawning to devour them.[27]

It remains an unknown of the Pennsylvania campaign that summer how many free blacks were captured and sent south by Lee's more zealous invaders. It could have been hundreds. Colonel William Christian of the 55th Virginia Infantry told his wife of his experience in a letter of June 28. "We took a lot of negroes [sic] yesterday. I was offered my choice but as I could not get them back home I would not take them." Then Christian adds, "In fact, my humanity revolted at taking the poor devils away from their homes ..."[28] However, most blacks in or near the path of Lee's forces, able to do so, packed up and ran as the Rebels approached, headed for Harrisburg and beyond.

Other Rebel formations had been reported moving in the vicinity and the residents were naturally apprehensive. Then on Sunday afternoon, June 28, to the great relief of Gettysburg's residents, two Michigan regiments of the 3rd Cavalry Division, Army of the Potomac, were seen approaching along Emmitsburg Road. James Kidd was one of the horsemen riding with this command. The two regiments were quickly told of General Early's stop over on Friday and the movement of his command to the east. The Federals were also alerted to the other sightings in the surrounding country. Commanding the two Michigan regiments was Brigadier General Joseph T. Copeland. The general reported from Gettysburg at 2p.m. on June 28:

> We have just arrived with the column at this place, and find no enemy. They destroyed the railroad bridge near here, and helped themselves to everything they needed in town. They went out on the road to York, and it is reported here that White, with his Cavalry, branched off to Hanover Junction from a place called Abbottstown …

Copeland continued:

> At the same time that the enemy arrived here, a large camp of them was seen on a road 4 miles north of this place, which also leads to York, and during that night the troops proceeded in that direction. The citizens who observed them report an estimated 6,000 infantry and twenty cannon (counted) … All the enemy came from Chambersburg, and they stated they were going to York, and to cut railroad communication at Hanover Junction.

Copeland passed this message up through the division's commander who in turn passed it to General Alfred Pleasonton, Commander of the Cavalry Corps, Army of the Potomac. The night before, while bivouacked at Emmitsburg, Copeland had sent a similar message through the command chain based on reports he had received from the Gettysburg vicinity. Pleasonton, when he received the message from Copeland dated June 28, continued it up the chain. By the next day at the latest it was among the many reports and messages piled on the desk of Major General George Gordon Meade, the new commander of the Army of the Potomac, at his field headquarters.[29] It was only about 24 hours earlier, on June 28, that General Meade had been ordered into command by President Lincoln. For the Pennsylvanian Meade, it was something of a shock as he was one of the few general officers in the army that did not take an active hand in army politics or try for promotion at the expense of other officers or the troops under his command. George Meade would, in a distinguished and capable manner, now lead the Army of the Potomac, but now

General George Meade who took over command of the Army of the Potomac only three days before the beginning of the battle at Gettysburg. (Library of Congress)

it was the morning of June 29 and the hours for which George Meade would always be remembered, and those that would define the army he led, were two days in the future when Copeland's report found its way on to his desk.

George Meade had commanded V Corps until early on the morning of June 28 when an officer direct from the president woke the sleeping general in his tent at Frederick, Maryland. It was bad news for him, the officer said. Meade at first thought he was being arrested or relieved. Regardless, he said, his conscience was clear and he had done his best. However, the documents brought by the officer from Washington were orders he had to obey. He was 48 years old at the time, tall and thin with gray sprinkled through his beard. Meade most often wore glasses and "might have been taken for a Presbyterian clergyman, unless one approached him when he was mad."[30] He was a man of high character, but he was irritable, petulant and dyspeptic.[31] George Meade had been ordered into command of the Army of the Potomac, relieving General Joseph Hooker. Within a short time, this was done and Meade spent the rest of the day and night trying to get a grip on what the army was doing, where its component parts were, and what were its plans. It was rumored other senior officers had recommended to the president that Meade be placed in command of the army, but the general himself had not encouraged it, if indeed he knew of it other than by rumor and camp talk, some of which he repeated in letters to his wife in Philadelphia. Now he was stuck with it and the Army of Northern Virginia waiting somewhere in the countryside ahead.

George Meade, a West Pointer, had been an engineer for nearly his entire time in the army since graduation, building lighthouses along the Florida coast among other projects. He had been with the army in Mexico but when the Civil War came it was the first time he had led a large number of troops. He did it well enough to command a brigade, a division and an army corps in battle and, as a non-participant in internal army politics, he was a different sort of ranking officer in this army. His political views were somewhat of a mystery. Although historians consider Meade to have been a conservative Democrat, one not inclined to look favorably upon abolitionists and the political party then in power, he had led his men in a competent manner in the fighting this army had done in the past year. While he had, at times, a volcanic temper, an aversion to the pomp surrounding the station he held, and while he was not an overly aggressive general, his competence and courage, his willingness to stand for the Union, and willingness to employ force to bring it back together, had gained the trust of his fellow generals. Described by a contemporary: "In manner he was often sharp and preemptory, but this was because of his utter absorption in great affairs."[32] George Meade, the fourth general to lead this army, would lead it until the war's end.

The soldiers outside of V Corps knew little or nothing about George Meade. They had been marching through heat and humidity or through rain and on muddy roads since leaving the north bank of the Rappahannock River, each man thinking of the meaning behind Lee's move north with few reaching a conclusion. To a man, these soldiers regarded Lee's move into Pennsylvania as an invasion and spoke of it as such, both then and later. Of their leader, who could say? In a letter dated June 16, more than a week before George Meade took command of the army, Major Henry Lee Higginson of the 1st Massachusetts Cavalry said in a letter:

> The rebel army will get well into Pennsylvania, will anger the people, and finally get a severe whipping.... It is a desperate move on Lee's part, but it can be checkmated by someone, and turned into a great and final defeat. We have yet to see who 'someone' is ...

Major Higginson was wounded the next day in the cavalry action at Aldie, Virginia.[33]

They had a new commanding general and it was hoped he knew what he was doing. They were out of desolate Virginia and into the rich and undisturbed north, hailed by the citizens as they passed along the road but as each mile rolled by the seriousness of it all seemed to grow more intense. An infantryman in III Corps remembered the march a decade later:

> The next place of any interest is the beautiful city of Frederick. As we near the place we observe some bodies dangling from the limbs of trees. They were rebel spies. We camped around the city and have nice times.

As this soldier's regiment is about to cross into Pennsylvania he comments on the mood of the troops.

> [E]very one is confident of victory ... besides, we are fighting on our own soil, and every man thinks that if Lee don't get a whipping here he never will.[34]

General Meade and everyone in the upper echelon of the Army of the Potomac knew that General Lee and his legions were out in front of the Union army as it moved through Maryland and into Pennsylvania. The reports of sightings and messages, like that of General Copeland's, when evaluated still did not pinpoint exactly where the elements of that army were at a given moment, but the three divisions of the Potomac Army's Cavalry Corps were ordered by Meade to get out ahead of the infantry and look for the Rebels. Spread across the front and flanks of Meade's army, they were certain to make contact with at least a portion of the Rebel force. Also, centered in the consciousness of each soldier making up this Union force was the knowledge that when General Lee and his army were found there would be a battle. If there ever was a battle that George Meade and the Army of the Potomac could not afford to lose—and they had lost a few—it would be the one fought against Robert E. Lee on northern soil. On June 30, General Meade advised cavalry leader Pleasonton of his true mission, advice having no need of being stated but for the fact that in the march north through Virginia, and until Lee got to the Potomac River, General Jeb Stuart, commanding the cavalry of the Army of Northern Virginia, had screened the advancing Rebel army so effectively the Union cavalry had been unable to break through and acquire solid intelligence on Rebel movements to and across the river. In fact, cavalry battles had been fought with Stuart on the roads and near the towns leading to gaps in the Blue Ridge, at Aldie, Middleburg, and Upperville, that prevented anything precise as to Lee's intentions from being reported to the commanding general and, therefore, the movement of Union forces had been a best guess as opposed to planned moves designed to counter the Rebel threat to the land above the Potomac. The information arriving at army headquarters was, for the most part, obtained from individuals encountered along the line of march or from scouts and/or agents reporting from the vast countryside the Rebels were moving across. On June 30, therefore, and yet unaware that Buford had already exchanged shots with Rebels near Fairfield, Meade advised the cavalry commander "… your cavalry force is large and must be vigilant and active. The reports must be those gained by the cavalry themselves, and the information sent in should be reliable … Cavalry battles must be secondary to this object."[35] Nevertheless, there would be a cavalry battle on June 30.

Despite being only two regiments, the residents of Gettysburg wanted General Copeland and his visiting Michigan troopers to stay for their protection against roving Rebels but the Michigan men were under orders to move early the next morning, Monday, June 29, for a rendezvous with the rest of their division at Littlestown, Pennsylvania. Copeland and the two regiments he led into Gettysburg were part of Pleasonton's new addition to the Cavalry Corps, the 3rd Cavalry Division. This division, under the command of Brigadier General Hugh Judson Kilpatrick, would camp at Littlestown the evening of June 29. Its mission was the same as Buford's 1st Division: locate and report the position of the Rebel army. The Michigan regiments got to Littlestown on time and reported to Kilpatrick by that evening. After resting overnight in the fields surrounding Littlestown and caring for their horses, Kilpatrick, on June 30, led his division to the northeast, on the road from Littlestown leading to Hanover, Pennsylvania. By mid-day, Kilpatrick and most of the division were through the town, but its last two regiments and supply train were yet to leave. As it turned out, Hanover, with its streets filled with Federal cavalry was directly in the path of Jeb Stuart's cavalry. Before leaving Virginia for the campaign above to the Potomac River, Lee had authorized a movement by Stuart's cavalry that by its discretionary wording left the Rebel general far afield and unable to report on the movements of the Union army. Stuart was attempting, on the morning of June 30, to unite with the army corps commanded by General Richard Ewell that was supposed to be moving in the direction of Harrisburg, with one element of it near York, Pennsylvania. This was the division commanded by General Jubal Early that had passed through Gettysburg the previous Friday. No doubt to Stuart's great annoyance, the encounter with Kilpatrick's cavalry would delay his uniting with his army. The accidental confrontation escalated, pistols and carbines were brought to bear, shots exchanged immediately on contact. The sound of the gunfight immediately brought the return of Kilpatrick and the rest of the division to Hanover and a bloody confrontation resulted that encompassed the streets and alleys of the town and the countryside just to the south and southeast. Artillery was deployed, and a duel started with the Rebels and after at least two charges into the Rebel force in regimental strength by the Yankees, the encounter became a standoff. As the Tuesday afternoon began to fade, Stuart disengaged and moved off to the east, trying to avoid further delay in finding his army. The 3rd Division did not pursue but reported the encounter to Pleasonton. Kilpatrick, known throughout the Cavalry Corps as "Kill-cavalry," reported his casualties in the encounter as "trifling." For Kill-cavalry, 19 dead and 179 wounded or missing was worth what he now believed was the approximate location of the Rebel army. He reported to Pleasonton that Lee's army had to be massed in and around the town of East Berlin, about eight or ten miles to the north of Hanover. He was to move in that direction the next day, July 1. This intelligence conflicted with what Buford was reporting at the same time from Gettysburg. By the evening of June 30 at the latest, Meade knew at least where Stuart had been that day and, generally, the direction he was headed. He knew where Buford was and that there had been contact with at least one Rebel element. Meade knew what he had in John Buford, but were the reports coming from Kilpatrick at Hanover correct intelligence also, "… gained by the cavalry themselves, and the information … reliable."[36] What to believe?

On that Tuesday morning, as Buford's division approached Gettysburg from the south along Emmitsburg Road, a Rebel force had been about to march on the town from the west via the Chambersburg Pike. For reasons the Gettysburg residents giving Buford this intelligence couldn't explain, these troops had stopped along the pike, observed the town for a while and then turned and marched back the way they came. These Rebels had probably seen Buford's scouts or the leading element of the division, a squadron of the 8th Illinois Cavalry that had approached the town well in advance of Buford and the division. It was 10am.

This Rebel column belonged to a division commanded by General Henry Heth of Lee's III Corps. General Heth and his division were in camp at Cashtown, eight miles from Gettysburg along the Chambersburg Pike. The general had heard a quantity of shoes could be had in the town just ahead, a commodity always needed in the Army of Northern Virginia. Either the night before, June 29, or quite early in the morning of June 30, General Heth called one of his brigade commanders, General J. Johnston Pettigrew, and gave him his orders. An aide to General Pettigrew at this time was Lieutenant Louis G. Young. In later years, the former lieutenant wrote an account of his brigade's actions during the time spent at Gettysburg that summer. It contains some detail on what he had witnessed on June 30, as well as his later reflections on its significance relating to the events of July 1. Heth's instructions to Pettigrew were for him to take three of his four North Carolina regiments from the First Brigade and some wagons and march to Gettysburg "… for the purpose of collection commissary and quartermaster stores for the use of the army." It was thought that there may or may not be some Pennsylvania home guard assigned to the town, helping to sooth the nerves of the worried residents with their presence. These Sunday soldiers Pettigrew should have "… no difficulty in driving away." However, if he encountered anything resembling "organized troops," he was not to engage them or bring about in any manner an engagement. This admonition was later characterized by Lieutenant Young as "peremptory." General Pettigrew and 2,000 troops were on the road by 6:30am. Doing picket duty along the road outside Cashtown that morning was the 55th Virginia Infantry of Heth's 2nd Brigade, led by Col. William S. Christian. Whether it was a more experienced unit than his or whether he believed he needed to add muscle to his command if there was trouble that could not be avoided, Pettigrew convinced Christian to join the march. At or about 9:45am, Pettigrew was outside Gettysburg, possibly as near as Seminary Ridge, to the west of town, and could see blue-clad horsemen moving along Emmitsburg Road.

As the column moved along the road to Gettysburg, Lieutenant Young later recalled, "… we were passed by General Longstreet's spy." This was a man named Harrison, employed by General James Longstreet, who had overtaken the army on June 28, riding hard from Virginia. Harrison had brought word that the Army of the Potomac had crossed its namesake river and was moving north, searching. This information had triggered a change of orders for Lee's army. Orders went out from army headquarters on the night of June 28 and early in the morning of June 29 for the scattered elements of the Rebel army to begin concentrating in the Gettysburg vicinity. Apparently, Harrison rode ahead into Gettysburg, but "quickly returned." He told Pettigrew that there were Yankee cavalrymen in the town. Lieutenant Young, in his recollection, has Harrison telling Pettigrew that the force in Gettysburg was Buford's and estimated to be about 3,000 troopers. Saying that Buford's entire division was in the town at the moment is probably a lapse of memory on Young's part, but no doubt Harrison did encounter some Union cavalrymen, mostly likely scouts or troopers from the 8th Illinois. Young goes on to relate, "This report was confirmed by a Knight of the Golden Circle who came out for the purpose of giving us warning."[37]

A courier was summoned and "General Pettigrew sent immediately to General Heth, a report of what he had learned and asked for further instructions." Evidently, while waiting for the courier to return, the brigade stood in the road, its distance from the town not being mentioned in the record left by Lieutenant Young. However, if Buford's entire division had been in Gettysburg at that moment, no doubt his scouts would have encountered these Rebels and John Buford would not have stayed in the town and done nothing.

It was not recorded how long it took the courier to make the round trip to General Heth, but on returning his message was "… simply a repetition of the orders previously given coupled with an expression of disbelief as to the presence of any portion of the Army of the Potomac."[38]

With orders not to bring on an engagement, Pettigrew reversed field and started back to Cashtown. He had been seen, however, not only by Gettysburg residents but also by whatever cavalry there was in the town at that time. An unknown number of cavalrymen followed Pettigrew's column for some considerable distance. Lieutenant Young and another officer rode at the end of the brigade and recalled:

> This we easily did, for the country is rolling, and from behind the ridges we could see without being seen and we had a perfect view of the movements of the approaching column. Whenever it would come within three or four hundred yards of us, we would make our appearance, mounted, when the column would halt until we retired. This was repeated several times … The cavalry made no effort to molest us.[39]

By 11am that morning, the 1st Cavalry Division was filling Gettysburg's streets and accepting refreshment from its citizens. Undoubtedly, Buford was informed of what had been seen along the Chambersburg Pike only a short time before. Digesting this news, and having already that morning skirmished with Rebels as well as hearing from residents of the town of the stop over by Rebels troops the previous Friday, John Buford knew for certain that Lee's army was near. Given the landscape, the Rebels were probably massed somewhere to the west, back along the pike that passed over South Mountain and connected Gettysburg with Chambersburg. Some Rebel elements might be headed this way or perhaps some elements were marching north and east from Chambersburg, through the Cumberland Valley, toward the Susquehanna River via Carlisle, Pennsylvania. No doubt about it, the Johnnies were in the neighborhood.

At the front of Buford's column as it entered Gettysburg that morning was the 6th New York Cavalry, and Captain William L. Herrmance of Company C remembered it well. Much later. he recalled:

> [the] … patriotic songs that made the blood flow quicker in our veins, as we thought of those at home, and that we were there to defend Northern soil from the desolation that we had seen so much of in the homes of our Southern brothers, who had forced us to fight against them.[40]

With the passage of time, Herrmance may be excused for the embellishments upon his memory and the language. Nevertheless, many contemporary accounts made by the men now converging on this town speak of the Rebel army's presence in

Pennsylvania as something that could not be tolerated, something that must be driven out.

Tillie Pierce remembered that Buford's men "... passed northwardly along Washington Street, turned toward the west on reaching Chambersburg Street, and passed out in the direction of the Theological Seminary."[41] Buford then set his picket line and sent scouting parties roaming along the roads radiating in every direction from Gettysburg. These parties rode to the northwest, north and northeast, in an arc of almost 180 degrees. Knowing that at least some Rebels were out along Chambersburg Pike to the west, the bulk of his pickets were positioned there. The countryside to the west was rolling, undulating with the pike first traversing Seminary Ridge nearest to town. Further west there was McPherson's Ridge, named for the farmer whose house stood near its crest, and further still Herr Ridge, 1,300 yards beyond McPherson's. The 1st Brigade under Colonel William Gamble took picket positions as far out as possible, on the eastern slope of Herr Ridge behind a stream called Marsh Creek. This position was roughly two miles from the center of Gettysburg. The further out his pickets were posted, the more time Buford would have to ready the command to receive an attack, if those Rebels decided to move on Gettysburg again. Elements of the 8th Illinois Cavalry manned the picket post this night, with one post covering the bridge over Marsh Creek. To the left of the 8th Illinois were pickets from the 8th New York and to the right, and further back, were troopers from Colonel Tom Devin's 2nd Brigade.[42]

With the pickets in place, Buford wrote a quick report on the intelligence he had obtained, informing both General John Reynolds, leading I Corp approaching from the south, and General Alfred Pleasonton, commanding the Cavalry Corps, who would be at or near the army's headquarters.

Buford framed his intelligence to Pleasonton as follows but did not note the time he penned this report:

> Gettysburg, June 30, 1863
>
> I entered this place to-day at 11 a.m. Found everybody in a terrible state of excitement on account of the enemy's advance upon this place. He had approached to within half a mile of the town when the head of my column entered. His force was terribly exaggerated by reasonable and truthful but inexperienced men. On pushing him back toward Cashtown, I learned from reliable men that Anderson's division was marching from Chambersburg by Mummasburg, Hunterstown, Abbottstown, on toward York. I have sent parties to the first-named places, toward Cashtown, and a strong force toward Littlestown. Colonel Gamble just sent me word that Lee signed a pass for a citizen this morning at Chambersburg. I can't do much now. My men and horses are fagged out. I have not been able to get any grain yet. It is all in the country, and the people talk instead of working. The facilities for shoeing are nothing. Early's people seized every shoe and nail they could find.
>
> I am, very respectfully, your obedient servant,
>
> JNO. Buford, Brigadier-General of Volunteers.
>
> P.S. The troops ... are the same I found early this morning at Millersburg or Fairfield. General Reynolds had been advised of all that I know.[43]

Here Buford has been made aware of the appropriations made by the Rebel force while in Gettysburg the previous Friday, correctly identifying the command. Also, he correctly places General Lee at or near Chambersburg.

***

Having entered Gettysburg via Emmitsburg Road, and after partaking of the refreshments offered up by the townsfolk, Colonel Tom Devin, commanding the 2nd Brigade, moved to a point about a mile and a half to the north and west, bivouacking near what was identified as McPherson's farm. The 6th New York Cavalry, part of the 2nd Brigade, was about a year and a half removed from its recruitment and, because Tom Devin had been its

Colonel Thomas Devin, original commander of the Sixth New York Cavalry and commander of Buford's Second Brigade on July 1. (Library of Congress)

original commander, was now an established and efficient organization. Devin's Brigade established a picket line running north from the Chambersburg Pike from Willoughby Run, a stream running in the low ground between McPherson's and Herr Ridges all the way to the road leading northeast toward York, Pennsylvania. Beyond these pickets, Buford's scouting parties were out until after dark cautiously looking for any sign of approaching Rebels. According to the early history of the 6th New York, John Buford, at a point either in the afternoon or early evening, decided to make a stand in the countryside surrounding Gettysburg. He had ridden the landscape surrounding the town, noting the terrain. To his professional eye, it was favorable for defense. At some point, probably in the late afternoon, Buford may even have ridden back to Moritz Tavern where General Reynolds had set up his headquarters for the night. Joseph Rosengarten was on the staff of the army wing commander and later wrote:

> General Reynolds was kept fully aware of the movements of the enemy by Buford, who had reported to him in person on the afternoon of the 30th, and through an aide of Reynolds's who had gone with Buford to the front and returned late at night with the latest news.[44]

When talking with Reynolds that afternoon, Buford, now familiar with the town's surrounding terrain, certainly would have consulted with him about his orders for the next day and what the general was planning. If nothing else, from what they already

knew, Reynolds and Buford had every reason to conclude that contact with at least a portion of Lee's army was likely, probably occurring the next morning out along Chambersburg Pike. It is not loose speculation to assume that Buford, with the concurrence of John Reynolds, would, early the next day, July 1, contest any movement by General Lee on Gettysburg. As a result, the great battle the Army of the Potomac expected, the one that must defeat the Rebel invasion, the one that could not be lost, most likely would start in the morning.

After the dispositions had been made for the night by I Corps, the infantry corps closest to Gettysburg and with which Reynolds was marching, he asked General Oliver Howard to join him at Moritz Tavern. Howard was in command of XI Corps that had marched that day to Emmitsburg. Some months after the battle, Howard summarized in a letter his meeting

General John Reynolds commander of three corps that advanced on Gettysburg in support of Buford's cavalry. (Library of Congress)

with Reynolds during the evening of June 30. Arriving at the tavern Howard remembered:

> I was just in time for supper and sat down with himself and staff in the front room of the house ... We had a cheerful conversation on ordinary topics during the meal, and then retired to a back room where the General read me some communications he had received from Gen. Meade, requesting us to animate our troops in view of the struggle soon to transpire ... General Reynolds treated me with the most marked confidence, and we conversed together till a late hour, being momentarily [sic] in expectation of orders from Gen. Meade for the next day ... The orders did not arrive by 11 P.M. and I returned to Emmitsburg.

It is a reasonable assumption that in the after-dinner conversation Reynolds told Howard of what had been learned during the day from Buford and his command; primarily that it was likely tomorrow would bring on a confrontation with the enemy.[45] This after-dinner meeting has also been detailed as including Reynolds showing Howard a number of maps of the Gettysburg area. Reynolds tells Howard that he intends to move on Gettysburg, and he wanted XI Corps in support. Also, III Corps, traveling behind XI was to move up with both I and XI Corps. From the tone of the conversations, and as recalled by Howard, Reynolds clearly expected contact to be made the next day. It appears Howard's understanding that Reynolds planned to "have reserved a position of my Corps" and "place me at once on the Cemetery heights, and then brought his own thither as soon as he found the enemy in large force." Reynolds planned to make contact and determine the Rebel strength. If it were too strong for I Corps, he would fall back to Howard's position on Cemetery Hill.[46]

Left unstated by Howard, but probably recognized then, certainly the next morning, was the unmistakable fact that John Reynolds was committing not merely the three corps under his command to a fight, but the entire Army of the Potomac and its new commander, George Meade.

Colonel Gamble's pickets from the 1st Brigade out on Herr Ridge were ordered not to fire on any advance by the Rebels but to report quickly to the picket reserve and to him so that the full brigade could deploy to the main line of resistance that Buford had determined would be set atop McPherson's Ridge. If contact was made at a point beyond Herr Ridge, a fighting withdrawal could be made back across Willoughby Run to McPherson's Ridge and then, when necessary, to Seminary Ridge, 400 yards to the rear and nearer the town. On top of this last ridge to the west of Gettysburg stood the Lutheran Theological Seminary, thus this high ground being called Seminary Ridge. The seminary building had a cupola, perfect for observation in any direction. When the Rebel infantry appeared in large numbers the next morning, coming out of the humid morning mist and the fighting withdrawal began, it would be observed from atop the Seminary, as would be the approach of any support by General Reynolds coming up the Emmitsburg road. The order for the pickets to hold their fire would be quickly forgotten.[47]

In the late afternoon, the scouts and patrols Buford had sent out on the various roads radiating from Gettysburg began to return and report to him. The early history of the 9th New York Cavalry of Devin's brigade recorded that, at about 5pm, a patrol of the regiment returned with one captured Rebel taken on the Hunterstown road earlier in the afternoon. Early the next morning, another patrol from the 9th would capture four more Rebels near Hunterstown. The information acquired from that afternoon's prisoner and his scouts probably made it into a report Buford sent later in the evening to headquarters and to General Reynolds.[48]

General Buford had made his headquarters in the Eagle Hotel and, at a point after the return of the division's scouting parties, the general wrote out his estimate of the situation. The report was timed 10:30pm and likely sent via the staff officer General Reynolds sent to Gettysburg earlier in the day. It said in part:

> I am satisfied that A. P. Hill's corps is massed just back of Cashtown, about 9 miles from this place. Pender's division of this (Hill's) corps came up to-day of which I advised you, saying, "The enemy in my front is increasing." The enemy's pickets (infantry and artillery) are within 4 miles of this place, on the Cashtown road. My parties have returned that went north, northwest,

and northeast, after crossing the road from Cashtown to Oxford in several places. They heard nothing of any force having passed over it lately. The road, however, is terribly infested with prowling cavalry parties. Near Heidlersburg to-day, one of my parties captured a courier of Lee's. Nothing was found on him. He says Ewell's corps is crossing the mountains from Carlisle, Rodes' division being at Petersburg in advance. Longstreet, from all I can learn, is still behind Hill. I have many rumors and reports of the enemy advance upon me from toward York. I have to pay attention to some of them, which causes me to overwork my horses and men. I can get no forage nor rations; am out of both. The people give and sell the men something to eat, but I can't stand that way of subsisting; it causes dreadful straggling. Should I have to fall back, advise me by what route.[49]

The 1st Cavalry Division was composed of three brigades, but Buford had led only two, the 1st and the 2nd, on his march in advance of Reynolds's left wing. The 3rd or Reserve Brigade, along with the division's supply wagons, was under the command of newly promoted Brigadier General Wesley Merritt. By order from General Pleasonton, this brigade had been sent to Mechanicstown, Maryland. There it stood on the evening of June 30.

After providing Reynolds with the latest intelligence, Buford sent a dispatch to Pleasonton noting the time as 10:40pm:

I have the honor to state the following facts; A. P. Hill's corps, composed of Anderson, Heth, and Pender, is massed back of Cashtown, 9 miles from this place. His pickets, composed of infantry and artillery, are in sight of mine. There is a road from Cashtown running through Mummasburg and Hunterstown on to York pike at Oxford, which is terribly infested with roving detachments of cavalry. Rumor says Ewell is coming over the mountains from Carlisle. One of his escorts was captured to-day near Heidlersburg. He says Rodes, commanding a division of Ewell's, has already crossed the mountains from Carlisle. Will the reserve [brigade] be relieved, and where are my wagons? I have no need of them, as I can find no forage. I have kept General Reynolds informed of all that has transpired. The enclosed is in reply to the last dispatch.[50]

These reports to Reynolds and Pleasonton are examples of why Buford was held in high regard as a cavalry commander. The information acquired because of his scouting is important intelligence, a commodity in great demand by the army and the new general that led it on this summer evening. The reply Buford speaks of from Reynolds in this report is not included in the record, but one can speculate that it was a note to Buford from the general, written earlier that evening, confirming that he would move on Gettysburg on the morning of July 1. As he wrote these dispatches, Buford had to have known that, early the next morning, his two brigades, totaling approximately 2,800 men, would be attacked by "a greatly superior force," to employ the wording most often used in Civil War reports by commanders that were forced to retreat. The Rebel infantry division camped out along the Chambersburg Pike—the pickets "are in sight of mine"—numbered about 7,400 men and there were more behind them. Despite knowing he would be facing, at a minimum, one full infantry division, the sentences Buford wrote that night are remarkably free of any apprehension on his part, denoting the professional he was. At some point during the night or before daylight on July 1, Buford sent Signal Officer Aaron Jerome to the cupola of the seminary to observe and report, telling him, "… see out the most prominent points and watch everything; to be careful to look for camp-fires, and in the morning for dust." Then Jerome added his impression of Buford at that time, "He seemed anxious, more so than I ever saw him." Another staff officer noted a similar mood about the general, saying he "… had never seen him so apprehensive[,] so uneasy about a situation as he was at this time."[51]

The pickets sent forward that night along the Chambersburg Pike were from the 8th Illinois Cavalry and they took position on Herr Ridge, east of March Creek, with an advance post on the pike where it crossed the creek. Back at the bivouac of Gamble's brigade, the men had eaten and stretched out in the valley between Seminary and McPherson's Ridges. A trooper in the 8th Illinois, John Beveridge, years in the future, would reflect on that quiet night and its acquired meaning for one man. The sun had set, and the stars were out, the weather mild:

> Thus picketed … beneath our own skies, on our own soil, with a sense of security and a feeling of homeness, thinking of loved ones, breathing praise and prayer to Him who had blessed us and our arms, we lay down upon the greensward, pillowing our heads on our saddles, to rest and to sleep,—little dreaming the morrow would usher in a battle, terrible and sanguinary, that would determine the destiny of the Republic and fix the fate of human liberty on the earth.[52]

Through the efforts of John Buford and to a lesser degree by Joseph Copeland, General Meade, during the evening of June 30, must at least have harbored a suspicion that in the early morning hours of July 1, Robert E. Lee and at least a portion of his army, somewhere to the west and northwest of the Union army, would collide with his command. It would not be a surprise to General Meade that a clash occurred, the only uncertainty was its exact location.

***

Despite Buford's concern for the situation he faced with large elements of the Lee's army close by, it is reported, while moving on Gettysburg on the morning of July 1, that I Corps Commander General Reynolds maintained he did not think a fight was likely that day. This impression was recorded in the diary of Col. Charles S. Wainwright, commanding I Corps' artillery. The colonel had asked Reynolds that morning as they rode up Emmitsburg Road if an encounter with the Rebels was likely that day. The general told Wainwright they were only moving on Gettysburg to lend support to Buford's cavalry as it continued its reconnaissance. A soldier in I Corps then marching up Emmitsburg Road remembered:

> The men were fresh … and the influence of a perfect morning and a beautiful landscape inspirited them … The mountains in the distance, gilded by the morning sun, left nothing lacking to the perfection of a summer morning scene.[53]

There appears to be a discrepancy in what Colonel Wainwright later remembered and what Reynolds probably knew early on the morning of July 1. In the *Official Record*, a message from Buford to Reynolds is dated and timed, June 30, 5am. However, the message speaks of events that occurred later on June 30 than 5am. It might be a copy of a dispatch Buford sent to Pleasonton the night before. In all likelihood, it was written either at 5pm, after some of Buford's scouting parties returned and reported, or at 5am on July 1. In it, Buford tells Reynolds:

> The enemy has increased his force considerably. His strong position is just behind Cashtown. My [scouting] party towards Mammasburg [sic] met a superior force, strongly posted. Another party that went up the road due north, 3 miles out, met a strong picket, had a skirmish, and captured a prisoner of Rodes' division. Another party that went toward Littlestown heard that Gregg [General, commanding the 2nd Cavalry Division] or Kilpatrick [General, commanding the 3rd Cavalry Division] had a fight with Stuart, and drove him to Hanover.[54]

The encounter between Jeb Stuart and Union cavalry occurred about mid-day June 30, therefore, this note had to have been written either late in the afternoon of June 30 or early on the morning of July 1. In any case, General Reynolds probably was in receipt of this information before I Corps infantry began their march up Emmitsburg Road early on July 1. That Reynolds thought a clash was unlikely, given what Buford had reported through all of June 30, seems remote. As further evidence of a strong Rebel presence in the surrounding country, Buford forwarded a note intercepted on the night of June 30. It was addressed to an unidentified Rebel Colonel:

> Get between Gettysburg and Heidlersburg, and picket Mummasburg and Hunterstown. Send in the direction of Gettysburg, and see what is there, and report to General Ewell at Heidlersburg. A small body of Yankee cavalry has made its appearance between Gettysburg and Heidlersburg. See what it is. J. A. Early, Major General.

Buford added his own words to this intelligence but did not note the time:

> This was captured last night [June 30/July 1] on the road to Oxford. The bearer of it said he saw Early last night [June 30] at [East] Berlin. All quiet here last night.[55]

If no others were aware of it as Wednesday, July 1, dawned, Generals Buford and Reynolds had to know a fight was coming with the rising sun. Reynolds's statement to Colonel Wainwright cannot be reconciled with the written record.

There is one other note, and possibly an alternative sequence of events, related to what Buford and Reynolds knew, as it grew dark on June 30 and may be related to the incorrectly timed note from Buford of either June 30 or July 1. The 12th Massachusetts Infantry was part of the 2nd Brigade, 2nd Division of I Corps and its regimental history, published in 1882, was compiled by the regiment's former lieutenant-colonel, Benjamin Cook. Speaking of the advance on Gettysburg on the morning of July 1, Cook included:

> ... Buford was that night [June 30] at Reynolds's headquarters, and came back to Gettysburg with one of Reynolds's staff, who returned to Reynolds with 'the latest news from the front' early in the morning of July 1.

The staff officer that had spent the remainder of the night at Gettysburg could, therefore, give Reynolds Buford's current thinking on what might happen that day. Then the 12th Massachusetts' history continues:

> Gen. [on July 1 Captain] James A. Hall avers that he saw Buford and Reynolds conversing at Marsh Run 'quite early' in the morning of July 1, 'before the batteries hitched up for marching.'

Cook at this time was captain of Battery B, 2nd Maine Light Artillery, part of the I Corps' artillery component.[56] This might be simply faulty memory on the part Captain Hall or Buford made at least one, and possibly two, trips from Gettysburg to consult with Reynolds before the fighting began.

George Meade and his plan of staging a fighting withdrawal from wherever Lee's force was encountered to behind a defensive line along Pipe Creek, a defensive position just south of the Pennsylvania state line, had been circulated on June 30. It had not, however, either during the night of June 30 or on the morning of July 1, reached either Reynolds or Buford. These two generals had already made the decision: their commands would engage the force under Robert E. Lee at Gettysburg this morning.

The legend is that it was all about shoes. The former Confederate general, Henry Heth, makes a point of saying so in an article he penned in 1877 and published in a volume of the *Southern Historical Society Papers*. Here General Heth is speaking of an immediate cause for the fighting to erupt when and where it did. As for his action on June 30, Heth said:

> Hearing that a supply of shoes was to be obtain in Gettysburg ... and greatly needing shoes for my men, I directed General Pettigrew to go to Gettysburg and get these supplies.[57]

An army, thousands of men marching hundreds of miles on mostly dirt roads, will wear shoes out far faster than normal. As with many other necessary items needed by the Army of Northern Virginia, shoes for the soldiers were always in short supply. Indeed, if there were time after an engagement, the corpses of dead Union soldiers were nearly always relieved of their footwear by the Rebels. Why it was thought that a supply of footwear was to be had in Gettysburg remains a mysterious loose end relating to the battle and will likely remain so. On June 26, as it marched towards Pennsylvania, the commander of the 1st Division of I Corps of the Union army rode ahead of his column into a town in Maryland to inquire if there were any shoes for sale by the local merchants. The reply he received from the male citizens was decidedly unfriendly and uncooperative. Given his reception and the fact that many of his men were marching with bare, bloody feet, General James S. Wadsworth appropriated 200 pairs of shoes from 200 secessionist leaning male residents of the town.[58] Now, early on July 1, an incident occurred that, because of its surreal nature and the time at which it supposedly took place, could just possibly be true. As remembered by General Abner Doubleday, in temporary command of I Corps, a staff officer from his corps rode into Gettysburg early in the morning. There he encountered John Buford who was about to ride toward Seminary Ridge, the sound of gunfire already discernable to the west. Buford saw the officer and asked, "What are you doing here, sir?" The staff officer answered hesitantly that he had been sent to inquire about getting shoes for some of the men of his command. Buford told him he had better quickly return to his command. "Why," came a hesitant reply, "what's the matter, general?" At that precise moment, the first loud report of artillery was heard from out beyond Seminary Ridge. Buford swung up on his horse and just before galloping off said to the officer, *"That's the matter."*[59]

***

As for being in Pennsylvania on that day, where two armies, one searching for the other and attempting to gain a tactical advantage; it was all the doing of General Robert E. Lee, commanding the Army of Northern Virginia. Now, having been in command of this force for one year, Lee's status within the Confederacy had already become the stuff of legend. During 1862, Lee had relieved the threat to the Confederate capital posed by the Union army under General George B. McClellan. It had taken seven days of heavy fighting, but in the end, McClellan was forced into a "change of base." Lee had essentially penned the general and his army in a harmless enclave on the Virginia Peninsula. Frustrated with the failure of McClellan's campaign, Washington ordered the general and the Army of the Potomac back to the capital as Lee marched north following Stonewall Jackson. Outside Washington in the closing days of August, Lee then defeated the Union forces under General John Pope at the Second Battle of Bull Run, while McClellan gave his attention to the city's defense with only a part of the Army of the Potomac marching to Pope's aid and doing relatively nothing to support him. In September 1862, Lee crossed the Potomac into Maryland, fought McClellan again outside the town of Sharpsburg and then left the field and returned to his native state, leaving some to conclude that the battle had been the decisive Union victory that it was not. It was decidedly not because of McClellan's failure to vigorously pursue Lee back into Virginia and bring him to battle again. The month of October slipped by, and November started with McClellan slowly advancing through northern Virginia, headed for the Rappahannock River. Lincoln's patience finally ran out; he relieved McClellan and put in his place General Ambrose Burnside. A prolific letter writer and Yale graduate, Lieutenant William Wheeler of the 13th Battery New York Light Artillery, summarized his thinking on the general's relief by the president at this time and may be taken as reflecting the opinion of the more reflective within the Army of the Potomac:

> I do not wish to triumph over the fallen, but I must say the removal of McClellan as just and necessary. He had been tried and found wanting in those qualities of swiftness, energy, and ready talent which are needful in a leader who would successfully combat the genius of Lee, the dash of Stuart, the daring of Jackson. Whatever else we may say of the rebels, we must confess that they have managed to pick out their best men, and have put them at the head of their army.[60]

In compiling the history of the 20th Massachusetts Infantry, also known as the Harvard Regiment because so many of its officers were graduates of the university, George A. Bruce attributed a comment on McClellan's relief to General Lee in which the Rebel leader admits he will miss General McClellan because "we always understood each other so well. I am afraid they will continue to make these changes until they find some one whom I don't understand."[61] The author gives no source citation for the statement he attributes to Lee speaking to General James Longstreet. Nothing like it appears in Longstreet's memoirs. Longstreet summarizes Lee's thinking on hearing the news of his opponent's dismissal as Lee "thoroughly understood" McClellan. But the Union commander "… was growing, was likely to exhibit far greater powers than he had yet shown …" This is taken to mean that McClellan was growing in the job of command, becoming a better or more able opponent with each confrontation.[62] A humble soldier in V Corps, writing after many years and probably absorbing the history written since the war's end, offered an assessment of McClellan that closely summarizes the consensus view of the general. In a long paragraph, Robert Tilney wrote:

> …the men idolized him … He was undoubtedly a great organizer and made a magnificent army out of the raw troops that were sent him … But notwithstanding his ability … there was wanting in him that decision and determination that distinguishes a great general … Afraid of himself; too timid to carry out his plans … Always at war with the government … always calling for more troops, even when his forces numbered nearly or quite double those of the enemy … hesitation to make a movement when to all appearances, everything was favorable.[63]

In any case, the Army of the Potomac would change generals again, and not too many months in the future. After writing of the battle of Antietam and anticipating McClellan's relief, regimental historian George Bruce adds, "of the fifty odd general officers exercising command of the Army of the Potomac at the time of its organization, only one, General Meade, was with it at Appomattox."[64] The other generals reporting to Meade in 1865 would rise through the army's officer corps and in the last two years of the war, it would be because of distinguished performance over politics.

December came, with new Union generalship in command. The result was another victory for Lee and his army, a bloodbath called the battle of

Fredericksburg, a contested river crossing followed by an uphill assault on an extremely well defended position manned by Lee's entire army.

During the campaign on the Virginia Peninsula, George McClellan had written his assessment of Robert E. Lee, when it was rumored Lee would replace General Joseph E. Johnston who was then commanding the army defending Richmond against the Army of the Potomac. McClellan wrote:

> I prefer Lee to Johnston—the former is too cautious & [sic] weak under grave responsibility—personally brave & energetic to a fault, he yet is wanting in moral firmness when pressed by heavy responsibility & is likely to be timid & irresolute in action.[65]

This was written at a time when McClellan and his army were within a handful of miles of Richmond and conveniently forgotten after a seven day "change of base" that found the general huddled on the bank of the James River with the navy's guns for protection. If ever there was a misreading of a general, this was it. Union officers all down the command chain tended to discount their enemy at first. On the Peninsula, one of the first encounters with Rebel soldiers by the 10th Massachusetts Infantry came by way of prisoners captured early in the campaign. It was recorded at the time by a company commander:

> The Carolina prisoners were an ignorant set and many, when asked if they could read or write, answered that they 'hadn't any book larnin';' [sic] they had no particular uniforms, unless being uniformly ragged and dirty could be called such. The Virginians were more intelligent, and better dressed.[66]

Now it was early 1863, the allusion of a quick victory over a rabble force long in the Potomac Army's past, and there was a new commander of Union forces in the Virginia springtime, Major General Joseph Hooker. The press called him 'Fighting Joe' and he led his force over the same Rappahannock to engage and defeat General Lee. In what was Lee's signature victory, the battle of Chancellorsville, one where he was outnumbered and outgunned by at least two to one, he and his legendary subordinate, General Thomas 'Stonewall' Jackson, out-maneuvered and out-fought the Union army, intimidating the commanding Union general to cross back over the Rappahannock River after a few days of fighting. Fighting Joe Hooker had become Mr. F. J. Hooker. The loss to the Army of Northern Virginia had been heavy, though. As more than one of his lieutenants would later remark, the Chancellorsville battle was won "at such a terrible sacrifice that half a dozen such victories would have ruined" General Lee and his army.[67]

Something wasn't right to General Lee's strategic thinking, however, even as his victories were celebrated throughout the Confederacy. Lee understood better than anyone that after each defeat in battle the Union army seemed only to get bigger and stronger, not weaker. Its commanding general might change in the hope of bringing the army a victory that would crush and end the rebellion, but Lee's defeating them had only prolonged the war, had not driven the blue host from the sacred soil of Virginia. It had only allowed the Northern army to acquire more men and more equipment and weapons. The South had not won a victory that would end the fighting and secure Southern independence. Lee's losses in battle could be made up only fractionally when compared with the North, and he knew it. There was always the problem of supply, food for his men and horses. One of Lee's division commanders, Henry Heth, remembered the long winter months:

> The ration of a general officer was double that of a private, and so meager was that double supply that frequently to appease my hunger I robbed my horse of a handful of corn, which, parched in the fire, served to alley [sic] the cravings of nature. What must have been the condition of the private?

Confederate cavalryman Luther Hopkins later remembered much the same thing as General Heth. Answering the question why Lee went into Pennsylvania in the summer of 1863, Hopkins expounded:

> ...for the same reason that the children of Israel went down into Egypt. There was a famine in the land ... Food was growing scarcer and scarcer in the South, and it became a serious question ... as to how the army was to be fed ...[68]

After the Battle of Chancellorsville in May 1863, General Lee traveled to Richmond to consult with the Confederate president, Jefferson Davis. Although there was no formal record kept of the talks he had with Davis, the issue of supplying his army in the field had to be prominent in the general's thoughts as were many other issues. To the general's thinking, and with the summer's campaigning season fast approaching, his army could accomplish nothing significant where it now stood. To remain behind the Rappahannock River and wait for another assault by Union forces was not an option to General Lee. He might again defeat another thrust across the river but in doing so he would not gain any advantage for the Southern cause. To retreat within the defensive perimeter of Richmond would only lead to a siege of the city and eventual surrender to the Union. For the aggressive minded Lee, the alternative was to drive north in a menacing matter, into Pennsylvania. The advantages of this option were that the move would free most of northern Virginia of Union forces, allowing residents to grow and harvest a crop without interference and pillaging by the Union army. It might induce the North to shift some troop strength from the west, thus lessening the pressure on Vicksburg and the state of Mississippi where General Ulysses S. Grant was then campaigning. Most prominent in the general's mind was the issue of supply. When in Pennsylvania the Army of Northern Virginia could provision itself completely from the undisturbed countryside and, additionally, send south supplies to be stored for the coming winter season. Of all the arguments in favor of the move north, the most persuasive was also the simplest: Lee "... could no long feed his army on the Rappahannock."[69] Crops, livestock, as well as shoes, would be dutifully paid for with Confederate cash or, lacking that, with promissory notes redeemable after the war from an independent Confederacy. Lastly, if a decisive battle was to be fought and won somewhere north of the Potomac, the political result might be to greatly enhance the Northern disillusionment with the war and increase popular pressure on the Washington administration to such a degree that it would move toward acquiescence regarding Southern independence.

General Lee habitually read northern newspapers whenever they got through the lines. From his reading of the press during the early spring he perceived a degree of Northern disillusionment with the war and its progress. War weariness had inspired peace rallies in the North and Democratic papers were offering their editor's ideas for ending the war. There could be a truce of some kind followed by some kind of negotiation leading to some kind of status for the Confederate states that their leadership could get their people to agree to. It was all somewhat vague, but a truce would at least stop the killing. Left generally unsaid in the press was any mention of the fact that every general, North and South, knew: while any talks went forward after the fighting stopped, the contending armies would simply melt away, the soldiers taking to the road leading home. The truce would lead to a de facto ending of the war regardless of the outcome of negotiations and independence for the South could not be guaranteed without an armed force in the field. To capitalize on the perceived weariness with the war in the North, Lee thought the South should encourage those elements in the North hoping and calling for a truce while at the same time a disciplined Confederate army was moving across their soil. Hopefully, this would show that the South could not be defeated, and that recognition of Southern independence was the only way for the fighting to be stopped. In one form or another, Lee advocated this theory to President Davis and the general's theory carried weight. To Lee's aggressive turn of mind, this ambitious course was the only one that could stave off eventual defeat of his army and the Southern cause. As a West Point graduate like Lee, President Davis had to appreciate the general's proposal, ambitious though it was. The plan was laced throughout with risk but the alternatives, as outlined by Lee, promised defeat, pure and simple. The Confederate president and his cabinet assented to the plan and Lee returned to his army and began preparations, one of which he had already seen completed. During the winter just passed, Lee had ordered Jed Hotchkiss, a mapmaker on General Jackson's staff, to provide a detailed map of the country from Winchester, Virginia, all the way to the Susquehanna River. The degree of detail was reported to be such that individual farmhouses along the road, with the names of the owners, were inscribed on it.[70]

Theories have a way of evaporating, or at least being modified, when put into practice. The further Lee and his butternut soldiers got into Pennsylvania, the greater the determination by all segments of the North's population to fight and defeat them. From the moment Lee began his march north, the soldiers of the Army of the Potomac and the citizens back home, some the very groups Lee hoped to influence, spoke of the movement as an invasion, and invasions, by inference, must be defeated and thrown back. As he was probably unaware of this quick turn of attitude in the North, or despite it, Lee, believing in his plan and its political element, marched. Almost a year after he had gone north, in the spring of 1864, Lee told one of his division commanders:

> If I could—unfortunately I cannot—I would again cross the Potomac and invade Pennsylvania ... I believe it to be our true policy, notwithstanding the failure of last year. An invasion ... breaks up all their preconceived plans, relieves our country of his presence, and we subsist while there on his resources. The question of food for this army gives me more trouble and uneasiness than every thing else combined ... The legitimate fruits of victory, if gained in Pennsylvania, could be more readily reaped than one on our own soil. We would have been in a few days' march of Philadelphia, and the occupation of that city would have given us peace.[71]

***

Now it was late in the day, June 30. After the hesitating Rebel advance on Gettysburg of that morning, the infantry brigade that had done the looking at the town was bivouacked back near Cashtown. Brigade Commander Pettigrew went to report to General Heth. Years later Heth remembered:

> On the 30th of June General Pettigrew, with his brigade, went near Gettysburg, but did not enter the town, returning the same evening to Cashtown, reporting that he did not carry out my orders, as Gettysburg was occupied by the enemy's cavalry ... that under the circumstances he did not deem it advisable to enter Gettysburg.[72]

It seems that the daylight was fading when Pettigrew reported to Heth. Perhaps while Buford was hearing reports from his scouting parties, Pettigrew reported what had been seen were not local militia, as might be expected, but regular troops. The overriding and standing order for the army under Lee was not to bring on an engagement without sufficient support at hand. Pettigrew and his command had followed orders and retired without starting a fight. Heth, as the division commander, heard him out and as he did so, the corps commander, Lieutenant General Ambrose P. Hill, rode up. General Heth related to Hill what had been reported by Pettigrew. Hill quickly dismissed the report, saying that what had been seen at Gettysburg was "... cavalry, probably a detachment of observation." It was recalled by Heth's staff officer, Lieutenant Young that it was at this point that Pettigrew called on him. Young was known to General Hill and would corroborate what Pettigrew had said:

> Neither General Heth nor General Hill believed in the presence of the enemy in force, and they expressed their doubts so positively to General Pettigrew that I was called up to tell General Hill what I had seen while reconnoitering the movements of the force which had followed us from Gettysburg ... General Pettigrew supposed that my report might have some weight with him.

Young told Hill the soldiers that followed Pettigrew were "... well-trained troops and not those of a home guard."[73] Hill again casually dismissed the intelligence, adding with an arrogant flourish for those assembled to hear: if Young was correct there was not a better place he cared to have the Yankee army than in front of him. Then Henry Heth said to his corps commander, "If there is no objection, I will take my division to-morrow and go to Gettysburg." Hill, without giving the proposition a thought, replied, "None in the world."[74]

It was decided that General James J. Archer and his 3rd Brigade of Heth's division would lead the way to Gettysburg in the morning. According to Lieutenant Young, Pettigrew conferred with Archer and "... described to him minutely the topography of the country between Cashtown and Gettysburg." Archer was informed "... of a ridge some distance out of Gettysburg on which he would probably find the enemy, as the position was favorable for defense." Young's judgment was "General Archer listened, but believed not, marched on unprepared ... his command routed and he himself taken prisoner." "For want of faith in what had been told, and a consequent lack of caution, the two leading brigades of Heth's Division marched into the jaws of the enemy ..." bringing on the great battle.[75]

Years in the future, a Gettysburg citizen would remember June 30, 1863, as the day:

> ... some four thousand of our cavalry came here, and, although we knew Lee was nearby, we felt then as if everything was safe. Oh, my goodness, yes! Our belongings were under Uncle Sam's protection ... The following morning the battle began on the edge of town ...[76]

General Henry Heth, at a much later date, summarized his thinking on what happened the next day. "The 'Battle of Gettysburg' was the result purely of an accident, for which I am probably more than any one else, accountable."[77]

CHAPTER SIX

Skirmishers Three Deep

Early Morning, Wednesday, July 1, 1863

> With God's help we expect to take a step or two toward an honorable peace.
> COLONEL ARMISTEAD L. LONG, OF GENERAL LEE'S STAFF, JUNE 29, 1863

> We must win or die here, was the watchword.
> LIEUTENANT EDWIN D. BENNETT, 22D MASSACHUSETTS INFANTRY

> Some bloody work done to-day. How many that was alive and full of life this morning now sleep the sleep of death.
> JOHN INGLIS, 9TH NEW YORK CAVALRY[1]

In the twilight and then the darkness of June 30, after the scouting parties returned, Buford considered the wording of the messages to be sent to his superiors. The majority of his troopers, having seen to the care of their horses, were now resting. The others were out on picket duty, covering the approaches to Gettysburg from the west, north and east. Almost every account written of these evening hours includes the following exchange between John Buford and the commander of the 2nd Brigade, Colonel Thomas Devin. Most likely it was overheard and later recorded by a division signal officer, Lt. Aaron B. Jerome. After dark, Buford spent an extended period with Tom Devin at his headquarters tent along Mummasburg Road, where it crossed a low point in McPherson's Ridge. Speaking with Devin by his campfire, he let his brigade commander know he expected a fight to start in the morning and the division would be greatly outnumbered, at least until infantry support from General Reynolds could move up. Tom Devin, a competent and well-liked commander, as well as the original leader of the 6th New York Cavalry, whether out of brashness or in an attempt to encourage his worried commander, reportedly told Buford that the next day he and his men could hold off anything the Rebels threw at them. It is said that Buford, in a calm voice, answered:

> No, you won't. They will attack you in the morning and they will come booming—skirmishers three deep. You will have to fight like the devil to hold your own until supports arrive. The enemy must know the importance of this position, and will strain every nerve to secure it, and if we are able to hold it, we shall do well.[2]

If Buford is quoted accurately, it is clear the cavalry general planned to resist a Confederate advance upon Gettysburg the next day, and his use of the words "until supports arrive," indicates he knew Reynolds with I Corps would be coming to join him in the morning's confrontation. The decision to fight at Gettysburg had been made.

Upon learning the Army of the Potomac had crossed its namesake river and was concentrating at or near Frederick, Maryland, General Lee had issued new orders to the Army of Northern Virginia. His army would gather at Cashtown or Gettysburg in anticipation of the next move by the enemy. "Dawn of July 1 broke with a gentle breeze and was sunshiny and clear, except for occasional showery clouds. Despite the uncertainty, Lee was cheerful and composed and called to Longstreet to ride with him."[3] The two generals often rode together and this morning they were on the Chambersburg Pike, headed up the western face of South Mountain. There still hadn't been any word from Jeb Stuart, and Lee, knowing the enemy was across the Potomac, would certainly feel more secure with his army in one place. Now all of his soldiers were then moving to do just that. As the two generals neared the crest of South Mountain, they heard intermittent booming, the unmistakable sound of cannons firing somewhere ahead. Once at the crest of the mountain the "… sound of firing came insistently from the east." Longstreet turned back, riding to alert his corps, while Lee quickened his pace, riding to Cashtown and there speaking with the commander of III Corps, General A. P. Hill. General Heth had gone on to Gettysburg earlier, yes, and yes, he was under orders not to bring on a general engagement if he should meet the enemy.[4] According to Henry Heth:

> On July 1st I moved my division from Cashtown in the direction of Gettysburg, reaching the heights, a mile (more or less) from the town, about 9 o'clock A.M.[5]

Lee continued forward from Cashtown and it is estimated that it was 2pm and about three miles from Gettysburg when Lee "came to open country." He could see the gun smoke ahead of him floating over the pike where it crossed a creek and then a flat-topped ridge the names of which Lee didn't know. General Heth's division was deployed on both sides of the pike and clearly had been in action. The army's commander strained to understand what had happened and what was then happening across the rolling Pennsylvania countryside. Various staff officers and others tried explaining, but then the sound of firing came from the north of the town, gray clad soldiers in formations were seen advancing. These troops were in division strength and were attacking the flank of the XI Corps troops that had arrived with General Howard in support of the Federal formation that was standing its ground in front of Henry Heth's division.[6]

The report of Colonel William Gamble, commanding the 1st Cavalry Division's 1st Brigade, in the *Official Record*, is an abbreviated recounting of his action on July 1, despite the size of the fight forced upon his brigade. He says that it was about 8am when he got word of the approach of the Confederate force, which was then about three miles west of his headquarters on the grounds of the Lutheran Seminary. The pickets stationed out on Chambersburg Pike, as it descended to Marsh Creek from Knoxlyn Ridge, an elevation to the west of Herr Ridge, began firing on the approaching Rebel force. As predicted by General Buford, the Rebels soon "… deployed skirmishers in strong force." Gamble said he immediately sent three squadrons forward to support his pickets as the division's artillery battery of six guns was deployed and the remainder of his brigade formed a line "… about 1 mile in front of the seminary, the right resting on the railroad [cut] track and the left near the … [Fairfield] road, the Cashtown road being a little to the right of center …" Gamble then described how his 1,600-man brigade, greatly outnumbered, began the Battle of Gettysburg:

> The enemy cautiously approached in column on the road, with three extended lines on each flank, and his and our line of skirmishers became engaged, and our artillery opened on the enemy's advancing column, doing good execution. The enemy moved forward; two batteries opened on us, and a sharp engagement of artillery took place. In a short time, we were, by overpowering numbers, compelled to fall back about 200 yards to the next ridge, and there make a stand.

From there Gamble's reinforced picket line fired from behind fences and trees. Gamble does not specify how long it was from the first exchange of shots and his eventual fall back to the next ridge to the east, McPherson's Ridge, and the arrival of I Corps infantry. The time purchased by his brigade was considerable, perhaps as much as two hours. He merely said:

> After checking and retarding the advance of the enemy several hours, and falling back only about 200 yards from the first line [of] battle, our infantry advance of the First corps arrived, and relieved the cavalry brigade in its unequal contest with the enemy.[7]

The first contact that morning came out of the mist to the west of Herr Ridge. The first firing came from the pickets of the 8th Illinois Cavalry. When word got back to Gamble, the reinforcements he sent forward to support the picket line appeared to be as many as a third of his command, approximately 500 troopers. The cavalrymen, with their horses held by every fourth trooper safely in the rear, were spaced along Herr Ridge a few yards apart, firing from whatever cover presented itself. They put down such a mass of fire from their Sharps .52 caliber, breech-loading carbines that the Rebels thought they had encountered a heavy force of infantry rather than a mere portion of a cavalry brigade. This was partly due not only to the rate of fire put down, but because the cavalrymen's horses were held out of sight. In that an artillery element was marching near the head of Heth's column, these guns were deployed as soon as shots started crossing Marsh Creek. If these were home guard or a detachment of cavalry, a couple of bursting shells should scatter them and Heth's soldiers could advance and not bring on a general engagement. This, at least, could be the thinking of General Heth giving the conversation of the previous evening.

It didn't turn out this way. The Rebel artillery fired and quickly received return fire from at least two of the six guns of Buford's artillery component. The skirmishing and exchanges of artillery fire continued for a time while General Heth added weight to his move on Gettysburg. The first two brigades of his division were deploying, one on each side of the pike, as the artillery shells flew overhead. Using his artillery and the advance of the two brigades should clear the ridge of any Yankee resistance, but the infantry deployment took time, by some accounts upwards of 90 minutes. Only then did the Rebels resume their advance on Herr Ridge. The time gained by the stout resistance of the reinforced picket line allowed the first elements of the Union infantry to get that much closer to Gettysburg.[8] It would become a general engagement when these soldiers arrived.

Captain Amasa E. Dana of the 8th Illinois reinforced the pickets out on Herr Ridge. The rebel skirmish line was strung out on both sides of the Cashtown Pike "a distance of a mile and a half, concealed at intervals by timber." Rather than retire eastward Dana later remembered that he had his men:

> … throw up their carbine sights and [we] gave the enemy the benefit of long range practice [;] the firing was rapid from our carbines and at the distance induced the belief of four times our number of men actually present. This was evident because the enemy [skirmish] line in our front halted.

When the cavalry skirmish line was about to be flanked, Dana would only then order a retreat to the next firing position. He recalled:

> The true character and length of our line soon became known to the enemy, and they promptly moved upon our front and flanks. We retired and continued to take positions, and usually held out as long as we would without imminent risk of capture. We were driven from three positions successively in less than one hour.[9]

At the same time as this fighting withdrawal by Gamble's men was taking place, Colonel Tom Devin reinforced his skirmish line on the north side of the Chambersburg Pike with about 100 men.

The fight for Herr Ridge, might well have consumed the critical hours from just after first light to possibly 9 or 10am. To the south, where I Corps had bivouacked, July 1 started like many others when troops were moving. An officer, who later in the day would win the Medal of Honor in the fight to the west of Gettysburg, remembered:

> … the day opened clear … but soon a drizzle came on and it became sultry beyond measure and to add to the discomfort, the supply wagons not having come up, it was difficult for the men to make out a good breakfast. There seemed to be no haste about moving, but by eight o'clock the First Division was on its way to Gettysburg.[10]

The 1st Division of I Corps marched toward Gettysburg along Emmitsburg Road. General Reynolds was riding at the head of the long column with division commander, Brigadier General James Wadsworth. Hearing the firing from the cavalry's artillery coming from the direction of Gettysburg and then encountering a courier sent by Buford, Reynolds left Wadsworth and, with his staff, rode ahead to town to see for himself the situation he was leading the infantry into and to consult with Buford. From his vantage point on top of the Lutheran Seminary, Lt. Aaron Jerome later related:

> We held them in check fully two hours, and were nearly overpowered when, in looking about the country, I saw the corps flag of General Reynolds. I was still in the seminary steeple … I sent one of my men to Buford, who came up, and looking through my glass confirmed my report, and remarked: 'Now we can hold the place.'

Some accounts have Reynolds and Buford meeting at the Lutheran Seminary atop the ridge, with the cavalry leader observing the fighting from the building's cupola, other accounts set their meeting further to the west, out upon McPherson's Ridge. One supposed contemporary account by Stephen Weld, an officer on Reynolds' staff says:

> When we reached the outskirts of Gettysburg, a man told us that the rebels were driving in our cavalry pickets, and immediately General Reynolds went into town on a fast gallop, through it, and a mile out the other side, where he found General Buford and the cavalry engaging the enemy, who were advancing in strong force.[11]

By the time John Reynolds got to the area of engagement, Buford's men had fallen back to McPherson's Ridge, the point the general hoped to hold until the infantry could become engaged. John L. Beveridge of the 8th Illinois left his remembrance of the soon to be hallowed patch of Pennsylvania. With Willoughby Run to the immediate west:

> To the north, south, and west, the country was open, stretching away in a succession of ridges, two miles westward to Marsh Creek … The green landscape was, dotted, here and there, with patches of grain, yellowing for the harvest. The cattle were feeding lazily in the fields.[12]

Like Buford, John Reynolds was a professional. Rumor had it that Lincoln had offered him command of the Army of the Potomac, but the general said no, recommending George Meade instead. John Buford had decided to fight on this terrain and Reynolds agreed. With Buford's division already committed, Reynolds was adding I Corps and Howard's XI Corps to the action, upward of 21,000 soldiers to the fight. It is thought by those most familiar with the events, a tale told many times, that after Reynolds rode through the town, he quickly arrived at the Lutheran Seminary. John Buford was climbing down from the cupola as Reynolds arrived. One can picture Reynolds reining in his horse, swirling dust and a sweating steed, firing to the west as background noise, Buford with a surge of relief running through his body and crossing his face, as Reynolds nonchalantly asked, "What's the matter, John?" "The devil's to pay," Buford shoots back. Regardless of where, or even if this exchange took place, Reynolds immediately grasped the situation as Buford outlined it. Understanding what Buford and his division were attempting to do, all he needed to ask of the cavalry was, can you hold? Buford's reply, pressed though he was, came easily. "I reckon I can."[13]

Reynolds turned and galloped back toward the infantry column marching on Emmitsburg Road, his staff members dismounting along the road, attempting to knock down the fence on the left side to allow the first infantry elements to cross the fields and mount Seminary Ridge by an oblique route rather than having to march through the town proper and out Chambersburg Pike.

As with most Civil War engagements, there is confusion and to a degree disagreement about when and how things came to happen. One concerns the decision to even fight a battle at Gettysburg that day and who was it that made the decision. In the voluminous literature concerning this battle, John Reynolds is often credited with the decision to fight at Gettysburg, given the terrain surrounding the town, especially Cemetery Hill and Ridge to the east of Seminary Ridge. Other authors place the choice of the battlefield upon Major General Winfield Scott Hancock, commander of II Corps, who General Meade sent from his headquarters at Taneytown, Maryland, to Gettysburg at a point in the afternoon of July 1 and who reported back that the positions where he found Union forces deployed when he arrived would be suitable for fighting defensively. Still another scenario credits John Buford with choosing Gettysburg and Cemetery Hill and Ridge as the battleground. William Herrmance, the captain of Company C of the 6th New York Cavalry, had ridden into the town the day before with Buford's cavalry. In a paper he delivered at Delmonico's in New York City in 1900, Herrmance maintained it was Buford who chose Gettysburg as the place to fight it out with the Army of Northern Virginia. According to this veteran of the 6th, "Buford alone selected the ground to be held, seeing on his arrival the day previous the advantage of its position."[14] This assertion must be given some credence. The cavalry general had already decided on fighting a holding action on July 1, as he indicated on the night of June 30 when speaking to Tom Devin. This decision probably resulted from the discussions he had had with Reynolds the morning of June 30, while he was passing through Emmitsburg headed for Gettysburg, or via dispatches exchanged with Reynolds via couriers during the afternoon. Buford knew the fight would swallow his division if Reynolds and at least two of the three infantry corps under his command didn't come to his support quickly. As Reynolds galloped up Emmitsburg Road, the sound of cannon firing ahead, he had only to glance to his right to see Cemetery Hill and recognize the position for what it was: a redoubt if one was needed. But Buford's division was already engaged, and I Corps would soon be. The weight of the evidence in the sources available to us seems to indicate John Buford, with the concurrence of John Reynolds, made the decision to fight at Gettysburg. In a quick message to Meade that Reynolds sent that morning, he seems to be confirming Buford had already arrived at the decision, as well as his own. Staff officer Stephen M. Weld carried the message. When compiling for publication his war diary and letters in 1912, he recalled the events of that July morning. Weld says Reynolds rode through Gettysburg and up Seminary Ridge, observed the cavalry firing and being heavily pressed. He then returned.

> General Reynolds rode back to the town, went into a field on the right side of the road and talked two or three minutes with General Buford, and then called all his staff around him. He looked at us all over, and said, 'Weld, I am going to pick you out to go to General Meade with a message' (the message as given in the diary).

In his war diary written at a point soon after the fact Weld recorded:

> He [Reynolds] sent me to General Meade, 13 or 14 miles off, to say that the enemy were coming in strong force, and that he was afraid they would get the heights [Cemetery Hill] on the other side of the town before he could; that he would fight them all through the town, however, and keep them back as long as possible.[15]

It is likely General Reynolds, with his possible passing acquaintance with Gettysburg geography had certainly, by now, acquired an appreciation of the topography, suited as it was for defense.

This, in addition to the fact that Buford's command was already in close contact with Rebel infantry and with Reynolds' infantry advancing rapidly—a corps of three divisions—the idea of disengaging and withdrawing in the direction they had come was a near impossibility. Buford, with Reynolds sitting on his horse next to him for those two or three minutes, merely had to nod in the direction of Cemetery Hill and military logic would proceed from there. The decision taken by Buford on June 30, and agreed to by Reynolds, was confirmed on the morning of July 1. The name Gettysburg would then be written into American history. Staff Officer Weld then rode off with a message for Meade.[16]

The battle at Gettysburg has long been called a meeting engagement and, within the overall context of two armies numbering many tens of thousands, it was. It was not, however, an unexpected, accidental encounter for the two generals, Buford and Reynolds. At the latest, as summer twilight faded, and it grew dark across the Pennsylvania countryside on June 30, Buford and Reynolds certainly knew they would encounter at least a portion of Lee's force the next day. General Oliver Howard, of XI Corps, in his autobiography, might inflate his role in the battle once it had begun, but what benefit would accrue to him by detailing a distorted encounter with General Reynolds at Moritz Tavern the evening of June 30. Howard, in meeting with Reynolds that evening, clearly got the impression that Reynolds would move in the morning on the town and that he would follow with XI Corps in support. As quoted by a historian of the battle, Allen C. Guelzo, Reynolds planned for Howard to "have reserved a position of my Corps" and "place me at once on the Cemetery heights …"[17]

The exact time of the consultation between Buford and Reynolds on the morning of July 1 was not officially recorded, but it was probably before the arrival of the leading elements of the I Corps infantry. At some point, Buford found the time to dash off a note to General Meade at his headquarters. Buford noted the time as 10:10am:

> The enemy's force (A. P. Hill's) are advancing on me at this point and driving my pickets and skirmishers very rapidly. There is also a large force at Heidlersburg that is driving my pickets at that point from that direction. General Reynolds is advancing, and is within 3 miles of this point with his leading division. I am positive that the whole of A. P. Hill's force is advancing.

Years later Gettysburg resident, Tillie Pierce, unofficially recorded that it was between 9 and 10am that "Soon the booming of cannon was heard, then great clouds of smoke were seen rising beyond the ridge."[18]

While Buford and Reynolds had been meeting, the Rebels had continued massing despite the amount of fire the cavalry was delivering. The Rebel advance pushed the Yankees from Herr Ridge, the troopers, at the last minute, jumping on their horses and galloping back to McPherson's Ridge. It had taken Heth some hours to accomplish this, though. At about 10:30 or 11am, the first elements of I Corps infantry began arriving, crossing Seminary Ridge and moving out to McPherson's. The infantry and cavalrymen mingled atop the ridge, firing into the Rebel regiments coming at them.

Captain James Stewart, commanding an artillery battery attached to I Corps, had ridden ahead of his command that morning and arrived about this time at an unspecified point close to the action. Recalling that morning years later, Stewart tells of meeting Colonel Tom Devin with his cavalry brigade. Stewart remembered that he:

> … watched the battle going on for some time, and soon found that our cavalry force was not equal to the enemies', although they were stubbornly holding every foot of ground. General (Colonel) Devens [sp] informed me that the cavalry was holding the enemy to give General Reynolds time to bring up his corps and also to develop their strength. Having the battery field-glasses with me, I took a good survey of the field, and was surprised to see their strength as they were advancing.[19]

William Herrmance with Company C of the 6th New York remembered that Devin's brigade was posted on the right of Gable's and:

> … held their position until Hill's advance had flanked their right on Mummasburg road and advanced their batteries, which opened on the skirmish line both from front and flank. The I Corps having come up and secured the Seminary Ridge, we had been fighting to hold for them, we were ordered back. I commanded the extreme right and returned under a severe fire down the Mummasburg road to a clump of woods north of the Seminary where we had left our horses; seeing that the enemy had gotten so far in rear of our flank, the men in charge supposed we had been gobbled up, and had gone back to the Seminary ground with them [horses], and exhausted as we were we had to double-quick another mile before we reached them[20]

Only a few of the Union dead at Gettysburg July 1. (Library of Congress)

There had already been casualties and there would be many more this day, foremost among them one of the two leaders in this action. General Reynolds was riding now among the infantry on McPherson's Ridge, moving from one arriving unit to another and placing them in positions. He had just shouted some encouragement to one group when he was hit and instantly killed.

As John Reynolds was carried from the field, Captain Stewart and his battery arrived on the ridge and deployed. Stewart recalled the infantry had become heavily engaged. One Rebel advance on McPherson Ridge had been beaten back but another was advancing:

> ... as we could see the bayonets of the infantry coming over the rising ground, the distance being about six hundred yards. They came on in fine style. Our men did not fire a musket until they came within a distance of about four hundred yards.

Stewart had ordered his newly arrived guns loaded with canister and waited:

> ... until the enemy had reached what we thought about three hundred yards ... It was more than they could stand. They broke to the rear, where they halted, faced about and advanced again, but meeting with such a storm of lead and iron, they broke and ran over the raising ground entirely out of sight.[21]

At almost the same moment, the momentum behind the Rebel advance seemed to dissipate and then, what only can be called a lull in the fighting settled over the fields. The time cannot be accurately determined other than it was after 11am. As more Union infantry arrived and the lull continued, Buford used this period of diminished firing to withdraw the bulk of Gamble's brigade from the fight.

The battle at Gettysburg would be resumed as more Confederate troops moved on the town from the north and northeast as well as from the west. I Corps would be forced to retire, first to Seminary Ridge and then through the town and on to Cemetery Hill and Ridge to the south. XI Corps, upon its arrival, deployed to meet the threat coming from the north and northeast, but was eventually forced back to the same positions occupied by I Corps. Casualties were heavy in both Union Corps.

***

Near the time of the Federal withdrawal from Seminary Ridge, at some unknown spot, Buford scribbled a note addressed to Cavalry Corps commander, Pleasonton. It apprised him of the situation, as Buford knew it at that moment. Buford noted the time as 3:20pm, and only in the last line does any anxiety show in his reporting:

> I am satisfied that Longstreet and Hill have made a junction. A tremendous battle has been raging since 9:30 A.M., with varying success. At the present moment the battle is raging on the road to Cashtown, and within short cannon-range of this town. The enemy's line is a semicircle on the heights, from north to west. General Reynolds was killed early this morning. In my opinion, there seems to be no directing person. JHO Buford. P. S. We need help now.[22]

What Buford didn't know at the time he scribbled his note was that a "directing person" had arrived. Major General Winfield Scott Hancock, commander of II Corps, had been at Meade's headquarters when news of the death of General Reynolds had arrived. This was remembered as being around 1pm. Thirty minutes later, Hancock was riding toward Gettysburg with Meade's written orders: take command of the battle and determine whether the topography favored fighting at Gettysburg or withdrawing to a more suitable place. It would only be a short time before Buford heard from Hancock.[23]

With the over running of the positions on Seminary Ridge, Buford led Gamble's brigade to the base of Cemetery Hill as Rebel infantry surged in from the west. At this point Buford was "asked" if he could do something to stem the Rebel tide overflowing Seminary Ridge while the retreating Union infantry formed a new line of resistance on Cemetery Hill and Ridge. The staff officer who delivered this message later recalled that Buford … rose in his stirrups upon his tiptoes and exclaimed: "What in hell and damnation does he think I can do against those long lines of the enemy out there!" The staff officer had no answer for this, and Buford knew it, his being just the messenger. "Very well," he then said, "I will see what I can do." Buford then gave an order and Gamble's brigade moved out.[24] He would stop the Rebel advance by having the brigade move forward slowly, sabers and pistols were drawn as if a charge was going to be ordered. The advancing Rebel infantry, seeing this, stopped their forward movement and quickly formed squares, a defensive posture designed to resist a mounted attack. It was all a bluff by Buford, but it allowed some of the retreating Union infantry to get to the high ground. More than anything else, Buford's feint against the Rebels had eaten up more time, allowing more Federal troops, now converging on Gettysburg, to get closer to the new Union line. It was now after 5pm and although there would still be summertime daylight for a few more hours, the Rebel thrust upon Gettysburg was approaching its twelfth hour, its internal momentum rapidly dissipating. Sometime near 6pm, the organized fighting had all but stopped and only occasional firing by individuals on both sides was heard until darkness engulfed the scene.

General Richard Ewell and his corps, coming in from the north and northeast was now almost fully on the field with the town of Gettysburg in his possession. Lee had urged Ewell to assault the Union force on Cemetery Hill to the south of the captured town, "if practicable." Ewell and his division commanders, particularly Jubal Early, looked the situation over and did not see the practicality of it. It is one of the several "what ifs" of this battle that an attack on the hill at this point in the afternoon might have carried it, the Union's defenses not yet fully formed. Theoretically, a successful assault on this high ground by Ewell's troops would have forced the Union commands into a full retreat from the Gettysburg area.

At a point in the early evening and probably responding to a verbal order, Buford reunited his two brigades and moved to the left on the Union line. The spot he and his men settled upon was just off Emmitsburg Road, close to a peach orchard, a place that would become notorious the next afternoon.[25]

John Buford and his command had rendered invaluable service to the Army of the Potomac and the Union cause as the July 1 engagement enveloped the quiet town of Gettysburg. The next two days would turn the town and surrounding landscape into a revered portion of the American landscape. Buford's handling of the 1st Cavalry Division, and the leadership of his brigade commanders, William Gamble and Thomas Devin, had shown itself to be the best use of cavalry thus far in the Civil War. The cost in casualties, never cheap, was approximately 127 men, killed or wounded, or about 4 percent of the cavalry force engaged. If John Buford hadn't already proven himself to be the finest cavalry commander serving with Union forces, the matter was settled by the time dusk settled over the fields surrounding Gettysburg that Wednesday evening.

That afternoon, when Gamble's brigade withdrew from Seminary Ridge it moved to the left flank, and almost immediately the Rebels attempted to move by that flank, attacking the Union infantry on the ridge. Deployed behind a stonewall, Gamble's men inflicted huge casualties before being forced from the position by a "greatly superior force." The colonel reported:

> ... we opened a sharp and rapid carbine fire, which killed and wounded so many of the first line of the enemy that it fell back upon the second line. Our men kept up the fire until the enemy in overwhelming numbers approached so near that, to save my men and horses from capture, they were ordered to mount and fall back rapidly to the next ridge [Cemetery Ridge], on the left of the town, where our artillery was posted. The stand which we made against the enemy prevented our left flank from being turned, and saved a division of our infantry.

In an after-action report lacking in detail, the colonel merely says the brigade fell back to where "our artillery was posted." Presumably, this was a move back to Cemetery Hill, were the guns of the arriving XI Corps, as well as those of I Corps, were being positioned.[26] Gamble skips entirely the charge demonstration against the Rebels that Buford led after the fall of Seminary Ridge.

John Buford, writing over a month later, said that while this was transpiring:

> ... Devin's brigade, on the right, had its hands full. The enemy advanced upon Devin by four roads, and on each checked and held until the leading division of the XI Corps came to his relief.[27]

This is as much as the general, who had remained close to Gamble's brigade all through the morning and afternoon, had to say of the engagement by Devin on July 1.

Weeks later, Tom Devin submitted his lengthy report on his command's action on July 1:

> On the morning of July 1, the pickets of the First Brigade [Gamble's], on the road to Cashtown, were driven in by a heavy force advancing from that direction, and the Second Brigade was ordered to prepare for action, and form on a crest of the hill on the right of the First Brigade. I immediately formed as ordered, with my right resting on the road to Mammasburg, and deployed a squadron of the 6th New York to the front and left as skirmishers, dismounted, and connecting with those of the First Brigade, at the same time connecting by skirmishers and vedettes with my pickets on the three roads on the right leading to Carlisle, thus establishing a continuous line from the York road, on the extreme right, to the left [right?] of the 1st Brigade, on the Cashtown road. The infantry not having arrived, and the enemy's artillery fire increasing, I was ordered to retire gradually, as they succeeded in getting the range of my position. This I effected in successive formations in line to the rear by regiment, in the face of the enemy, the troops behaving well, and forming with perfect coolness and order.
>
> About this time, my skirmishers on the right were forced back by the advance of the enemy's line of battle, coming from the direction of Heidlersburg. Knowing the importance of holding that point until the infantry could arrive and be placed in position, I immediately placed the Ninth New York in support, and, dismounted the rest of my available force, succeeding in holding the rebel line in check for two hours, until relieved by the arrival of the XI Corps, when I was ordered to mass my command in the right of the York road and hold that approach. While in that position—immediately in front of the town, the command faced to the front and my pickets on the York road advanced three-quarters of a mile—a heavy fire of shells was opened on us from one of our own batteries on Cemetery Hill, immediately in my rear. The fire becoming very hot and persistent, and many of the shells bursting among us, I was led to suppose for a moment that the enemy had succeeded

in gaining that position, and I immediately removed my command into the town, the column being shelled the whole distance. After I retired, the battery turned its attention to my pickets on the road, and shelled them out. I was then ordered to the Emmitsburg road, where the brigade was formed in line, in rear of the batteries of the division, with its right flank resting on the town.

The enemy, having gained the York road, entered the town immediately after my pickets retired, and, passing through with their sharpshooters, attacked the flank of the brigade, killing and wounding several men and horses. I immediately dismounted one squadron of the Ninth New York, who, with their carbines, drove them some distance into the town, punishing them severely. The brigade was then ordered to the extreme left, where it bivouacked for the night.[28]

Lieutenant Hillman Hall was regimental quartermaster and, years later, would help assemble the 6th New York's early history. He remembered the action of his brigade on the morning of July 1. As the Rebels advanced along Chambersburg Pike, and according to plan, Devin's 2nd Brigade formed a line to the right of Gamble, extending from the railroad cut parallel with Chambersburg Pike and bending around to Mammasburg Road, with a skirmish line out to the front. "The Sixth New York was placed on the right of the brigade, on the road to Mammusburg, where it dismounted and deployed, holding the enemy in check for two or three hours until the arrival of the infantry [elements of XI Corps]." Then, Hall recalled, the cavalrymen responded with a rapid carbine fire from behind trees, rocks, and stone walls, their sturdy resistance giving the enemy the impression that he had infantry before him, and causing him to advance slowly and cautiously.[29]

When elements of I Corps arrived under Reynolds, the 2nd Brigade moved off from the railroad cut, to the right covering the roads coming into town from the north:

> As Rodes' and Early's divisions successively arrived, Devin retired gradually, effecting this movement to the rear by successive formations in line by regiment. In executing these movements in the face of the enemy, his troops behaved well, and formed each time with perfect coolness and order, the small losses in the brigade being due largely to the admirable manner in which it was handled.[30]

It had developed that the main threat was Early's division advancing on the road coming from Heidlersburg. With the 9th New York out as skirmishers, the 6th New York and the rest of the brigade were formed into a line of carbineers. As the first elements approached, the 9th's troopers blasted away and were able to hold until the infantry of XI Corps came up. This was reported to be about noon by Hillman Hall. Immediately after this, the early regimental history details:

> ... the cavalry formed in line of battle on the hill north of the town, while a portion of the Sixth New York went forward as skirmishers. It soon met the rebel lines, long and strong, advancing from the woods beyond, and immediately the cavalry fighting commenced, and shot and shell flew fast and thick. When the infantry came up, the fighting, of course, became more furious, and soon two entire rebel regiments came into town as *prisoners*.

This action lasted for about one hour. Then, according to the early history, at 1 p.m.:

> ... the brigade was formed in close column of squadrons, north of town, dismounted, when suddenly a battery on a commanding eminence east of town opened fire upon it—a terrific fire, equal to any it had ever been exposed to. Colonel Devin promptly headed the brigade toward town, on a double quick, while the shot flew thick and fast over and about, killing a number of horses, but none of the men. That any escaped was a miracle ... The battery belonged to the XI Corps and had mistaken us for the enemy. The mistake had broken the infantry line as well as the cavalry line, and shortly after the enemy got possession of the town ...[31]

Hillman Hall continues:

> During the fire of the battery, Adjutant Easton of the Sixth New York dashed to Cemetery Hill and informed the Captain of the guns that he was firing on our own troops. Not receiving assurance that it would be stopped, the Adjutant called to General O. O. Howard, who was at some distance on the right, 'Howard, Howard, for God's sake, stop this firing on our own men!'

In 1907, Adjutant Easton asked General Howard if, by any possibility, he remembered the incident, and was assured that he did "perfectly well." The adjutant expressed surprise that a major-general should recall such a minor matter, and was answered with a smile, by Howard, "Oh, you did not give me my title."[32]

"In the afternoon of July 1st," Hall continued, "after the Union forces had fallen back to and taken position on Cemetery Hill, Buford, having reunited his two cavalry brigades, of his division in front of Cemetery Ridge, southwest of the town, near the low ground east of Stevens' Run, where he occupied an advanced but firm position."[33]

At this point the 6th's early history is somewhat confused and gives no detailed account of the regiment's or Buford's division's movement, the orders it received, or how it, late in the day, found itself somewhere to the west of Round Tops facing Emmitsburg Road. But as the command took its position in this area, the leading elements of General Daniel E. Sickles's III Corps, the last of the corps that had been commanded by General Reynolds, began arriving and took a position to the left of the troops then on Cemetery Ridge, extending the Union line south along Cemetery Ridge toward Little Round Top. It was on the left flank of III Corps that Buford's division went into position. Elements of this corps would continue to arrive throughout the night.

Dan Sickles, in his long life, has proven to be one of the more interesting, one of the more controversial and one of the least likable personalities to emerge from a war full of characters of all stripes. As a measure of Lincoln's apparent willingness to do almost anything early in the war to get volunteers to fill out an army to fight for the Union, the president, in September 1861, recommended ex-Congressman Daniel Sickles of New York for a general's commission. Having no prior military experience, Sickles had raised a volunteer regiment and then another, eventually gathering six regiments into a brigade, named "Excelsior" after the state's motto, with himself hoping for command of it. That he was a Democrat, that he had, before the war, shot and killed his wife's lover on a street blocks from the White House, that he had pleaded temporary insanity (the first successful pleading in American Law) and been acquitted, that Lincoln had to twist arms in Congress to get Sickles his general's commission, all seemed not to matter at the time to the president. It took until May 1862 to get the commission approved due to the unsavory view of Dan Sickles among many in Congress and his lacking any military experience. Sickles had the men and, for better or worse, he would lead them, obviously having to learn as he went along. His courage was evident from the beginning and the men he led liked him, even if the West Pointers throughout the army were skeptical. As familiar with controversy as he already was, Dan Sickles would create the biggest of his career beginning on Thursday, July 2, and, as for his actions influencing the Gettysburg battle, the fact that historians still write of it today should be enough said.

The early history of the 6th New York speaking of this time period, states:

> The [second] brigade was then ordered to the extreme left, where it bivouacked for the night, but remained on duty as pickets at the Peach Orchard, watching the enemy, and directing the different commands where to go.

This refers to the brigade directing the arriving elements of III Corps to the Cemetery Ridge line.[34]

Confusion in the early histories extended into the morning hours of Thursday, July 2. Precisely where Buford's division was in the early morning is speculation. The best that can be deduced is that it was somewhere west of the Round Tops facing Emmitsburg Road, with pickets out to beyond the road some distance. The exact time the division retired from its flanking position is not known with certainty, but it was before Sickles's Corps was advanced in an ill-conceived creation of a salient that was to have serious consequences for the Army of the Potomac late that afternoon. Indeed, it may have been the withdrawal of Buford's command that gave impetus to the general's thinking with regard to advancing his corps as he later did. Hall, in the early history says of July 2:

> The next morning, while reconnoitering in the rear of the enemy's right, our sharpshooters became engaged with a division of the enemy advancing to feel our line in front of the position held by Devin's brigade. Two squadrons of the Sixth New York were dismounted and deployed in support of the ... sharpshooters, while the [Second] brigade was formed into line on the left of the First [brigade] with one section of Tidball's battery in position. The enemy not pressing his advance, and the III Corps coming in to position, the brigade was ordered to march to Taneytown, where it bivouacked and marched the next day [July 3] to Westminster.[35]

Tom Devin's report on Gettysburg is essentially the same and Hall may have lifted his version from the *Official Record*. Devin said:

> The next morning, July 2, while I was engaged reconnoitering in the rear of the enemy's right, our sharpshooters (Berdan's Sharpshooters) became engaged with a division of the enemy advancing to feel our lines in front of my position. I immediately dismounted and deployed two squadrons in support of Berdan's Sharpshooters (who were engaged in my front), and formed the brigade into line on the left of the First, with one section of Tidball's battery in position.

John Calef commanded this artillery section. He reported, "… the attack commenced directly in front of where my battery was parked." This was skirmishing between the sharpshooters and Rebel infantry pickets.

> Notwithstanding the severe work of the 1st, every one showed himself ready for a continuation on the morning of the 2d. We had hardly got into position when an order came from General Buford for me to follow with my battery the First Brigade …

A trooper in the 8th New York of Gamble's brigade wrote to his hometown newspaper about the encounter on the morning of July 2, saying:

> … while we were drawn up in line to support skirmishers, that our company lost one of its faithful and truest soldiers. Jonathan Macomber of Livingston County, who was nearly directly behind myself, being struck full in the forehead by a bullet, killing him instantly, without a word or a groan.

Devin then reported:

> The enemy not pressing his advance, and the III Corps coming into position, we were ordered to march to Taneytown, where we bivouacked …[35]

Here is an explanation concerning Sickles relative to his movement and Meade's reaction to it. According to Lieutenant Hall of the 6th New York:

> To the surprise and embarrassment of General Sickles, Buford's division of Cavalry, which had been posted on his left, had moved off the field, General Meade having authorized General Pleasonton to send the division to Westminster, 30 miles distant. Meade supposed that Gregg's division of cavalry had relieved Buford, but he had been incorrectly informed. As soon as he was aware of his mistake, he [Meade] instructed Pleasonton that Sickles' flank should not be left unprotected by cavalry, but it was then too late.[36]

Having recorded this in the 6th New York's early history, yet in a subsequent paragraph on page 143, the author then writes:

> The regiment engaged the advance of Longstreet's corps at Round Top. The Confederates appeared to secrete themselves in every available position not directly exposed to Union lines. Whenever the effect of their deadly aim uncovered their hiding-places, the Sixth New York, with the other regiments, was employed in dislodging them from their strongholds. At 11 a.m., having been relieved by the III Corps, the regiment left the field and marched to Taneytown, Md, twelve miles, and encamped.[37]

This confusion, perhaps, may be the result of Buford's division leaving the left flank position by regiment at different times during the late morning or early afternoon. The early history of the 8th Illinois of Buford's 1st Brigade speaks of leaving the field at about "… one o'clock P.M. (just as the battle was being renewed) …" In addition, its author says that at this time "Sickles' division [corps] was advanced across Emmitsburg pike, and all the movements betokened a renewal of the engagement …"[38] Two companies of the 9th New York remained posted to the southeast of Round Top while the battle of July 2 played out. Only after darkness did they start for Taneytown.[39]

***

As the Union soldiers marched toward Gettysburg, knowing there would be a fight, they were also aware it all depended on them. They had a confidence, in part stemming from knowing that the fight would be on their soil, in their country. In those brief moments of rest along the way, or while they waited on the battlefield for the shooting to start on July 2, they spoke of it to their loved ones, penciled scribblings, while out beyond Emmitsburg Road the invaders were moving. "This AM says this is to be the Battle of the war and every man must stand." "Our troops were determined not to be drove …" "We are well prepared to meet the rascals." "I hope that none of them will escape." They "are arrogant and think they can easily conquer us with anything like equal numbers. We hope that in this faith he will remain and give us final and decisive battle here."[40]

General Daniel Sickles and his two III Corps divisions had occupied the lower part of Cemetery Ridge, the land sloping into the base of Little Round Top. He didn't consider it a good position in that he could see, directly in his front, high ground, between where he was then standing and Emmitsburg Road further to the west. He advanced to this higher ground, creating a salient, the crest of it reaching into a Peach Orchard, located on the east side of Emmitsburg Road. III Corps troops occupied the orchard and the area surround it. Officers in II Corps that had been on Sickles's immediate right along Cemetery Ridge were astounded as they stood and watched the forward movement. The thought briefly surfaced: had there been an order from Meade to advance? No, couldn't be. Moving forward would weaken the position already established. A cautious General Meade, and new to army command, would not do that. Accounts generally agree that it started at 4pm. In the attack that was launched by Lieutenant General James Longstreet at that time, the Union III Corps under Dan Sickles was decimated.

Accounts that speak of Buford during the morning hours of July 2 say it was he that asked Pleasonton to withdraw the division for refit and that the corps commander gave his approval. It is unclear when exactly this happened or when the orders filtered down to the individual regiments to mount and withdraw.

The best estimate is between 11am and noon. Buford and the 1st Cavalry Division apparently then marched out of the battle, to Taneytown, Maryland, about 12 miles away. Pleasonton's agreeing to allow Buford to withdraw was followed by nothing to compensate for the loss of his division. Pleasonton in agreeing did not order Gregg's 2nd Cavalry Division to fill the left flank position Buford had held.[41] At that moment Gregg's division was the only mounted command with the army. As one historian of the battle summarized the situation, "Meade approved this action on the unspoken assumption that another mounted force would come up to protect the army's left flank." Months later Pleasonton explained Buford's withdrawal before the Joint Committee on the Conduct of the War. He said that Buford's division "had been 'severely handled' on July 1 (which was untrue) and asserted that he had promptly moved up another cavalry unit to replace it (a bald lie). No one took over for Buford's men after they began pulling out around midday. Not until Dan Sickles complained about losing his flank protection did Meade realize that Pleasonton had not followed through. Dispatches demanding corrective action were forwarded to the cavalry chief at 12:50 and 12:55 P.M.; an hour later."[42] Meade's Chief of Staff, Major General Daniel Butterfield, in a note to Pleasonton at 12:50am said:

> The major-general commanding directs me to say that he has not authorized the entire withdrawal of Buford's force from the direction of Emmitsburg, and did not so understand when he gave permission to Buford to go … the patrols and pickets upon the Emmitsburg road must be kept on as long as our troops are in position.

Five minutes later, Butterfield told Pleasonton:

> My note, written five minutes since, is a little confused, I find. The general expected, when Buford's force was sent to Westminster, that a force should be sent to replace it, picketing and patrolling the Emittsburg [sic] road. He understood that all your force was up.

Only at 1:45pm did Pleasonton react, noting to Gregg's 2nd Cavalry Division:

> You will detail a regiment from your command to picket on the left of our line, lately occupied by General Buford …[43]

Gregg reacted by sending the 4th Pennsylvania Cavalry led by Lt. Col. William F. Doster. Doster recalled it was 3pm when he was ordered to move and was placed near to Little Round Top. He then went to see Pleasonton at army headquarters:

> Pleasonton begged my pardon for having me ride so far. There was no need of exposing the cavalry in front. I should rejoin Gregg on the right …

It was all too late by the time the 4th Pennsylvania got in place; the day's Confederate attack had already begun.[44] By the evening of July 2, Sickles's Corps, because of its forward move, had been wrecked. It's doubtful, however, given the strength of Longstreet's assault, that Buford's division, if retained, would have been able to avert the ravaging of III Corps.

General Sickles, testifying later before the Joint Committee on the Conduct of the War, summarized his view of the matter before he ordered the advance of his Corps out to the vicinity of the Peach Orchard:

> I had strengthened and supported my outposts in order to give me timely notice of the attack, which I knew was very imminent. Buford's cavalry, which had been on the left, had been withdrawn. I remonstrated against that, and expressed the hope that the cavalry, or some portion of it, at all events, might be allowed to remain there. I was informed that it was not the intention to remove the whole of the cavalry, and that a portion of it would be returning. It did not return, however.

By all accounts, the withdrawal had been at Buford's request and consented to by both Pleasonton and Meade. but as commented upon by one cavalry historian, "If he [Pleasonton] believed

General Daniel Sickles Commander of the Third Corps that was wrecked fighting the Confederate advance of July 2. (Library of Congress)

that other mounted units would take Buford's place, he could not have said where he would find them; he must have known that replacements were not immediately available." The 3rd Division under Kilpatrick was moving on Hunterstown five miles to the north and would soon become engaged with Stuart's returning cavalry. The 2nd Division, under Gregg, was out on Hanover Road and Merritt's Reserved Brigade was still in Maryland. Years later, Dan Sickles was still trying to cover his precipitous advance from the Union mainline of resistance and into the Peach Orchard, blaming Meade. Meade's order, Sickles wrote:

> …deprived me and himself of the most effective support he had on his left flank by the unaccountable withdrawal of Buford's division of cavalry, which held the Emmitsburg road and covered our left flank, including Round Top, until a late hour on the morning of the 2nd.[45]

By nightfall, III Corps was wrecked, many hundreds killed and wounded, among them Dan Sickles who had a leg amputated that night and would not again command in the field during this war. However, being directly responsible for the avoidable damage to his corps, Sickles would devote a good portion of the years remaining to him blaming George Meade for the disaster of July 2. While he still lived, Meade did not stoop to answer. A staff officer in II Corps who witnessed the July 2 fighting wrote within weeks of the battle, the point of his pencil sharpened when he spoke of Dan Sickles. The general's movement:

> … was a gross, and came so near being the cause of irreparable disaster that I cannot discuss it with moderation. I hope the man may never return to the Army of the Potomac, or elsewhere, to a position where his incapacity, or something worse, may bring fruitless destruction to thousands again.[46]

During the late morning or early afternoon of July 2 then, Buford moved off the battlefield and the bulk of his two brigades marched to Taneytown, Maryland. The cavalrymen had been on the end of the Union line and were perhaps miles away when that day's major confrontation started and miles further still when it ended. The ground they had left would, in later years, be remembered by a Gettysburg resident as the location of:

> … my uncle's farms, just below Big Round Top, eighteen hundred of the dead were buried in a single trench. There were covered very shallow, and at night you could see phosphorescent light coming out of the earth where they were buried.[47]

After bivouacking overnight, on July 2, Buford's command started for Westminster, Maryland, where, according to a trooper in the 9th New York of Devin's brigade:

> … feed and supplies were obtained, horses were shod, and the men had an opportunity to do their washing. The heavy cannonading at Gettysburg, thirty miles away was distinctly heard on the afternoon of July 3.[48]

Lieutenant Frank Haskell was on the staff in II Corps and in a later recounting of the events of these July days, wrote the following regarding the events of this second day of July:

> From the position of the III Corps [on Cemetery Ridge from which Sickles advanced to his new position] the distance is about a thousand yards, and there Emmitsburg road runs near the crest of the ridge. Gen. Sickles commenced to advance his whole corps … straight to the front, with a view to occupy this second ridge, along, and near the road [Emmitsburg]. What his purpose could have been is past conjecture. It was not ordered by Gen. Meade, as I heard him [Sickles] say, and he disapproved of it as soon as it was made known to him. Generals Hancock [II Corps commander] and Gibbon [a division commander], as they saw the move in progress, criticized its propriety sharply, as I know, and foretold quite accurately what would be the result. I suppose the truth probably is that General Sickles supposed he was doing for the best; but he was neither born nor bred a soldier.[49]

With this advance and the withdrawal of Buford's cavalry, he exposed the left flank of his corps to attack. Haskell went on to say:

> So when this advance [of the III Corps] line came near the Emmitsburg road, and we saw the squadrons of cavalry mentioned, come dashing back from their position as flankers, and the

smoke of some [Rebel] guns, and we heard the reports away to Sickles left, anxiety became an element in our interest in these movements.[50]

This testimony appears to confirm not all of Buford's cavalry marched away at one time prior to the III Corps advance as Sickles seems to testify or that part of it—squadrons—remained for a time after the division moved toward Taneytown and withdrew only when Rebel artillery began firing at the beginning of the July 2 attack.

The officers of II Corps stood on Cemetery Ridge gaping at the inexplicable advance of III Corps ordered by General Sickles. Time passed, Rebel artillery opened on Sickles and his corps followed by a surge of infantry that, over the next two to three hours, would push III Corps back to the area it had originally been intended for it to defend. In the late afternoon, calls for help from III Corps were sent out as the Confederate army was sweeping the Union force before it. Next in line along Cemetery Ridge was General Winfield Scott Hancock's II Corps and the closest element at hand for the general to call upon to help in blunting the attack was the 1st Division's 2nd Brigade. This force was the Irish Brigade, already a command famous for its fighting ability and courage. Hancock called on them to get ready to march to the support of III Corps, into battle clearly going in favor for the Confederates at that moment.

Father William Corby was the brigade's chaplain and when he saw the brigade preparing to march into the battle he asked if he might have a moment. When Father Corby wrote a memoir of his time with the Irish Brigade his modesty made him quote mostly from the words used by Major St. Clair Mulholland, commanding a Pennsylvania regiment in the brigade. "I proposed," Corby later wrote, "to give a general absolution to our men." Then in his memoir he turns the telling over to Mulholland. Corby stood "on a large rock ... he explained what he was about to do, saying that each one could receive the benefit of the absolution by making a sincere Act of Contrition and firmly to resolve to embrace the first opportunity of confessing his sins, urging them to do their duty."[51] With Father Corby before them, the brigade knelt with Mulholland noting, "I do not think there was a man in the brigade who did not offer up a heartfelt prayer. For some, it was their last; they knelt there in their grave clothes."[52]

At the ceremonies at Gettysburg during the 25th anniversary in 1888, Mulholland recalled, it was "... one of the most impressive religious ceremonies I have ever witnessed." Then:

> ... as he [Father Corby] closed his address, every man ... fell on his knees with his head bowed down. Then stretching his right hand toward the brigade, Father Corby pronounced the words of absolution ... the scene was more than impressive, it was awe-inspiring ... and while there was profound silence ... yet over to the left ... the roar of the battle rose and swelled and re-echoed through the woods ...

General Winfield Scott Hancock Second Corps commander at Gettysburg. (Library of Congress)

Many of the officers from other commands within II Corps, as they watched this scene, also went to their knees and even the hard core and profane Winfield Scott Hancock, Corby observed "removed his hat, and, as far as compatible with the situation, bowed in reverent devotion." When the priest and the former regimental commander met at Gettysburg in 1888, Corby relates that as the quick religious ceremony took place, Mulholland noticed a soldier kneeling near him "... and praying with more fervor than [he] had ever before witnessed. Twenty minutes later that poor soldier was a corpse!"[53]

***

As for the attack by General Longstreet and his corps during the afternoon of July 2, a lieutenant in an Alabama regiment left us with his impression of it:

The sun was fiercely hot and there was no shade or other protection for the men. Here they sweated, sweltered and swore … our brigade commander during the morning took occasion to explain to the officers the general plan of attack in so far as our immediate front was concerned, stating that the movement would be by echelon. Beginning with the right of Longstreet's corps and extending to the left as each brigade came into action, and that owing to our situation the Alabama brigade at the proper time would move by the left flank rapidly, to give Barksdale's Mississippi brigade, which would be in our rear, or rather on our immediate right, room to move forward in proper line.

It was near to 4pm, the Confederate artillery opened and then the troops, aligned to the west of Emmitsburg road, began moving forward:

As the fire and clamor reached the Alabama brigade, Barksdale threw forward his Mississippians in an unbroken line in the most magnificent charge I ever witnessed during the war, and led by the gallant Barksdale, who seemed to be fifty yards in front of his boys. The scene was grand beyond description.[54]

In the attack, two Union lines were overrun. At the third line, the attack stalled, reserve Rebel infantry, it is suggested by the Alabama brigade, were called for but did not appear and, therefore, a retreat was ordered. The Confederate force returned to the line they had advanced from. General Barksdale was killed in the action at the head of his Mississippi brigade. One of the regiments from II Corps that ran to support III Corps was the 126th New York. Lieutenant R. A. Bassett, advancing to meet Barksdale's brigade, saw his brother, advancing with the regimental flag, fall at the head of the regiment. That night Bassett had time to write a few lines of a letter:

> I have not the time to give many particulars, neither do I feel inclined to say much at present; my heart is too full and sad to say anything; and I do not know what to say to console the afflicted, for I am as afflicted as any one.

Bassett knew the fight would continue the next day, adding to his letter, "We expect to give the rebels another time tomorrow."[55]

The fighting on July 1 had been a defeat for the Union force engaged, pushed as they were from the positions they had occupied, through the town of Gettysburg, and up and on to Cemetery Hill and Ridge. Reinforcements came up by the end of the day and on through the night and next day. The day's fight had been large and expensive with an estimated 7,000 Union casualties. The next day would be worse, the day after, worse still, but the Union's Army of the Potomac would not be driven from the position it found itself holding at the end of July 1. In the late afternoon of July 2 and, again, in the afternoon of July 3, the outcome of the Civil War would be decided. Those men didn't know it then, but they would later, it would be the turning point in this war. As noted by Bruce Catton:

> The perplexing mists and shadows would fade and Gettysburg would reveal itself as a great height from which men could glimpse a vista extending far into the undiscovered future.[56]

Some miles to the west, Randolph Shotwell was waiting with his regiment to join the battle. They were to march to Gettysburg beginning at 3am on Friday morning. As night descended, Shotwell made a note in his diary:

> Little Jimmie Bose came to me a few minutes ago, and laid down on the edge of my blanket. Seeing him rather depressed, I asked him what troubled him. Said he: 'I wish you would take my money, and this little Journal and give it to Mother if I get killed tomorrow.' I tried to reason him out of his presentment, but he seems almost certain of death. Says he was barefooted and … wanted to come on with the Army and get himself a pair of new boots in Baltimore. His mother told him before he left: 'I fear you will never live to see Baltimore, Jimmie!' And said Jimmie:—'*I expect she was right.*'

Writing of the next day Shotwell said:

> The slaughter can be imagined without any effort at word painting. My regiment was almost destroyed—only 17 (seventeen) men escaped untouched … Little Jimmie Bose, whose presentment of death caused him to urge me to take his money and blank book, was shot through the heart at the first volley.[57]

CHAPTER SEVEN

Maybe This Time

Friday, July 3, 1863

> For every Southern boy fourteen years old, not once but whenever he wants it, there is an instant when it's still not yet two o'clock on that July afternoon in 1863, the brigades are in position behind the rail fence, the guns are laid and ready in the woods and the furled flags are already loosened to break out and Pickett himself with his long oiled ringlets and his hat in one hand probably and his sword in the other looking up the hill waiting for Longstreet to give the word and it's all in the balance, it hasn't happened yet … This time. Maybe this time with all this much to lose than all this much to gain …
>
> WILLIAM FAULKNER, *INTRUDER IN THE DUST*[1]

> We dozed in the heat, and lolled upon the ground, with half open eyes. Our horses were hitched to the trees munching on some oats. Time was heavy, and for the want of something better to do, I yawned, and looked at my watch. It was five minutes before one o'clock. I returned my watch to its pocket and thought possibly that I might go off to sleep and stretched myself upon the ground accordingly.

It hasn't happened yet.

These words are a remembrance by Lieutenant Frank Haskell, at the time a staff officer in II Corps. Within weeks of this afternoon, Haskell wrote in detail about his time spent in Pennsylvania this summer. When he finished, he had a lengthy letter. He mailed it to his brother in Wisconsin. It is a remarkable account of events as he saw them, one that even the most casual rendering of the day's events should not ignore.

Earlier, at about 11am, Haskell remembers, "… the sky is bright, with only white fleecy clouds floating over from the West. The July sun streams down its fire." The Army of the Potomac is in its position on Cemetery Hill and Ridge. This is the third day of the battle. The dead from the first two days are scattered in all directions, all over the landscape surrounding the town of Gettysburg. If not that morning, soon there would be an odor of death floating in the summer breeze along with the sulfurous smoke, the smell of spent munitions. There had been fighting on the right flank this morning, over and around Culp's Hill, but it is quiet now, positions checked, everyone just waiting on events. Sometime before noon a few of the generals gathered for some lunch. Frank Haskell, as hungry as anyone else, was there and remembered:

> There was an enormous pan of stewed chickens, and the potatoes, and toast, all hot, and the bread and the butter, and tea and coffee … Our table was the top of a mess chest. By this the generals sat … We were just well at it when General Meade rode down to us from the line … and by General Gibbon's invitation … joined us.

Only Lieutenant Haskell left remarks concerning the meal:

> I think an unprejudiced person would have said of the bread that it was good; so of the potatoes before they were boiled. Of the chickens he would have questioned their age.
> [The] generals ate, and after, lighted cigars, and under the flickering shade of a very small tree discoursed of the incidents of yesterday's battle and of the probabilities of today.[2]

The generals finished their cigars and mounted, each riding to see that everything was as it should be. Everyone on that ridge knew something was bound to happen. Frank Haskell remembered:

> General Gibbon called up Captain Farrel, 1st Minnesota, who commanded the provost guard of his division, and directed him for that day to join his regiment. 'Very well, Sir,' said the captain, as he touched his hat and turned away. He was a quiet, excellent gentleman and a thorough soldier. I knew him well and esteemed him. I never saw him again.[3]

***

American history is replete with rumblings, tremors and upheavals. If one subscribes to the historical proposition that the Civil War was the central seismic event in that history, the point from which things are measured, the before and the after, then the epicenter, the moment where precise measurements may be taken came between 1 and 4pm on July 3, 1863. Happenstance allowed the moment to be played out on a summer afternoon in Pennsylvania.

Men of the Army of the Potomac started writing about the battle at Gettysburg as soon as it was over; the words continuing to flow into the next century. Those who had marched to the town knew that in the approaching battle there could be no substitute for victory. Beforehand they suspected it would be a desperate encounter, a suspicion that proved correct. Those that wrote searched for words to describe what had happened, what it had been like. Some, frustrated, said only that there were no words to describe both the fighting and the landscape strewn with corpses after it was over, but all were aware of the immensity of the battle, its horrific casualties and its significance. II Corps was officially under the command of Major General Winfield Scott Hancock who this day also had command of III Corps with Dan Sickles being wounded the day before. He, Lieutenant Haskell and II Corps would stand at the epicenters of events this afternoon, Hancock marked as one of the day's heroes while being one of its casualties. The corps was arrayed along the crest of Cemetery Ridge, facing west, waiting for something to happen. In Haskell's record of events, it is noticeable that he spent considerable time thinking of and remembering the events of that day and then labored with his pen to mold the proper, appropriate sentences containing the facts as he had seen them; his participation in them. For that we are grateful, but even as he put word to paper while memory was fresh, Haskell was, like Walt Whitman, already a skeptic about history, about the real history never getting in the books. A paragraph or two from the end of his account, Haskell remarked:

> ... of this battle ... a history, just, comprehensive, complete will never be written. By-and-by out of the chaos of trash and falsehood that the newspapers hold, out of the disjointed mass of reports, out of the traditions and tales that come down from the field, some eye that never saw the battle will select, and some pen will write what will be called *the history*, with that the world will be and, if we are alive, we must be, content.

After Gettysburg, Haskell was promoted to command the 36th Wisconsin Infantry and was killed leading his regiment on June 3, 1864, at Cold Harbor.[4]

Twenty-six years later, one surviving witness, Major St. Clair A. Mulholland, commanding the 116th Pennsylvania of the Irish Brigade, would remember this moment and speak at the dedication of his regiment's monument at Gettysburg. The memory of Frank Haskell and that of Major Mulholland are somewhat different, perhaps embellished by the major in his dedication speech. We, at this distance, cannot know. It was quiet along Cemetery Ridge between 11am and 1pm, with Generals Gibbon and Hancock asking for something in the way of lunch be brought up. Mulholland recalled:

> It was a warm summer day and from Round Top to Culp's Hill hardly a sound was heard, not a shot fired. The men rested after the fighting of the previous evening, no troops were moving to and fro ... But during those two hours we could see considerable activity along Seminary Ridge. Battery after battery appeared along the edge of the woods. Guns were unlimbered, placed in position, and the horses taken to the rear. Our men sat around in groups and anxiously watched these movements.

Then the lunch for the generals was brought up. Mulholland:

> The bread that was handed around, if it was eaten, was consumed without butter, for as the orderly was passing the latter article to the gentlemen a shell from Seminary Ridge cut him in two.[5]

It would all be over by sunset. By dark the gun smoke and the sulfurous smell would have drifted off. The temperature dropped by a few degrees, small campfires started behind the firing lines, coffee boiled. Some of the wounded had been gathered in and the oil lamps would burn all night above the contrived operating tables manned by the surgeons. The lucky ones, those not wounded, tried not to hear the moans of those waiting for the surgeon's knife. The lucky talked in hushed tones, gnawed on hard tack and sipped coffee as the daylight faded to black. What they had seen and done that afternoon was recounted. Now, maybe now they could get some sleep.

Lieutenant Haskell later wrote of this day saying it was "… second to none … in importance, which I think I saw as much as any man living …" That morning, "As the sun arose to-day, the clouds became broken, and we had once more glimpses of sky, and fits of sunshine—a rarity."[6]

E. F. Palmer of the 13th Vermont, later noted:

> It is nearly noon; firing soon ceases all over the field, and the sun which has been obscured much of the day by clouds, now shows his splendor, as if to smile on this signal triumph of the friends of liberty.[7]

On the other side of the valley, to the west, perhaps 1400 yards off, beyond Emmitsburg Road, the Confederates waited under the trees, the dread pervasive. An old Rebel veteran years later remembered, "We held our breath waiting for the signal guns were to let us know when the ball was to open." It would be over an hour before these troops would be called to advance, but when they did "the regiments fell in just like clockwork, lots of the boys lookin' white around the gills, and not a word was spoken above a whisper except as the commands were given."[8]

"What sound was that?" Haskell, dozing on Cemetery Ridge, asked himself. It was the first shot, the first of many hundreds, perhaps many thousands of cannon shells fired in the largest and most intense artillery action to ever occur in the Western Hemisphere. Everyone on the Union line atop Cemetery Ridge scrambled for cover.

The numbers would be something these men would have dwelled on if they knew them at the time, the number of guns, the number of Confederate soldiers, the number of dead when it was over. A Confederate attacking force would step out from the woods along Seminary Ridge, march to and across Emmitsburg Road, across undulating farmland sloping up to the crest of Cemetery Ridge to where their attack was aimed. In preparation for this, Confederate artillery pounded Cemetery Ridge for well over an hour—for two hours by some accounts—using over 150 guns. Samuel Fiske was on the receiving end of the bombardment and noted the next day, "… such a cannonade as, I believe, no battle of this war has yet begun to compare with …" Another soldier recalled:

> … the bombardment opened with a fury beyond description. The earth seemed to rise up under the concussion, the air filled with missiles and the noise of all was so furious and overwhelming that one had to scream to his neighbor beside him to be heard.

The artillerists manning the guns "… could be seen … bleeding at both ears from the effect of concussion and the wreck of the world seemed to be upon us." Lieutenant Haskell recalled it was:

Half-past two o'clock. An hour and a half since the commencement, and still the cannonade did not in the least abate; but soon thereafter some signs of weariness and a little slacking of fire began to be apparent ... What next, I wonder?[9]

Damage was done but the smoke from their barrage and the Union return fire from Cemetery Ridge obscured the aim of many of the Rebel guns and consequently they fired long, over the heads of the Union defenders along their main line of resistance.

A staff officer of a Maine regiment had watched the bombardment and recalled:

Then suddenly all the firing ceased, and there was a lull. The smoke clouds were rising from the opposite crest, the sunlight again glistening on the long line of brass guns; but what was that gray mass that seemed to be moving scarce distinguishable from the smoke wreaths about it? On they came: it looked to me like three lines about a mile long each, in perfect order. They crossed Emmitsburg Pike, and our guns ... opened first with shot and then with shell.[10]

The actual number of men in the assault force cannot be known exactly, history now estimating it in round numbers, somewhere between 12,500 to as many as 14,000 troops stepping off. Their line of battle estimated as being from 800 to 1,000 yards in width. It must have been an awesome and frightening sight for those waiting to receive their attack. They marched as if on parade and the Union batteries on the ridge fired at will, tearing gaps in the advancing lines. A witness that would in a few minutes time become a combatant on Cemetery Ridge later remembered the Confederate skirmishers appeared from the woods, then troops in line of battle, a second line of battle followed by a third line. The Union soldiers on the ridge "... watched this never-to-be-forgotten scene,—the grandeur of attack of so many thousand men." The Union troops "... looked with admiration on the different lines of Confederates, marching forward with easy, swinging step..." "Here they come," someone said. In the 19th Maine's history, it was written that the advancing Confederates presented "one of the most inspiring sights ever seen on a field of battle." In their advance, "there was a coolness, and air of discipline and a precision of movement that called forth from the Union soldiers a spontaneous expression of admiration." Alexander Hays, a general commanding a division of II Corps at the point where these Confederates were marching, recalled in his report, "Their march was as steady as if impelled by machinery." As the Confederate infantry emerged from the woods along Seminary Ridge, a soldier in the 14th Connecticut waited behind the stone wall atop the opposite ridge and looked around him. In later years the regiment's history would vividly recall the scene:

It was, indeed, an anxious moment. One you can see is looking at the far off home he will never see again. Another is looking at his little ones, as he mechanically empties his cartridge-box on the ground before him, that he may load more quickly, determined to part with life as dearly as possible. Others are communing with Him before whom so many will shortly have to appear.

There was difficulty at the post and rail fence running along Emmitsburg Road and there were casualties among the Confederate troops struggling with the obstacle. Once across Emmitsburg Road, part on the battle line marched into an undulation in the ground and then advanced out of it and coming out "… they seemed to rise out of the earth, and so near that the expressions on their faces were distinctly seen." The artillerymen switched ammunition. "Shrapnel and canister from the batteries tore gaps through those splendid Virginia battalions." The Union line opened with rifle fire and "Nothing human could stand it." Disorganized return fire came from the Confederate mass and "… that portion of Pickett's division which came within the zone of this terrible close musketry fire appeared to melt and drift away in the powder-smoke of both sides."[11] Samuel Fiske noted the fire from the Union line:

> … swept them down as hail does the growing grain, till human courage could no longer stand against such a tempest of lead and iron; their steady line wavered, rallied, quailed again, and began to break and flee.

Speaking of his regiment, the 14th Connecticut, Fiske wrote:

> Its position was in the center of the enemy's advance, and nowhere did the heaps of rebel dead lie thicker than in its front.[12]

"More than half a mile their front extends," Lieutenant Haskell recalled. Men turned "ashy white" as they looked on the Rebel advance. "Right on they move, as with one soul, in perfect order …"[13] The soldiers on the ridge had passed around extra ammunition and cannons were rolled up to the stonewall behind which the soldiers would fire. Haskell could see the Rebels headed directly for the two divisions of his corps arrayed on the ridge. The lieutenant, at a glance, knew he and his men were outnumbered. Also, a call for reinforcements, if assented to, could not get to the point of attack before the advance would overwhelm the ridge. Two II Corps divisions with their artillery would have to defeat the attack. General Gibbon wrote a quick note of General Meade, "The enemy is advancing his infantry in force upon my front."[14]

Men in an Alabama regiment were being aligned for the assault in the woods on Seminary Ridge by their brigade commander and it was remembered:

> …there were ominous shaking of heads among the boys as to the wisdom of the move, and expressions were heard on all sides to the effect that [the brigade commander] not satisfied with having lost half his brigade the day before, but was determined to sacrifice the 'whole caboodle' today.[15]

Colonel William Christian, who had written to his wife from Pennsylvania on June 28, and his 55th Virginia were positioned on the extreme left, or left flank, of the Confederate assaulting force. His regiment and another, the 47th Virginia, were under the temporary command of Colonel Robert Mayo and did not start forward with the rest of the force. It was later noted that the late start by these two regiments was because Colonel Mayo "could not be found to give the order to advance." Years later, Colonel Christian wrote that the command eventually went forward, but "We were a long ways behind, and had to run to catch up with the rest of the Brigade."[16] The two regiments caught up with its brigade as they struggled with the post and rail fence running along Emmitsburg Road. At the fence, or a short distance beyond it, Christian's men received a continuous hail of canister fired from Cemetery Hill. Standing within the Union position was Franklin Sawyer of the 8th Ohio Infantry. Sawyer later wrote that what was Colonel Christian and the two Virginia flanking regiments:

> … were at once enveloped in a dense cloud of smoke and dust. Arms, heads, blankets, guns, and knapsacks were thrown and tossed into the clear air. A moan went up from the field. Distinctly to be heard amid the storm of battle.

On the receiving side was a sergeant in the 55th Virginia who later said, "We could see it was useless …" And still later, "I feel no shame in recording that out of this corner the men without waiting for orders turned and fled, for the bravest soldiers cannot endure to be shot at simultaneously from the front and side." The 55th and 47th Virginia regiments retreated. Colonel Christian and others from the two regiments found some shelter in a ravine some distance further back, possibly near Emmitsburg Road. Later, either Christian or Mayo claimed the two regiments remained on the battlefield until what was left of the assault force returned.[17] The estimate on casualties for these two regiments for the action on July 3 is not known, but for all the three days of battle there were 97 casualties suffered by the two regiments out of an estimated total of 477 troops.[18]

The most effective munition employed as these Southern soldiers closed on the Federal lines was canister, a type of tin can filled with iron balls each about an inch, or an inch and a half, in diameter. Some guns were loaded with two canisters that when fired turned the cannons into massive shot guns, spewing iron that would rip through the lines of advancing troops, eviscerating some, severing limbs or simply blowing a huge hole through an infantryman, leaving many dead on the ground in the same order as they had been marching.

This munition was used all along the Union line as the Confederate assault advanced. At about 200 yards, Union rifle fire from infantry began; more attackers dropped. Union infantry on the flanks advanced and poured enfilading fire into the assault force as it passed. When the 14th opened with rifle fire, the barrels became so hot the soldiers could not reload and had to pour water from canteens on their rifles to cool them. The assault came to be known as Pickett's Charge, for the division commander that had been ordered to lead it. It is calculated in one recounting that 53 percent, or 2,669 men of General Pickett's division alone became casualties. The 13th Vermont, one of the regiments that advanced on the flank, had the Rebel columns then crossing in its front. E. F. Palmer was with his regiment:

Down the slope forty or fifty rods to the lowest spot between the contending batteries, about half way. Here in a strip of low brush they construct a small breastwork out of an old rail fence the best they can.[19]

Firing from Rebel artillery, coming at the Vermonters, overshot and the enemy was moving "directly in our front. They have marched but a short distance before the order comes, 'Fire, Fire!'" The "rebel line wavers and diverges to our right, staggering and falling rapidly from flank to flank." These troops are firing at the passing ranks of Rebels at about a 90-degree angle. The fire from the Vermonters was at close range and it was "poured into them, and before they have faced many volleys, the rebel column is broken to pieces … "how the 'rebs' jumped and staggered and 'tipped over' as we opened fire on them." The Rebel line broken, they are "… throwing down their arms, running into our line, some crying 'Don't fire, don't fire.'"[20] General Hays of II Corps later reported from his front:

When within 100 yards of our line of infantry, the fire of our men could no longer be restrained. Four lines rose from behind our stone wall, and before the smoke of our first volley had cleared away, the enemy, in dismay and consternation, were seeking safety in flight. Every attempt by their officers to rally them was vain … The angle of death alone can produce such a field as was presented.[21]

Palmer of the 2nd Vermont Brigade related, "The next morning I went" to where the enemy had advanced against the massed artillery, "and the mangled dead in long lines, showed how they came in triple columns." That day, Palmer penned a quick letter to Vermont, saying "I wrote you last when at Emmitsburg." The story of the battle should be in the newspapers; "I cannot describe the battle, only to say, that for more than fourteen hours both days, we were under fire."

Randolph Shotwell and the 8th Virginia had marched from near Cashtown that morning and now waited behind Seminary Ridge for the bombardment and then the order to advance. Some of the men chewed on whatever was in the haversack and "Others spread their blankets on the gravelly hillside, and stretched themselves for a nap. Everything looked quiet, dull and lazy,—as one sees the harvest-hands lolling under the trees at noontime." There was the artillery bombardment and then the order to move and align forward. And Shotwell remembered:

… ten regiments in front, and Armistead's five following, directly after. Colonel on horseback lead the way; behind them a moving wall of steel; at intervals of half a hundred yards, the red battle flags floating high above the bayonet-points; here and there an officer motioning with his sword to perfect the alignment, which, as a general thing, is as fine as on a holiday parade … Stirring the dry stubble into a cloud of dust as they move; the flags flutter and snap, the glaring sunlight gleams upon the burnished bayonets and officer's sword…

Then:

… a ponderous shell screams across the valley, striking the ground in front of the advancing line, bursts, and 'cuts a swath' of ten men out of a company. Four of them all flat on their faces, never more to rise, five or six others limp away to the rear, or lie moaning and groaning in agony.

The advancing line continues on:

Whizz-z! Whistles the grape-shot, and its crashing of bones tell that it has found a victim …

Once past Emmitsburg Road, Shotwell:

Looking up the slope, I see a dense blue line raising from behind the earthworks on the crest … For an instant sheen of the bright musket barrels contrast with the red clay of the works, and then all was hidden by the fearful, withering, blinding blaze that burst forth from the myriad muzzles … The slaughter can be imagined without any effort at word painting.[22]

Although the assault did succeed in momentarily getting over the stonewall and among the defenders on the ridge, most of these were captured in the ensuing struggle. Those left retreated, running, walking, limping or crawling back in the direction of Seminary Ridge. During that night and into the next day preparations for withdrawal, a return to Virginia, were set in motion by General Lee. It would take until July 15 and more fighting for this to be accomplished. The histories written soon after and those appearing a hundred or more years after, all will recognize the heroism of the Southern soldier in what was General Lee's last attempt for a complete victory over Union forces. If one or more, or a series of improbable, imponderables, had gone Lee's way, what may have been the result for his army and the Confederacy struggling and suffering as a newborn species in a world not really suited for it? The histories, some of them, would note that there would remain many more months of heroism and valor for the Army of Northern Virginia but ultimate defeat of it and the Confederacy it sought to sustain was now inevitable, the result of the battle at Gettysburg.

General George Pickett was never the same after the afternoon of July 3. He fought out the war until its last few days, his command being roundly defeated on April 1, 1865, at Five Forks, west of Petersburg, in the final surge by Grant and Sheridan to close out the war. He never could reconcile the pain of that day in July 1863 and Lee's ordering of the assault that later had his name attached to it. Pickett encountered General Lee as the surviving troops staggered back from Cemetery Ridge and the army commander called on him to reform his division in case there should be a counterattack. "General Lee," Pickett answered, "I have no division now." The bitterness remained. Some years after the war, when asked to accompany a friend to pay a courtesy call on General Lee, he did so, but reluctantly. The call was a brief one and uncomfortable and after Pickett remarked to his companion, "That old man had my division slaughtered at Gettysburg."[23]

That morning, as the massive assault on Cemetery Ridge was in preparation, there was significant fighting in the right of the Union line, on and around Culp's Hill. The noise and firing were heard by those on the ridge and commented on. The

150th New York Infantry was known as the Dutchess County regiment and it was in the thick of it. Several letters from participants were later published in the county's newspapers. An officer in the regiment wrote, presumably to the Poughkeepsie, New York, newspaper, of the action the regiment saw at Culp's Hill. It was dated "July 4, 8:20 a.m., in the Rifle Pits about a mile from Gettysburg. Bless the Lord, Oh my soul. I am safe and well! But oh! What a day was yesterday! July 3d will never be effaced from my memory!" The regiment stormed a breastwork occupied by Rebels and drove them out, and then "ordered to fire until relieved." The officer then remarked, "Our boys all did work splendidly ... The boys used about one hundred rounds each before we were relieved." But there had been return fire from the Rebels:

> Charles Howgate ... was struck with a shell on the top of his head ... He breathed only a few gasps, and all was over ... John P. Wing and Levi Rust ... were struck by the same ball, it going through John's breast and then striking Levi Rust. The latter fell at once. John looked up to me, I thought as much as to say 'That was close,' when he fell over on his hands and knees and settled down in death with only a groan.[24]

The regiment's chaplain, the Reverend T. E. Vasser, wrote to the local newspaper soon after the battle:

> The uniform testimony of those who witnessed the fight is that the Dutchess regiment deported itself nobly ... It stood without flinching under the hottest fire, and from the number of dead gathered up opposite that point on the following morning, there is reason to believe that they left their mark. Saturday night ... I superintended the burial of the dead of the 150th. Your readers doubtless know that we had seven killed. Close by the edge of the woods we dug their graves. The flicker of the dying campfires streamed up amid the deep darkness as we wrapped around our heroes their blankets for a winding sheet, and silently laid back the earth ... It lacked not much of midnight when we rounded up the last mound ...[25]

Another missive from the battlefield from a Dutchess county officer picks up the story on the night before the climatic day:

> We lay on our arms that night ... and at daylight the great battle of July 3 commenced. The roar of artillery and musketry was beyond description, but I suppose you have the details more fully from the papers than I can give them.

This officer's letter stops there and resumes on July 6 as the regiment is on the march in pursuit of the Lee and the Confederates:

> We got away from the battle-ground in good time, for the stench had already began to be sickening. Most of the dead men had been buried before we left, but the dead horses and mules lay thickly about ... You know my nerves are pretty strong. I always had a desire to witness a great battle; I have now seen one, and am satisfied not to see another ...[26]

Generations later the numbers resulting from these three days of battle at Gettysburg can cause a casual reader of history to stop, go back and read the sentences again. After commenting about the large barns of Pennsylvania farmers had on their property, George Benedict of the 12th Vermont Infantry years later noted, "Each of them was a field hospital; its floors covered with mutilated soldiers, and surgeons busy at the lantern-lighted operating tables."[27] In rounded numbers, of the three days of fighting, the Army of the Potomac sustained 23,000 casualties, close to 20 to 25 percent of the estimated total force engaged at Gettysburg. It was worse for Robert E. Lee's Army of Northern Virginia because it was the smaller of the two armies. It lost 28,000 or about 33 percent of its men, again an estimate based on the number Lee brought to the battle. Lieutenant Haskell wrote that a day or two after the battle, Union soldiers, "by count," buried 1,800 Confederate soldiers in the area in front of the stonewall defended by II Corps.[28]

The 13th Massachusetts had been lucky on July 3 and had been held in reserve most of the day. This is probably why the aftermath of the action on that day was recorded as it was in their regimental history. The men along the ridge were all cheering as the prisoners were gathered up and marched off:

> The army was boiling over with enthusiasm. It seemed as though the pent-up feeling of two long years had been suddenly released, so boisterous were its demonstrations. Everywhere in that much-abused army was expressed the wish to be led forth to finish up the bloody business.

However, on the next page of the regiment's history, referring to the absence of a counterattack late in the afternoon, the author remarked

> To our minds this seemed one of those moments when a Sheridan or a Stonewall Jackson might have annihilated Lee's army ... An opportunity such as the Army of the Potomac never had before nor after.

For the attitude of the 13th Massachusetts, it author says, "It was not so with us. There must be more slaughter, as if the gods were not already appeased."[29]

It took Calvin Haynes of the 125th New York Infantry until July 19 to get around to writing to his wife:

> Not having heard from you in a great while, I did not know but what you would like to hear whether I am dead or alive. I am enjoying good health at present. We have had an awful march and a terrible battle ... Our regt. lost 100 men in 10 minutes.

On July 3:

> At 2 p.m. they opened on us–with a 100 cannons. We lay flat on our faces for 2 hours ... The battery that lay in front of us had 44 horses and 80 men killed.[30]

Haynes then went on to tell his wife that he did not have the words to describe the battlefield the next day, but only that he never wanted to see another.

As twilight crept over the battlefield, the Union soldiers on top of Cemetery Ridge, from private to general, were exhausted. There were many, many Confederate dead from this day's assault and related fighting, a number too many for them to count in the growing darkness. The majority lay between Emmitsburg Road and the stone wall atop Cemetery Ridge. Tomorrow they could start the burying if those across the way didn't attack again. When he later walked the field, a soldier wrote:

> For the most part the dead were lying on their backs with wide-open expressionless eyes. In a few instances the features were drawn and distorted in a manner which gave an expression of great pain and horror.

Rufus Dawes of the 6th Wisconsin spoke of the casualties in a letter written two days after the battle:

> Our bravest and best are cold in the ground or suffer on beds of anguish … One young man, Corporal James Kelley of Company 'B,' shot through the breast, came staggering up to me before he fell and opened his shirt to show the wound, said, 'Colonel, won't you write to my folks that I died a soldier.'[31]

There were other dead too, many off to the east near Rummel's farm, to the west in and around the town of Fairfield and those to the south in the area in front of Big Round Top. It was cavalrymen that lay in these areas. While the great assault was in preparation, while it was happening, and after it was over, the cavalrymen had had their fights. The 2nd Cavalry Division had defeated an attempt by Jeb Stuart's cavalry force to strike into the rear of the Potomac army close to the Rummel farm. A regiment was sent on a probe in the direction of Fairfield and was turned back by a larger Confederate cavalry force. It is asserted by some that if an attack in that direction had gone forward in greater strength, serious damage might have resulted to the rear of Lee's force. To the south, under the slope of Big Round Top, the 1st Brigade of the 3rd Cavalry Division, in a useless and almost criminally ordered charge on fixed Rebel infantry and artillery positions, achieved nothing but lengthening the casualty list. As an example of the hold some incidents occurring during the war had on veterans, what many chose to later remember in writing, this cavalry action in the shadow of Big Round Top, known as Farnsworth's Charge, provides an excellent case in point. The charge was later named after the young general who led it, Brigadier General Elon Farnsworth, a general only since June 28. The charge was ordered by the 3rd Division's command, Brigadier General Judson Kilpatrick, Kill-cavalry, also promoted to command the 3rd Division on June 28. If he hadn't already earned that nickname, Kilpatrick did so late in the afternoon of July 3. Although all the regiments in Farnsworth's brigade suffered casualties during that afternoon, the 1st Vermont Cavalry took the most. By the best estimate, reported by the regiment's commander, Lt. Col. Addison W. Preston, the Green Mountain boys lost 67 troopers of which 14 were killed. The charge went forward at about 5pm with Farnsworth having no hope of success other than adding to the horrific number of casualties already sustained that day and no hope of materially contributing to the already won Union victory. Kilpatrick, a Civil War glory-seeker first class, by ordering it, deliberately cause the death of the leader of the charge and many others riding with him. In the decades to come, many survivors of the 3rd Cavalry Division, as well as many Confederates, would contribute their remembrance of that afternoon to the historiography of this one action. The most common recollections appeared in the *National Tribune* and *Confederate Veteran*, periodicals subscribed to by many of the war's veterans. By a rough count, at least 12 articles appeared in the *National Tribune*, and eight in *Confederate Veteran*, referring to this one action. These estimated numbers are derived from one excellent and authoritative book, *Gettysburg's Forgotten Cavalry Actions*, published in 2011, that devotes over half of its pages to a detailed study of Farnsworth's charge and its historiography. The articles and their numbers spoken of here are in addition to the pages devoted to Farnsworth that appeared in troopers' personal memoirs and recollections, regimental histories, and the letters written after the fact as well as the formal article most often referenced in the uncounted histories written about the events of July 3, the article by C. H. Parsons of the 1st Vermont Cavalry, "Farnsworth's Charge and Death," contained in *Battle and Leaders of the Civil War*.[32] Doubtless there are many other actions, of little or no contribution to the war's eventual outcome that, nevertheless, were preserved in ink by active, pen wielding veterans concerned with recording their past.

***

In the small farmhouse that was his headquarters, and by the dim light of a candle, George Meade wrote a dispatch to the army's general in chief, General Henry Halleck, and those in Washington that were no doubt desperate for news of the day's events. It was dated July 3, 8:35pm and was received in the capital on July 4, at 6:10am. A courier had to carry it from Meade's hand to the nearest telegraph to be sent. It can be assumed President Lincoln read it soon, if not immediately, after receipt. In his message, General Meade doesn't say he won the battle, only that the attack on his army on July 3 was "handsomely Repulsed":

> The loss upon our side has been considerable … At the present hour all is quiet. My cavalry have been engaged all day on both flanks of the enemy, harassing and vigorously attacking him with great success, notwithstanding they encountered superior numbers of both cavalry and infantry. The army is in fine spirits.

In that Meade was with the force on Cemetery Hill and Ridge all day, only General Pleasonton could have provided the words about the cavalry's action on that day. As for the accuracy, only the action on the right flank by the 2nd Cavalry Division can be labeled a Union victory.[33]

When it was getting dark, the 13th Massachusetts was ordered to send a lieutenant and 50 men out to form a skirmish line near the fence running along Emmitsburg

Road, connecting with other lines from other regiments on its right and left. Lieutenant Edward Rollins of the 13th was in charge and later recorded the ground was covered with bodies as they moved forward and:

> Arriving at the rail fence, we saw beyond a pile of dead and wounded, struck as they exposed themselves clambering over, while on the charge.

Then there was the noise coming from the rear of the line set out by Rollins:

> The whole night a wounded and probably insane rebel, in the rear of the skirmish line, walked back and forth like a sentinel, singing religious hymns, in a clear, calm voice, and paid no attention to requests' to keep quiet.

Another unit ordered out on the picket line that night came from the brigade commanded by Regis de Trobriand of III Corps. He remembered the portion of the field covered by his men:

> The greater part of the dead were terribly lacerated, for it was here particularly that the artillery had done its dreadful work. There were the dead, with heads carried away, breasts torn open, limbs gone, entrails protruding on the ground.[34]

***

Suddenly it is 30 years later. Former general Daniel E. Sickles, III Corps Commander when he first arrived on the battlefield, is speaking before an assembled crowd of veterans returning to Gettysburg for the dedications of regimental monuments and a huge column overlooking the 861 graves of the fallen from New York State. Dan Sickles, the politician, had been instrumental in getting the monuments placed and the dedication ceremonies scheduled. His negligent deployment of III Corps on the afternoon of July 2 cost the lives of many more men than would otherwise have been the case. This day, Sickles was saying that the many New Yorkers distributed through his corps on July 2 "… sustained the many fierce combats that ended in the final repulse of the enemy on the left flank" of the Union army. He was speaking of the fighting on July 2 in his then area of responsibility. His words might be construed as glossing over the facts to a certain degree, For Sickles maintained his positioning of the troops under his command that day actually led to the Union victory at Gettysburg, despite anything George Meade may have done, either before or subsequently. Perhaps inadvertently, Sickles, later in his oration, noted a fact he thought relevant at the time that reflected on the public position he hoped to maintain for himself regarding the battle. "There is a day and an hour in the life of every nation when its fate hangs on the issue of a battle," he told the assembled veterans, and "such a day and hour—thirty years ago—was the crisis of the battle of Gettysburg on the afternoon of the 2d day of July 1863." Then he added that darkness closed the fighting during which the killed and wounded for July 2 "were larger than on the 1st and 3rd combined."[35] Sickles was correct, but he never admitted, perhaps even to himself, that it was he who was largely responsible for the numbers being what they were.

In 1893, Dan Sickles, the politician, was chairman of the New York State Monuments Commission, one of whose missions was to "supervise the design and execution" of the 83 monuments on the battlefield commemorating New York commands that fought at Gettysburg, as well as seeing that these 19th century carvings and sculptures "shall not be deemed unworthy of the culture and art of the epoch in which we live." Sickles also used his dedication address to advocate that the battlefield be made a National Park. This was accomplished two years later with Sickles, as a congressman, successfully having legislation passed making a greater portion of the battlefield a National Military Park.[36] Fully aware his audience was almost all veterans and from New York, Sickles added a paragraph to his remarks that he knew was close to all veterans and their families. This was on the sensitive subject of pensions for the veterans and widows. Although the figure he cites may not be totally accurate, it is the second half of the sentence Sickles wanted remembered. "We give more than $100,000,000 a year to the soldiers of our wars," he says, "and let no man be chosen to rule over us who will take a dollar from the pension of a worthy veteran. (Applause.)"[37] Veterans' pensions had, in elections previously, played a significant role among the electorate eligible to receive, or trying to receive, them.

Lieutenant William Wheeler was not there the day Dan Sickles spoke before the monument. He had commanded an artillery section, had fought at Gettysburg with XI Corps and a month later was still speaking about the battle, in one form or another, in his many letters. On August 4, near the banks of the Rappahannock, he wrote:

> You see, dearest mother, this war has become the religion of very many of our lives, and those of us who think, and who did not enter the service for gain ... have come more and more to identify this cause for which we are fighting, with all of good and religious in our previous lives, and so it must be if we are to win the victory.

Then later, but within the same letter, he said that during the battle:

> The captain of the other battery ... would not believe that they were not our own men at first, although their blood-red battle-flag was plain enough in sight and at last asked me, 'Wheeler, which are the rebels and which are our men?' Whereupon I retorted ... 'you pays your money and you takes your choice.' Somehow or other I felt a joyous exaltation, a perfect indifference to circumstances, through the whole of the three days' fight, and have seldom enjoyed three days more in my life ...[38]

For perhaps a majority of the men who were there during those three days of July, Gettysburg would be the moment around which everything else in their lives would revolve. For Robert E. Lee, he would never again have the offensive power he had possessed on Wednesday morning as his men marched out of mist along Chambersburg Pike to confront Buford's troopers. For the general and his Army of Northern Virginia the next 21 months would be a gradual descent to ultimate defeat, all the while showing himself a master of defense, capable of bleeding his enemy enormously, and thus prolonging the war all the while. The fighting to follow and the numbers would prove this.

***

Some of those that survived the war and who had witnessed the massed Confederate attack during the afternoon of July 3 would, as the years passed, desire to leave to others a picture as clear and correct as their memories could provide. These memories as they put them on paper were a commitment to the truth as they recalled it from where they had stood that summer afternoon. Their degree of success can only be measured by what historians have taken and done with these remembrances.

CHAPTER EIGHT

Pursuit to the Potomac

In the years to come the controversy would center around whether the pursuit of Lee's army to the Potomac River by General Meade and his army was as fast and as energetic enough to have enabled it to confront the Confederate force and destroy it before it was able to get over the river. That this did not happen, and the ensuing blame, inevitably fell on George Meade. Whether it all was something of which the Army of the Potomac was capable of doing after having fought at Gettysburg and having sustained the casualties it did, is a question debated among historians, beginning with those of the 19th century that had at hand the near-contemporary recollections of the actors in the events as well as personal memories of it. Generations of subsequent historians, down to the present, still discussed whether it was possible and the inherent "what ifs." The telegraphic exchange cited above clearly shows the president considered it achievable, then and days later. The often-quoted letter Lincoln wrote to Meade and never sent, says, essentially what the president believed at the time; to have closed on Lee above the river and wreck or destroy his army would probably have ended the war. General Meade, obviously, took exception, while many under his command at the time thought otherwise.

The army of the Potomac moved from Gettysburg and moved slowly, but still desirous of catching Lee's army before it got over the Potomac River. Captain Richard Auchmuty of V Corps scribbled a quick note to his mother soon after the battle:

> A merciful Providence has preserved me through another battle, and for a second time I have seen a battle-field after the fight was over.

Captain Auchmuty, after the battle, prevented Gettysburg residents from wandering over the field in his area of responsibility, it all being too horrid for the civilians, although he had no liking for the people he had encountered in Pennsylvania. "The people here are all Pennsylvania Dutch, and being mostly Copperheads," he wrote. Of the hungry Union soldiers, "the soldiers help themselves in spite of orders to the contrary." Once across the river and into Maryland, Auchmuty was in a better frame of mind:

> I am Glad to be in Maryland, as the Pennsylvania Dutch are a hard set. The Marylanders are Americans, live in a land of plenty, and are either friendly or subdued.[2]

John Buford and the bulk of the 1st Cavalry Division were on the road to Taneytown during the afternoon of July 2. In the late afternoon, the day's great battle was being waged and not to be concluded until twilight had settled over the summer countryside south of Gettysburg. If allowed to stand by itself, the inconclusive battle of July 2 would be counted among the largest clashes of the war. Thousands had been killed or wounded. The next day, July 3, the day that seared the battle into the collective memory of the nation, made it the turning point of the war, and later caused the president to praise those that fell as offering up their last full measure of devotion, was when General John Buford and his division reached Westminster, Maryland.

At a point late in the day, July 3, with the Rebel attacking force back within its lines on Seminary Ridge and only random shots being exchanged between the contending armies, Robert E. Lee decided to end his army's sojourn in Pennsylvania. The fighting that day had clearly decided the issue in the Union's favor and now, for the defeated, retiring to Virginia without further loss was essential. Lee and his men would have to return to the crossing point on the Potomac River they had used when marching north. It would be a difficult maneuver. The wounded that could travel were loaded into wagons for the journey. Other wagons, carrying the army's remaining ammunition and essential equipment, had to be organized and started south. Then there were the wagons carrying the supplies appropriated by the troops from the well-tended Pennsylvania landscape. All these had to be saved. The infantry and artillery, seriously depleted during three days of intense combat, had to maintain unit cohesion and march to, and get over, the Potomac, specifically at Williamsport and Falling Waters, Maryland.

On this Friday night, Lee called to his headquarters Brigadier General John D. Imboden, commander of an independent cavalry brigade that had been guarding the army's supply trains as the climatic action of that day went forward. Imboden remembered:

> I shall never forget his language, his manner, and his appearance of mental suffering. He invited me into his tent, and as soon as we were seated he remarked, 'We must now return to Virginia. As many of our poor wounded as possible must be taken home. I have sent for you, because your men and horses are fresh and in good condition, to guard and conduct our train back to Virginia. The duty will be arduous, responsible, and dangerous, for I am afraid you will be harassed by the enemy's cavalry. How many men have you?'

General Imboden answered that he had 2,100 men and a six-gun battery. After his personal briefing, orders were written out by Lee's staff and 17 additional pieces of artillery were added to Imboden's brigade.[3]

Throughout the remainder of the night and into the next day the great column of wounded was organized, the supply trains assembled, their routes of retreat mapped out. At about noon on July 4, thunder and lightning began hammering the scene, then the rain, coming down "in blinding sheets." Imboden watched from beside the road leading to Cashtown as the column began its journey. He, or one of his subordinates, estimated the train to be 17 miles long. It wasn't to stop until it reached Williamsport. It rained, with accompanying sound and fury, all night turning the way to the Potomac into a swamp. The next afternoon, and despite some harassment by a small detachment of Union cavalry with the inevitable loss of a portion of the wagons, a victory of sorts was won by Imboden; his command and those suffering in the wagons began rolling into Williamsport.

If he hadn't already suspected as much, on arriving at the river, Imboden was confronted with the consequences of the rain that had been drenching this part of Pennsylvania, not only the day before, but periodically for weeks. The torrential rain had caused the river to be at least 10 feet above the level where a man, a horse or a wagon could ford. The pontoon bridge spanning the river that Lee's engineers had put in place on their way north had been burned by Federal cavalry from Harpers Ferry on July 4. Getting his command over the river to Virginia quickly was impossible until the water level dropped. There were, however, two small ferries at Williamsport and those were pressed into constant service. The wounded that were able to walk were sent over on the ferries and told to start walking to Winchester.[4]

***

At Westminster, on July 4, there was a moment for troopers to rest themselves and their horses. A trooper in the 8th New York noted in his diary:

> Here I am writing to you on a piece of hard tack box. Now about the battle. I can say it is the hardest fight I was ever in, and I suppose the reason we were called away on the second day was that ourselves and horses had lived for five days on two days' rations; but we did well enough, for we bought bread and butter, and had plenty of coffee and sugar …

As this trooper wrote, orders found their way to John Buford and his 1st Division. It is probable the orders were written when it became known, or at least suspected, that Lee and his army were leaving the Gettysburg vicinity. The 8th New York trooper added while at Westminster, "we are anxiously awaiting news from the front, and the battle was raging yesterday with fury."[5] Possibly with the orders for Buford came news of the Union victory of the day before. At Westminster, Buford's command was the Federal force nearest to the river crossing point that Lee would use. The orders directed Buford to Frederick, Maryland, about 25 miles southwest, but still more than 20 miles from Williamsport. One of Buford's troopers later remembered, "The regiment moved, July 4, 1863, from camp, four miles in the direction of Frederick, and bivouacked for the night. A very rainy time."[6]

Orders were also directed to Judson Kilpatrick, commanding the 3rd Cavalry Division, in position to the south of the Gettysburg battlefield early on July 4. He and his division were to move southwest, toward Emmitsburg and then to Monterey Pass. There, during the night of July 4/5, Kilpatrick's division caught a retreating wagon convoy, wrecked it, and took hundreds of prisoners. General David Gregg's 2nd Cavalry Division was sent individually by brigades after the retiring components of Lee's force.

When Buford's request to refit his division away from the battlefield on the morning of July 2 was approved by Generals Pleasonton and Meade, he was told to go to the army's forward supply base at Westminster. There, late on July 3 and into July 4, rations were drawn, the horse unsaddled and cared for. The shoes of many of the horses were looked after and, of course, expended ammunition was replaced. Troopers quickly washed their shirts and hung them, hoping they would dry before it started to rain again. While they went about their tasks, and with Gettysburg 30 miles distant, a sound, a rumbling cannonade, the roar from a distant wild animal, caught the ears of the men and the general on Friday afternoon. The battle was joined.

After stopping along the way for some sleep, the division got to Frederick on July 5 and went into bivouac. The road to Frederick was slop from the rain that had fallen during the afternoon and evening of the 4th, yet somewhere along the way a citizen approached Buford, described as a Dutchman, the owner of a prosperous nearby mill. The man wanted Buford to speak to the contradictory rumors then circulating through the countryside. Were the Union forces beaten and retreating or was it the Rebels? Buford told the citizen the truth as he knew it; the Rebels were retreating after a good beating. Seeing the mill owner was pleased, Buford was quick to capitalize. The Dutchman offered Buford whatever flour and grain he needed for the hundreds of men and horses standing behind him. No doubt the citizen was thanked in the most sincere terms as the general gave the signal. Troopers were quickly into the mill helping themselves. Buford wrote out a voucher for the amount of goods his men took so at some point the owner would be reimbursed by Washington. The owner, glad to know the Rebels were leaving Maryland, refused payment. On Buford's command, the division spread out in the area around the mill, started fires and cooked buckwheat cakes and fed the horses.[7]

When everyone had eaten, the division continued toward Frederick. The condition of the road caused by the rain made many troopers in the column dismount and walk with their horses. Still, many horses simply gave out. Finally, Buford had to call a halt in order to save further loss in horses. He was about five miles from Frederick; but the mud seemed to pose a greater threat to his command than any Rebel force he was likely to encounter. The column dismounted and the majority of the men fell asleep where they landed, too tired to care.

An interesting incident occurred during this roadside stop, one that foretells what the rebellion would become in the year to follow. A man of about 60 years old came into Buford's camp. A supposed peddler of songbooks, he had been under suspicion the previous year when the command had ridden in Maryland because of his persistent questions about military movements. As related by one cavalry historian:

> The old man found Buford sitting on a log. True to form, he began asking Buford questions about his camp and the Federal army. After listening silently for a few moments, Buford called out his provost marshal, Lt. John Mix, and told him simply, 'Arrest this man, he is a spy.'
>
> The peddler, William Richardson, was grabbed by several staffers and thoroughly searched. Detailed drawings of Federal troop dispositions, passes from both Lee and Longstreet, and large sums of Confederate and Federal money were all found sewn into his clothing. For the first time, Buford looked up from his log and stared Richardson in the eyes. 'You have three minutes to pray.'
>
> Buford was well within his authority to carry out drumhead courts marshal [sic] and perform executions in the field according to a Congressional act passed in March 1863. After the tense three minutes expired, while Richardson begged for his life, Buford ordered he be hanged.

A tent rope, a nearby tree, the shuffling of the executioners and the condemned and the deed was done. "Buford never got up from his log, nor stopped smoking his pipe, while the man was being executed," one of the witnesses noted.[8] The spy hung from the tree for several days with a sign attached warning other potential Confederate agents to beware.

Brigadier General Wesley Merritt and his brigade of regulars had joined Buford after marching from Gettysburg where they had seen action near Kilpatrick on July 3. Reunited, the 1st Division was again composed of three brigades. Buford had his orders to harass and prevent, if possible, Lee and his army from crossing the Potomac. Beyond Frederick, the division passed through Middletown, climbed over South Mountain and entered the village of Boonsboro before approaching Williamsport. Along the march to Williamsport, many wagons and battalions of prisoners were encountered, all headed in the opposite direction. These were the spoils resulting from Kilpatrick and his division overtaking a retreating supply train in Monterey Pass and on the road that descended into the Cumberland Valley to the west. A trooper with Buford, known only as Charlie, later wrote of an encounter along the road that day. The command:

> … met an infantry guard coming in with nearly 1,000 prisoners, and such a starved lot of men I never saw. We shared our [hard] tack with them, and they said we were the best lot of fellows they had met. One old haired man said, 'You are in good fighting condition boys, if I am a judge.'[9]

It was July 6 and while still a distance from Williamsport, Buford's advance met Rebel pickets. Skirmishing began and soon after it grew into a serious engagement. General Imboden had done an excellent job navigating the wagon train under his command to the river without serious loss, getting there with time to establish a defensive position, but the good work he had done might be negated if this Yankee cavalry force wasn't driven away, or at least held off until the leading elements of Confederate infantry got to the vicinity.

What had delayed Buford—indeed, had played a role in every engagement in the retreat from Gettysburg—were the roads, the condition of which is spoken of by every contemporary source that at all touch on this aspect of the campaign. "You know the country well enough to tell me whether it ever quits raining about here?" General Lee asked a subordinate. "If so, I should like to see a clear day soon." Lee is reported to have spoken these lines "laughingly."[10] However, one cannot avoid thinking the general was frustrated to the point where only an attempt at humor would relieve it. The roads were converted by rain into mud, rain in near biblical proportions transformed mud into bottomless, never-ending quagmires that inhibit movement of any kind; can swallow a horse or sink a wagon to its floorboards. The weather in June and July of this year was expected to be hot and humid, as it always is, but the rain, its frequency and amount, was beyond anything in living memory. General Lee, whatever his mood relative to the atmospherics, and therefore the road and river, had been hoping for a positive answer from the subordinate. The record is blank as to any answer he might have received.

The participants, the soldiers on both sides, endured conditions that we today might consider intolerable or impossible. But we have the written record and the testimony of those that were there, and one can only be impressed by their ability to endure and carry forward the orders of their superiors. One cavalryman described the road as being "… one immense hogwallow the entire distance." Translated, this trooper meant he was moving in at least ankle-deep mud that sapped his strength and eventually that of his horse.[11] The soldiers and horse-drawn vehicles and weapons were so impeded by road conditions that the retreat after the great battle probably took more days than otherwise would have been the case in dry conditions. One might speculate on what might have been if the movement of the contending forces had not faced mud-filled roads and a swollen river.

As for events as they unfolded, and despite what had transpired at Gettysburg, the retreat of the Army of Northern Virginia to the Potomac and its eventual escape under these conditions could arguably be considered one of General Lee's finest field performances. This is said despite Lee's considerable head start from the battlefield. In this retrograde movement, two of Lee's subordinates stand out for special mention. General John Imboden, along with his cavalry command, proved more than competent in leading the innumerable wounded from Gettysburg to Williamsport and to within sight of Virginia in relative safety. The other Rebel acting in a supporting role, as well as a redemptive one, was Lee's prodigal cavalry commander, General Jeb Stuart. Absent for days before the battle at Gettysburg and leaving Lee lacking accurate information as to the position and strength of his adversary, Stuart's performance during the retreat can only be considered one of his more commendable contributions to the Army of Northern Virginia. His proactive screening of his army's movement during the retreat and the intensity of his spoiling attacks on Union cavalry bent on preventing Lee's escape is an effort most often underrated, if not ignored, when the Gettysburg campaign is discussed.

Once at Williamsport, John Imboden and his cavalry force, augmented by a thrown together force of teamsters and walking wounded armed with rifles carried from Gettysburg, were able to stymie the July 6 attack by Buford's cavalry division. Imboden had adequate warning of Buford's approach and posted his men and guns on high ground covering the lines of approach to the town. The approximate 700 teamsters were organized into 100-man companies "officered by wounded line-officers" where possible. At about 1:30pm, as the cavalry approached on the roads coming from both Hagerstown and Boonsboro, the Rebels opened with artillery and small arms. Buford quickly put his horse artillery battery into action, and just as quickly some of the 23 guns Imboden had dragged from Gettysburg ran out of ammunition. Luck was with the Rebels this day, though. Two wagons with artillery ammunition, driven from Winchester, had been ferried across to Williamsport, arriving just in time. It was this ammunition and the skill of the artillerymen, along with the mixed Rebel command of cavalry, wagon drivers and wounded, that held Buford and his command at bay. However, there was one disgruntled participant, not fully cogniscent of the deployment of forces or the dire situation. This member of the Texas Brigade later inaccurately recalled:

> … just as the Yankees were fairly on the run, General Imboden came creeping up with a brigade of Confederate Cavalry, and, without a blow to win them, coolly appropriated all the honors of the engagement.

During the fight, Imboden received a message from Fitzhugh Lee at the head of this cavalry brigade, encouraging him to hold for another 30 minutes, by which time he and his troopers would be in a position to help him.[12]

A trooper in the 9th New York Cavalry of Devin's brigade, when he wrote his reminiscences, didn't devote much ink to the encounter at Williamsport. Late in the afternoon, July 6, a:

> … sharp fight with the Confederate cavalry. The 3rd Indiana of Buford's Division charged and captured 27 wagons and 46 prisoners. The skirmishing continued till after dark and the Division remained saddled all night, the men lying by their horses.[13]

Probably because Devin's brigade was in reserve during the action, the fighting that day made little impression on this trooper.

The action and the details of the fighting are as vague and lacking in detail as are most after action reports written after the fact and encompassing events covering many days in the field. The historian desires as much detail as possible, so that an event may be recreated on a page of his history, but more often than not the historian working with Civil War material must work with quickly drawn overviews of what happened. In most cases then, the descriptions and detail needed to draw a full picture are lacking and therefore our view of the picture is hazy. Sometimes, much later, some detail of an event might be included in some veteran's reminiscence that, if able to be verified, adds color to the story, might be sewn into the fabric of the event's history. The officer ordered to write a report of his unit's activities that cover several days, in most cases, would rather be doing something else in the limited free time between active operations. Therefore, the barest essentials are committed to paper and near the end the names of a few are mentioned for meritorious or invaluable service. One can only admire the skill, craft, the art and dedication of those historians that have scoured scanty sources in years past and produced narratives, the roots of which lie in the *Official Record* and personal testimony of those that lived the event.

Because of his brigade's reserve status, Tom Devin, in his report, only detailed, essentially, the deployment of his command for the next 18 hours. Of riding into the Williamsport area, he wrote:

> I found our batteries engaging the enemy, supported by parts of the First and Reserve brigades, a part of which were also dismounted and engaged with the enemy's infantry. I was ordered to mass my brigade in the woods in the rear of the position and await instructions.

After an indeterminate amount of time had passed, Devin detailed what orders Buford gave him:

> At 7 P.M. I was ordered to relieve the 1st Brigade, then engaged on the left front, and at dark to retire my command again to the woods, which I was to hold until daylight, to enable the other brigades to return on a suitable position near the cross-roads. Retiring as ordered, I withdrew my skirmishers to a line 500 yards in advance of my position, and connecting with the woods at the same distance on each flank, completely covering the road. I had previously strongly picketed the roads in rear toward Sharpsburg on the left and Hagerstown of the right. Lieutenant Blunt, of the Sixth New York, whom I had sent to the right to reconnoiter, ascertained the presence

of a strong force of infantry and artillery in close proximity to my right flank. The enemy's skirmishers also commenced to feel their way on my left.

About midnight, the enemy advanced on my front, and engaged the skirmishers. He was repulsed, and soon after retired. Our loss was Captain Van Buren, Sixth New York, 2 sergeants, and 1 private.

Just at daybreak [July 7], I made a demonstration on the enemy's front by charging down a squadron of the Sixth New York, driving in his skirmishers and pickets on the reserve, and throwing them in confusion under cover of which movement I withdrew the main body 1 mile to the rear, and took up a position in front of the road running from Hagerstown to Sharpsburg. I then withdrew my skirmishers from the front and the pickets from the roads, and retiring slowly, the enemy followed very cautiously, and halting when my rear guard face about. After retiring about 2–3 miles, I was ordered to halt, rest men and horses, strongly picket the roads to the rear, and, if possible, hold the position until the division had crossed Antietam Creek.[14]

Colonel Gamble's 1st Brigade was more actively involved in the engagement of July 6 in front of Williamsport. The colonel's report gives the essentials as he thought them to be in his report:

This brigade was ordered to engage the enemy on the left of the Boonsborough [sic] road, near Williamsport, the Reserve Brigade being on the right of the road. The Third Indiana was ordered to capture and destroy a train of seven wagons of the enemy on our left, on Downsville road, which was successfully accomplished, making prisoners of the drivers and those in charge of the train. The brigade was then placed in line of battle, and three-fourths of it dismounted to drive in the enemy's skirmishers; and Tidball's battery of four guns, placed in position, supported by the balance of the mounted men, opened on the enemy, many times our superior in numbers, and did excellent execution; the dismounted men in the meantime, keeping up a sharp carbine fire, drove in the rebel pickets on their reserve. The dismounted men were under the immediate command of the gallant and lamented Major Medill, 8th Illinois Cavalry, who fell mortally wounded.

We held our position until dark, and were then relieved by Colonel Devin's brigade, and ordered to fall back to Jones' Cross-Roads; in the direction of Boonsborough [sic], which we reached about midnight, the delay being caused by Kilpatrick's division having been driven back in confusion from the direction of Hagerstown, completely blocking the road in our rear, making it impassable for several hours.[15]

The reports of the two brigade commanders were written within weeks of the events described. Realistically, some events were not included simply because the officers did not recall them from memory in the rush to finish the report and get it off their desks or they were unaware of some incidents altogether. Neither report mentions the approach of Fitz Lee and his brigade to Imboden's support. Both say darkness forced their withdrawal. Imboden credits the movement of the teamster-trooper companies from place to place during the fighting making it appear to Buford and his men that there were many more Rebels than there really were. The Rebel commander admitted later that he never had more than 3,000 men committed to the action and that the 23 guns with ammunition made the difference in the fight. In addition, during and after the fight, 4,000 Union prisoners were ferried over the Potomac and started on the way to Richmond.[16]

William Herrmance of Company C, 6th New York, in a recollection written decades later recalled:

> Strangely circumstance will work together.

While riding toward Gettysburg with the 1st Division, the command stopped at Boonsboro and:

> … the Union sentiment was shown by the young girls giving flowers to our soldiers, and I was favored by receiving a bunch, with a small American flag, from a young lady, in front of whose house I had stopped. About ten days later, in an engagement there, I was wounded and carried to the same house where this young lady lived, and after the surgeons cut the bullet from my breast, she gave me all the care a sister could until I was able to go home, but it did not end as such events should, for I have not seen her since, but often look at the faded flowers and flag given me, with pleasant remembrance of the care and kindness of Annie Wecker.[17]

***

There had been cavalry actions in the countryside surrounding Williamsport, Hagerstown and Boonsboro of varying sizes and levels of intensity every day for the past six. The seven infantry corps of the Army of the Potomac were in position to cross a no man's land in front of Lee's defensive enclave, bayonets fixed. General Lee, in random moments, may have wished George Meade would order it so that July 3 could be replayed with roles reversed. George Meade was aware of this when he called his corps commanders together on the evening of July 12. Meade was under significant pressure. General Henry Halleck—a synonym for Lincoln—far to the rear in Washington, was encouraging the army commander to attack and finish Lee and his army on the north side of the river. Obviously, Halleck was remote from the precise problems facing the army commander, the risks, the danger, the blood and, of course, what to do in the immediate aftermath of failure. Meade had Lee in his front and Halleck at his back. It would not be Halleck who would be relieved of command after a failed Union assault on Robert E. Lee.

George Meade knew he had won a significant victory at Gettysburg, the importance of which he had as yet fully to gauge from a national perspective because of his ongoing responsibilities with an army still in the field and maneuvering. He was, however, aware that whatever benefit to the Union, large or small, the victory at Gettysburg engendered, it all could be lost if he was in turn defeated by General Lee before an obscure town in Maryland. Handling, for its day, a massive army in a trying and difficult pursuit of the enemy, the weather and road conditions were only two of his problems. Each new telegraphic message from Washington spoke to him in a not too oblique manner that he had better finish the job and fast. And Williamsport was close enough to Washington that important visitors could show up, one being the vice-president, not here to interfere, mind you.

Despite this, Meade, with everything with which he had to deal, was exhibiting exemplary management skill, skill from someone whose elevation to this level of command could be counted in days, not months. On July 7, Meade was informed the president had authorized his promotion to brigadier general in the regular army for the victory in Pennsylvania. Within hours he received Halleck's encouragement from Washington, "You gave the enemy a stunning blow at Gettysburg. Follow up, and give him another before he reaches the Potomac." Later the same day, and again from Halleck, "Push forward, and fight Lee before he can cross the Potomac." And still later the same day, when the news about the fall of Vicksburg reached Washington, Lincoln himself, through Halleck, was adding his encouragement. "Now, if General Meade can complete his work, as gloriously prosecuted thus far, by the literal and substantial destruction of Lee's army, the rebellion will be over. A. Lincoln."[18] On July 10, Meade told his wife in a letter:

> I am of the opinions that Lee is in a strong position and determined to fight before he crosses the river. I believe if he had been able to cross when he first fell back, that he would have done so, but his bridges being destroyed, he had been compelled to make a stand, and will of course make a desperate one.

Lieutenant Colonel Dawes of the 6th Wisconsin gave his opinion in a letter dated July 21:

> General Meade did wisely in not attacking General Lee in his entrenched position ... I examined the rebel fortifications ... and I think General Meade would have certainly failed to carry them by direct assault.

The Rebels:

> ... were worn out and tired as we were, but their cartridge boxes had plenty of ammunition, and they would have quietly lain in their rifle pits and shot us down with the same coolness and desperation they showed at Gettysburg.[19]

Washington wanted an attack, now while the river was swollen. On July 8, having digested the encouragement from Washington, Meade replied with carefully chosen words, trying to alert his superior officer, as well as Lincoln, of what Halleck should have known as a matter of course:

> Be assured I most earnestly desire to try the fortunes of war with the enemy on this side of the river, hoping ... to settle the question, but I should do wrong not to frankly tell you of the difficulties encountered. I expect to find the enemy in a strong position well covered with artillery and I do not desire to imitate his example at Gettysburg and assault a position where the chances were so greatly against success.

Meade finished again referring to the chances, good and bad:

> I wish in advance to moderate the expectations of those, who, in ignorance of the difficulties to be encountered, may expect too much. All I can do under the circumstances I pledge this army to do.[20]

Now on July 12, with all his troops in position, his corps commanders with him, Meade spoke of attacking the next morning, despite or because of the telegraphic noise from Washington. When told of the next day's operation, Meade subordinates exhibited less enthusiasm than he thought should be the case. There was a discussion and then a vote. Five of the nine generals were against an attack. It was decided to further examine the enemy's position the next day, deferring the attack decision for a day. Of course, the commanding general could have overruled these generals, but George Meade respected these men, perhaps because just a handful of days before he had been one of them. These subordinate commanders retained in their memory, as Meade did, the events of only nine days previous. A massive infantry assault, no matter how well prepared and supported with artillery, proceeding uphill against a well-entrenched force, would produce casualties on a scale so large that the attack might fail. A similar attack nine days before had failed, not to mention the affair the previous December at Fredericksburg. It all looked too familiar to these generals, too much like the reverse of the Gettysburg coin. These generals, Meade's subordinates, were not squeamish men lacking in courage or zeal for the cause. Nor were they averse to spilling blood. They were experienced, conservative veterans, not inclined to wager the loss of the nation's most prized possession—the Army of the Potomac—on the single turn of an event over which they would have no control once they ordered forward their regiments, brigades and divisions.

A diarist in the 8th New York scribbled for July 12, while he waited for the commander to order an attack, "we laid in camp all day in sight of the enemy's pickets. Had a terrible rain storm."[21] Meade took another look at what he faced on a rainy July 13. At 5pm he notified Halleck:

> Upon calling the army corps commanders together and submitting the question to them, five of them were unqualifiedly opposed to it. Under these circumstances, in view of the momentous consequences attendant upon a failure to succeed I did not feel myself authorized to attack until after I had made more careful examination of the enemy's position, strength, and defensive works. These examinations are now being made. So far as completed, they show the enemy to be strongly intrenched [sic] on a ridge running from the rear of Hagerstown past Downsville to the Potomac. I shall continue these reconnaissance with the expectation of finding some weak point, upon which, if I succeed, I shall hazard an attack.[22]

Henry Halleck immediately telegraphed back:

> Washington, D.C., July 13, 1863—9:30 P.M.
> Maj. Gen. George G. Meade,
> Army of the Potomac
>   Yours of 5 p.m. is received. You are strong enough to attack and defeat the enemy before he can affect a crossing. Act upon your own judgment and make your generals execute your orders. Call no councils of war. It is proverbial the Councils of war never fight. Re-enforcements [sic] are pushed on as rapidly as possible. Do not let the enemy escape.
>   H. Halleck, General-in-Chief.

No doubt considering things as they were, and as they were desired in Washington, and without further discussion, Meade ordered a reconnaissance in force to go forward the next morning, July 14. At 11am Meade telegraphed Halleck:

> On advancing my army this morning, with a view of ascertaining the exact position of the enemy and attacking him if the result of the examination should justify me, I found, on reaching his lines, that they were evacuated. I immediately put my army in pursuit, the cavalry in advance. At this period my forces occupy Williamsport, but I have not yet heard from the advance on Falling Waters, where it is reported he crossed his infantry on a bridge. Your instructions as to further movements in case the enemy are entirely across the river, are desired."[23]

It was George Meade's misfortune—perhaps plain back luck—that during the night of July 13/14, Robert E. Lee, at not only his most skillful but also at his most lucky, slipped away. A trooper in Buford's division remembered that on July 14, "… we found the enemy's earthworks evacuated. They had just left, and their fires were all burning."[24]

While it had been raining in the days pervious and the river still too high to ford, Lee's engineers had constructed another pontoon bridge, salvaging what remained of the previous one and cannibalizing homes and warehouses in town to build the remainder. The engineers built 16 pontoon boats in two days while the connecting pieces and flooring was fabricated. Kettles taken from homes were used to boil tar to be used as a sealant for the boats. While this went forward, the ferry made up to 70 crossings of the river each day. The wounded, some wagons and the Union prisoners all were sent south, and some supplies brought up. When the rain lessened, and the water level began to drop, Lee could start his men across.[25]

The view from among the soldiers that would meet any advance on Lee's defensive position was summarized by one Rebel cavalryman. Luther Hopkins remembered:

> … the whole northern army gathered in our front and threatened us with destruction, but they seemed to be about as afraid of us as we were of them; for instead of attacking us, they began to throw up breastworks.

An artilleryman with Stuart's cavalry commented on the situation as he saw it on July 12. He observed:

> General Lee's army is still in line, with breastworks thrown up along the front. The Yankee army is in the immediate front of our line, and both sides have been skirmishing all day. It looks to me as if the Yanks are afraid to attack General Lee when he is prepared for their reception.[26]

Meade was criticized for his non-attack upon an entrenched Army of Northern Virginia. This emanated largely from an officer corps—junior and field grade officers—anxious to end the war and return to other pursuits. Those in the volunteer ranks thought much the same thing. The newspapers took a dim view of it all. The president was beyond disappointed. He believed that Gettysburg, coupled with a victory at Vicksburg and capped with another victory that pushed Lee and his army into the Potomac, might well see the war ended. Two weeks passed, yet a trooper in Buford's division was still irritated by Meade's apparent delay in attacking. Writing on July 28 to a New York newspaper he said:

> … our forces remained nearly four days idle spectators of the enemy's lines, who of course, were busily engaged in perfecting their means of escape across the Potomac. It is not perhaps for me to criticize the plans of our generals. The only reason I could give was that they were afraid to attack, with the force at hand; if so, there had been some tremendous lying on the part of the administration papers, and the people and soldiers have been much deceived.[27]

Perhaps a minority view at the time, but with the passage of years a somewhat less emotional view was penned by an enlisted artilleryman. It would have been he that would have done the fighting at Williamsport. Augustus G. Buell believed that if Meade had ordered the attack:

> … the troops … would have obeyed sullenly, as they had so often done before, hopeless of success and convinced that they were to be murdered once more to satisfy the screaming editors in the North and the blatant politicians at Washington. Meade did exactly right. His caution saved many a gallant life that a rasher commander would have wasted, and the result was the same. Without doubt, if we had assaulted the Rebels along [their] line on the 12th or 14th of July, we would have suffered a bloody repulse, which, so soon after the carnage of Gettysburg, we were in no mood to endure.[28]

General Charles Wainwright, commander of I Corps artillery saw the Rebel defensive line after it was abandoned. His opinion was noted in his diary at the time:

> These were by far the strongest I have seen yet, evidently laid out by engineers and built as if they meant to stand a month's siege.[29]

Buell's opinion, formed years later, was, however, a minority view at the time. Many others in the Army of the Potomac held differing views, among them a trooper from the 8th New York. Writing to a New York newspaper, he said:

> … it is too bad for Meade to allow them to cross, for if we had only pitched into them on Sunday or Monday we might have prevented it, as we had them nearly surrounded.[30]

The Union army was in position before Williamsport, waiting all through July 13. A soldier in a Connecticut regiment noted in his diary:

> … I fear we may wake up one fine morning, the Potomac subsides a little, to find ourselves closely investing *the place where he was!*

And then the next day:

> There is a beautiful door up here, open, and with the appearance of having been passed through lately a very fine road, with tracks in it, leading away from us, a fine fox-hole, but no fox in it.[31]

Justus Scheibert, a foreign observer with Lee's army, was among those waiting by the Potomac for either a Yankee attack or an opportunity to cross to the Virginia side. In his recounting of events written shortly after the war he recorded:

Thus the retreat was ordered on the 14th, and it began suddenly, since the Potomac had subsided for the moment and could now be forded. Men rode along the lines now as if to reconnoiter, so that neither the troops nor the enemy would be made aware of anything, but outposts were not withdrawn until night.

It rained constantly during the crossing, and the weather was bitter cold and unpleasant. In view of this, the infantry and artillery went across the bridge, the wagons brought across on two old ferries. But the worst was the fact that the roads south of the river were so miserable that the wheels sank down to the axles, and they were so congested that no one could walk along beside the vehicles. The night was pitch-black. One could not see his hand before is face. Men would fall. They would get between the wagons, and the horses would get in the ditch or would come to a stop at some places ... A fire was built for light at a crossroads, where specially great confusion might arise and the General stood here with us throughout the night to regulate and enliven the march, to keep all in high spirits and on the track.[32]

It was 1pm, July 14, when Meade heard from Washington, lightning speed after his message that Lee was over the river, a message seen by Lincoln. Halleck told Meade:

The enemy should be pursued and cut up, wherever he has gone ... I cannot advise details, as I do not know where Lee's army is, nor where your pontoon bridges are. I need hardly say to you that the escape of Lee's army without another battle had created great dissatisfaction in the mind of the President, and it will require an active and energetic pursuit on your part to remove the impression that it had not been sufficiently active heretofore.

Halleck was pushing hard, and Meade knew it. He pushed back just as hard immediately. Meade, with stunning speed, telegraphed back his request to be relieved of command. Of course, the general in the field had to be calmed down and Halleck quickly responded. After an equally stunning victory over Robert E. Lee mere days before, George Meade could not then be relieved, not in the middle of a campaign.

With as much tact of which he was capable, Halleck telegraphed back almost immediately—4pm—saying no censure was implied, his phrasing only meant as encouragement. In an oblique way, Halleck told his general there was not "... sufficient cause for your application to be relived."[33]

General John Sedgwick, commanding VI Corps, had a member of his staff write to his sister on July 17, saying:

At Hagerstown Lee had a very strong position, which Meade, with his certainly not superior force, could not with safety attack. He could not be morally certain of success, and dared not risk failure which would entail such serious consequences as a defeat would not have failed to bring about.[34]

During the night of July 13/14, Stuart's cavalry covered the infantry positions along the line as the troops quietly withdrew and marched to Falling Waters and the pontoon bridge. The falling rain was an asset, muffling the noise as the brigades and divisions formed up and moved off. At daylight, and with occasional rain still falling, Buford's 1st Division moved forward. Colonel Gamble's report contains the most detail of the action on July 14, after the absence of the defending force was known. Devin's brigade moved on Gamble's left, toward the Rebel rear guard, capturing some stragglers, while from the opposite bank the Rebels lobbed artillery shells in their direction. Gamble reported:

> We ... found the enemy's earthworks ... abandoned, and were informed that the enemy had retreated toward Falling Waters and Williamsport, to cross the Potomac during the night. The brigade marched rapidly toward Falling Waters, and when near there observed a division of the enemy entrenched on a hill, covering the approach to the ford. While the brigade was moving around the flank and attack the enemy in rear, to cut them off from the ford and capture all of them, in connection with the other two brigades of the 1st Cavalry Division, which we could easily have accomplished, I saw two small squadrons of General Kilpatrick's division gallop up the hill to the right of the rebel infantry, in line of battle behind there [sic] earthworks, and, as any competent cavalry officer of experience could foretell the result, these two squadrons were instantly scattered and destroyed by the fire of a rebel brigade, and not a single dead enemy could be found when the ground there was examined a few hours afterward.[35]

Abner Hard of the 8th Illinois Cavalry later wrote that he saw something of this action also. It was part of Kilpatrick's Michigan Brigade and whether he or George Custer ordered the action the result was as Gamble described. According the Abner Hard:

> ... the brave men rode up to the muzzles of the rebel guns; and some actually went over their works, alas! Never to return. The enemy slew them by scores, and few returned to tell the tale.[36]

During this action, General J. Johnston Pettigrew, who had led the initial approach to Gettysburg on June 30, was killed.

At a point in time close to this charge by Kill-cavalry's men, Gamble's men moved forward dismounted, the result being a fire fight at the end of which the colonel reported the capture of 511 prisoners:

> ... 61 of whom, together with 300 stands of arms were turned over to an officer of Kilpatrick's division by mistake; also a 3-inch Parrot gun, captured by the Eighth New York Cavalry, which was afterward sent by General Kilpatrick to the camp of this brigade, where it properly belongs.

It was during this action at Falling Waters that Colonel William Christian of the 55th Virginia Infantry was captured.[37]

Lee was across the Potomac; the three cavalry divisions of the Army of the Potomac moved downstream from Falling Waters and crossed. Some refitting was needed, but only a day, July 18, was allocated before the pursuit was renewed. The cavalry moved along the eastern side of the Blue Ridge, blocking the gaps and harassing Lee's army as best it could. It was obvious the Rebels were moving to re-establish themselves behind the Rappahannock River. There it could reconstitute itself as best as it could, drawing on resources from further south and contemplate future operations. July was more than half over; the year's campaigning season approaching its midway point and the armies were back where they started, minus many thousands, casualties scattered across the landscape from the Rappahannock to Gettysburg and back. Everyone knew the war would continue, but no one knew for how long, how many more months, how many more years.

***

General Dan Sickles was operated on for his Gettysburg wound later on July 2. His leg was removed and by Sunday, July 5, was resident at a private home on F Street in the capital. That afternoon, President Lincoln and his young son Tad stopped by for a visit. After the obligatory questions about the general's wound and the care he was receiving, "Mr. Lincoln dropped into a chair, and, crossing his prodigious arms and legs, soon fell to questioning Sickles, as to all phases of the combat at Gettysburg." Accompanying Sickles from the battlefield was III Corps Staff Officer, James Rusling, who many years in the future would write of the president's visit. Rusling remembered that "… it was easy to see they both held each other in high esteem. They were both politicians." The president inquired and:

> Sickles, recumbent on his stretcher, with a cigar between his fingers, puffing it, leisurely, answered Mr. Lincoln in detail but warily, as became so astute a man and soldier; and discussed the great battle and its probable consequences …

Rusling said Lincoln asked the general in substance, given the victory at Gettysburg, "what General Meade proposed to do with it." The answer Sickles gave slipped through Rusling's remembrance. Knowing that III Corps had been decimated on July 2 and knowing also that he was responsible for it, Dan Sickles, despite his wound, must have calculated his military and, more importantly to him, his political stance when the dust settled after the Gettysburg campaign. The Joint Committee on the Conduct of the War was no doubt waiting for him to recover sufficiently to talk with them. And although Dan Sickles was a War Democrat, he was still a Democrat. Staff Officer Rusling, perhaps inadvertently, provided a comment on the character of the conversation between President and general that afternoon:

> He certainly got his side of the story of Gettysburg well into the President's mind and heart that Sunday afternoon; and this doubtless stood him in good stead afterward …[38]

With the knowledge of his otherwise greatness as a war president, and yet with the memory of his meeting with Dan Sickles still fresh, the exchange of telegraph messaging between Meade and Halleck in the second week of July, with the president seeing each word and no doubt nodding his approval, marks for one studying the record left to us the most disappointing moment in Lincoln's presidency. One cannot help thinking that Sickles and his no doubt twisted version of Gettysburg, delivered the week before, clouded to some degree the president's thinking relating to Meade's actions and matters as they stood along the Potomac a week later. Lincoln had received only quick and scattered accounts of the fight in Pennsylvania from hurried individuals who had been in or near the event, each with a partial knowledge and an opinion. Certainly, he had not talked with Meade directly. The president was too far away to have acute knowledge of the logistics, the wet terrain, the degree of exhaustion hanging over the army and to appreciate what the loss of men like Reynolds and Hancock meant; in general, all the many problems General Meade faced. As Lincoln said later, he should have gone to Williamsport himself—the vice-president did and was there on July 14—and once there seen the situation and talked with the general commanding. Also, there was reporter Noah Brooks, a friend of Lincoln. Surely these men must have at least talked with the president when they returned to Washington.

In asking to be relived, was Meade playing a game of bluff with Halleck? It cannot be known with certainty, but the speed at which these communications shot over the wires raise the thought that, somehow, Lincoln was involved. Perhaps the president, as he sat is the telegraph room of the War Department as was his custom, saw Meade's request to be relieved and told Halleck calm things down. How could a general that had given the country its most significant victory thus far in the war be gotten rid of so soon after his and the army's success? The answer: Meade would stay commanding the army. The general knew he had won a significant victory, but he wrote to his wife on July 10:

> I also see that my success at Gettysburg has deluded the people and the Government with the idea that I must always be victorious, that Lee is demoralized and disorganized, etc., and other delusions which will not only be dissipated by any reverse that I should meet with, but would react in proportion against me. I have already had a very decided correspondence with General Halleck upon this point, he pushed me on, and I informed him I was advancing as fast as I could. The firm stand I took had the result to induce General Halleck to tell me to act according to my judgment.[39]

Nevertheless, Halleck continued to prod Meade. Writing to his wife on July 16, Meade said:

> They have refused to relieve me, but insist on my continuing to try to do what I know in advance is impossible to do. My army (men and animals) is exhausted; it wants rest and reorganization, and no reinforcements of any practical value have been sent. Yet, in the face of these facts, well known to them, I am urged, pushed and *spurred* to attempting to pursue and destroy an army nearly equal to my own, falling back upon its resources and reinforcements, and increasing in *morale* daily.[40]

Although Meade greatly over-estimates Lee's strength at the time, the exhaustion of his army was clearly evident to all, even those with the most rudimentary military background. General Halleck should have known that getting the army from Gettysburg, after a tremendous battle, to Williamsport, getting it supplied, getting it into a position to attack, would take time, more time given the condition of the roads. Instead of coaching Meade from the far sidelines, Halleck could have been coaching the president on the intricacies of logistics and command. That General Meade at Gettysburg and after was a reactive rather than a proactive general may be a true assessment, but this and the previous sentence fall into the trap of hindsight. Consider what Meade knew on the evening of July 3 and through to July 12. He had fought and won a meeting engagement on a colossal scale, with no advance planning as to how to fight it or any prior knowledge of the terrain on which it was to be fought, against an enemy of unknown size and power. At Williamsport, the enemy's position could be seen and appreciated, the size and composition of his force and its power still an unknown. George Meade was not the best general in the rebellion's pantheon of bearded men in blue, but for the Army of the Potomac from July 1 and after, he was the best of those still alive.

***

As for General Lee's objectives for the summer campaign he had led, they were only partially realized. Overall, the negatives totaled many more than the positives. The move north had precluded another offensive by the Army of the Potomac during at least June and July. For a time, it got Lee's army out from behind the Rappahannock, and the Army of the Potomac out of northern Virginia for at least a short time. While Lee and his men were in Pennsylvania, they ate well and sent south for future use large amounts of grain, cattle and other commandeered products, but the minus side of the ledger negated all of this. The casualties Lee suffered, possibly as many as one-third of the force he had led north, could never be adequately replaced by the Confederacy. The campaign did nothing to relieve the pressure on Vicksburg. The city was surrendered on July 4. The campaign had not furthered to any degree a Northern slide toward acquiescence regarding Southern independence, and the myth of the invincibility of the Army of Northern Virginia had vanished with the gun smoke of July 3.

Lieutenant Randolph McKim of the Army of Northern Virginia wrote to the folks at home on July 15. Writing from Martinsburg, Virginia, he told his mother:

> We remained in Maryland ten days after the battle, and yet our enemy dared not attack us, though we lay in line of battle three days within half a mile of him.

But as for the collision at Gettysburg he confided in his diary on July 11 something not included in the letter home.

> I went into the last battle feeling that victory *must* be ours—that such an army could not be foiled, and that God would certainly declare Himself on our side. *Now* I feel that unless He sees fit to bless our arms, our valor will not avail.[41]

CHAPTER NINE

Return to the Rappahannock

I think I told you confidentially that Halleck had ordered me to halt and cease pursuing Lee, that I had given my judgment against the measure, but had been over-ruled.

GEORGE MEADE TO MRS. MEADE, AUGUST 6, 1863

There is no news. General Meade, I believe, is repairing the railroad, and I presume will come on again. If I could only get some shoes and clothes for the men, I would save him the trouble.

R. E. LEE TO MRS. LEE, OCTOBER 25, 1863[1]

The casualties continued even after the Potomac army's return to the Rappahannock. Northern newspapers often contained notices such as one about a trooper in the 2nd New York Cavalry.

Brought Home Dead,—The body of Thomas McCutchen was brought to the village yesterday. He was wounded in the shoulder on the 13th inst., in the successful attack upon Culpepper [sic] Court House, a bullet passing entirely through his shoulder. He was taken to a hospital near Washington, where an operation was performed, and he seemed to be doing well. A short time after, however, what is termed hospital gangrene set in, and terminated his life on Tuesday, the 22d inst. He was a brave young man, and performed his duties with great courage and energy. His funeral will be preached in the 2d Presbyterian Church to-morrow, and his body buried in the Old Church Cemetery.[2]

It was July 1863 and there was nearly 20 more months of war to fight before notices in newspapers such as this would end.

The Army of the Potomac was back where it started over a month before, deployed along the north bank of the Rappahannock, General Lee's pickets on the south side occasionally trading tobacco for coffee with the better-supplied Yankees who were watching them. If their generals were loath to admit it, both armies needed at least a brief period of rest and refitting. For General Meade, the rest period came in a form of an order from Washington not to advance and bring on another encounter with Lee. On August 3, he told his wife:

The Government, for some reason best known to itself, had ordered me to cease the pursuit of Lee, though I strongly recommended an advance. This is confidential … I don't know what this all means, but I suppose in time it will all come right.[3]

Having been ordered not to advance, the Army of the Potomac rested as best it could and went about refitting itself. Also, there had been riots in New York City related to the draft imposed by Congress and many troops from Meade's army were detached and sent there to stabilize the situation. It can be easily assumed the New York rioting did not sit well with the troops, the volunteers in the field, and particularly after having lived through Gettysburg. A soldier in the 120th New York Infantry wrote in August to his hometown newspaper in New Paltz:

> Major Tappen has gone to New York, with a detail of men from the regiment to aid in enforcing the draft, and to bring on the conscripts—three hundred and fifth-five of whom will be placed with the 120th ... Great indignation is felt by the members of the brigade at the dastardly conduct of the Copperheads in our native state. We have some respect for the rebel soldiers who will stand up, face the bullets and fight like men; but words cannot express the contempt with which we regard those home traitors, who seek to stab in the dark and fire in the rear.[4]

Near the end of July, nine regiments composed of men at the expiration of their terms of service were discharged. The detached troops and the discharge of others had depleted the Army of the Potomac by more than 15,000 men. Draftees and new recruits would be added in the coming months, but these had to be assimilated and that would take time.

With the army motionless, William Wheeler of the 13th New York Light Artillery wrote that he had started a school for his artillerymen:

> My school is in a flourishing condition ... the schoolmaster, an old corporal whom I detailed for the purpose, fetches the spelling books and the writing materials, and set his classes their lessons. You would be pleased to see the eagerness with which the men from twenty to forty years of age seize upon the opportunity for repairing the defects of their early education ... I am hoping that very few men, if any, will have to call upon officers to sign their names for them on the next pay-day.[5]

***

In early October, the Army of Northern Virginia started a movement to the right flank of Meade's army. Meade was forced to retreat from the Rappahannock line, covering his supply line, the Orange and Alexandria Railroad, and keep his army between Lee's advance and Washington. This movement, which ended with the Army of the Potomac in a strong defensive position at Centerville, became known as the Bristoe Campaign, because the largest fight that took place during this autumn maneuvering took place near the railroad stop of Bristoe Station. Lee and his army retired behind the Rappahannock and Rapidan Rivers to await further movements by Meade.

While manning the position at Centerville, the army, and presumably Meade, had a visitor. It was the late commander of III Corps at Gettysburg, Major General Dan Sickles. With crutches to support him, Sickles visited what was left of his boys in III Corps who cheered him enthusiastically. Apparently, Meade and Sickles had a conversation, no doubt the corps commander wanting to return to lead his men, but George Meade wanted no part of the politician/general in a command position and tactfully suggested that Sickles "… was not yet able to endure the hardships of service and fulfill all the duties incumbent on the position" and also noting that he had to use crutches and "… could not yet support the pressure of an artificial leg."[6] As far as George Meade was concerned, Sickles had, on July 2, caused the Potomac army to suffer an inordinate number of casualties by his forward movement and wrecked III Corps in the process. Dan Sickles could begin his post-war career immediately as far as the army commander was concerned.

After the movement to Centerville and back, and with the Army of the Potomac now occupying the territory between the Rappahannock and Rapidan Rivers, thought was given to an offensive before winter shut down operations until the spring of 1864. While this process went forward, however, Warren Freeman of the 13th Massachusetts Infantry had just received the news of the death of a friend in another command:

> Yours of the 10th was received … announcing the death of Joseph P. Burrage. This is Sad news indeed … for he was a noble, generous, and brave soldier—yielding up college honors, a luxurious and cultivated home circle, to meet death upon a battle-field that his country may live … I shall always cherish his memory and his friendship … You will recollect that in a previous letter I spoke of our last meeting and of his apparent rather reserved or taciturn, for which I could not account. Now it may be that it brought up thoughts of home, the church and Sabbath—school where we had always met, and the possibility that we might never meet again on earth; such thoughts may have produced such results, which is the only way I can account for the want of that cordiality manifested at previous meetings.[7]

Freeman, in a later letter, dated December 7, spoke of the movement of the army under General Meade in November, with obvious disapproval. After all the campaigning that had started in May, and despite a long interval of non-action in August and September, the soldiers were not eager for another campaign. Freeman wrote:

> … our general suppose it would be necessary, in order to satisfy the press and public, for the 'Army of the Potomac,' before going into winter quarters, to offer battle to the rebel army on our front, whether we gained anything by it or not.[8]

General Meade brought the army to the banks of the Rappahannock and Rapidan Rivers and, in November, attempted another lunge at Lee. However, because of the slowness of the advance among some of the army's elements, General Lee was able to quickly counter and when Meade's men approached a stream called Mine Run, a tributary of the Rapidan, they found the Army of Northern Virginia had entrenched itself and continued to do so as the Union soldiers watched. The front positions of Meade's army were within yards of the Rebel earthworks and anyone looking at their position could see that any attack would prove costly and probably would not succeed. However, General Gouverneur Warren, temporarily commanding II Corps, thought an assault by his corps would carry the Rebel position and Meade reinforced him and ordered the assault for the next morning, November 30.

While this attack was in preparation, the chaplain of the 102nd Pennsylvania Infantry was with his men and later recorded:

> Never have I spent a more solemn day … Ere the hour set for the battle came, all my pockets and even haversack, were filled with sacred mementoes in case of death in the conflict—pocket-books, money, watches, lockets, rings, photographs. Each one as I passed by, as he came and handed me his treasure or his keepsake, would say, in substance, 'Chaplain, this is going to be a bloody business. In it half of our regiment must no doubt fall, as we are in the front line. Of these, I may be one. God, we are sure, will spare you. Take this, and should I fall, give or send it to such and such a loved one, telling them I fell with my face to the enemy, and this is to them—my last earthly memento and pledge of love!' During many of these, perhaps, final interviews, my emotions were unutterable, being only able to grasp the brave, generous hand, and turn away.

A VI Corps staff officer recalled the minutes before the assault was due to start; his apprehension waiting for the order to attack:

> But what are the little white patches on all these overcoats of army-blue? For the first time I saw the men had pinned their names on their breasts, that their bodies might be recognized in the carnival of death they expected, but did not shun.[9]

Early on the morning of the planned attack, General Warren and a member of his staff crawled forward of his front line for another look at the Rebel position. The looking changed Warren's attitude relative to carrying Lee's position. The Rebels had made improvements to their position during the night. When he crawled back within his line and on his own authority, he cancelled the attack and notified General Meade. The general immediately rode to Warren's position and the record is not clear whether his famous temper was under control or not when he arrived, but after he talked with Warren and heard his explanation about the defensive line of the Rebel army, he concurred and cancelled the operation.

Needless to say, there was relief within the ranks. The 6th Wisconsin had done their own scouting of the Rebel position beyond Mine Run and Rufus Dawes later recalled:

> … the run was breast deep with water … and the opposite side bank was protected by a heavy abattis, made by trees felled from the opposite bank into the stream, and also that beyond the abattis covering the slope were batteries in position … Our line was formed and arms stacked, with big fires on the front to keep from freezing, while we waited for the order to move on to almost certain death.

Then the order canceling the attack came down, with Dawes remarking:

> All honor to General Meade, who … had the moral courage to order a retreat without a day of blood and national humiliation to demonstrate its necessity to every dissatisfied carper among the people.[10]

The Battle of Mine Run never happened, the army withdrew and returned to its camps. A soldier in Warren's Corps wrote home a few days later:

> ... the enemy's work could never have been taken where we were; it was worse than Fredericksburg. I felt death in my very bones all day, while the impending command of advance was hanging over us ...[11]

Meade was expecting an explosion in Washington, followed by relief from command. While he waited, he outlined his reason for the non-attack, an argument to use in a defense against the recriminations coming from Halleck and Lincoln. In a lengthy and detailed letter to his wife dated December 2, we get a glimpse of his position. The advance of the army had been delayed, particularly by an infantry corps hours late in moving and therefore holding up the troops behind them. As a result, Lee's army was able to entrench and strengthen their position to such a degree that when Warren's corps was ready to attack the Rebel position had become too strong to assail. Then he says, "I expect your wishes will now soon be gratified, and that I shall be relieved from the Army of the Potomac," he began. Meade was certain that he faced "certain personal ruin!" Then came his thinking and his certainty concerning the course he had chosen:

> I would rather be ignominiously dismissed, and suffer anything, than knowingly and willfully have thousands of brave men slaughtered for nothing ... I am willing to stand or fall by it at all hazards ... I shall write to the President, giving him a clear statement of the case ... I have acted from a high sense of duty, to myself as a soldier, to my men as their general, and to my country and its cause.[12]

Days passed, but there was nothing from Washington. General Meade only reported to Washington officially and did not write to Lincoln concerning the non-attack. However, his actions at Mile Run had the effect of seriously strengthening the opinion of him among the army's rank and file.

In late 1876, one Porter Farley sent Gouverneur Warren a copy of an article he wrote about the Mine Run affair and received a reply from the former general. "I believe you spoke the general sentiment of the army about the matter," Warren wrote referring to his recommendation to call off the attack. Then Warren adds, "I never attend any army gathering that numbers of officers and men do not come forward and personally thank me for taking the stand I then did."[13]

The weather was turning and, regardless of it being stated officially or not, the army needed a rest. They had been training since Hooker had taken command of the army early in the year, had conducted two major campaigns, Chancellorsville and Gettysburg, and one minor one, Bristoe, and had marched from the Rappahannock to Pennsylvania and back. Winter quarters, despite the cold and damp, would be welcomed. Beginning roughly on January 1, in the bleak and barren landscape between the Rappahannock and Rapidan Rivers, the Army of the Potomac went in winter quarters.

The wind drove either the snow or the rain and made the cold temperatures all the worse, but the trains running on the Orange and Alexandria Railroad brought fresh meat, some fresh and dried vegetables, and newspapers and illustrated magazines. Soft bread again became available. Whatever trees still standing were cut down and any building not being used as a headquarters was cannibalized for material to construct crude huts, each with an equally crude chimney slapped together with any non-combustible material and the sticky Virginia mud. An officer in a New Hampshire regiment had lived in a similar camp the winter before and later penned his remembrance:

> In the course of time the pine woods which covered the hill disappeared before the axemen, the houses which had not the protecting care of a commanding officer were carried away piece-meal to fit up the soldiers' quarters ...

The surrounding landscape became barren with "... no vestige of vegetation remained ... So complete a change would not be wrought by a quarter of a century of peace." The regimental historian of the 1st New Jersey recalled, the "... scouting parties from the different companies impressed every loose board to be discovered within five miles of the cantonment." Open spaces between the logs were "... plastered with the stiff red clay which formed the soil, the buildings were rapidly made impervious to wind and rain ..." This regiment was in camp close to a brick schoolhouse that was now temporarily abandoned. Brick chimneys for fireplaces for the cabins were therefore provided despite orders not to disturb the building. The 1st New Jersey threw up a stable for its horses, but ... no covering could be procured for them ... To save the cost of a few tarpaulins the lives of many horses, worth thousands of dollars, were sacrificed during the winter.[14]

Newspapers and magazines gave the men news of the events going on around them as well as what was going on at home. There were family and friends to be written to. There was drill, weather permitting, but the men in the infantry were mostly left alone, to write letters, read or listen to lectures on all subjects. Regimental chaplains proselytized, temperance petitions circulated, and Sunday services held. With the army stationary, food in quantity and quality superior to that consumed in the field was available and as a captain from Massachusetts remembered:

> We always had an abundant supply of soft bread and Bordin's condensed milk in cans was one of the luxuries invented at this time for our delectation and comfort.[15]

When the troopers were paid, the money could be sent home by an express service. If there was money to spare, there was the local sutler, a merchant of sorts peddling to the soldiers items not among those things issued by the army. A sutler's inventory included, but was not limited to, items of convenience and specialty foods, paper and ink, envelopes, stamps and the like, and, of course, liquor, cheap liquor, retailed at prices far above what would be charged in a normal civilian environment.

Although chaplains throughout the Potomac army encouraged temperance, directly through their preaching to attendees at services and informally whenever the occasion permitted, nevertheless, recreational use of spirits was common whenever it was available, from the most humble private to general officers. Thomas Livermore of a New Hampshire infantry regiment recalled the on-going situation within II Corps during the latter half of 1863:

> Old General Hayes, our commander, used to be very fond of whiskey, with sugar and water, particularly so when mixed in a delectable way by Lieutenant Haskell. The general, however, made it a rule not to drink before 10 A.M., but about 9.30 A.M. he would be seen at his tent door, his red nose shining in the morning sun, while he questioned what the hour was from its altitude. Finally, he would loudly, but moderately, say, 'Mr. Haskell!' When the following colloquy would take place. 'Yes, General!' 'What time is it?' 'Half-past nine, General.' A long pause. 'Suppose we call it ten, Mr. Haskell!'—and there upon the aide would come out of his tent and gravely go into the general's and mix the morning toddy.[16]

The 1st New Jersey Cavalry, as depicted in its regimental history, seems to be a command that swam against the current. In winter quarters near Warrenton, it was recorded that "The facilities for intoxication were as small as they ever can be among a crowd of soldiers." This may be the result of so many wives of officers visiting through the winter that the regiment "… set a commendable example of sobriety and decency." It must be noted, however, that the author of this comment, Henry R. Pyne, was the regiment's chaplain.[17]

While winter camp was significantly better than being in the field, marching and fighting, it still had its moments on loneliness for most of the army. It was a Saturday night and one officer, writing to his parents, spoke of a wish that lingered with him as he wrote the news from his camp:

> A feeling came over me … I thought of you gathered around your cheerful fireside, and with your work laid aside for the pleasant Sunday books, and the papers in each and all of your hands. I could see you perfectly. I thought you looked very comfortable. I only wish I could step in on you for a moment …[18]

In winter camp the infantry sat out the winter with only drilling and guard duty to perform to keep them from thinking of home. The cavalry rotated picket duty among regiments out on the army's perimeter and along the rivers. The campaigning season of 1864 was still some months off when trooper George Benedict of the 1st New York Dragoons wrote to his wife:

> Jan 26th, 1864
> My dear wife I take this opportunity to inform you that I am well at present and I hope these few lines will find you the same. It is very warm nice weather here for the season. We hear no war news of any importance. Only the Rebel soldiers are a deserting every day and coming into our lines and declare that they will fight against the Union no longer. Sarah T. J. Thorp is with us now. We do not like him because he drinks. The officers most all drink and gamble and do not regard the Sabbath day at all. Oh. So much evil in the army the good lord

have mercy upon us … Sarah my dear wife I have not had a letter from you in 4 or 5 weeks. Oh my dear wife what can the matter be [?] I do not know but hope I shall get one soon or I shall think something awful is the matter. I have written you 4 or 5 letters to you and have had no answer. One of them had 10 dollars in money in it and another with 5 dollars in it which I hope you have … I shall endeavor to write once or twice a week while we remain in camp. We have been marching so much and been so busy that I had to neglect writing but now we are in winter quarters. Still we have picket duty and camp guard to do. Many other things to do. We can see the Rebs and their camps across the river. They have pickets along the river the same as we do only about 3 quarters of a mile apart. There is no fighting here. It is all quiet now … Jan 27. My dear wife. I am well this morning and hope these lines find you the same. No more at present. Sarah write often your husband. Geo D. Benedict.[19]

But there was also a dreariness stemming from repetition. As noted by an officer in II Corps: Being "… engaged in daily drills, guard-mounting, and parades, is 'monotonous' and even card-playing, horse-racing, and kindred intellectual amusements became 'stale and unprofitable' when a steady occupation." Another officer recalled along the same river the year before:

[I]n the evening we sat around our fires and drank, sang, and told stories, or played cards, frequently for heavy stakes. Our favorite game was 'poker.' … and so fascinated was the game that I once sat for twenty-four hours at the game …"

Then the officer confessed he "… spent a good deal of money in this way," never saving any of his $125 a month pay or giving any thought to life after the army, "… for I presumed it very likely that I should be killed before the war was over."[20]
    A cavalryman noted as he recalled this winter:

Visits to friends in distant camps, and long rides along the picket lines, leaping fences and ditches to try the mettle of our horses; or down to the fords to have a chat with the Johnnies on their outposts; failed to be exciting after a while.[21]

That serious rivalries developed between regiments brigaded together was normal while in camp for extended periods. Most often this was stimulated or encouraged by commanders as a way to bolster morale. In the late winter and early spring, weather permitting, the regiments would field baseball teams. In the cavalry, naturally, there was horse racing with the obligatory wagering. The chaplains held religious services and welcomed all regardless of denomination or previous condition of piety. It may be myth, but it seems the rivalry among regiments spilled into the religious arena as well. According to Private Warren Goss, there was a great rivalry between a Brooklyn infantry regiment and their New York neighbors. A chaplain from the Brooklyn Regiment asked the colonel of the New York regiment if he might hold a service for his men. The colonel is reported as having said in answer, "You might just as well preach to the horses. They are good fighters but make dreadful saints." The chaplain, perhaps unknowingly, then remarked that he had held a service among the men of the Brooklyn regiment that also prided itself as a fighting command, one having little or no piety, and that he had enticed 13 men from that command to be baptized. When the colonel heard this his attitude regarding a religious service quickly changed. He authorized the service and ordered the entire regiment to attend and to maintain a pious demeanor throughout. At the conclusion of the service the colonel rewarded the chaplain. The colonel called out, "Adjutant, detail twenty men and have them baptized. This regiment isn't going to let that damn Brooklyn regiment beat them at anything." A nearly identical event is reported as an "actual occurrence" within the 10th New York Cavalry, only the number of converts is much greater. The chaplain of the 10th New York had witnessed the baptism of 21 troopers during a service held by the 16th Pennsylvania Cavalry. The chaplain, speaking of this to a company commander in the 10th New York, caused an order to be issued. The captain's entire company was ordered out, a total of 60 troopers. All were duly baptized with the captain remarking, "No damned Pennsylvania regiment is going to get ahead of the Tenth New York."[22]

Out in the outskirts of the areas occupied by the winter camps there was still picket duty to perform and the presence of "bushwhackers" and Mosby's partisans to contend with. The Johnnies on picket across the river might be docile enough, but as cited in the regimental history of the 1st New Jersey:

> Incessant vigilance had to be exercised against guerrillas, and squadrons kept always under the saddle, ready to dash out on the slightest alarm. Whether it not have been more economical to the main picket work by a brigade of infantry, and retain the cavalry for other service with an eye to their efficiency in the spring, was a subject which has not yet met with consideration of the ruling spirits of our military organization.

And the town of Warrenton was full of families whose husbands and sons were all serving with General Lee. However, being under a form of occupation and dependent in many cases on the Union forces in the area for some of the necessities of life, they made the best of the situation. It was appreciated, as recorded in the history of the 1st New Jersey Cavalry. "The Virginians," said Chaplain Pyne, "though marvelously ignorant, prejudiced, and narrow-minded, are a people of kindly impulses and quick sensibilities prompting them to a responsive good feeling toward those who went out of their way to do them service." This history goes on the remark that "An almost unprecedented instance of good behavior, it may be stated the poultry fed around a house adjoining a Massachusetts' camp without fowl being abstracted; and even cows went to and from pasture with no interruption beyond an occasional milking."[23]

***

In the early months of 1864, the men of many regiments were packing and preparing to go home. Those that had enlisted during 1861 would be entitled to discharge during 1864, three years of service having been completed. But in December and January, many had reenlisted and were now Veteran Volunteers, entitled to a

35-day furlough. All of it, the reenlistment and those incentives attached to it, had been the center of discussion from the moment the army announced its plan, one designed to keep within the ranks its most experienced and committed soldiers. Barring the unforeseen, Washington knew the war would continue into 1864 and many regiments raised in 1861 would be so depleted they probably could not be classified as regiments any longer. The army announced a program—generous for its time—it hoped would coax many of those committed to the cause to continue in the service. It included a large Federal bounty as well as the furlough. If enough of them did so, their existing regiment would be retained and keep its officers if they too reenlisted. Regimental commanders were required to speak to their men about reenlistment, it being known as one soldier recalled, "… old soldiers were worth so much more than new ones." However, while "it was sweet to hear all this," most old soldiers were "… not easily moved by this kind of talk." Each soldier wrestled with the pros and cons of reenlistment. Edwin Wentworth of a Massachusetts infantry regiment wrote to his wife telling her that he didn't plan to sign up again:

> There are plenty of men at home, better able to bear arms than I am, and I am willing they should take their chance on the battlefield and have their share of glory and honor.

Then Wentworth considered the bounty money, enough to acquire a home and some acreage; "… it will enable me to provide you a good home and a chance to live comfortably." Wentworth re-enlisted and was killed at Spotsylvania Court House that spring. Nevertheless, an estimated 28,000 men did re-enlist.[24] Commands with good officers tended to have high re-enlistment rates. Those that did not disappeared.

The army during this winter was being augmented with new recruits, draftees and draft substitutes. The draftees, of course, didn't want to be there and many were escorted to the front under guard, but as soon as they arrived many deserted, or tried to. One soldier remembered:

> The sewers of recruits and substitutes that had received enormous bounties … continually flowed into, or, to speak with more accuracy, through the army … A number that arrived at the camp after sunset escaped before morning … [if not under guard] … [These] Deserters exhausted their ingenuity in finding ways to reach the cavalry vedettes. And some gladly swam across the Rappahannock in the coldest nights of the year.

And those that stayed were sometimes regarded as "outlaws," because "They robbed each other as freely as they did others."[25]

It was now February and a routine had settled over the uncomfortable winter camps. Veteran Volunteers were going on furlough, officer's wives were visiting and, in Washington, President Lincoln was thinking about a general from the west taking command of all Union forces, as well as some other things that interested him. Then, at the headquarters of the Army of the Potomac on February 11, an order arrived, General Meade passing it on to cavalry commander Pleasonton:

> The commanding general directs that you at once order General Kilpatrick to proceed to Washington and report to the President, as requested by the latter.[26]

General Judson Kilpatrick, ambitious and wanting to exit the war with a combat record that might be of such renown that it might propel him to the governorship of New Jersey, his home state, or even to the White House, had concocted a plan to help along his port-war career. As everyone was aware, the conditions of the Union prisoners held in Libby Prison in Richmond and at Belle Isle in the James River were awful, the mildest descriptive word employed by those with direct knowledge provided by inmates that had escaped or been paroled. Inadequate food, medical care, clothing and blankets for the prisoners were all problems stemming from the failing Confederate economy. Kill-cavalry thought a quick strike at Richmond with a strong cavalry force could free the prisoners and just as quickly escort them to Union line. That it could be done in this way stemmed from the thought that Richmond was lightly defended and, if the raid was mounted, a diversion by the Potomac army to the west of its winter camps would at least hold in place any interference from General Lee or Jeb Stuart. Kilpatrick went to Washington at Lincoln's request and made his proposal. The president had an additional task for Kilpatrick and probably this was the reason he called Kilpatrick to the capital in the first place. Lincoln had recently issued an Amnesty Proclamation aimed at those in rebellion, primarily the Confederate soldiers. He wanted copies distributed as Kilpatrick went about his raid. Of course, the general accepted the proposal and then he met with Secretary of War Stanton. Within days of this meeting a former staff officer, Colonel Ulric Dahlgren, in some manner, volunteered or was authorized to accompany Kilpatrick on the raid. Although Pleasonton was not in favor of the raid, in that Washington consented to it, Meade had Kilpatrick begin detailed planning. Cavalry details from across the corps were selected to participate and the word quickly spread throughout the army that there was to be a raid.

As preparations went forward among the cavalry commands, others were preparing for what would be remembered in later years as the highlight of the winter season. For the activities related to Washington's Birthday and the guests that would be descending upon the army, arrangements were being made, parties at various headquarters were being planned and decorations hung. There would be a review after the celebrations.

Theodore Lyman was a wealthy natural scientist from Massachusetts. He met George Meade in Key West, Florida, in 1856, he on a scientific expedition and the future general supervising the building of lighthouses. Meade and young Lyman became "congenial companions" in the then wilderness of the Florida Keys. Later, Lyman's work took him to Europe, and he did not return until the summer of 1863, just prior to the great Gettysburg battle, fought and won by the new commander of the Army of the Potomac. Lyman wrote to Meade inquiring about a staff position at his headquarters. Meade, familiar with Lyman, his Harvard education, his "charm," "good humor" and "well-storied mind," quickly recruited him.[27] The newly minted staff officer bought horses and camp equipment and headed for Virginia, noting at this time, "A man must march when it is his plain duty, and all the more if he has had, in this world, more than his slice of cake." Left unsaid, was the fact that his wife's cousin, Robert Shaw, colonel of the 54th Massachusetts Infantry, had been killed leading his "colored regiment" that summer and this may have had an influence on Lyman's application to Meade.[28]

Theodore Lyman's letters and journal entries, beginning in September 1863 and continuing through to the end of the war are a literate, insightful and a necessary, if occasionally prejudiced, source for life and outlook, at least at the command level, within the Army of the Potomac during this time.

From Lyman we get a glimpse of the general and life within the army while in winter camp. With the parties about to start, Lyman wrote:

> General Meade is in excellent spirits and cracks many jokes and tells stories. You can't tell how different he is when he has no movement on his mind, for he is like a firework ... There is something sardonic in his natural disposition, which is an excellent thing in a commander; it makes people skip around so. General Humphreys [Meade's chief of staff] is quite the contrary. He is most easy to get on with, for everybody, but, practically, he is just as hard as the Commander, for he has a tremendous temper ...[29]

Lyman also recorded at this time the impression of headquarters as preparation for Kilpatrick's move went forward. The atmosphere at headquarters changed, and despite the attempt at secrecy, everyone knew what was going on:

> For some days General Humphreys had been a mass of mystery, with his mouth pursed up, and doing much of the writing himself, all to the great amusement of the bystanders, who had heard, even in Washington, that some expedition or raid was on the tapis, and even pointed out various details thereof ... But they should not have known *anything* ... Kilpatrick is sent for by the President; oh, ah! Everybody knows at once, he is a cavalry officer it must be a raid.

And finally, Lyman presents his assessment of Washington security, "All Willard's chatter of it."[30]

Speculation wasn't confined merely to army headquarters or Willard's bar. As far down as regimental level, perhaps further, there was talk. Major James Kidd was in command of the 6th Michigan Cavalry and in mid-February he made note of a "daring expedition." Many prominent statesmen would be visiting the army soon, most of whom would be attending the Washington celebration. Kidd noted at the time, "it did not take a prophet to tell that something of unusual importance was in the wind."[31] It was only a few days later that Kidd provided 300 men to the raiding force, a component of which he would lead.

It was February 22, and it seems that most of the army took the day off. For part of the day, Lyman attended a gathering at the tent headquarters of General Marsena Patrick, the army's provost marshal:

> There are a perfect shoal of womenkind now in the army—a good many, of course, in Culpeper, where they can live in houses … Likewise came some of the red-legs, or Zouaves, or 114th Pennsylvania, who finally had an air of men who had gone to a theater and did not take an interest in the play. There too were some ladies, who were accommodated with a tent open in front, so as to allow them to see and hear. The band of Zouaves sang hymns and were quite musical … To-night is a great ball of the 2d Corps. The General has gone to so also General Humphreys. None of the Staff were invited, save George Meade [the general's son and aide], to the huge indignation of the said staff and my great amusement.[32]

It appears every division and corps throughout the army had a celebration honoring George Washington on February 22. There were parties and dinners across all the winter camps. Music and dancing suppressed thoughts of the fighting soon to begin again. As gathered from the record left to us for that day, no expense seems to have been spared. There was food and beverages in abundance, field rations and army coffee not being in evidence. Ladies, mostly the wives of officers visiting husbands, were shuttled about in ambulances to keep their feet dry and mud free. Finally, there were the notables, special invited guests and more ladies imported by train from Washington. One officer, noting the many ladies now moving about winter camp, recalled:

> The enemy has had the good taste not to disturb the festivities by any ill-timed demonstration on the approach of a party of ladies and their attendants; they have frequently saluted them and have always refrained from firing or other disagreeable attentions.[33]

One invited guest was Hamilton Howard, the son of a senator from Michigan. Howard attended the first president's birthday celebration hosted by General Kilpatrick and held at the 3rd Division's combination training center, recreation hall, church and theater. Later, Howard reminisced:

> Kilpatrick was eager to be confirmed as a full major general … In order to ingratiate himself with senators, he extended a large number of invitations to them and their families to pay his headquarters a visit and witness a general review of the Second Army Corps. Many accepted … Quite a trainload started, properly guarded, and in due time we were deposited at Brandy Station. Kilpatrick was happy, and as active as a flea and almost as ubiquitous. Wines, liquors, and eatables were in profusion. His hospitality was unbounded. He was a little man, with loud, swaggering voice, full of fun and profanity, florid face, square, prognathous jaw, firm, large mouth, prominent nose, quick, deep-set, piercing, fearless gray eyes, full, square forehead …[34]

Later, Howard apparently attended the II Corps ball held "… in a newly erected large wooden pavilion … The dancing continued till long into the morning." It was early the next day, "After a most enjoyable evening spent in dancing and music," when the

A Sketch of the Washington's Birthday ball hosted by the Second Corps. (Library of Congress)

officers and their guests retired.[35] Of all the celebrations scattered across the army that day and night, the affair hosted by II Corps seems to have attracted the most attention and the largest number of guests. A II Corps officer later recalling that winter in camp:

> We became quite aristocratic, and resolved to celebrate Washington's birthday by a grand ball. So we built a hall 90x30 feet in extent, with a 'lean-to' running the whole length, properly divided for dressing, and cloak-rooms, and a spacious supper-room.
>
> Many of the officers' wives and daughters enlivened the camp by their presence, and hundreds more came expressly for the occasion. The Vice-President and a number of senators were there with their wives, and Governor Curtin and wife acted as a convoy for a bevy of beauties from Philadelphia, Washington, Baltimore, and New York.
>
> Generals Meade, Hancock, Warren, Pleasonton, Kilpatrick and Gregg were there, and so was one-legged Dahlgren, whose sad fate it was a few days later to be killed on his raid on Richmond. It was a scene of beauty, gallantry, and chivalry and the dawn paled the thousand tapers which lighted the hall, before the dance ended. It was the vision of a night, and seemed altogether unreal—as if it were some fairy palace risen in a night where reveling occupants, after tripping gayly in the fairy dance, fled with the ushering in of day.[36]

Of course, with something this big going on and the Vice President in attendance, General Meade would have to attend the ball that evening. However, the day before, and having just returned from a quick trip to Washington, he wrote to his wife:

I believe half of Washington is coming down to attend … As the ball is nearly five miles from my headquarters, I don't think I shall have the courage to go. I don't mind the going, but it is the coming back which is unpleasant.

Meade changed his mind and after the event, he reported to his wife:

Since writing last we have had a gay time. The ball … was quite a success … There were present about three hundred ladies, many coming from Washington for the occasion, an elegant supper furnished … everything in fine style. I rode over in an ambulance a distance of five miles, and got back to my bed by four o'clock in the morning.[37]

Another attendee, younger than Meade and severely lower in ranks recalled the affair that night:

The great ball, reception … it came off with the utmost distinction … Nothing could surpass the kindness of the ladies, there were in no wise exclusive, and the youngest lieutenant received as much consideration as the oldest and most conspicuous general.[38]

Another officer from a Pennsylvania regiment recalled:

The ball was a compliment to the many ladies, families of officers, who were in camp, and many more came down from Washington for the occasion. It was a very brilliant affair, to which handsome dresses of the ladies and the showy uniforms of the officers greatly contributed. No thought was given to the dangers of the past, or those of the near future, but all gave themselves up to the enjoyment of the hour.[39]

Septima Collis was the wife of an officer in V Corps that also hosted a ball that evening. In later years, and with the knowledge of what was coming in the spring, she remembered:

The handsome uniforms of the officers, to say nothing of their handsome faces and figures; the clashing of their sabers, the jingle of their spurs, and the universal expression upon every face and in every gesture to 'be merry while we may,' made it a scene of enchantment which was to me so novel and so suited to my years and my tastes that I consider it a great privilege to have been part of it … I don't believe a thought ever entered my mind that many of these splendid fellows were dancing their last waltz, and I am very sure such gloomy forebodings never entered theirs.[40]

After circulating among the guests at the ball and getting to bed at a late hour, General Meade was at the II Corps Review the next morning at 11am. Kilpatrick's Cavalry Division would be playing a supporting role this day before the invited guests and assorted generals. Theodore Lyman was, of course, in attendance and wrote:

Then there was his Excellency, the Vice-President, certainly one of the most ordinary-looking men that ever obtained the suffrage of his fellow citizens … Likewise were there many women kind in ambulances discreetly looking on. The cavalry came first, headed by the valiant Kilpatrick, whom it is hard to look at without laughing. The gay cavaliers themselves presented their usual contribution of Gypsy and Don Cossack. Then followed the artillery and the infantry. Among the latter there was a good deal of difference; some of the regiments being all one could wish, such as the Massachusetts 20th, with Abbot at its head, while others were inferior and marched badly. Thereafter Kill-cavalry (as scoffers call him) gave us a charge of the 500, which was entertaining enough, but rather mobby in style.[41]

Senator Howard's son recorded:

What a thrilling sight that was to a young, peaceful collegian who had never before seen anything more formidable than football and baseball! With sabers all drawn and carbines dangling by the side, and beginning with a slow forward movement, the skirmishers out in advance on the front and sides, the buglers at intervals sounding the orders in silvery, clear, high notes, the pace quickening as the squadrons approached the hill, the skirmishers gradually drawing closer and closer to the main body. At last the bugles sound the charge, and with one mighty shout, the glittering sabers held high up in the flashing sunlight, every man rising in his stirrups, the vast column rushes on like a mighty river that had overflowed its banks and sweeps everything before it. That sight stirs our blood the most of all … It seems as if nothing could stop those reckless, brave, death-dealing troopers and their horses.[42]

An officer noted for February 23:

It [the review] was a brilliant and imposing spectacle, and honored by the presence of a pretty large number of infantry, and lady spectators … the day was cold and bitter, and a flake of snow falling occasionally.[43]

After the parties, the review and seeing off the guests, Kilpatrick and his command returned to their preparations. Ulric Dahlgren had been wounded while fighting at Hagerstown, Maryland, during Lee's retreat after Gettysburg. The wound required that his leg be amputated below the knee. He seemingly recovered quickly, was fitted with an artificial leg and was able to ride a horse by the time he arrived at Kilpatrick's headquarters in mid-February. The planning called for a force of about 4,000 troopers. Dahlgren would lead a strike force of 500 and approach Richmond from the south, force an entrance and release the prisoners. Kilpatrick would attack the city's defenses from the north distracting and holding in place whatever number of defenders there were while Dahlgren liberated the prisoners. That was the plan, the one that George Meade knew of, the one apparently that was supported in Washington and, therefore, the one that would be carried out.

No written record has ever come to light relating to the discussion between Kilpatrick and Secretary Stanton in Washington, but after the raid's miserable failure, the retreat from Richmond of the raiding force, and the death of young Colonel Dahlgren, a good many questions surfaced, both at the time as well as when the history of this episode was written. No prisoners were released but no doubt they heard the gunfire along the city's defenses. Neither Dahlgren nor Kilpatrick had entered the city and after some hours they abandoned the mission and retired. Their plan was to retire to within the lines of General Benjamin Butler's forces on the Virginia Peninsula. As Dahlgren headed for Butler's lines, his force became separated, there was an ambush and the young colonel was killed and others from his command captured. On Dahlgren's body was found papers among which was an address he supposedly was to have read to his command at some point before entering the city. It called for releasing the prisoners, burning the city and finding and killing Jefferson Davis and his cabinet. The papers were turned over to the Confederate President and subsequently the text was published in the Richmond newspapers. Everyone in the Confederacy was outraged. The Confederate Secretary of War sent copies to General Lee along with a note asking whether he concurred with him that those troopers captured from Dahlgren's command ought to be hung. Lee advised against this fearing Union retaliation, But the general sent copies of the incriminating papers to George Meade under a flag of truce and asking whether the murder of Davis and his cabinet was something authorized by him or his government. Meade responded after reading Kilpatrick's report and denied having any knowledge that Dahlgren planned to carry out what was written in the address or other papers. It is evident that Meade did not completely believe Kilpatrick, but there was nothing further he could do.

The following year, after the Confederate surrender and the capture of the fallen government's archives, Secretary of War Stanton ordered all the documents related to the Dahlgren affair be brought to the War Department from Richmond. According to historian Stephen W. Sears, the documents haven't been seen since.[44]

That Meade was suspicious of Kilpatrick's denial is evident in a letter dated April 18, written to his wife, "This was a pretty ugly piece of business for in denying having authorized or approved 'the burning of Richmond, or killing Mr. Davis and Cabinet.' I necessarily threw odium on Dahlgren." Going on, Meade says, "… I regret to say Kilpatrick's reputation, and collateral evidence in my possession rather go against this theory." The theory purported that Dahlgren acted alone, and Meade says, I "… was determined my skirts should be clean." General Andrew Humphreys, Meade's chief of Staff, in a remembrance of this period of the war, written years later, said only "The release of the prisoners was the chief object of the expedition, which was sanctioned by the Secretary of War and the President."[45]

Samuel Merrill rode on the raid with the 1st Maine Cavalry and in 1866 published a history, *The Campaigns of the First Maine and First District of Columbia Cavalry*. He included a summary of events following Kilpatrick's withdrawal from Richmond. Apparently, according to Merrill, Kilpatrick was not yet beyond trying to get into Richmond. Merrill wrote, "The night was dark, the wind furious, and the rain pouring down in torrents." Nevertheless, at about 10pm, Kilpatrick called on Major Taylor of the 1st Maine. "Colonel Dahlgren and his party had been heard from. He had been unsuccessful." According to Merrill, even the lateness of the hour and weather would not force "… abandonment of the object so long as a possibility remained of securing it was not to be thought of." Taylor was told to select 500 men and advance by the Mechanicsville Road to Richmond, the pickets along the road were of such a number that he and his men could easily overpower them. The command was then to enter the city and split into two groups, "One was to liberate our prisoners, confined in Libby [prison], and the other was to secure Jeff Davis." Taylor's command was to start for Richmond at 2am. Kilpatrick would follow with another force and cover Taylor's withdrawal and, it might be assumed, help along the prisoners and greet the Confederacy's president. This plan never got started. An hour after giving this order, Kilpatrick's force was attacked by Rebel cavalry and he was forced to retreat further toward General Butler's lines.[46]

In might be that Meade supported Kill-cavalry not so much in the role of commander defending a subordinate, despite the "collateral evidence," but because the truth, if made known, would set off a political "firestorm," by indicating that Dahlgren or Kilpatrick, or both, had planned the killing and burning with an approving nod from Washington. After all, this was an election year. The "collateral evidence" spoken of by Meade and in his possession at the time has never surfaced, but historian Stephen W. Sears points to one possible related loose end:

> That collateral evidence was very likely the testimony of Captain John McEntee of the Bureau of Military Information who was posted to Meade's staff. McEntee had ridden on the raid with Dahlgren and evaded capture. General Marsena Patrick, the army's Provost Marshal, recorded in his diary at the time of the affair a conversation with McEntee after he returned from the raid. 'Captain McEntee had only contempt for Kilpatrick,' wrote General Patrick, 'and says he managed just as all cowards do.' He further says, that he thinks the papers are correct that were found on Dahlgren, as they correspond with what D. told *him*.[47]

So, the Dahlgren affair ended, another of the many unresolved episodes of this war.

***

The winter continued through the month of March and then the weather began to improve. There were changes, some the result of doings by Washington. New soldiers began arriving in the regimental camps, draftees, unenthusiastic participants in the efforts to save the Union. A former general later recalled the winter of 1863–1864:

> The draft had started the previous summer and the results were now showing up in the camps in Virginia. This time the abuses of the conscription system were made manifest … by the character of a large part of the recruits who were sent through the agency. The professional bounty-jumper and the kidnapped emigrant and street boy, … came in large numbers, the professional with the intention of deserting at the earliest opportunity.

The bounty jumpers would, when ordered onto the picket line, often steal away. This happened so frequently that additional cavalry was posted just to catch them. This led to more work for the provost marshal and the army's legal system. A former general recalled:

A gallows and a shooting-ground were provided in each corps, and scarcely a Friday passed during the winter while the army lay on Hazel River and the vicinity of Brandy Station that some of these deserters did not suffer the death penalty.[48]

A reorganization of the Cavalry Corps was necessitated with the arrival of James Wilson, newly promoted to brigadier general, to command the 3rd Division. Wilson received his promotion in April and, therefore, was junior in rank to every other one-star general in the corps. Therefore, Custer, as a brigade commander, could not serve under a divisional commander his junior in rank. Custer and his Michigan men were transferred to the 1st Division, and Custer's early biographer, probably making more of it than it was at the time, added another element to the situation. The 1st Division was to be commanded by General Alfred Torbert, and Custer then:

> … found himself under an infantry general, side by side with [Thomas] Devin, an old, steady-going man, not given to dash, in a place where his enthusiasm must necessarily be cooled to conform to slower movements of his commands.[49]

Custer wrote at the time, Wilson "… is an engineer officer of Grant's staff and had never even commanded a company of men." Custer goes on the say "Had [Pleasonton] remained in command of the Cavalry Corps I would now be in command of a division." Pleasonton was on his way to Missouri, replaced at the instigation of Secretary of War Stanton and General Grant. He was replaced by an unknown quantity from the western theater, Major General Philip Sheridan. Of Pleasonton's relief, Custer says "… without apparent cause … I know the reason but do not wish to state it on paper."[50] Wilson was an upper classman when Custer was at West Point and for whatever reason or cause, the two young generals could not get along, be it personalities or some event from their days at the academy that was remembered but never found its way into a record.

There were other changes within the Cavalry Corps when Sheridan assumed command. Wesley Merritt, who had been acting commander of the 1st Division since John Buford had been forced from command by illness and subsequently died, was returned to command of the Reserve Brigade, supplanted by General Alfred Torbert. James Kidd of the Michigan Brigade, and now part of Torbert's command, passed judgment on the new commander some 50 years later in a memoir. Torbert was "… an infantry officer whose qualifications as a commander of cavalry were not remarkable." There were "… subordinates more deserving, Custer, Merritt, and Thomas C. Devin."[51] Kidd also directed a kindly and rare positive remembrance of the deposed Alfred Pleasonton. The former Cavalry Corps commander in "… the campaign of 1863 had performed most meritorious and effective service and certainly deserved a high place in the list of union [sic] leaders of that period." Kidd continued that if, under General Grant, "… Pleasonton could have been permitted to serve loyally under Sheridan, who was his junior in rank, it would, doubtless, have been better for both of them."[52] Here Kidd is most likely unaware of Meade's negative feeling toward Pleasonton given the stance he had taken that winter before the Joint Committee on the Conduct of the War.

And there were good words for the new corps commander too, the years having mellowed Kidd's probable first impression:

> There was nothing narrow or mean about Sheridan. Conscious of his own greatness, he was too broad to begrudge recognition to others. When a subordinate deserved commendation and Sheridan knew it, he always gave it.[53]

***

That George Meade was, at times, "a snapping turtle," his staff hesitant in their approach to him, is underscored by too much contemporary testimony not to be absolute truth. And that in a less stressful setting Meade may have enjoyed the company of dogs and children, possibly even young staffers, is beside the point. He was a general and this was war. Orders were necessary and had to be executed exactly, on time and in the fullness of their spirit. Meade's career prior to the war had been in engineering where the totality of the project, its full concept, had to be brought to its planning, to underlay everything else. All contingencies and/or alternate plans recognized, accounted for, and ready for use before the first shovel of dirt was pried from the earth. Perhaps it was something he said or inferred when George Meade first met with Lieutenant General Ulysses S. Grant that made the newly appointed commander of all United States armies decide to keep the victor of Gettysburg in command of the Army of the Potomac. Meade had been prepared for reassignment before Grant arrived at his headquarters, thinking that he would prefer an army commander that he knew, but Grant quickly decided to retain Meade.

With General Grant, President Lincoln had now found a general, brought him from the western theater, promoted him and simply told him in so many words to go out and win the war. Of course, the president would help with all things that were within his power to provide, but Grant had to finish off the war. The new lieutenant general began at once planning for a coordinated spring offensive.

All the generals and all the men were waiting on the weather while collecting an immense stockpile of supplies, rations, ammunition and fresh horses. Along the picket line there was a continuing trickle of Rebels from across the river, Rebels that had had enough. A correspondent from the 8th New York Cavalry wrote home at this time:

> Deserters come into our lines quite frequently, and of course bring a variety of intelligence, the most important of which seems to be the reported re-enforcement [sic] of Lee by a portion of Longstreet's army, also that Lee had but 45 or 50,000 men with him, however, the stories of deserters and intelligent contrabands should be taken with many grains of allowance, especially those of the latter class, as cavalrymen have often found by a toilsome and fruitless midnight ride.[54]

The weather somewhat dictated events with General Grant issuing orders that both the campaign in Virginia, and that led by General Sherman in Georgia, would begin on the same day. On April 25, therefore, camp life would remain quiet at least for a few more days. The trooper from the 8th New York wrote:

> With the exception of a heavy rain storm last night, we have had very pleasant weather for several days past, vegetation displayed itself in the form of flowers, grass, and fruit bloosoms [sic] quite rapidly. During our leisure hours the men amuse themselves with ball playing, quoits, etc., and I will here take occasion to give a brief report of a game of base ball played a few days since, between the commissioned officers, and the men …

Following a list of the players on each side, this trooper from the 8th New York reported the score: Officers 41, Men 22.[55]

CHAPTER TEN

Again, the Wilderness

Preparations are making on every hand for the spring campaign, which threatens to be the most momentous and bloody of all the series we have made. Grant is in full command of all the armies in the United States and is to be with our army in person.

JOSIAH FAVILL, *DIARY OF A YOUNG OFFICER*

I hear to-day that the Yankee army is crossing the Rapidan in great force, and that General Lee is on the march to meet it; if that is true, we will soon be in the middle of some bloody work.

GEORGE NEESE, ARMY OF NORTHERN VIRGINIA, MAY 4, 1864

It was wonderful how much killing those Irish and Dutch in the Federal army could stand. But the Federals always managed to get some more men to fill up the places made vacant.

JOHN LEWIS, CONFEDERATE OFFICER, RECOLLECTIONS

Gen. Grant will have to remember that the best army of the Confederacy is in front of him commanded by one, if not the best, General on the Continent of America.

UNIDENTIFIED OHIO OFFICER[1]

It was April, springtime, and all the soldiers in their winter camps were wondering, speculating, when were the orders were coming down to march against the Rebels. The army's Judge Advocate's Office had been working for weeks to clean up affairs before the start of the spring campaign. Josiah Favill of the 57th New York Infantry, remembered:

By dint of steady and indefatigable work we have managed to empty the guard house, straightened out the muster rolls, relieved the oppressed and punished the guilty.

The II Corps' veteran Irish Brigade required special attention:

The Irish Brigade was for a time in a most chaotic state, nearly every officer and man had charges preferred against him, thereby stopping their pay and taking them off the roster of duty; by assiduous labor we have gone through the entire command, dismissing the charges in most cases as frivolous and unworthy of attention.[2]

But there were other instances not so frivolous. A few decades in the future, Father William Corby, chaplain of the Irish Brigade, would leave his recollection of a quick trip to Washington in April 1864. The man behind the desk in the capital listened and acknowledged to the priest that it was a "hard case." From him came a mild promise that consideration would be given, a notation made on the paper the chaplain had given him. A few more words were exchanged and then came a question. "What had I to say in extenuation of the crime?" "I answered that I could but say anything on the score ..." Moments passed, a few more words and then Corby made a final plea:

> I said, almost in despair of my case: 'Well, Mr. President, since I have seen from the start that it was out of the question to plead the innocence of this man, or to say anything in mitigation of his crime, I have confined myself to pleading for his pardon; but, since Your Excellency sees fit not to grant it, I must leave his life in your hands!' This was too much! His tender heart recoiled when he realized that a man's life depended upon his mercy. As I started across the 'green room' to take my departure he turned in his chair, and, throwing one of his long legs over the other, said: 'Chaplain, see here! I will pardon him if General Meade will, and I will put that on the petition.' Then under the note ... he wrote: "If Gen. Meade will say, in writing, he thinks this man ought to be pardoned, it will be done. A. Lincoln April 19, 1864."[3]

Father Corby then left the White House and quickly returned to the army's winter camp carrying the petition with Lincoln's notation written on it.

There were many men under a death sentence this April, prison terms for others would be spent as hard labor on Dry Tortugas in the Florida Keys. Former captain, John G. B. Adams, contributed his *Reminiscences of the Nineteenth Massachusetts Regiment* in 1899. The book, Adams says, was mostly "written from memory." "I do not dignify it by calling it a history. It is simply a soldier's story, told by one of the boys." The affair that Father Corby had been called upon to lend his support and had caused him to visit with the president in the White House had originated in the 19th Massachusetts, as Adams relates. "The discipline of the army at this time was very strict. So many substitutes were being received that the death penalty for desertion was often executed."[4] But the state of affairs was a good deal worse than Adams relates. In his reminiscences, Captain Adams only refers to the final act in the case of Private Thomas R. Dawson of the 19th Massachusetts, and no other detailed telling of the affair is readily available except for Father Corby's:

> Early in April, 1864, the case of a soldier named Thomas R. Dawson, not of my brigade but of the 19th Massachusetts Regiment, then in the II Corps, came up. He had been court-marshaled [sic] and condemned to die—to 'hang by the neck until dead.' He sent for me, and before I began to do anything for him he told me his story, in a simple, candid way, that left no doubt in my mind as to the truth of what he said. Still, the sentence had been passed and he must die. Still, the facts as given to me were as follows: He with two other soldiers wandered from camp, and, coming to a house, they found there wine or liquor of some sort, and, needless to say, they indulge freely. He said he became so stupid he knew not what followed. Some men and officers on duty, passing that way, arrested him on a charge rape made by an old woman of

about sixty. The other two got away and escaped arrest; but he was so 'full' that, unable to move, he became an easy victim. His being under the influence of liquor was not, in the eyes of the law, a sufficient excuse, for many reasons; especially because he was out of camp, and, besides, he had no business to be intoxicated. Still, taking human nature as it is, and in consideration of the other excellent qualities of Dawson, the officers of the regiment did not wish to see him die. They manifested the greatest sympathy for him … His friends were not idle. The officers of the regiment drew up a petition to the President, Abraham Lincoln, and came to me and asked me if I would be so kind as to go to Washington and present it.[5]

Father Corby got back to the army with the petition containing Lincoln's notation and quickly took it to the officers of the 19th Massachusetts. Rather than present it themselves to General Meade, Corby recalled:

…they were shy of such duty, and begged me to do it. I did, but with little hope of success. I called on General; Meade, and producing the document with the name of the President, I told the general the whole story in a few words. He looked at the paper for a few moments, and then said: "Father, I know that your mission is one of charity; but sometimes charity to a few means cruelty to many. If our discipline had been more severe, or cruel, if you will, in the beginning, we would not have so many cases for execution now. Besides, the President has the final acts of that court-marshal [sic] in his possession, and he should have given that final and positive decision. I will *not* act."

"Then the man must die," I said.

"You may see the President again."

"There is not enough time left. The execution is set to the 25th, the day after tomorrow."

"Well," he said, "you may use the telegraph; I will give you use of the military wires."

"No," I said, "the case seems to me to be now between you and the President. I have done all I could."

Father Corby goes on to relate that some generals in the army at the time felt that Lincoln had pardoned too many men already and Meade "could not see his way clear to do what had been found fault with in the President." The priest continues with possibly an opinion formed during the years before he penned his memoir:

The fact of the matter is, at that time the generals in the field, or some of them at least, thought that the kind-hearted President was too good in pardoning so many, and some blame was attached to him on this account.

Corby returned to the regiment's headquarters and related what had happened to the officers that had signed the petition. They encouraged him to use the telegraph that had been offered. Then Corby turned to II Corps commander, Winfield Scott Hancock, whom he called "our good friend." Hancock told Corby to use the telegraph. "You can do so from my headquarters," and he wrote out an order allowing the priest to do so. "I telegraphed," Corby said, "but I was told afterward that, in all probability, the message never reached the President. The secretary of war, very likely, put the dispatch in the fire, for I never received an answer."[6]

Louis Boudrye, the chaplain of the 5th New York Cavalry, was ordered to witness the execution of Private Dawson. In the journal he kept, Boudrye writes for April 25:

Went to witness the execution of a private, Co. A, 19th Mass. Vols. He was hung by the neck, till he was dead. The arrangement of the troops and the music were very imposing and impressive. The execution was bad, on account of the scaffold being too low or the rope too long, as that the feet of the man struck the ground as he fell. It was a solemn and impressive hour, one I had never seen before witnessed nor as I hope to see another.[7]

Between the date of Private Dawson's execution on April 25, and April 29, something or some attitude changed, either in the White House or at General Meade's headquarters. While Father Corby struggled for a pardon for Private Dawson, the 5th New York Cavalry had a man under a death sentence, one Private John Crowly, for desertion. On April 28, in his journal, Boudrye wrote the following:

I saw Mr. John Crowly who had been pardoned or rather had his sentence commuted from being shot to hard labor on the Dry Tortugas for term of service. He was a happy man and grateful.[8]

Nowhere does Chaplain Boudrye indicate that any one either in or out of the 5th New York was trying to get a commutation of sentence for Private Crowly for it certainly would have been mentioned in the chaplain's journal.

Lieutenant John G. B. Adams was one of the officers of the 19th Massachusetts that had signed the petition to the president, and he, along with the entire regiment, was ordered to march and witness the execution. Adams says that until he was accused, Dawson had been a good soldier and had won medals for bravery while with the British army during the Crimean War, but this was outweighed by the accusing woman testifying against Dawson at his court-martial. Adams published his reminiscences in 1899 and in his retelling of this story he adds a comment concerning the thinking within the army at this time relative to executions. This comment also cannot be said to be resident with army commanders at the time or formulated by Adams in years following:

The President would have been pleased to grant our prayer, but he said the complaint from many officers was that he was destroying the discipline of the army by so often setting aside the findings and sentences of court-marshals [sic], and he dare not do it.

After the execution, Adams says he was forever after against execution by hanging and some of the men of the regiment who were, and had been, for Dawson's sentence being set aside said "that it was too bad to hang men when they were so hard to get, and if they had let him alone for a few weeks Johnnie Reb would have saved them the trouble."[9]

***

Now it was May again, Virginia in the springtime. The army drilled, administrative loose ends cleaned up, supply requisitions written and filled. Everyone was now simply waiting for orders. Theodore Lyman of Meade's headquarters wrote at the beginning of May:

> At last the order of march, for to-morrow at 5 A.M.! Of it more when it is over—if I am here to write … May God bless the undertaking at last and give an end to this war!

Earlier and before returning from a leave at home, Lyman, thinking of the forthcoming campaign everyone with the army expected to be the bloodiest yet, wrote in his notebook:

> … I sometimes try to realize a death on the field, but I cannot. My poor mind cannot take in this one great Certainty for us all. One fruit is broken by the wind, green from the tree; another in its full time, falls, ripe, in the pleasant autumn. All fall. To me all close creeds seem like futile attempts to grasp the infinite, but it cannot be the Life with all its intense Reality of Beauty, Goodness, and Religion, should be a thing that passes into nothing.[10]

To be exact it was Wednesday, May 4, and the soldiers of the Army of the Potomac boiled coffee, ate an early breakfast and got ready to move. Today's move would be against their old nemesis, Robert E. Lee and his army. A soldier named Wilkeson remembered:

> It was a beautiful morning, cool and pleasant. The sun arose above an oak forest that stood to the east of us, and its rays causes thousands of distant rifle barrels and steel bayonets to glisten as fire points. In all directions troops were falling into line. The air resounded with the strains of martial music. Standards were unfurled and floated lazily in the light wind.

Another soldier, he was young then, and all the planning and preparations were done, the orders written and issued and at that moment being followed, with no one knowing what the day would bring. Then it was years later and that one veteran, old now, was still trying to capture in words the morning of May 4. It was the Army of the Potomac and:

> As I recall the scene of the old army in motion … a solemn spell comes over my heart … while I look back through the past at the magical pageant, I hear above me the notes of slowly passing bells.[11]

Writing and waiting for something to happen, a West Point-trained infantry officer, Emory Upton, remembered his army's past and wanted better. "The spring campaign will soon be inaugurated," Upton wrote on April 10. "The Army of the Potomac deserves a better name than it has, as we will soon prove." Upton was, at this time, a colonel leading a brigade and was expecting a promotion to brigadier general, as any ambitious West Pointer would during this war. But in the same letter Upton says, "General Meade has informed me that without 'political' influence I will never be promoted." Soon after he wrote, "I have despaired of receiving it [promotion] in the manner honorable to a soldier."[12] The campaign in Virginia then began and Upton survived the horrific fighting in the Wilderness and at Spotsylvania

Court House, where, on May 10 he led an assault where he was told, "Upton, you are to lead those men upon the enemy's works this afternoon, and if you do not carry them, you are not expected to come back, but if you carry them I am authorized to say that you will get your stars."[13] The attack was initially successful but miscommunication on the Union's side prevented support from being given and a stiff Rebel counter attack, threw Upton's force back. Nevertheless, Upton got his promotion. But by June 4, and with the thought of promotion still present, as well as that of Spotsylvania and Cold Harbor, Upton wrote with frustration at the way the campaign has been handled thus far:

> I am disgusted with the generalship displayed … Our men have, in many instances, been foolishly and wantonly sacrificed. Assault after assault has been ordered upon the enemy's entrenchments, when they knew nothing about the strength or position of the enemy. Thousands of lives might have been spared by the exercise of a little skill; but, as it is, the courage of the poor men is expected to obviate all difficulties. I must confess that, so long as I see such incompetency, there is no grade in the army to which I do not aspire.[14]

Upton's opinion made sense, especially among historians of the campaign. The slaughter was horrific, the casualties far in excess of anything thus far suffered by the Potomac army, and might have, in many cases, been prevented if different tactics—"the exercise of a little skill"—had been known to at least some generals and employed by them.

The chaplain of the 15th New Jersey remembered in later years the start of the campaign and the soldiers as they left their winter camp and as they marched in the Wilderness. "They were well aware of the fierceness of the struggle into which they were entering," Chaplain Alanson Haines wrote in the regiment's history, "yet they heard with readiness the order to advance, and stepped with alacrity toward the regions where they knew certain death awaited many thousands of their number." Haines's regiment crossed the Rapidan on May 4 and noted, "From the summit of the swells of ground we could see the big dark lines, which looked like fences dividing up the country, but the glitter of many thousand musket-barrels showed them to be massed men moving in column."[15]

The months in winter camp were at an end. The army had been augmented with new recruits and draftees. In September 1863, Washington had sent XI and XII Corps to the western theater and during the winter Meade had reorganized what remained. I and III Corps were folded into the three-remaining corps, II, V and VI. A corps commanded by General Ambrose Burnside, a former commander of this army but now leading IX Corps, was brought to the east from Tennessee but remained under the direct control of the Grant. This was the third springtime of this war, the fourth if the spring of Fort Sumter was included. If there was hope in the North that this year's campaign would be the last, the one that ended the war, that person with such a hope need only to be reminded that the two contending armies in Virginia stood now only 50 miles from where they had first clashed in 1861. Also to be remembered was that, in December 1862, the army had left its camps around Falmouth, crossed the river and attacked General Lee; its plan to destroy the enemy's force. It was a failure in which there had been twelve thousand casualties. In April 1863, the same army had left the same camps at Falmouth, crossed the river, got into position and this time allowed General Lee to attack it, with the hope that its numbers and weapons would prevail. It was a failure. The river crossing had cost seventeen thousand casualties. A different general had commanded each of these efforts. Now in May 1864, the same army, or what was left of it from the year before, and with a third general commanding, and another overseeing all, left its camps and crossed the river with the same intention. There was little reason to expect that the third time would be the charm. Lee attacked it as soon as he could march his men within rifle range. There were seventeen thousand more casualties by the time Meade exited the Wilderness.[16] The only difference this time was that the Army of the Potomac didn't re-cross the Rappahannock or Rapidan, but maneuvered south, and this was the doing of the new man in charge, Ulysses S. Grant. The president's decision to put Grant in charge was based on the campaigns he had led and victories he had won in the western theater during the past two years. The Congress had voted Grant's appointment in the affirmative and reauthorized the rank of lieutenant general, held previously only by George Washington and Winfield Scott by brevet. Everyone knew Grant's story, news of his victories also included background about the newsmaker. Grant was the victor of Vicksburg, the operation that had essentially cut the Confederacy in two, but he had resigned from the army in 1854, it was said, at the strong suggestion of superiors, serious drinking being the issue. In early 1862, Grant had captured Confederate forts on the Tennessee and Cumberland Rivers and won, narrowly—the opposing forces having retired—the battle at Shiloh. In 1863, after Vicksburg, he lifted the siege of Chattanooga in the fall. But from leaving the army, now a long decade in the past, and until he had won victories leading western troops against those river forts early in 1862, he had floated from civilian job to farming to working as a clerk in his father's business. The coming of the Civil War had given the West Point-trained, Mexican War veteran, ex-captain of U.S. Regulars, a second chance, and although he never truly admitted it, one suspects he knew it, appreciated it and was taking full advantage.

Everyone knew the spring campaign led by this general would produce a confrontation with Robert E. Lee that would probably be the most violent and therefore the bloodiest yet. Perhaps if more Rebel blood was spilled than Union, the war might be brought to an end. The year 1864 was an election year and mentioned only in the most hushed of voices of the political class, from the foremost to the lowliest, was the realization that if the war was ended by the autumn, or if significant victories were won by that time, Lincoln might win re-election. As things political now stood, if the election was held in the first week of May, he would not. But before any of that, "The summer days are almost here," wrote a soldier from V Corps, "when we shall be wearily plodding over the road once more in search of *victory or death*. Many a poor fellow will find the latter, and may it be a solace to him, I dread the approaching campaign. I can see horrors insurmountable throughout the summer months."[17]

Orders came down to break camp, for the mounted regiments and brigades to assemble. Inspections were made, ammunition and rations were brought forward, and all the creature comforts collected through the winter discarded. Late in the afternoon of May 2, the Potomac army was poised, waiting only for the order to move, its "… white tents covering the territory as far as the eye could reach." Then about 6pm, "Something was moving toward the camps, hiding from view the entire landscape in its passage … It was a cloud of dust—Virginia real estate on the rampage. As the hurricane struck the camps it leveled the tents and trees, filling the hearts of the men with consternation and their eyes with dust. Rain followed in generous supply, and the dust was again transformed into its native element—mud."[18] Some may have looked upon the storm as an omen. It was a violent storm on the eve of a hurricane of violence, engulfing the months of May and June, surpassing anything that had gone before in this war.

The fighting in the Wilderness over the next few days was more ferocious than the battle fought there the year before, if that were possible. On May 8, after three full days of bloodshed, a Confederate soldier, George Neese, remarked in his diary:

> The fierce, sharp roar of deadly musketry filled our ears from morning till night, and the thick white cloud of battle smoke hung pall-like over the fields and woods all day along the battle line … at midday the smoke was so thick overhead that I could just make out to see the sun … a thousand fires blazed and crackled in the bloody arena.[19]

Stephen Weld of a Massachusetts regiment noted on May 5:

> … all this time the musketry firing was fearful. It was one continuous roll, at long intervals broken by the loud booming of a cannon. We went up what was called the Brock Road … Trees were cut down by the bullets, and the bark knocked into my face time and again by the bullets. There are quite a few instances of trees being cut down by sustained rifle fire.

A short time later, Weld's regiment was in contact with a Confederate force and drove them back some distance, then:

> When we were advancing on this morning we passed several rebels lying on the ground, who had been wounded a little while before. One of them asked one of our men for some water. The man stopped at the brook, got him some water, and then went ahead. As soon as we had gone some fifty yards or so, the fellow we had given water to drew himself up and shot one of our men. Some of the others went back and quickly put him out of the world. It was a mean, cowardly thing for a man to do who had been treated as we treated him.[20]

Only darkness slowed and then stopped the rifle fire and the artillery. The soldiers on both sides scrambled then for something to eat and drink, but it was there for them only if they carried it with them. "The night is dark, and the woods around us are all on fire; all the dead trees scattered through the woods are a blaze from bottom to top ..." And all this among "... the wailing moans of the wounded and the faint groans of the dying, all loudly acclaimed the savagery of our boasted civilization and the enlightened barbarism of the nineteenth century."[21]

***

Grant had kept Meade in command of the Army of the Potomac, but he decided his place for the spring campaign was to be with that army. In reality, a field army can only have one commander. In this campaign, Meade got his orders from Grant, but how he carried them out was largely left to him. It worked well enough, and there was something else, something left unsaid at the time but written later into reminiscences. There was, beneath the surface, resident with at least the veterans going back to 1861, if not others of lesser longevity, that "... there was more at stake ... than in any other battles between Northern and Southern armies ... with perhaps the single exception of the battle of Gettysburg. The Army of the Potomac had never won a decisive battle on Southern soil." In every major encounter with General Lee "... a larger army with superior equipment suffered humiliation and defeat from Southern generals commanding a ragged and half-starved army."[22] If this war was ever to end, this had to change.

Reaction within the ranks to Grant's arrival with the Army of the Potomac was mostly of the waiting and seeing sort. The troops, of course, knew of Grant's successes in the west, but Virginia, they believed, was different. "We have never complained that Lee's men would not fight," wrote Frank Wilkeson, a private in a New York artillery outfit. "Whatever faults they may have, cowardice is not one of them. We welcome Grant. He cannot be weaker or more inefficient than the generals who have wasted the lives of our comrades during the past three years." Another veteran of eastern campaigns later reflected:

> ... all the Potomac veterans knew Lee's Army of Northern Virginia was an altogether different institution from the western armies that Grant had beaten or captured, still we felt that the Army of the Potomac was quite equal to the situation ... They knew that the Rebel army was inferior to them in numbers and equipment. And it was the almost unanimous opinion of the rank and file that this would be the last campaign of the war, and that it wouldn't last long either.

Another soldier recorded his thoughts, as he got ready to cross into Rebel territory:

> All look forward to this campaign as the last of the series and expect Grant to spare neither life nor material in reducing the rebel army to submission ... This is the beginning of the end, and in a few days our camp near Stevensburg will be a thing of the past, and where shall we be, who can tell? ... The army is ready to march with eight days' cooked rations.

In the 1st Maine Cavalry it was remembered that, with Grant in command, "it was evident that the government meant business." However, the troopers "could not help qualifying their belief and their hope with the fact that he [Grant] had never yet had the Confederate general, Robert E. Lee, to contend against." That 1864 would see the last of this war came also from a trooper in the 1st Massachusetts Cavalry who later remembered:

> We all believed that the Union cause would triumph. But When? Three years had rolled round since the Rebel fired on Sumter. And 'Uncle Robert; with his veterans in butternut, still flaunted the stars and bars defiantly as ever …'

"The feeling about Grant is peculiar," wrote cavalry officer Charles Francis Adams of Massachusetts, "a little jealousy, a little envy, want of confidence—all in many minds and now latent; but it is ready to crystallize at any moment and only brilliant success will dissipate the elements. All, however, are willing to give him a full chance and his own time for it." Another officer from Massachusetts remembered, "A hopeful spirit prevailed, but it was not demonstrative. The fact that General Grant was simple and unaffected in his manners and easily accessible was gratifying." Having said this, the same voice added, "as a whole our infantry was not in average merit equal to that under General Hooker in the Chancellorsville campaign." But then another officer in the same regiment added, "… events would soon decide whether his name is Ulysses or Useless." "We are on the verge of a decisive campaign," wrote a soldier, "a campaign which will bring the rebellion to an end or cover with disgrace and confusion the government and the loyal states."[23] Nearly every memoirist of the Overland Campaign that was now beginning left a comment concerning General Grant's assumption of command, either when he first arrived in the east or as the 1864 campaign was beginning. Captain Mason Tyler of the 37th Massachusetts Infantry was from Amherst and the son of a professor at the college. In the recollection he was to write years in the future, Captain Tyler spoke of his thinking at the time:

> He [Grant] was to be matched against the ablest commander that the war produced. We knew it meant a battle royal, but we had no conception of what was before us. The past was mere child's play in comparison in what we were now to encounter. Little did we reck[on] that within thirty days after the campaign opened fifty thousand of our comrades would be numbered among the killed and wounded.[24]

Quotes concerning Grant and the expectation resident in the minds of the soldiers he was to lead across the river can be quoted in the hundreds. Many of these reflect the individual's assessment, stated or not, of the leadership then resident in the force across the river. Also, for an army operating so close to its national capital there was bound to be closer observations of it and suggestions for it than for an army functioning at a greater distance would necessarily have to endure. Grant had been given full and complete control by Lincoln, but a staff officer waiting for the campaign to begin remembered:

... we thought people north hardly comprehended that the Army of the Potomac had been fighting the choicest leadership and the best army by far of the Confederacy, and all the time with a rope around its neck tied to the doors of the war department. But Grant came, and brought the little fellow with him named Sheridan to command the cavalry, and we began to think that perhaps they would do the business after all.[25]

There were expectations too on the other side of the river. General Lee's army was confident that 1864 would see the realization of Southern independence and defeat of the Northern army. A soldier from Georgia wrote home while waiting for Grant to strike:

All we want you to do is to be hopeful & continue to ask God for aid & Gen [.] Grant will go down like the rest of [the] yankey [sic] Gens, that have bin [sic] brought against this army.

The men of the Army of Northern Virginia had at this time a profound faith in God and in General Robert E. Lee. The colonel of the 31st Georgia, while he too waited for the move by Grant, wrote:

General Robert E. Lee is regarded by his army as nearest approaching the character of the great & good Washington as any man living. He is the only man living in whom they would unreservedly trust all power for the preservation of their independence.[26]

The offensive-minded Lee would have liked nothing better this spring than to start north on another campaign. The offensive was "... a role appealing strongly to his disposition," noted Edward P. Alexander, an artillery officer. The supply and logistic deficiencies that had plagued his army through the winter would not allow it, though. Even launching a spoiling attack across the river could not be sustained logistically and the numbers were all against him. The general had approximately 65,000 troops facing General Grant whose strength ran beyond 100,000. Lee, therefore, would be on the defensive, and to the general this "... was to invite the enemy to accumulate his resources to the points at which their very weight would crush us."[27] In the struggle soon to begin, soon to be called Grant's Overland Campaign, Robert E. Lee would, nevertheless, show himself as capable in defense as he had on offense; the casualties inflicted would prove the point.

After the fighting had gone on a few days, Theodore Lyman, of General Meade's staff, reflected upon the Confederate soldier. Decidedly biased as the New England patrician was, he wrote of the Rebels of 1864:

These Rebels are not half-starved and ready to give up— a more sinewy, tawny, formidable looking set of men could not be. In education they are certainly inferior to our native-born people; but they are usually very quick-witted within their own sphere of comprehension; and they know enough to handle weapons with terrible effect. Their great characteristic is their stoical manliness, they never beg, or whimper, or complain; but look you straight in the face, with as little animosity as if they had never heard a gun.

236 • VOICES OF THE ARMY OF THE POTOMAC

Another New Englander, from a New Hampshire infantry regiment, wrote later the Southern soldiers "… were infinitely better than the order of things which they represented; they were the best men the South possessed, and I cannot, and would not if I could, detract from or wipe out their bravery, courage and honor."[28]

As for the changes, the one that would prove to be the most fortuitous for the Union cause over the next several months was the appointment of General Philip Sheridan, replacing Alfred Pleasonton, as commander of the Cavalry Corps. Sheridan had served with distinction under Grant in the west but had limited cavalry experience. Whether it was Meade's or Grant's idea, or that of the secretary of war, and then having General Halleck purposely propose Sheridan's name so Grant could seize it, remains cloudy in the record, but Pleasonton, in any case, had to go. The commander of the Army of the Potomac might very well insist. During the winter just past, Pleasonton had shown himself to be a conniving and obscene political back stabber. He allowed rumors to circulate as the army rested in camp in late 1863 and early 1864; that it would be Pleasonton replacing George Meade as commander of the Army of the Potomac. Meade's experience before the Joint Committee on the Conduct of the War was one that did not help his outlook. As the committee surmised, someone had to be guilty for allowing Lee to get away after Gettysburg, get back to Virginia and remain constituted as an armed force arrayed against the United States. A head had to roll as a result and, typically, it was the general under whose command the event occurred. General officers serving under Meade clearly understood this and some allowed the memories of those July days to conform to what was thought to be the wishes of the Radical Republicans comprising the majority of the committee. The most notable of these was General Daniel Sickles, now minus a leg lost during the battle, telling anyone that would listen that it was he who saved the situation as it had developed on the afternoon of July 2. Left out of this version of history spoken by Sickles was the fact that his III Corps had been wrecked that afternoon because of his handling of it. III Corps had fought heroically on July 2 despite Sickles's placement of its divisions and brigades. But by his maneuver and deployment of the corps, placing his command as he did on July 2, Sickles had exposed the rest of Meade's force unnecessarily and it had required a supreme effort and many more casualties that otherwise would he been the case in resisting and turning back the Confederate assault that ruined III Corps. Indeed, there was so little left of III Corps that General Meade, that winter, took what remained and distributed it among his other corps organizations. Thankfully for the Potomac army, and probably before his testimony to the committee, it had been decided by George Meade that he would never allow Daniel Sickles to command troops again, at least if he were still commanding. Beyond Sickles, there were others. Pleasonton's self-serving testimony when he was called to the committee seemed designed to leave the impression that, once the infantry assault of July 3 had been turned back, only the cavalry leader appreciated the significance of the victory and how to follow it up. According to one officer remembering Pleasonton as he took command of the cavalry in 1863, the general "… afterwards, at Gettysburg, according to his own account, offered to give General Meade a lesson as to how to make a great general out of himself."[29] Of course, what was said before the committee didn't remain confidential and after processing by the army rumor mill, the commanding general soon heard all about it. There had been many changes in command of the Army of the Potomac in the years past and although he was the only Union general thus far to have ever beaten Robert E. Lee, Meade worried for his position as the winter dragged on. On March 9, 1864, Meade wrote to his wife telling her that Generals "… Birney and Pleasonton have appeared in the maintained ranks. The latter's course is the meanest and blackest ingratitude, for I can prove, but for my intercession he would have been relieved long since."[30] With Grant's arrival in the east, after whatever was spoken of between the general-in-chief and the army commander, Alfred Pleasonton was sent to Missouri and Phil Sheridan given the job.

As it turned out, the diminutive Phil Sheridan proved the perfect choice for a cavalry commander. Sheridan is "… a small broad-shouldered, squat man, with black hair and a square head. He is of Irish parents but looks very like Piedmontese," Theodore Lyman reflected upon meeting the new cavalry commander. "If he is an able officer," this officer opined, "he will find no difficulty in pushing along this army, several degrees …"[31] Coming from the western theater, Phil Sheridan may have only had a hint of the political and unmilitary undercurrents that swirled within an army operating so close to the national capital and populated in its upper echelons with so many conservative and ambitious personalities. Years later, in his memoirs, Sheridan does not say Pleasonton's removal from command was related to his testimony before the Joint Committee on the Conduct of the War or anything in particular, but there were "Many jealousies and much ill-feeling, the out growth of former campaigns, [that] existed among officers of high grade in the Army of the Potomac in the winter of 1864, and several general officers were to be sent elsewhere in consequence."[32] However, be it unhistorical speculation, Phil Sheridan might never have been called from the west if John Buford had not succumbed to typhoid fever in December 1863. As a contemporary wrote at the time of his death and quoted by cavalry historian Stephen Z. Starr:

> The army and the country have met with a great loss by the death of … Buford. He was decidedly the best cavalry general we had, and was acknowledged as such in the army … [He was] rough in his exterior, never looking after his own comfort, untiring on the march and in the supervision of all the militia of his command, quiet and unassuming in his manner.[33]

A year before, it had been seniority that had kept John Buford from Cavalry Corps command and, at the time, there was nothing glaring from the record that would bar the "Knight of Romance" from the job.

Philip Sheridan, not the tallest, strongest or most accommodating, was, nevertheless an innovative leader and not overly reticent when a superior or a policy he considered wrong or out of date got in the way. A young officer, a West Pointer like the new cavalry commander, after some years of accumulated hindsight said that Sheridan "… never could have permanently maintain pleasant official relations with his fellow commanders on any field; he had to be the chief control, tolerating no restraint from equals. Grant alone he bowed to …"[34] But at first many troopers asked, "Who this Sheridan was no one seemed to know, only that he came from the west, which was some recommendation."[35] However, once the men he led became familiar with him and his ways, a bond was formed through victories, one not to be broken with coming of peace, but stretching into the decades to come.

The regiments and brigades making up the three divisions of the Cavalry Corps, prodded by Sheridan and through its officers down to each trooper, used the remaining time before the start of the campaign to get prepared for field operations, operations lasting indefinitely. The horses were fed and cared for, giving them strength and weight. Horseshoes were looked after. Sabers were sharpened, carbines and pistols cleaned. The essential equipment a trooper needed in the field, a tin cup, a small frying pan, as well as any extra rations and extra coffee, however acquired, were packed along with a rubber blanket if one could be had, a poncho and any extra cloths an individual might need and could carry.

With the possible exception of McClellan's amphibious move to the Virginia Peninsula in 1862, the Overland Campaign of 1864 may be said to have been the largest military operation undertaken by the U.S. Army to that time. Indeed, nothing like it had ever been seen in the western hemisphere, possibly anywhere. To support a Federal army of 119,000 men with food and ammunition, forage for its animals, along with ambulances to haul off the wounded, a supply train of 4,067 wagons pulled by 24,250 horses and mules was required. The protection of this train was a primary concern of General Meade, and to his thinking therefore, also a primary responsibility of Sheridan's cavalry. Meade was willing to let Sheridan use any offensive tactics he thought proper in the campaign, but the cavalry's ultimate purpose was to protect the supply train.[36] Sheridan disagreed.

The Overland Campaign would last 40 days during which there would be bloodletting on a scale that made the battles that had gone before, Antietam, Chancellorsville and Gettysburg, pale by comparison. All the casualties of those three battles combined would not equal those of this campaign. The army of Lee and the army of Grant would clash repeatedly over the 40 days. And it had become a reflex, when the soldiers of either army stopped marching, they began digging field works to shelter and defend themselves. Without proper entrenching tools, tin cups, bayonets and hands were employed whenever the marching stopped. If the stop was long enough, and tools became available, trees were cut, the trunks used to strength the works, trenches were dug deeper, and obstacles fashioned as personnel obstructions placed in front of the trenches to entangle attacking infantry.

The weather was good, there were flowers blooming along the roadside, the birds sang. It happened on the morning of May 5. A chaplain of a Pennsylvania infantry regiment, who had crossed the Rapidan the day before, noted of May 5:

> Thursday morning … arose in all the exquisite loveliness of opening May—tree, shrub, plant, grass bursting into bud and flower. Numerous birds caroled forth their songs, unaffrighted by the presence of so many invaders.[37]

But the birds flew off at the sound of gunfire and the new green leaves became spotted with blood as the clash came. General Lee chose to fight within the Wilderness at the opening of the campaign in order to lessen Grant's advantage in men and artillery. The Wilderness restricted movement and vision, concentration of force and firepower and gave General Lee a fighting chance.

General Lee had set his army in motion for the Wilderness on May 4, as soon as the river crossing was confirmed. The infantry corps of Generals Richard Ewell and A. P. Hill marched to within easy striking distance of the Federals by the end of the day and bivouacked. Their orders, ironically, were the same as at Gettysburg: not to bring on a general engagement as the corps commanded by James Longstreet had a greater distance to march and would not get to the Wilderness until at least the end of May 5, and possibly later than that. Again, the order would not be consciously disobeyed. Contact came early on May 5 near a place called Parker's Store. The picket line along the Orange Plank Road placed by the 5th New York Cavalry was struck by the advance elements of A. P. Hill's corps. Isolated carbine fire evolved into a skirmish, then a pressing attack by the Rebels, and then a fighting withdrawal by the New York cavalry. Within an hour or two, the encounter became a full-throated battle as infantry brigades advanced into the area. If finest hours are to be remembered, this single incident, occurring when it did, with the New York regiment playing the overture in advance of the main performance, should be remembered. The 5th New York, staging its fighting withdrawal, in all likelihood inflicting many more casualties than it received from Hill's advancing infantry. William Parker was the chief of staff for the Confederate corps advancing along the Orange Plank Road this morning. He later wrote of this opening action:

> … we came to a heavy line of dismounted cavalry. They were picked men and hard to move. We had to thicken our skirmish line. The enemy's officers behaved with the greatest gallantry, on horseback encouraging the men, and exposing themselves to hold their line; finely they gave way. We captured a number of men, and many fine horses and moved some distance below Parker's store while waiting for Heth's division to form.

Only after resisting for upward of three hours and now out of ammunition for their Spencer carbines did the 5th New York retire. Infantry from VI Corps were by that time filing into place and attempting to stem the Rebel tide. The chaplain of the 5th New York, in his regimental history, quoted from an article written at the time for the *New York Herald*. After retiring to replenish ammunition and getting the wounded to the rear, General Meade ordered the regiment to hold itself near his headquarters and await his orders. "This was a compliment well earned by the gallant conduct at Parker's Store. It is under the command of Colonel Hammond, one of the best officers in the service."[38]

Generals Meade and Grant had wanted to transit the Wilderness and get into the open country to the south, but it was dangerous for the infantry to get too far ahead of its supply train. The monstrous supply train would need more than a day to transit the Wilderness. As a result, the army bivouacked in the Wilderness on the night of May 4 and in the morning Lee was there and attacked. Lee was using the Wilderness to his advantage, hoping to spoil Grant's offensive. He did not cling to a hope of pushing the Union force back across the river, as he had done against Burnside and Hooker, but he would inflict casualties on his enemy to such a degree that its forward movement might stall. The aggressiveness of General Lee and his advantageous use of the Wilderness terrain were not fully appreciated or allowed for in Union army's the plan of movement. General Lee was outnumbered, his losses almost non-existent deleter not replaceable, at the end of a weak and inadequate supply line supporting his men and with subordinate commanders, many of whom were replacements for others lost in battle the year before. Nevertheless, during the days following the opening encounter with the 5th New York, Lee was to show himself a master of aggressive defensive warfare.

Before the sun was very high in the eastern sky, Lee's forces were engaged along the Orange Turnpike and Orange Plank Road, the fighting spreading out to the left and right of each. Colonel A. L. Long, General Lee's military secretary, recalled at a later date the remark made by his general over breakfast on the morning of May 5, as the Wilderness battle was beginning:

> In the course of conversation that attended the meal he [Lee] expressed himself surprised that his new adversary had placed himself in the same predicament as 'Fighting Joe' had done the previous spring. He hoped the result would be even more disastrous to Grant than that which Hooker had experienced. He was, indeed, in the best spirits, and expressed much confidence in the result …[39]

May 5 and 6 witnessed the bloodletting the soldiers had expected but, nevertheless, astounded them. It came in massed attacks and in small unit skirmishes, often at close range given the obstructions caused by trees and undergrowth. Morris Schaff, a young ordinance officer, remembered the Wilderness:

> Chiefly of scrubby, stubborn oaks, and low-limbed, disordered, haggard pines … with here and there scattered clumps of alien cedar … But generally, the trees are noticeably stunted … The surface of the ground resembles a choppy sea more than anything else … As is in all the woods of Virginia, there are many dogwoods scattered about. Both they and the huckleberries were in

full bloom when the battle was going on, the dogwoods, with out spread, shelving branches, appearing at times through the billowing smoke like shrouded figures.

A chaplain from Pennsylvania recalled:

> *The Wilderness*; undulating with occasional swamps, technically *sloughs*—through which, if a man attempts to walk, he sinks leg deep; some large trees, but generally a thick growth of pine, cedar, oak, and hickory, with scarcely a field or house.

The same was true for the Rebel soldiers that marched into the Wilderness from the west. It left an impression on General John B. Gordon, who later said:

> Field glasses and scouts and cavalry were equally and almost wholly useless in that dense woodland. The tangle of underbrush and curtain of green leaves enabled General Grant to concentrate his forces at any point, while their movements were entirely concealed.[40]

Along the Orange Turnpike, the wounded that were able to walk trudged to the rear looking for any medical attention available. Staff officer Theodore Lyman watched as the firing to the west along this road intensified and more soldiers advanced against the stream of retiring wounded. "I saw coming toward me, a mounted officer—his face covered with blood," he noted, "and he was kept in the saddle by an officer who rode beside him … 'Hullo, Lyman!' he cried, in a wild way that showed he was wandering; 'here I am; hurt a little; not much; I am going to lie down a few minutes, and then I am going back again! Oh, you ought to have seen how we drove 'em—I had the first line.' It was my classmate, Colonel Hayes, of the 18th Massachusetts … I was afraid Hayes was mortally wounded, but I am told since, he will recover. I trust so."[41]

Two days of close contact produced about 17,600 Union casualties, while General Lee lost 11,000 men, only a fraction of which could be quickly replaced. Illustrative of the casualties sustained by Union forces in the Wilderness is that of the 19th Maine which, in its later history, detailed its 137 casualties for the two days. They had crossed the Rapidan with 490 officers and men and left the Wilderness 29 percent weaker. During the actions at Spotsylvania Court House, the regiment would accumulate an additional 82 casualties. It equates to a casualty rate of 44 percent.[42]

Some within the Union army at the close of these two days might have thought what some had expressed in April when the new general-in-chief had first arrived with the army in Virginia. General Grant might have had much success in the west, but he had yet to encounter Bobby Lee. The regimental history of the 19th Maine Infantry makes mention of what some thought might be the army's next move after the close of combat of the past days. The Rebels expected that the Wilderness fighting would result in "… the usual order of events, they confidently expected the General Grant would re-cross the Rapidan after the battle … Indeed, they felt hurt because our new commanding General … would not recognize the customs and precedents so firmly established." This was not to happen and as this regiment's history relates, it was resting by the side of the road near General Hancock's II Corps headquarters between nine and ten in the evening of May 7. It was there the regiment witnessed the arrival of Generals Meade and Grant:

> The burning woods lighted up the scene, and the faces of the Commanders were recognized, wild cheers echoed through the forest. Tired as they were, the soldiers shouted with renewed enthusiasm. The enemy must have thought a night attack was intended, for they opened fire upon us with shells, which had the effect of silencing the cheering.[43]

George D. Benedict of the 2nd New York Dragoons, who during the winter had not heard from his wife for weeks and wrote of his concern in a letter to her, was wounded in an action near Todd's Tavern in the Wilderness on May 7. A casualty, Benedict was evacuated to Fredericksburg and received medical treatment.

> Fredericksburg Va 18 May 1864
> Mrs. Sarah Benedict
> I have visited your good husband twice. He sends his love. He told me you were a blessed good woman. He loves Christ his savior. I held a service in his room this morning. He is in the house occupied once by the mother of Gen. Washington. Your husband is comfortable, severely wounded in the shoulder and back.
> Your letters at present cannot reach him. I like him very much.
> Very truly your servant for Jesus sake,
> James Hall,
> Episcopal clergyman of the Philadelphia Delegate of the Christian Commission.

A Wilderness casualty, George Benedict died on May 25, 1864.[44]

Hospital attendants and volunteers often wrote letters to the families of wounded soldiers while they recovered, and to the families of those that did not. Katharine P. Wormeley, a volunteer with the U.S. Sanitary Commission, wrote many letters during the Peninsula Campaign in 1862. In two of her own letters, she commented on this duty:

> We receive such pathetic, noble letters from the parents and friends of those who have died in our care, and to whom it is a part of our duty to write. They will never cease to be a sad and tender memory to us. The mothers' are the most noble and unselfish; the wives' the most pathetic,—so painfully full of personal feeling.

But some of the wounded did not want those at home to know how bad it all had been and possibly Ms. Wormeley misconstrued this writing:

> Some few told the horrors of the march; but as a rule they were all about the families at home. Did you ever notice how people of limited education seem unable to relate anything that is happening about them? They go over a string of family details quite as well known to their correspondent as to themselves.[45]

It was on the third day of fighting in the tangled Wilderness, the battle essentially a stalemate, that General Grant decided to move out of the trees and undergrowth and slide to the left, hopefully out to somewhere his army could confront Lee's and bring to the meeting more men and artillery. It would be a move south, deeper into Virginia; its first waypoint the Village of Spotsylvania Court House. He issued the orders and Meade began moving when it got dark.

Sheridan's 1st and 2nd Cavalry Divisions had fought most of the day, May 7, in the area surrounding Todd's Tavern, at the intersection of Brock and Catharpin Roads, and driven the opposing Rebel cavalry some distance in the direction of Spotsylvania Court House. The territory gained during the day, however, was abandoned when it grew dark, the cavalry withdrawing back to the Todd's Tavern area, to replenish ammunition. The cavalry settled in for the night unaware that Meade had ordered the infantry to advance along Brock Road that night. The planned move would be impeded with the cavalry divisions, commanded by Generals Merritt and Gregg, still occupying the road. Either Sheridan was not fully informed of the infantry move on Spotsylvania scheduled for that night or, if he had, he failed to clear the way for them. It was 1am, May 8, when Sheridan wrote out orders for Merritt and Gregg to move again along Brock Road, clearing the way for the infantry to follow and secure Spotsylvania Court House. This move was to start at 5am. At about the same hour as Sheridan was writing his order for the coming day, George Meade, in advance of his infantry, arrived at the Todd's Tavern intersection. There he encountered Merritt (General Torbert was then on medical leave) and Gregg with their divisions blocking the road and being "without orders." General Meade's volatility likely rose several degrees when he encountered the two cavalry generals uninformed as yet about what to do next. As the army commander, Meade issued his own orders to the cavalry: Move forward without blocking or delaying the infantry from using the road, and get to and beyond Spotsylvania, holding the bridges over the Po River. Merritt and Gregg obeyed as Meade sent a copy of his order to Sheridan. They [the two cavalry divisions] are in the way of the infantry, and there is no time to refer to you. I have given them the inclosed [sic] orders which you can modify to-day after the infantry corps are in position.[46] In like measure, upon receipt of Meade's order to his command, Sheridan's temper must have risen significantly.

It was 3:30am on May 8 and Wesley Merritt was trying to clear Brock Road of Rebels so his division could carry out Meade's orders for the move on Spotsylvania; little progress was being made, the enemy fighting from behind field works. A seriously annoyed Sheridan, now arriving on the scene, and to speed things along, asked for help from V Corps that was waiting back along Brock Road. The infantry came forward and helped the cavalry drive the Rebels out of the way.[47]

It was about 8am when Wilson's 3rd Cavalry Division arrived at Spotsylvania Court House from another direction, he had received Sheridan's order timed at 1am that the other two cavalry generals had not received when General Meade encountered them. As Wilson attempted to secure the village and the crossings of the Po River to the south, the Confederate I Corps made its initial presence known. Grant and his move on Spotsylvania had been anticipated and General Lee had ordered his own move on the village the previous night. The race to Spotsylvania seemed to have resulted in a tie, but in the Civil War ties went to the infantry corps over a cavalry division. According to the historian of this campaign, Gordon Rhea, General Grant lost the race to Spotsylvania and any advantage the position might hold was negated because he had followed "too ambitious a plan." And the blame extends to Meade also, for "… neglecting the details, failing to insure that Brock Road was clear and even obstructing the way with his staff and provost guard." Subordinates reporting to Meade "seemed oblivious for the need for haste." Artillery General Wainwright commented on the move in his journal:

> The fact that our march was at night was enough to tell every man that we wanted to reach some place without Lee knowing it; and one would think that desire for their own safety would spur them all to do it, so as to avoid a fight.[48]

At Spotsylvania, Wilson could see his position was less than tenuous and an order from Sheridan, reaching him that morning, told him to withdraw. Wilson retreated from Spotsylvania by the road leading north to Fredericksburg.[49] The result of these hours of confusion, delay and frustration denied Grant a favorable position outside the inhibiting Wilderness and caused him in the succeeding days to attack Lee's army arrayed behind entrenchments. Exact casualty figures for the days that followed are only estimates, some made at the time of the fighting and some resulting from fine scrutiny of unit records in succeeding years. George Meade estimated his casualties for May 10 in the attack he made on Lee's fortified position to be 4,000 men. For May 12, and another Union assault on the Confederate position, the combined casualties were estimated to be 17,000, the majority of which were from the Army of the Potomac.[50]

George Meade blamed Sheridan for the delays and the extra fighting along Brock Road during the move on Spotsylvania. Although it is likely Meade did not know all the details resulting from the foul up on the night of May 7/8, he was probably aware Wilson's cavalry division had been ordered out of the village when faced with superior numbers of Rebel infantry. Now Lee was in possession of the place that Grant had ordered Meade to secure and the army had essentially lost the initiative in the near term. Given the pressure of leading an army in combat operations, given Meade's incendiary temper and given his cavalry subordinate's known combative and firmly held opinion on the employment of his troopers, there could be no disguising the commanding general's frame of mind as May 8 wore on. Meade sent for Sheridan. The cavalryman rode to Meade's headquarters, arriving at about noon. "Sheridan strode into Meade's tent, and things went downhill from there."[51]

Lieutenant-Colonel Horace Porter, a member of Grant's headquarters staff, happened to be at Meade's command post when Sheridan arrived. Porter later recorded in a memoir the essence of the meeting between the two generals and no doubt related the episode to General Grant later in the day. It is Porter's rendition of the meeting that is most often cited in any recounting of the May 8 "discussion between Generals Sheridan and Meade." According to Porter:

> [Meade] had worked himself into a towering passion regarding the delays encountered in the forward movement [of the army the night before], and when Sheridan appeared went at him hammer and tong, accusing him of blunders, and charging him with not making proper disposition of his troops, and letting the cavalry block the advance of the infantry. Sheridan was equally fiery ... His language throughout was highly spiced and conspicuously italicized with expletives.[52]

At a point during this "conversation" Sheridan, dissatisfied with the role assigned to his corps, told Meade that if he had his way he would not block any more roads used by infantry but take his corps out and away from the army, find Jeb Stuart's cavalry and defeat them thoroughly. Officially, Sheridan's record of the "discussion" with Meade only surfaced in the 1880s in a few brief sentences in his *Memoirs*:

> I found his peppery temper had got the better of his good judgment, he showing a disposition to be unjust, laying blame here and there for the blunders that had been committed. He was particularly severe on the cavalry, saying, among other things, that it had impeded the march of the V Corps by occupying the Spotsylvania road. I replied that if this were true, he himself had ordered it there without my knowledge. I also told him that he had broken up my combinations, exposing Wilson's division to disaster, and kept Gregg unnecessarily idle, and further, repelled his insinuations by saying that such disjointed operations as he had been requiring of the cavalry for the last four days would render the corps inefficient and useless before long. Meade was very much irritated, and I was none the less so. One word brought on another, until finally, I told him that I could whip Stuart if he would only let me, but since he insisted on giving the cavalry directions without consulting or even notifying me, he could henceforth command the Cavalry Corps himself—That I would not give it another order.[53]

Apparently, the meeting ended at this point.

George Meade did not write a memoir, but his son, who in 1864 was a member of his staff, in later years, compiled a biography of his father that included many of his letters. The biography does not speak of anything relating to the May 8 meeting. Theodore Lyman's letters and reflections, as he also did duty on Meade's staff at this time, are silent also. However, the editor that compiled Lyman's account of life and events at Meade's headquarters was obliged to include a reference to the Sheridan-Meade discussion in a note he added to his text. The following was added from the journal Lyman kept at the time:

> Sheridan now came to Headquarters—we were at dinner. Meade told him sharply that his cavalry was in the way, though he had sent him orders to have the road clear. S[heridan] replied that he never got the order. Meade then apologized, but Sheridan was plainly full of suppressed anger, and Meade too was in ill temper. S[heridan] went on to say that he could see nothing to oppose the advance of the 5th Corps, that the behavior of the infantry was disgraceful, etc. etc.

Lyman then concluded with the following, obviously written at a much later date:

> May be this was the beginning of his dislike of Warren [V Corps Commander] and ill-feeling against Meade.[54]

Eleven months in the future, Sheridan would be in command of a significant portion of the Army of the Potomac in the war's closing campaign. A few days before Lee's surrender, Sheridan relieved General Warren from command of V Corps for reasons a Board of Inquiry at a much later date thought wholly insufficient.

The confrontation between Meade and Sheridan is summarized by cavalry historian Starr:

> This underlying set-to between the two generals may be ascribed at least in part to weariness, neither of them could have had much sleep the night before. In any case, Meade was notorious throughout the army for his vile temper. Still, Sheridan's tirade was not only insubordinate; it was also grossly unfair to Meade. Sheridan's statement in his *Memoirs* that Meade modified the orders he [Sheridan] had given Gregg and Merritt is contradicted by the record, and is simply incorrect, or false, as one prefers.

Fatigue as one factor in the foregoing is testified to in at least one contemporary source related here. According to Theodore Lyman, writing 11 days later and speaking generally, May 8 had been a rough day. "I think there was more nervous prostration to-day among officers and men then on any day before or since, the result of extreme fatigue and excitement."[55] Nothing was settled, although Meade had been well within his rights to order the two cavalry divisions to move in compliance with the known orders at the time, even though Merritt and Gregg had yet to receive them through Sheridan, their immediate commander.

Not long after, possibly within some minutes, Meade related the details of his meeting, and the heat generated by it, to General Grant. The cavalry general wanted to ride away and take on Stuart. Detouring gingerly around the spicy language and seemingly ignoring the insubordination of Sheridan, and also bypassing the fact that it was then known that Lee had gotten to Spotsylvania ahead of him, Grant went straight to cavalryman's forceful suggestion. If he wanted to go out and find Stuart and defeat him, then by all means go. It would be an improvised mini-campaign, one that would lead to the death of the Confederate Cavalry Commander Stuart, the guiding spirit and heart of the Rebel mounted force. Grant surely knew the cavalry force of the Army of the Potomac was better armed, equipped, and mounted and if he had not previously seen it in action in the field, still he was aware that Stuart and his men were not now a match for the vintage 1864 Union cavalry.

With lightning speed, orders were cut. Sheridan would assembly his Cavalry Corps, obtain the necessary supplies and ammunition and head away from the army and confront Jeb Stuart. Of interest also, as it may relate to this episode and, generally, to the campaign as it had progressed thus far, is the fact that Grant, on May 13, five days later, wrote the following to Secretary of War Stanton:

> General Meade has more than met my most sanguine expectations. He and Sherman are the fittest officers for large command I have come in contact with. If their services can be rewarded by promotion to the ranks of major-generals in the regular army the honor would be worthily bestowed, and I would feel personally gratified. I would not like to see one of their promotions at this time without seeing both.

Two days later, on May 15, Meade, writing to his wife, said:

> General Grant showed me a dispatch he had written to the War Department, speaking in complimentary terms of my service, and asking I be made a major general in the regular army. I told him I was obliged to him for his good opinion, but that I asked and expected nothing from the Government, and that I did not myself attach any importance to being in the regular army, so long as I held an equal rank in the volunteer service.[56]

Grant's recommendation was approved.

The Wilderness as part of the Overland campaign was in large part a series of clashes, some involving small units while others engulfed divisions in a dense, wet and swampy forest; individual stories and experiences of the men doing the fighting would later emerge. One of the most poignant occurred on May 7. The day previous the cavalry brigades of George Custer and Tom Devin had fought off an attack by Fitzhugh Lee and his cavalry near the intersection of Brock Road and Furnace Roads, driving Fitz Lee a considerable distance from the field. The next day, May 7, Gregg's 2nd and Merritt's 1st Cavalry Division fought Lee and Wade Hampton at Todd's Tavern at the intersection of Brock and Catharpin Roads and again drove the Rebels from the field. During this action, a 6th New York trooper recorded an incident, never to be forgotten by him and, in one aspect, illustrative of this springtime and what the war had become in 1864. The 6th New York Cavalry was ordered into the fighting near a road intersection embracing Todd's Tavern. Alonzo Foster, riding with the regiment, recorded in his diary for that day:

> Left the Foundry this morning and marched to Todd's Tavern. Our regiment was ordered to gallop to the left and support the troops that were falling back. Went into the fight about 3 P.M. and soon became heavily engaged; drove the enemy back more than a mile, and held the position until relieved by infantry late at night; lost five men. Thomas Carr, of Company F, was shot by my side; we buried him where he fell.

Thomas Carr enlisted at age 29 in the 6th New York on October 17 1861 and re-enlisted with the other veteran volunteers in December 1863.[57]

Years later, Foster when writing a memoir of his service in the 6th New York, mentions the battle primarily in relation to one event and the life-long impressions it left with him, here quoted in full:

'The Foundry' and 'Todd's Tavern' were located in the 'Wilderness,' and that terrible battle was raging all around us while the entry in my diary was being made. To better show our position I will quote the entry of the following day:

Sunday, May 8, 1864—After being relieved from our position on the line late last night we went on picket; the second and fifth corps moved to the left and relieved the cavalry; heavy firing on the right, the army slowly advancing; the woods are on fire all around us and many of our dead are being burned; we were obliged to fight dismounted as there is no open ground here; we are certainly in a wilderness.

In the early part of the day, and before we were ordered on to the line of battle, Carr rode up to my side, and in the most impressive manner said: 'If we get under fire to-day, I shall be killed.'

I made some jesting reply and thought no more of the remark. A little while later Carr came to me with a card on which was written his wife's name and address: Handing it to me, he said: 'There is my wife's name and address; If I am killed to-day write to her and tell her how I fell and the circumstance of my death.'

Seeing that he was in earnest, and that the premonition had taken strong hold of him, I tried to reason him out of his fears, but to no purpose. The conviction that he would be killed was upon him, and no words of mine could dispel it.

Soon after noon orders came for us to gallop to the left, where the Sixth New York was in action. After a sharp gallop we reached the point designated, and knew by the rapidly approaching volleys that our men were falling back. The woods were so dense that we could accomplish nothing mounted; the orders were hastily given to dismount and prepare to fight on foot. In such cases—the men being in sections of four—Nos. 1, 2, and 3, after strapping their sabers to the saddle, pass their bridles to No. 4; and dismount, leaving every fourth man in charge of the three horses belonging to the dismounted men; thus, one-fourth of the regiment is left in the rear to care for the horses, while the others advance on the line of battle. Carr's number was 2; he dismounted and the line was formed, our men rapidly falling back, and the Confederate infantry was advancing through the woods, firing and shouting as they came, the order was given to advance; the crack of a musket sounded nearer than the others, and Carr fell with a bullet through the heart; his presentment had been verified; the man who fired the shot—a gray haired Confederate—fell at almost the same instant with a bullet in his side from Harry Sharp's carbine; as he lay in the agony of death he said to Sharp that he was ready to die now, since he had killed a Yankee.

After the battle, late that night, while the fire crackled through the woods and underbrush of the 'Wilderness,' we dug a shallow grave, and wrapped the body of Carr in his gray blanket, placed it in the grave and covered it with sand and sod; there it rests to-day in company with the nameless dead, who so thickly strew that battlefield.[58]

While there was confusion and traffic snarls, the troopers waited, some no doubt dozing off, others gnawing on a hunk of hard tack. James Kidd, of Custer's Michigan Brigade, long after, recalled one of those sentimental Civil War moments so many veterans carried from the conflict and later, thankfully, were shared for posterity:

Later in the evening, away to the left where the infantry was going into bivouac a union band began to play a patriotic air. This was the signal for loud and prolonged cheering. Then a confederate band opposite responded with one of their southern tunes and the soldiers on that side cheered. Successively, from left to right and from right to left this was taken up, music and cheering alternating between federals and confederates, the sound receding and growing fainter and fainter as the distance increased until it died away entirely. It was a most remarkable and impressive demonstration under the circumstances and lingered long in the memory of those who heard it.[59]

On May 7, staff officer Lyman observed what was for him a strange sight and later wrote of it, not knowing, realizing, or perhaps caring, whether his contemporary prejudices drip from the page:

> At five this morning a novel sight was presented to the Potomac Army. A division of black troops, under General Ferrero, and belonging to the IX Corps, marched up and massed in a hollow near by. As I looked at them, my soul was troubled and I would gladly have seen them marched back to Washington. Can we not fight our own battles, without calling on these humble hewers of wood and drawers of water, to be bayoneted by the unsparing Southerners? We do not dare trust them in the line of battle. Ah, you may make speeches at home, but here, where it is life or death, we dare not risk it. They have been put to guard the trains and have repulsed one or two little cavalry attacks in a creditable manner; but God help them if the gray-backed infantry attack them …[60]

This is representative 19th century as it relates to the use of black troops, a perspective held by many in the Army of the Potomac at this time.

The order for the cavalry to ride out and fight Jeb Stuart was written and issued with lightning speed. It was in Sheridan's hands as the Cavalry Corps gathered along the Orange Plank Road that afternoon. Of more significance, as it relates to the progress of the Overland Campaign, is not the raid led by Sheridan that followed the meeting of the two generals and with Grant's allowing it to go forward, but the fact that when he rode off with the Cavalry Corps, neither of the three generals took into account that the Army of the Potomac was being left with cavalry insufficient for its needs and its imminent engagement with Robert E. Lee, his army at that moment digging entrenchments just down the road at a court house village called Spotsylvania.

Later in the month, on May 28, Charles Francis Adams, commanding General Meade's cavalry escort and therefore not engaged in the Wilderness fighting directly, wrote to his father, the U.S. Ambassador to Britain. Part of his letter contained his thoughts concerning the overland campaign as it had developed thus far:

> [T]hough Grant expected hard fighting, I have no idea that he expected anything like the fighting and the slaughter which took place in the Wilderness and at Spotsylvania. He had never seen anything like it in the West … These two great armies have pounded each other nearly to pieces for many days; neither had achieved any real success over the other on the field of battle … The Wilderness was a most fearfully discouraging place—an enemy always in front, against whom the fairest attack we could make made no impression; incessant fighting day after day; no progress forward, and the hospitals cleared out only to be filled again, while the country was becoming peopled with graves.

A week earlier, from V Corps had come:

This is the 9th day of uninterrupted fighting, the most fearful and protracted that has ever taken place on this continent, no doubt.[61]

Adams was not overstating the case. The colonel of the 56th Massachusetts Infantry had been killed in the Wilderness and Lieutenant-Colonel Stephen Weld had taken over. Weld wrote home on June 2 of the campaign, but only in general terms, "I know that no one staying at home can have any idea of what this army has been through. Any one who gets through safely may consider himself lucky." Then, speaking of his regiment in the campaign just short of one month old he says, "We have lost 300 men in killed, wounded and missing since the beginning of the campaign." But quickly Weld turns his attention to his rank—a most important subject within the army during these years—fearful that he will not be made colonel of the regiment because it is now considerably under strength because of the casualties it had suffered. To his father he wrote:

Do you know whether I am to be commissioned as colonel of the regiment or not? No other person, were he to be commissioned, could take the place, as there are not enough men for him to be mustered. If I am commissioned as colonel and my commission dates from the 6th or 7th of May, I can probably be mustered back to that date, as I have been acting as colonel since then. I had over the minimum regiment on the 7th of May.

Weld was made colonel of what was left of his regiment on June 4, but two days later said, "I am afraid that I cannot get mustered as colonel, as I have not enough men."[62]

Before marching into the Wilderness, a soldier added to the end of his letter home, "the hour has come, and God grant success to Liberty! Good-Bye!" Then just before actually marching off there was "Be assured that no opportunity on my part will be lost to informing you of my whereabouts and well being." There was the Wilderness and then Spotsylvania Court House, horrific confrontations that he somehow survived. On May 13, the soldier wrote:

I hardly dare to write you of my safety, lest I am a dead man before this vain assurance reaches you, many wrote yesterday, and to-day they lie a few hundred yards from here, stiff, blackened corpses.[63]

Despite the blood, his commitment to the cause survived:

… if I should fall, I desire to lie in Virginia, in the very grave my comrades dig for me (if I should be so fortunate after death), it will signify at least amidst the haunts of treason, that there are men who stand by their country, and they may take warning.[64]

Words such as tremendous, monstrous, obscene, inconceivable, unconscionable can be put before the word casualties for these weeks during the Civil War. The above letters tell us something of what some thought of the coming Overland Campaign and then of the battleground. The words that follow tell us something of its aftermath, its cost. Henry Nightingale of the 183rd New York took a Rebel bullet in the shoulder on May 6 as II Corps fought in the tangled undergrowth of the Wilderness. Nightingale kept a diary and at some point, soon after being wounded, recorded some of his experience. May 7:

> Lay in the hospital all day and in great pain as the ball is still in me somewhere—at 10 the surgeon examined me and said my arm should come off but I will not wish it off and refuse to allow him to take me to the amputating table.

Henry is later taken by wagon to Fredericksburg and recorded:

> ... the sound of the battle gets nearer and the woods are afire. How much I ought to be thankful for that I am not lying in the burning woods ...

May 8. Still being moved by wagon, Henry noted that he passed

> ... a brigade of Colored troops. They treated us very well and emptyed [sic] their canteens for us ... couldn't stand much more, I have to lie on my back and if I undertake to raise my mouth will fill with blood, how I wish the ball was cut out, I can feel it in my back.

May 9, at Fredericksburg:

> I had my wound dressed for the first time and the ball taken from my back. The Dr. says I was right in not allowing my arm to be taken off and says he thinks it will be allright [sic] in a few months. This is cheerful news for me ... My wound is less painful but the maggots are in it.

Henry spent the rest of the war on light duty in Washington after his shoulder healed, was discharged at war's end, went home with a pension and lived until 1919.[65]

Peter Ostrye was with the 22nd New York Infantry and his family preserved some of the letters received from him while with the Army of the Potomac. Only one of the following is directly from Peter, but through his and those penned for him by others some of his story can be told:

> Washington, D.C. 12 May 1864
> Dear Sir: I found your son Peter Ostrye in Douglas Hospital today. He was wounded in the ankle, not dangerously—on Tuesday May 10. He is in good spirits and having good care and will be about in a week or two. He has been a brave man so his commander says and deserves all the care he needs at the present and a warm place in the hearts of all patriots for his bravery and sacrifice. D. G. Morgan.

> Washington D.C. 31 May 1864
> Dear Mr. Ostrye: Your son is very ill ... He wants to see you <u>soon</u>. He has had his leg amputated. He is at Stanton Hospital Ward I. Oh! He wants to see his family so bad. Anna Shuman

> Washington D.C. 31 May 1864
> My Dear Father: Please, come to see me immediately for I am very sick and if anything should happen to me or if I should die then you could take me home ... Your affectionate son.

Washington D.C. June 2, 1864

Mr. Paul Ostrye: I suppose you have received my letter of the 29th of May. My previsions were but too correct. Your son Peter died this morning at 2 o'clock. I do sincerely and earnestly pray God to comfort you in this sad circumstance ... His only regret was to leave his father, mother, sister. Most respectfully yours, G. Rocoffort, S. J.

Washington D.C. 1 June 1864

Paul Ostrye, Esq: Dear Sir: It has become my painful duty to announce to you the death of your son Peter Ostrye ... He will be buried at the Soldiers Home burying ground. His effects, if any, will be at your disposal. Yours. E. E. Breaking

Washington D.C. June 6, 1864

Dear Sir: Your son Peter died in this city on the first of this month ... As his father and heir you are entitle to certain amount of money since now due. It is our business to attend to such cases and for your interest that it be done immediately. If such be your wish please send us a letter to that effect ... We will promptly send you the necessary papers. John Stevens.[66]

CHAPTER ELEVEN

Spotsylvania, Cold Harbor and Across the James

> Before you get this you will know how immense the butchers bill has been … I doubt if the decisive battle is to be fought between here and Richmond—nearly every Regimental off[icer] I knew or cared for is dead or wounded.
>
> OLIVER WENDELL HOLMES, 20TH MASSACHUSETTS, MAY 16, 1864[1]

Each time the Army of the Potomac had crossed either of the two rivers, the Rappahannock or Rapidan, and engaged Robert E. Lee, they had returned, bloodied if not thoroughly defeated. In May 1864, the troops huddled among the scrub oak and underbrush of the Wilderness; after all the attacks and counterattacks, thoughts surfaced, not without precedent, that history would again repeat itself. General Lee had indeed spoiled the hoped-for speedy transit of the clogged and dense woodland, now the resting place of how many more thousands.

When the order to move filtered down, a movement by the army to be executed, in the dark, many, not yet in the know, expected a march back to the pontoon bridges, back to some place where they had spent the winter. Then, somewhere off in the distance, there was a sound. What was that? Chaplain Louis Boudrye of the 5th New York Cavalry, the regiment covering the extreme right and rear of the army, was busy in the command's bivouac for the night of May 7:

> While we were cooking our supper by our bivouac fires, suddenly the wilderness before us became vocal with deafening cheers. Extending up and own our vast army lines. Lee had been outgeneraled, his line driven back, his right almost broken, and Grant was prepared for his first left flank movement.[2]

There would be no re-crossing of the rivers. Grant was moving on. In the journal Chaplain Boudrye kept, he noted the rumors rippling through the men. The talk quickly became action:

> …we are to move forward, somewhat on the Rebel's right flank during the night. We knew this at once, for the moving began almost as soon as the echo of cheering ceased … To General Grant, under a Kind Providence, I feel to trust the issues of this terrible conflict. Tonight, there are reported not less than thirteen thousand (13,000) killed, wounded or missing! This is terrible indeed![3]

George Stevens, a surgeon with the 77th New York Infantry, in a remembrance he later wrote, quotes a letter written by an unnamed doctor who was working with the wounded that were continually being evacuated to Fredericksburg where many of the town's buildings had been converted into hospitals. For May 11, the surgeon wrote:

> All day yesterday I worked at the operating table. That was the fourth day that I had worked at those terrible operations since the battle commenced, and I have also worked at the tables two whole nights and part of another … It does not seem as though I could take a knife in my hand to-day, yet there are a hundred cases of amputation waiting for me.

Two days later, this surgeon recorded:

> Captain of the Seventh Maine is dying tonight. He is a noble good man, and he looks in my face and pleads for help. Adjutant Hessy and Lieutenant Hooper of the same regiment died last night. All were my friends, and all thought that I could save them.[4]

The move was to Spotsylvania Court House; a place that would become another killing ground, massed troops attacking entrenched defenders, massed defensive fire and, inevitably, massed casualties. In the Smithsonian in Washington, among the memorabilia in its collection, there is the stump of an oak tree taken from the ground behind the Rebel defensive line. It is two feet in diameter. The stump was exhibited at the Centennial Exposition in Philadelphia in 1876. The once stout oak tree standing above the stump was cut in two by the rifle fire of the assaulting Union regiments.[5]

The denouement came on May 12 with an attack on the Rebel entrenchments by two infantry corps. It was initially successful, broke the Confederate line and the Union troops advanced about half a mile. General Lee, himself directing the defense from among his troops, decided to counterattack and would lead his reserve force himself.

The troops were readied, and Lee rode the front rank. General John B. Gordon saw this and quickly approached the general, taking in his hand the bridle of Lee's horse. Speaking loudly so the men nearby could hear, Gordon assured his commander the men of his command would not let him down in their attack. Hearing this the men began shouting, "General Lee to the rear," the men shouted, "General Lee to the rear." As Gordon later recalled, soldiers:

> …gathered around him, turned his horse in the opposite direction, some clutching his bridle, some his stirrups, while others pressed close to Old Traveler's hips, ready to shove him by main force to the rear. I verily believe that, had it been necessary or possible, they would have carried on their shoulders both horse and rider to a place of safety.

General Lee got the message and retired, allowing the attack to go forward.

The Union force was pushed back in a close quarters battle that is reported to have lasted 18 hours, bodies and parts of bodies, blue and gray, trampled upon and layered in the mud in the bottom of the trenches of the contended ground. When night fell, the Rebel force withdrew to a new defensive line laid out by engineers while the fighting of May 12 was in process. The attack and the killing had secured for the Union about half a mile of Virginia territory lying in front of the Army of the Potomac. The next day Captain Oliver Wendell Holmes of VI Corps commented in a letter on the trenches captured from the Confederates:

> In the corner of woods referred to yesterday the dead of both sides lay piled in the trenches 5 or 6 deep—wounded often writhing under superincumbent dead—The trees were slivers from the constant peppering of bullets.

V Corps on the right of the Union line got "peremptory" orders from Meade early on the morning of May 12 to attack, to its front, an elevation called Laurel Hill. The corps, commanded by Gouvernueur Warren, went forward, sustained horrific casualties and achieved nothing, yet its commander was criticized for being slow—if not unwilling—to assault an impregnable position. After, when the fighting was over and the enemy was out of rifle range, Adam Badeau, one of Grant's aides, walked the Spotsylvania field. His remembrance is typical of many who wrote of the aftermath of Spotsylvania:

> … the grounds was hidden by corpses, lying in heaps, three of four on each others.

Then in a footnote, Badeau adds:

> This is no rhetorical exaggeration but a simple statement of what no man can forget.[6]

The analysis has been done. By one calculation, the fighting at Spotsylvania on May 12, a two corps assault on Lee's entrenched line, resulted in 9,000 Union casualties. For the one springtime week, May 5 through 12, the Army of the Potomac, by one figuring, sustained 32,000 casualties.[7]

Not until May 16 did VI Corps staff officer Oliver Wendell Holmes write at any length about the Overland Campaign going on around him. In his words there can be detected what might be characterized as moral weariness with the war. His regiment's three-year terms would expire in July, and, after reflection, Holmes writes that, in essence, he has had enough:

> I have made up my mind to stay on the staff if possible till the end of the campaign & then if I am alive, I shall resign. I have felt for sometime that I didn't any longer believe in this being a duty & so I mean to leave at the end of the campaign as I said if I'm not killed before.

The editor of the letters written by Holmes, in a footnote, quotes another letter written just the month before, on April 17, where he says the war is "the Christian Crusade of the 19th century." He then adds what might be his thinking about the war just weeks before:

> If one didn't believe that this war was such a crusade, in the cause of the whole civilized world, it would be hard indeed to keep the hand to the sword; and one who is rather compelled unwillingly to the work by abstract conviction … must feel his ardor rekindled …[8]

After the carnage of the Wilderness and Spotsylvania, the ardor once felt by Holmes seems beyond rekindling. Holmes left the army at the end of his three-year enlistment and went back to Harvard where he received a law degree in 1866. He developed into one of the premier legal minds of his generation and was appointed to the U.S. Supreme Court by Theodore Roosevelt, serving until the age of 90.

There would be no retreat. Grant again maneuvered to his left, toward and then across the South Anna River. The next great confrontation came in early June near a small place called Cold Harbor. Sheridan's cavalry had seized the place on May 31 in heavy fighting and by June 2 the army had come up and entrenched, now standard procedure as soon as marching stopped.

There would be a battle at this place in Virginia called Cold Harbor, General Grant no doubt thinking there might be a chance at Lee's army, a chance to destroy it. There was more marching in the heat, dust clouds raised by thousands of men and horses choked the throats of the soldiers, men nearing exhaustion after nearly a month of moving and fighting. The infantry columns stopped, the digging began, with or without the implements needed to make it somewhat less labor intensive.

F. W. Morse of VI Corps, in a memoir written soon after he returned to his home in Cherry Valley, New York, spoke concisely of his feeling concerning the battle of Cold Harbor. The Rebel army was entrenched with artillery studding their line. In front of the earthworks there:

> … was a plain nearly seven hundred yards in width, over which their guns had full sway. As soon as the rebel position was fully known, the decision was made to charge them.

VI Corps was arrayed in three lines of battle with Morse remarking, "The situation was as dubious a one as I ever saw [and] seemed almost madness." The move forward succeeded in gaining the first trench line, but there was a second, about 250 yards behind the first. Another assault was called for by the commander of VI Corps, with Morse recalling, "What could General Wight mean by murdering our men in that manner?"[9]

Since the beginning of this campaign, brigade commander, Colonel Emory Upton had been critical of the tactics employed by his superiors in these actions, particularly those at Spotsylvania and Cold Harbor. Upton wrote to his sister on June 4, echoing the same refrains that had surfaced from staff officer Morse. Upton wrote:

> Our loss [at Cold Harbor] was very heavy; and to no purpose. Our men are brave, but cannot accomplish impossibilities. My brigade lost about three hundred men.

For conspicuous gallantry, Emory Upton was promoted soon after to brigadier general and deservedly so. Upton would go on with his distinguished career and later became commandant of West Point.[10]

The chaplain of the 15th New Jersey, Alanson Haines, witnessed the assault of Friday, June 3, at Cold Harbor and wrote of it 18 years later. From where his regiment was located, a glance to the left took in an advance by a force Haines numbered at 2,200 men, many former heavy artillerymen converted to infantry, now in II Corps and "in bright new uniforms ..." "When we first saw them the enemy did also, and opened fire upon them. They had to cross the same wide field we had passed on [June] the first, every inch of it swept by the enemy." The battle formation:

> ... advanced in a handsome line, and was cut down like mown grass ... Their destruction so complete and so sudden. It was the most sickening sight of this arena of horrors; and the appearance of their bodies, strewn over the ground for a quarter of a mile, and in our view for days, can never fade from our recollection.[11]

General Grant ordered a second assault be made that afternoon, but after riding along the lines and speaking with the corps commanders, he rescinded the order.

General Grant realized his mistake at Cold Harbor and years later said so but without admitting the tactics employed (a direct assault on an entrenched position), those Emory Upton complained of so bitterly, was practically useless. "I have always regretted that the last assault at Cold Harbor was ever made," Grant wrote, adding only, "At Cold Harbor no advantage whatever was gained to compensate for the heavy loss we sustained."[12] At Cold Harbor the resulting casualties were inexcusable, even if the general was a prisoner of 19th century infantry tactics. The engagement cost the Army of the Potomac another 7,000 casualties added to the totals for the Wilderness and Spotsylvania.[13]

A surgeon with the 20th Massachusetts took note of the casualties at Cold Harbor in a letter written on June 4, saying:

> If the Confederates lost in each fight the same number as we, there would be more chance for us; but their loss is about one man to our five, from the fact that they never leave their earthworks, where our men are obliged to charge even when there is not the slightest chance of taking them.[14]

Lee had been able to gather some reinforcements from forces to the south of the James River and arrayed his army for another defensive stand. Grant had augmented his army with a corps taken from Butler's Army of the James. After the fighting and the repulse of the Union force at Cold Harbor, the armies stood in place, reflecting on the battle and its cost and with Grant thinking of what he would do next. Lieutenant-Colonel Tyler of the 37th Massachusetts recalled:

I well remember the sickening odors that greeted my nostrils on the second and third day after the battle. Then a truce was arranged, and for two or three hours the men of the two armies mingled while each attended to the burial of their dead.

Joseph Ward of the 106th Pennsylvania recalled the truce and the scene in front of the position held by II Corps. The soldiers readily talked to each other and at one point:

… members of both sides were washing together in the same small run, and joking each other on the result of the previous days. It seemed very odd to see these men mingling with each other, laughing and joking and very friendly, that only a short time before were watching for an opportunity and trying their best to kill each other, and would so soon be trying it again. About eleven o'clock an officer on the Confederate side called his men back to their lines, and told ours he would 'give them five minutes to get behind their works.'[15]

It was not only the Virginia heat but also the continuous marching and the mental stress that was wearying on Grant's force. This was also being reflected on the home front where the names of the dead and wounded appeared in the press. And not to be forgotten, this was an election year. Added to this was the fact that some of the army's best officers had become casualties and morale within the ranks was eroding, despite the forward movement.[16]

On the night of June 12/13, the Army of the Potomac quietly began a withdrawal from the Cold Harbor line and marched for the James River. Engineers had put a pontoon bridge across the river and by June 15 advance elements were across and marching on Petersburg.

Petersburg was a railroad hub with the lines coming from further south and west bringing food and ammunition to Lee's soldiers. Capture of this hub would mean the Confederate's hold on its capital city could not be maintained. The city of Petersburg was defended by a stout line earthworks and artillery, all under the command of General Pierre Gustav Toutant Beauregard. Like so many other battlefield situations of the Civil War, the "if only" came in to play outside of this vital logistic hub. The capture of Petersburg might have brought the war much nearer an end. Orders were issued for an assault scheduled for early morning, June 15, by two corps. It did not go forward until 7pm. The attack captured some territory and entrenchments and should have been pushed forward even after it got dark, but it wasn't. Later, it could only be labeled a humiliation. At this moment the city was held by only about 2,500 troops. Failure to capture Petersburg was later ascribed to the command structure of Meade's army, the exhaustion of the troops and their immediate commanders, or a combination of all three with an ample dose of simple bad luck. The primary reason for crossing the James River, the capture of Petersburg, was a failure.

After several more attempts to break into the city, on June 18, Grant decided to stop ordering assaults on the Petersburg defensive lines. In assaults ordered in the preceding days, some infantry units refused to commit suicide attacking

Rebel defensive works. The commanding general would lay siege to the city. The "if only" of all this was that trains continued to roll both into Richmond and up to Lee's supply lines. George Meade, in a letter home begins at this time to reveal some frustration with the role he is playing in the command. On June 21, speaking of the battles fought to take Petersburg he said:

> In all this fighting and these operations I had exclusive command, Grant being all the time at City Point, and coming on the field for only half an hour on the 17th, and yet in Mr. Stanton's dispatch he quotes General Grant's account and my name is not even mentioned. I cannot imagine why I am thus ignored.[17]

The crossing of the James River marked the end of Grant's Overland Campaign and the beginning of the siege of Petersburg. Because of the loss of many energetic and capable junior and field officers, it was perceived the army no longer fought with "vigor and force" as it had when in the Wilderness. In many units, enlistments by men that had not taken the offer of re-enlisting were due to soon expire. Over and above this, no army could continue to sustain the casualties this army had suffered and continue to be considered a potent offensive threat. Mason Tyler reported in a letter from in front of Petersburg on June 20:

> The 37th [Massachusetts] has, I believe, only a little over 200 [men]. We started out in the campaign with over 600 strong.

And, he added, the entire brigade now numbered only 407 men.[18] Historian James M. McPherson, an authority on the subject, notes that, from May 5 through June 18, the casualties in the Army of the Potomac "… amounted to three-fifth (60%) of the total number of combat casualties suffered by the Army of the Potomac during the previous three years."[19]

The siege of Petersburg would continue through the summer and fall and into the next year. With the army investing Petersburg from the east, Grant tried to extend his line to the left, curving around to the south of the city and cutting the rail lines coming from the south. His efforts were stalled by a vigorous Confederate defense indicating the vital importance of the life-sustaining railroads to General Lee and his men. From a position toward the southern end of Grant's lines, Mason Tyler reported on June 26 in a letter:

> … we have been sweltering in this hot Virginia sun with the temperature at 102 in the shade now for three days. It seems as if the perspiration runs in streams all the time and bring not relief … I ought to be happy that I am well and able to endure, and have been saved from sickness and wounds during this terrible campaign.[20]

Benjamin Clark of the 12th Massachusetts, writing almost two decades later, gave his summation of the Overland Campaign in his regimental history:

> … the fact will ever remain unshaken that the overland route from the Rapidan to the James cost more than it was worth, and that the loss inflicted upon the enemy was much smaller than

Entrenchments at Petersburg. (Library of Congress)

our own ... The continual flanking movements, fighting at every opportunity, tended greatly, no doubt, to weaken and discourage the rebels, and make final success in the spring of '65 possible.

Clark listed the regiment's casualties for the period May and June 25 as 46, killed, 125 wounded, and three missing. This three-year regiment was mustered out and returned home on July 8.[21]

Blame, some historians believe, has to be placed somewhere for the horrific number of casualties this campaign produced. Head long charges against an enemy were not new to this war, but one after another without appreciable results soon had an effect, a demoralizing, if not fatalistic pall hovering over the troops. Contemporaries, the ones doing the marching and the charging felt it, if not able to put exact words to it. Ulysses S. Grant must assume at least a portion of the blame for the lengthy lists of dead and wounded being printed in hometown newspapers in the North. Although George Meade was, by title, in command of the Army of the Potomac, Grant gave the orders, the where, the when and the how to attack being left, generally, to Meade. At Spotsylvania and Cold Harbor, it was straight ahead, massed frontal assaults into prepared defensive positions. The odds of defeating or destroying Lee's army, lengthened with each defensive volley the Rebels fired into the ranks coming at them. That General Grant was aware of this, beyond merely regretting the losses it caused, remains questionable.

Union and Confederate dead at Petersburg. (Library of Congress)

CHAPTER TWELVE

Petersburg

> This morning, as for some days past, it seems exceedingly probable that the Administration will not be re-elected. Then it will be my duty to so co-operate with the President elect, as to save the Union between the election and the inauguration; as he will have secured his election on such ground that he can not possibly save it afterward.
>
> ABRAHAM LINCOLN.[1]

While the movement across the James River went forward, a Lieutenant Lincoln of a Pennsylvania regiment was writing home:

> With you I would like to be sitting at this hour, listening to the preaching of the gospel; but instead I hear only the sounds that tell of death and destruction … My time, energies and life are not too good to be given for the preservation of the Union … I am here, and if necessary, I suppose I am to be sacrificed for my country; yet I have faith in God that he will preserve me through it all.

Lieutenant Lincoln was sacrificed on June 16 in the attempt to capture Petersburg. For June 17, there was another advance, trench lines guarding the city taken by the Union force, but it did not achieve a breakthrough. By June 18, Lee had reinforced General Beauregard and another attempt at breaking the Rebel lines went forward. Theodore Lyman of Meade's staff wrote in a letter dated the same day:

> It was as I expected—forty-five days of constant marching, assaulting and trenching are a poor preparation for a rush! The men went in, but not with spirit, received by a withering fire, they sullenly fell back a few paces to a slight crest and lay down, as much as to say, 'We can't assault but we won't run.' The slopes covered with dead and wounded bore testimony that they were willing to give proof of courage even in circumstances that they deemed desperate.[2]

It is on this day, with both Grant and Meade on the scene, that both agree the army needed rest while they thought of another approach that would lead to the capture of Petersburg.

Charles Banes, an officer in the Philadelphia Brigade, prefaced his use of journal entries in the brigade's history of this action before Petersburg with a telling remark concerning the brevity and lack of color in the notes jotted at the time, an example, he said, of the state of mind of men after three years of fighting:

> The annexed entries from a journal will show the character of these operations, although they will give but a faint conception of the severity of the work and the conditions under which it was performed.

Banes then adds:

> Few of the soldiers … will fail to remember the impression produced by the sight, for the first time, of comrades dead on the field. Frequent repartitions of similar scenes wrought great changes in the tender sympathies of the men while they still felt true sorrow at the death of comrades, they became indifferent to the terrible scenes of a battle-field.[3]

On June 18, Mason Tyler of VI Corps recorded that his division was within three-quarters of a mile of Petersburg. "We could see the church spires very plainly." And the next day, June 19, Tyler included in a letter:

> The men, however, look rather haggard and after their terrible campaigning experience, and they don't have the same amount of spirit they had when they started out. The charges made yesterday lacked spirit, and the organizations of the army are so thinned out it is not to be wondered at.[4]

The next morning, June 19, General Meade sent Lyman forward to request a truce so the wounded could be gathered in. The only item resembling a white flag that could be found was the army's Inspector General's "new Damask tablecloth." It was attached to a pole and Lyman cautiously approached the Rebel line, asked for the truce and waited most of the day as the question went up the command chain to General Beauregard. The truce was refused in writing, with Lyman commenting that it was "signed by Beauregard, and was a specimen of his mean Creole blood." Beauregard said in his note that he did not know there had been an action the previous day. "He lied;" Lyman wrote, "for he knew full well there had been heavy fighting and that we at least had lost thousands. But he wished to show his dirty spite. Lee does not do such things."[5]

**

As reinforcement from the Richmond area hurried to Petersburg, on the Union side there had been a series of mistakes, accidents and poor communications coupled with the general exhaustion of the attacking forces after more than a month of campaigning and bloodletting that prevented the outright seizure of the Petersburg. Between June 15 and 18, with each day adding troops to the Union force before the city, the soldiers had pushed Rebel forces out of some entrenched positions, but failed to achieve a breakthrough, faulty coordination primarily cited as the cause. As summarized, Grant's failure to capture Petersburg was because his "… corps commanders failed him." Also, it was noted at the time, if not back in the Wilderness, that Generals "… Beauregard and Lee were not Pemberton and Johnston," two Confederate generals Grant had faced in his Vicksburg campaign. It appears at this time the push to capture Petersburg lacked aggressiveness and coordination and this stemmed, primarily it seems, from the exhausted troops themselves. Before one line of trenches, a brigade of II Corps, when ordered to stand and attack the Rebel works, "refused to get up and charge the bullet-swept open ground." Yet, in the same action, a regiment of converted heavy artillerymen pulled into the infantry from the defenses of Washington, in position next to this brigade, when ordered to charge the same works, "… went in … and were shot to pieces, losing 632 of 850 men in this one action."[6] The excuses were noted in the reports that were filed later.

With their decision to allow the army to rest, Generals Meade and Grant had moved from a campaign of maneuver to a siege. Engineers on both sides moved to dig more trenches and earth works and to strengthen those already excavated. The defensive lines of the Rebels would, it was hoped, insulate the city from any further advance.

It had been a long 45 days since the Army of the Potomac, anxious for a fight, had crossed the pontoon bridges over the Rapidan. Every time a Rebel or Federal command had been told to halt on a battlefield, the troops started digging. Entrenchments had become standard procedure, protection of a kind from the bullets fired by the enemy. Sheer numbers might overrun one line of quickly dug trenches, but there would always be a second line. After 45 days, it should not have been a surprise that the men, some of them at least, wouldn't get off the ground when ordered. After all the battles and bloodletting, to say the troops were exceedingly reluctant to assault entrenched Rebel positions over open ground, manned by any number of troops supported by artillery, should have been not only known to the commanding generals, but appreciated for what it was. From the perspective of distance, it must be that even the dimmest of lights among the Union officer corps, after the engagements fought at Spotsylvania Court House and Cold Harbor, had to realize and appreciate these most recent examples of the futility borne of 19th century infantry tactics running a distant second place to the weapons employed in defense, massed rifle fire and cannons loaded with double canister, all firing from entrenched, protected positions. There seemed to be developing among the massed assaulting forces what one historian has called a "Cold Harbor Syndrome," stemming from these previous attempts at carrying a fortified enemy position. The origin of this might conceivably be traced as far back as Fredericksburg in December 1862.[7] The soldiers on the ground, while not knowing the exact number, were fully aware the casualties their army had sustained since leaving winter quarters had been massive. Since crossing the Rapidan River, the argument can be made that the Federal forces under General Grant had been engaged in the most intense combat during one defined time period that the U.S. Army had ever experienced to that time. The number of killed and wounded proved the point. Further, it was at least as intense, if not more so, than some prolonged engagements faced by American soldiers in subsequent conflicts.

What had been accomplished since the crossing of the Rapidan? From the perspective of the Union side, Lee's army, having only marginal ability to maneuver offensively when the campaign began, was now locked into position, movement limited to the shifting of troops to meet localized thrusts by Union forces. The Army of Northern Virginia had suffered an estimated 35,000 casualties that could be replaced only by stripping other Confederate commands of men and they being of lesser quality. The Confederacy had also lost about 80 miles of territory in Virginia. With Lee's force immobilized, Grant could entrench his force before Petersburg and extend those trenches south and westward, gradually cutting the railroad tracks over which rolled Lee's food and ammunition. At a point, hopefully in the near term, Lee would be forced to attempt a breakout, where in open country the Army of the Potomac could destroy the Confederate force.

All of this was being reported in the Northern press. The reports from the field and the editorials of one persuasion or another were having, to an unknown degree, an effect on the voting public.

Part of Grant's overall offensive plan in Virginia had included a drive down the Shenandoah Valley by a force under General David Hunter. This offensive had been thwarted. The Army of the James, supposed to have moved on Richmond, had been pinned down in an enclave known as the Bermuda Hundred along the James River. Only Sherman and his army in Georgia was moving on its objective, but with its own casualties littering the roadside.

***

The Union engineers directing the work before Petersburg were creating elaborate trench complexes, bunkers and bomb proofs with artillery positions studding the line. Trees were cut and hauled into reinforcing positions. Artillery pieces were hauled into position, and mortars placed behind the lines, and sighted to lob shells over the friendly trenches and into those of the enemy. General Grant established his headquarters at City Point on the James River, and the surrounding area became the army's supply base and its primary medical facility. Supply Officer Morris Schaff noted in his diary at the beginning of the Petersburg siege, that he ordered 2,325,000 rounds of rifle and pistol ammunition "… as a reserve for what was already on hand" as well as 11,000 artillery rounds.[8] General James Wilson's 3rd Cavalry Division and the cavalry division commanded by August Kautz from the Army of the James were ordered out on a raid to cut the railroads running into Petersburg. Beginning on June 22, this cavalry force of over 5,000 troopers, was out ripping up tracks, bending rails and burning everything else for over a week. Considerable damage was done, and a lengthy interruption of rail transport achieved, but Wilson's command, on returning to Union lines was forced to fight a mixed force of Rebel cavalry and infantry that resulted in the loss of upwards of 1,000 men. Most of Wilson's losses were men captured during this fight to get within Union lines. It was during this action that Wilson was forced to abandon 12 pieces of artillery, supply wagons and the ambulances with his wounded.

It was during these weeks that General Lee sent General Jubal Early to the Shenandoah Valley to deal with General David Hunter and his advance on Lynchburg. General Early's appearance near Lynchburg caused Hunter to retreat into the West Virginia hills, opening the Valley northward to the Potomac. Early then mounted an offensive that initially looked suspiciously like that of Lee's of the previously year, a Confederate force headed for some unknown and under-defended target. Troops from the Petersburg front might have to be dispatched to counter this move. General Early, marching north, got to the Potomac on July 6. The authorities in Washington grew more nervous with each forward step. Once in Maryland, General Early turned to the east and was confronted by a composite force at the Monocacy River near Frederick on July 9. Early pushed this force aside and continued his march, increasing the panic in Washington. In the build-up for his Overland Campaign, Grant had pulled nearly all of the defensive manpower from the defenses of the capital for use with the Army of the Potomac and now urgent messages from the authorities in Washington were arriving at his headquarters before Petersburg. The capital of nation was under threat by a Rebel force, Grant was advised; something must be done. Walking wounded were pulled from hospitals and government clerks pulled from their desks, given rifles and sent to man the city's defenses. By July 11, Early was appraising the defenses of Washington from the city's outskirts while VI Corps was pulled from the siege of Petersburg and rushed north. The troops came off the boats and were run into the forts and defensive line of the city as Rebel sharpshooters peppered the city's defenses at long range. There was skirmishing on July 12 by a strong picket force from VI Corps in the open area in front of the city's defenses. An individual who should not have been present, but whose curiosity had gotten the better of him, watched the action from a parapet of a fort. Early's troops were moving in a threatening manner and rifle fire from the enemy was well aimed and lethal. Then an officer from VI Corps that had just arrived saw the tall stranger, standing, looking at the action. He wore civilian clothes topped with a tall hat. Major Oliver Wendell Holmes shouted at him: "Get down, you damn fool, before you get shot." Major Holmes got President Lincoln's attention and he got down.[9]

One of the elements of VI Corps that had arrived late the day before included Dr. George Stevens of the 77th New York. On his arrival he found the fort defended by:

… a small force of heavy artillery, hundred days' men, and detachments of the Invalid corps … clerks and employees of the quartermaster's department, with convalescents from the hospitals …

Some of the action Lincoln watched from the parapet the next day took place along the picket line established outside the fort by the then arriving VI Corps. There were sharp exchanges of fire and casualties before General Early decided to withdraw. Stevens noted in his remembrance the aftermath of the July 12 encounter:

> We gathered our dead comrades from the field where they had fallen, and gave them the rude burial of soldiers on the common near Fort Stevens. None of those in authority, who had come out to see them give their lives for their country, were present to pay the last honors to the dead heroes … We laid them in their graves within sight of the capital [sic], without coffins, with only their gory garments and their blankets around them. With the rude tenderness of soldiers, we covered them in the earth; we marked their names with our pencils on the little head-boards of pine, and turned sadly away to other scenes.[10]

It was obvious to General Early that storming the city defenses would be useless given the number of troops under his command and with VI Corps in his way. He ordered a retirement, marching back to Virginia. Stopping along the way at Frederick, Maryland, Early extorted $200,000 in greenbacks from the town with a promise not to burn it. Hagerstown was good for an additional $20,000, in return for not burning the citizens out of house and home. Soon he and his men were back in the Valley resting and refitting as best they could.

General Early's march on Washington, brief though it was, further added to the depression being felt in the North. Whether it was adding to the public's dissatisfaction or merely reflecting it, the nation's press was selling papers and having its say on the course of things as the summer days of 1864 passed one after another. The prospects for peace seemed as elusive as ever and the election clock was ticking inexorably toward November. Nevertheless, General Sherman was still active in Georgia and in a few days Grant would send Philip Sheridan to the Shenandoah Valley with orders to clean it out, not only of Jubal Early and his men, but of any and everything that could in any manner contribute to the Confederate cause. This meant taking all the crops and livestock his men encountered. What crops they couldn't carry away, they would burn. The livestock would feed the troops. And in the trenches at Petersburg, there was a man with a Pennsylvania infantry regiment that had an idea.

Before the war, Colonel Henry Pleasants had been a mining engineer. Now he was in front of Petersburg serving with IX Corps. One of the regiments in this corps was the 48th Pennsylvania Volunteer Infantry and many of its men had been coal miners from Schuylkill County. Across the dead zone, in front of the section of trench the Pennsylvanians held, was a Rebel strong point, or fort, studded with cannon, with trenches running out on both flanks. One day, a soldier in the 48th suggested a mineshaft should be run under the Union trenches and across the intervening open ground and under the Rebel strong point. At the end of the mine, explosives could be placed that could blow the Rebel line high into the air. Pleasants heard the comment, thought of the possible result if the explosion was combined with a swift follow-up attack by infantry. The stalemate might be turned into a Union victory, cutting Lee's army in two, capturing Petersburg and dealing the Rebel army a defeat from which it couldn't recover. Pleasants went with the idea to the division command and, in turn, was send to the corps commander, General Ambrose Burnside. The scheme got Burnside's endorsement, and then the reluctant approval from Meade with Grant going along. The digging began on June 25. Army engineers pronounced the plan 'hum-bug' and provided no support. The Pennsylvania soldiers did all the work. By July 30, the mine had been run under the Confederate strong point with 40-foot extensions leading off to the left and right. Four tons of gunpowder was packed into the end of the mine with a fuse ready to be lit.

General Burnside's IX Corps was made up of four divisions, three of which were composed of white troops. The fourth, referred to as a "Colored Division," or United States Colored Troops, had not seen action thus far in the campaign, primarily having guarded the army's wagon trains since crossing the Rapidan. Burnside, therefore, thought to use this division in the follow-on attack. It was fresh and at strength, having had no significant casualties thus far in the campaign. The division, about 3,000 men, received some specialized training as the digging went forward and the plan for the infantry assault was worked up. The Colored Division would spearhead the assault, followed by the other three IX Corps divisions. Diversionary actions would be conducted at other points along the line with an eye to pulling some Rebel troops away from the point of attack. Late in the day, July 29, a change in the attack plan was ordered, the alteration coming because of concern having been expressed by both Grant and Meade. If the attack failed, went the thinking, and the black troops were in the lead, the press, and therefore the public, could add to the inevitable recriminations that the generals had deliberately used the black troops, and had many of them killed, because they suspected all along that the entire affair would be a failure. Generals Grant and Meade and the Army of the Potomac didn't need this kind of publicity and, besides, at this time in the conflict, many of little faith saw the fighting capabilities of Black troops as being not on the same level as white troops, the prejudice of the era underlying this belief. A white division was substituted and, as the sun rose on July 30, the fuse in the mineshaft was lit.

The explosion shook the ground and wiped out the Confederate strong point, blowing it over one hundred feet in the air and making a huge crater. Rather than bypassing the crater as they had been instructed, surging through the break in the Confederate line and driving into Petersburg, hundreds of men went into the crater. The Confederates quickly recovered and counterattacked and by early afternoon had driven the Union attack back to where it started. Theodore Lyman of Meade's staff witnessed the explosion and the follow-on advance and noted:

> ... the assaulting column moved forward, in a loose manner. This was ... a brigade composed of dismounted cavalry and demoralized heavy artillery ... the whole good for nothing ...

In the crater filled with men who should have been passing around it and moving forward, confusion reigned, no one advancing. More troops moved forward, clogging both the crater and the surround area. Lyman commented:

> ... the troops of the 18th Corp and the black division of the 9th came back in confusion, all mixed with the whites in and about the crater. Their officers behaved with distinguished courage, and the blacks seem to have done as well as white—which is faint praise.

Then Lyman listed the various reason the other men that had watched the attack gave for its failure, concluding, "But I can give you *one* reason that includes and over-rides every other—*the men did not fight hard enough.*"[11]

In his letters in the days after the mine explosion and attack, Lyman reveals a distinct prejudice that many making up the army at this time carried with them relating to those not deemed as quite Yankee—a mild exception being made for the Irish—and yet, for whatever reason, they were fighting with the army in front of Petersburg. In early August he expounded, the particulars of his observations going unstated:

> As soldiers in the field the Germans are nearly useless ... they have no native courage to compare with Americans. Then they do not understand a word that is said to them ... Send bog-trotters, if you please, for Paddy will fight—no one is braver ... every worthless recruit [sent] to this army is one card in the hand of General Lee and is the cause, very likely, of the death of a good soldier.

Lyman's comments reek of mid-19th century anti-immigrant prejudice that had taken political form 10 years earlier in such organizations as the Know Nothing Party. As for the other soldiers in the army, the men signing on, in part, for the bounty money offered by the states, he said "the very men that desert the next day will fight the day before, for sake of avoiding shame." And the "faint praise" Lyman bestowed on the Colored Division that was pushed into the fight at the crater in the last echelon instead of the first had, by the end of August, dissolved, with his letter of the 26th:

> I say, as I always have, that you never, in the long run, can make negroes [sic] fight with success against white men. When the whole weight of history is on one side, you may be sure that side is the correct one.

Then Lyman returned to the Germans saying:

> I told General Meade I had expressed myself strongly, at home, against the imported Dutchmen, to which he replied: 'Yes, if they want to see us licked, they had better send along such fellers as those!' As I said before, the Pats will do: not so good as pure Yanks, but they will rush in and fight.[12]

With each morning's edition of the North's newspapers, there was the latest list of the dead and wounded, from Early's movement across the Potomac, from the crater at Petersburg and Sherman's seemingly endless struggle in Georgia. Each paper also freely offered opinion, from a Democratic paper hoping, and each Republican paper fearing, that the President would be taking a train back to Springfield in March after seeing his former army commander, General George McClellan, sworn in as chief executive of the nation, that might very well become only half a nation if what were thought to be his policy regarding the war was brought to fruition. At army headquarters, Theodore Lyman reported that General Meade took the defeat at the crater as well as could be expected and laughed when a newspaper reported he was to be relieved and replaced by General Hancock of II Corps. He commented to his staff sardonically that it all would be too bad; he would have to go home and live in Philadelphia. At the headquarters of IX Corps, Lyman found the post-battle mood lighter than expected. Lyman was informed that "Burnside and his Staff were all going on a thirty-day leave, which will extend itself, I fancy, indefinitely, so far as the army goes." The newspapers also reported the rumor that General Grant had gone to the capital. "I presume our father Abraham," Lyman noted, "looks to his election prospects as waning, and wants to know of Ulysses, the warrior, if some *man* or some *plan* can't be got to some *thing*."[13]

Since settling before Petersburg, the army had been trying gradually to move to the left, flanking Lee's force and permanently cutting the Weldon and the Richmond and Danville railroads. In August, along the Weldon railroad, running directly south from Petersburg, there had been heavy fighting, with Lee trying desperately to maintain a hold on this vital artery. In a letter written at this time, Lyman noted a twinge of guilt at being a staff officer and not getting shot at constantly and commented that he felt "… as the late T_____ remarked, when he proposed, 'I am good for ten years'; which turned out to be true (to the regret of Mrs. T)." Then Lyman added a quote from a Major Miller and his comments on the casualties sustained in an action at Reams' Station on the Weldon Rail line in late August. The major said, "The Rebels licked us, but a dozen such lickings and there will be nothing left of the Rebel army."[14] The numbers were all running against the Confederate forces, as they had been for over a year. Essentially, the South was running out of men, the draft age had been expanded and there began to surface in whispered form, and from the most radical Rebel lips, the suggestion of arming slaves in defense of the Confederacy. Of course, all that could be offered to such black men that would accept such a proposition would be service in exchange for freedom after independence was successfully achieved. Such a proposition illustrates fully the desperation facing the South: the elimination of at least part of the institution for which, in part, they had gone to war, to be exchanged for the maintenance of independence. By the time the Confederate Congress gave grudging approval to arming slaves, the Confederacy had only weeks to live and, essentially, nothing came of it.

**

In the weeks before the November election, the soldiers in the field enthusiastically cast their votes and then waited. Some regiments from states that did not allow absentee balloting were sent home to vote. George B. McClellan, the Democratic nominee, had disassociated himself from his party's platform peace plank, but most voters didn't take this recommitment seriously. President Lincoln had been anxious all through the spring and summer, hoping the field armies would prove successful, provide victories that would turn into votes for his administration in November. Without victories, he believed he could not win re-election. As the stalemate continued at Petersburg into September, Sherman in Georgia captured Atlanta; Sheridan defeated Early in a battle outside the town of Winchester, Virginia. The following month, Sheridan again defeated the Rebels, decisively at the Battle of Cedar Creek, again in Shenandoah, some miles south of Winchester. These field victories, and the votes of the troops in the field, decided the issue in the public's mind in favor of the Lincoln administration.

In a lengthy discourse included in a letter to his sister, written after the election, Lieutenant Henry Howe, of the 13th Massachusetts, spoke of an exchange of letters with a Miss C. G. He had received a letter from her and from its tone, Howe tells his sister, "I did not think she admired the present administration, so I asked her who was her choice for President." Howe says that she answered, "She was a Democrat, a peace Democrat, did not like Abraham Lincoln ... did not like McClellan, but would have peace on any terms." Lieutenant Howe says he answered, "If such are your feelings, for such is the result of unconditional peace, I must call you a Copperhead." Miss C. G., in a return letter, said Howe, tried to be "penitent," but signed her letter "Your Democratic (not McClellan) friend." This was apparently it for Howe, saying to his sister, "I tell you what, no woman, if she be a woman, can write such sentiments to me and not hear of it." "I cannot retract anything for Democrats," says Howe, "especially McClellan Democrats, whom I consider traitors." Howe then closed the discourse saying, "However, she writes good letters and is a nice young lady, but no patriot."[15]

Cavalry officer Charles Francis Adams somehow got leave from the army and went home at election time. On November 14, he wrote:

> I am disposed to believe that I have just witnessed the most sublime moral spectacle of all time. As you know I got home in time to throw my vote and found myself one of some 5000 superfluous majority in the solid city of Boston. Think of it! The state of Massachusetts, as the result of four years of war and bloodshed and taxes and paper money, reviews her action

and declares it good, and reordains [sic] the ministers of that action by a majority hitherto unknown in her annals.[16]

When the votes were counted in the 2nd Ohio Cavalry, trooper Luman Tenney wrote in his diary:

> The decisive day of the nation. If the cause of the Union prevails today, liberty and union will be ours forever. God grant the right success ... Voted. 201 for Lincoln, 4 for McClellan. Glorious of the 2nd Ohio.[17]

Theodore Lyman, writing from Meade's army besieging Petersburg, was content with the people's decision, but not overly so. On November 10 he noted:

> They have been singularly niggardly to us about election returns; but we have reliable intelligence to-night that Lincoln is re-elected, the course, honest, good-natured, tolerably able man! It is very well as it is; for the certainty of pushing the war to its righteous end must now swallow up all other considerations.

As for those states that went for McClellan as opposed to the president, Lyman says. "This will caution him [Lincoln], or better, his party, to proceed cautiously, and to make no fanatical experiments, such as we too often have seen ..." Robert Tilney of V Corps noted on November 13:

> The Fifth Corps has always been considered a McClellan Corps ... when the corps gives a majority for Lincoln against McClellan it speaks volumes for its good sense and patriotism. Some of the Democratic election agents have been arrested for issuing spurious tickets, in which the names of the electors were wrongly spelt and one name omitted, so that all the votes on them would be thrown out on examination. Such is Democratic, or more properly speaking, Copperhead honesty.[18]

***

Others were writing letters during this fall and winter and in a few we catch a glimpse of what concerned one John Green from New York. Trooper Green had been with Sheridan's cavalry divisions at Winchester, Virginia, but an undisclosed illness had put him in the Invalid Corps, officially the Veteran Reserve Corps. Sheridan and his cavalry divisions would be returning to the Army of the Potomac late in the winter for the final campaign against General Lee. Trooper Green had been sending money home and had plans for when the war ended and he left the army. On December 1, 1864, in a letter to his mother, John said, "Ma I want you to put my money away ... I keep it for a want it when I get home to go to School with." At the end of January 1865, his concern about the money has grown somewhat:

> Ma if I send a letter to you in your name I want you to read it to yourself for you know that I make you my bank and if I send anything to you I want you to keep it to yourself or you may be relieved of it some night.

John Green's mother apparently had put the money he sent home in the local bank, but trooper Green still had concerns. In March 1865, he wrote:

> Ma I want you to tell me what kind of bank it is where you have deposited my money. I want to know if it is a National Bank or some upstart.

Three of Mrs. Green's sons had volunteered in 1862, two of them, Marvin and Levi, joining from Wellsville, New York, on the same day. The previous June, their regiment, the 1st New York Dragoons, was part of the force Sheridan led on his raid to Trevilian Station and into a fight with Rebel cavalry. When Marvin returned from the raid, he wrote home:

> Dear Parents I received your letter 2 or 3 days ago. But have not answered it for I wanted to see whether Levi would get in or not[.] But he has not. He is tacon [sic] prisner [sic]. I got out all right. We have had a hard Battle here I tell you ... Levi is all rite [sic] only he is a prisner [sic].

Now from winter quarters near Winchester, Marvin wrote on January 9, 1865, two troopers who had been captives of the Confederates had returned to the regiment by some means and told Marvin of his brother's death:

> I rite [sic] these few lines to you for I have bad news. Levi is dead[.] [H]e died in Savanah [sic] and what he died with was starvation and he had Scurvey [sic] ... He died last October.

Marvin also informed his brother John and he wrote home on January 28 saying:

> I received a letter from Marvin the other day in which he said that Levi was dead at Millican, GA. It was rather hard but is the fortune of war and the way we must all go in time but it is hard to die in a strange land and among enemies.[19]

***

It was late in February 1865 and Phil Sheridan began his movement from near Winchester, Virginia, back to the Army of the Potomac. General Jubal Early, and what was left of his command, retired to an entrenched position outside the town of Waynesboro in the days after the Battle of Cedar Creek in October. It was in the Cedar Creek battle that Sheridan's Army of the Shenandoah, its bulk composed of two cavalry division and VI Corps from the Army of the Potomac, had thoroughly defeated the Rebels in the valley. Early had remained in his Waynesboro position through the winter. If he needed to escape, there was an escape route, through a gap and over the Blue Ridge, that would get him back to Richmond, but the general seemed content to remain as ordered at Waynesboro and write his report.

Phil Sheridan, after the October battle, continued north in the valley and prepared for a winter that promised little organized military activity, but much in a non-conventional sense. Colonel John Mosby and his partisan raiders were still active and a continuing and annoying threat to Sheridan's command. Mosby's partisans usually retreated to the Loudon Valley after a foray against Union forces. There to feed and rest men and horses. Sheridan was determined to deny this area of refuge and ordered Wesley Merritt and his 1st Cavalry Division into the valley to gather or destroy all the grain, forage and livestock there that potentially could help support Mosby's guerilla band. Merritt and his men left the Winchester area on November 28 and returned on December 3 after burning barns and mills and herding into Sheridan's camps 2,240 cattle, 400 hogs, 1,000 sheep and 400 horses, according to the regimental history of the 1st New York Dragoons. While in the valley, there had been some contact with Mosby's men, but not one that put his command out of action.

Before the 1st Division left for the Loudon Valley, however, there had been Thanksgiving Day in the camps around Winchester:

> Sometime previous to Thanksgiving day, reports appeared in the Northern papers that every soldier was to be furnished a good Thanksgiving dinner—a regular lay-out of roast turkey or chicken, with trimmings of cranberry sauce and mince pie. As the time drew near, our anticipation of the joyous feast ran high.

However, before anything got to the field troops the goods had to pass through a rear echelon, through the hands of support troops composed of "mule whackers and rear bummers who habitually pried open and robbed boxes," reported James Bowen. For the 1st Dragoons, "… our dinner consisted of the old standby—hardtack and pork."[20]

If Thanksgiving was disagreeable for the troopers in the field, it was so much more so for civilians in the path of the moving armies. The winter months were on the horizon with little prospect of any relief by an end to the war. George Custer's 3rd Cavalry Division continued scouting in the valley and at the end of November the 2nd Ohio crossed and mountains into West Virginia and passed through a town named Moorefield where Luman Tenney's encounter with a local resident was preserved in his diary:

> Camped 13 miles from M [Moorefield] on an old gentleman's farm. I had quite a talk with him. He owned a farm, sterile and poor, of 200 acres in among the hills. He was 70 years of age. Move here 34 years since when all was a wilderness. Had never owned a slave. Had cleaned up the farm, built a log house and made all the improvement with his own hand. It made him almost crazy to see all going to destruction in one night—all his fences, outbuildings, cattle, sheep and fowls. An only son at home, an invalid. Had always been true to the government. Only wished that God would now call him, that he might be with his many friends in the church yard—pointing to it near by—and this aspect of suffering and starvation be taken from him.[21]

The only other major operation during the winter started in mid-December. Two divisions under the overall command of General Alfred Torbert were sent by Sheridan over the Blue Ridge to Charlottesville to rip up the railroad leading to Lynchburg, as well as destroying anything else of possible use by the Confederates.

The 8,000 cavalrymen suffered severely in rain and sleet, in wet clothes that froze on them when the temperature dropped. There were minor skirmishes with Rebels encountered along the way and the capture of prisoners and two artillery pieces, but "The expedition, under a competent leader might have been a success; but under Torbert proved a failure." Even after 30 odd years, one regiment's appraisal, that of the 1st New York Dragoons, on General Torbert remained negative. "Aside from his incompetence, his tyrannical treatment of the soldiers made him an object of detestation." This regimental history didn't stop there. The end of the war was clearly in sight for these men and they remained bitter about the waste they continued to see about them:

> It was a ten-days' raid of hard tramping and suffering, in which we lost men and horses, with many men injured for life; and no one has ever been able to point to even one compensating result.[22]

CHAPTER THIRTEEN

Closing Out the War

Warren was deposed from his command at Five Forks mainly, I have no doubt, under the irritation of his being slow in getting up to Sheridan the night before from White Oak Road.

GENERAL JOSHUA CHAMBERLAIN, ON THE RELIEF OF GENERAL GOUVERNEUR WARREN

General Warren was no more to General Sheridan than was any other general in the galaxy of stars which would disappear at the end of the war.

FREDERICK C. NEWHALL, SHERIDAN STAFF OFFICER

I trust, therefore, that I may yet receive some unequivocal acknowledgement of my faithful service at the battle of Five Forks.

MAJOR GENERAL G. K. WARREN[1]

The Army of the Potomac had arrived before the city of Petersburg just days before the summer solstice. The sun would shine down for the next three months, drying the soil upon which little rain would fall. Dust clouds of enormous size would form whenever any group of men or any wagons or horses moved about. Then fall arrived, the leaves on whatever trees were left standing turned color, and then there was the transition to winter, cold and damp, rain and then mud, week after miserable week. Now another spring was beginning, the spring of 1865, with the sun warming the Virginia air and coaxing the orchards into bloom and wildflowers closer to blossom. The army was still there, before the city, the siege it had maintained all during the summer and winter past still in force, the casualties still accumulating.

Joshua Lawrence Chamberlain was one of the many heroes in the defense of Little Round Top during the Battle of Gettysburg. One of the others was Gouverneur K. Warren. On that July afternoon, Warren, then Chief of Engineers for the Army of the Potomac, recognized the threat to Little Round Top posed by the Confederate attack and saw to it that troops were deployed—just in time—to prevent the capture of this imposing high ground. Chamberlain that day was in command of the 20th Maine Infantry, one of the regiments deployed on the summit of Little Round Top that played a large role in holding the important

General Joshua Chamberlain, officer in charge of receiving the surrender of the Army of Northern Virginia. (Library of Congress)

elevation. Now it was the spring of 1865 and Warren was commanding V Corps and Chamberlain a brigade commander in one of the corps' three divisions. In the opening movements of the campaign that would lead to the eventual surrender of General Lee's army at Appomattox, there occurred an engagement known to history as the Battle of Five Forks. General Phil Sheridan would be in command, directing his three cavalry divisions as well as V Corps. For Joshua Chamberlain more than 50 years would pass, he now past the age of 80, and despite drinking from the cup of victory in that battle and campaign, there remained a bitter taste, a memory, left by Phil Sheridan by his treatment of Major General Warren at Five Forks.

Chamberlain produced his remembrance, *The Passing of Armies* in 1915, calling it "An interior view" as opposed to a history that is "… usually written for the most part from the outside," by a non-participant. For Chamberlain, an engaged participant, his interior view tells of what was important to him at the time as well as important to him at the time of his putting pen to paper. He hoped to provide with his memory only what was known, done, thought and felt at the time, but events during the campaign were to be such that even the passing of years would not, or could not, change an opinion formed at that time and held into the next century. He wrote:

> It may be permitted to hope that this simple recital may throw some light on a passage of history of the Corps, the record of which has been obscured in consequence of the summary change of commanders early in the campaign.

Here Chamberlain refers to Sheridan, in immediate command of the forces engaged, and his relief of Corps Commander Major General Gouverneur Warren at the close of the battle for not doing what Sheridan had in mind, regardless of the on-the-ground conditions. That bitter taste that Sheridan's action left with the Corps' officers remained half a century later and is mild proof, try as one might, that interior views or reminiscences cannot be wholly unprejudiced.[2]

As General Grant had done since arriving before Petersburg the previous summer, he wanted to extend his line to the left thereby severing the rail lines coming into the city from the south and southwest; the lines that brought food and ammunition to the Army of Northern Virginia. With the supply lines cut, Lee would have to abandon Petersburg and Richmond. One of the last unbroken rail lines running into Petersburg was the Southside Railroad, coming in from Lynchburg. Sheridan would lead his Cavalry Corps to the left, passing the end of Lee's defensive position and then turn north advancing on the Southside Railroad and cutting it. The path north would pass through a road intersection called Five Forks and when it became known to the Rebels that Sheridan was moving, General Lee rushed a force to the Five Forks road junction to block it. The cavalry's advance on the intersection was stalled,

Confederate General George Pickett commander of the Confederate force at Five Forks. (Library of Congress)

with Chamberlain long afterward saying Sheridan hadn't attacked the Rebel force in sufficient strength. Sheridan had to retreat to his starting point at Dinwiddie Court House, followed by the Rebels. When he reported that he planned to advance again on the intersection he was given control of V Corps to help secure the intersection. V Corps was ordered to move to Sheridan's aid late on the night of Friday, March 31. Before Warren's troops could get to Dinwiddie, the command had about six miles to travel over rain-soaked roads and across a flooded creek over which a bridge had to be re-built, all in the dark. Grant's headquarters had told Sheridan to expect the corps' arrival only about two hours after sending Warren his initial order to move in support of the cavalry force. This totally unreasonable calculation was someone's fault, perhaps even that of the commanding general, Grant, but Sheridan took this information and spent the remainder of the night and part of the next morning waiting, all the time his temper escalating and his attack plan for the day being delayed.

During this night, the Confederate force opposing Sheridan and under the command of General George Pickett, had withdrawn from near Dinwiddie and moved back to Five Forks, assuming a defensive stance. After arriving at Dinwiddie

General G. K. Warren commander of the Fifth Corps at Five Forks and the officer who called off the assault at Mine Run in November 1864. (Library of Congress)

and receiving a briefing on the attack plan by an annoyed Phil Sheridan, Warren and V Corps moved to the position from which it was to attack. The movement to the attack position was hampered by the broken terrain, soggy from rain that had soaked the area for the better part of two days. It wasn't until about 4pm that the attack on the Rebel position at the Five Forks intersection by V Corps went forward. Because of an alleged faulty reconnaissance, the corps positioned itself for its assigned attack in the wrong place and only by advancing and coming under enfilading fire did it locate the true enemy position. When it did, it attacked and thoroughly defeated the Confederate force. In his report, Warren said the corps had taken 3,244 prisoners, four artillery pieces and eleven battle flags while suffering 634 casualties.[3]

Sheridan, rather than being pleased with the victory, was still smoldering, unable to get over the apparent slowness of V Corps' arrival hours after he had been told to expect it but also the again apparent slowness of the corps getting into position to attack, all the while his Cavalry Corps was fighting dismounted with the same Rebels Warren was supposed to be attacking. As soon as the Five Forks victory was assured, as the prisoners were rounded up and the captured battle flags collected, Sheridan sent a written order to Warren via a staff officer relieving him of his command and ordering him to report to General Grant.

Unlike General Chamberlain, William Locke, chaplain of the 11th Pennsylvania of V Corps, did not wait 50 years to speak of Warren's removal. In Locke's 1868 history of his regiment, he said:

> With the splendid achievements of General Sheridan fully acknowledged, and with an admiration of his dashing soldierly qualities second to none, the men of the V Corps have never forgiven him for his hasty action toward their well-tried commander.

Five Forks was "a victory which belongs as much to Warren as to Sheridan." Sheridan's action was "Regarded at the time as a freak of temper rather than the dictate of calm and sober judgment, the removal of General Warren remains to this day without justification of reason or expediency."[4]

A soldier in V Corps that fought at Five Forks, writing years later, would say that in the last charge made against the Confederate position, Warren was on the field and "seizing the corps flag he led the division [General Crawford's] across the open field up tight on the entrenchments under severe fire, and sent the only remnant of all Pickett's brave battalions from it last abiding place." General Warren, mere minutes later, was confronted with the order sent to him by Sheridan. The same soldier, after indicating his disapproval both at the time and when he was writing of it, quotes Warren, from the report on the battle he wrote after being relieved. "I trust, however," Warren says, "that I yet receive some unequivocal acknowledgment of my faithful service at the battle of Five Forks that will ever free me from opprobrium, even among the superficial."[5] A year after the war's end there appeared in print *With General Sheridan in Lee's Last Campaign*. Its author was only listed as "a Staff Officer," but later attributed to one Frederick C. Newhall of General Sheridan's staff. Newhall says of his employment of the pen name "Staff Officer" that "if the famous names now upon the title page fail to receive attention, it would avail very little to add his own." This explanation appears weak when one reads the 45 pages of the book devoted to the Battle of Five Forks. This version of events contains a severe, even harsh, critique of General Warren's conduct during the battle. The staff officer, in his preface, announces that his book was not written at the request of Sheridan and has as its purpose only to provide a "Sketch" and "has no object in the world but to fairly present the general and his campaign to such readers as the book shall find."[6] The actions of General Warren and V Corps are detailed move by move from the time of its receipt of the order to march to the support of Sheridan through to the close of the battle. One takes from reading this account the impression that its author is protesting—or praising—too much. This officer's unqualified, loyal and unquestioning defense of General Sheridan and his actions on April 1, 1865, and his portrayal of Warren, might have, at the time, been intended as first strike at potential criticism others may be planning to write as well as a kind of preliminary brief to submit to a court of inquiry that may be convened in the near future. Such a court, requested by Warren, was more than a decade in the future. The laudatory praise showered upon Sheridan by this devoted staff officer is such as to color negatively and cast doubt upon the worth of anything detailed in the work relating to the remainder of the Appomattox campaign.

Joshua Chamberlain expended considerable ink speaking of this incident in his later memoir of the campaign. V Corps had been delayed in its attack, Chamberlain admits, and Sheridan considered it Warren's fault. It may be summarized, in Chamberlain's words as follows, a Captain Gillespie of Sheridan's staff performed the faulty reconnaissance:

It would appear that the staff officer making the reconnaissance had not examined the whole field [where Warren's attack was to be directed] or all of the enemy's position ... But a discrepancy of a thousand yards in a report of such consequence is a pretty wide error. It might be said that Warren was responsible for assuring himself perfectly of the conditions in his front of attack. But Sheridan saw and approved the diagram; and if anybody is to be blamed, he must be considered ultimately, and in a military sense, responsible for these misapprehensions. At any rate there was a very imperfect reconnaissance, from which we all suffered, but it would be very unjust to place the blame on the Fifth Corps or its commander.[7]

After the fighting was over, after several thousand prisoners were marched to the rear, the force under General Pickett's command essentially ceased to exist.

As ordered, General Warren reported to Grant's headquarters where the commanding general upheld Sheridan's decision even after hearing the extenuating circumstances surrounding it, reasons Warren obviously thought well founded. The decision was painful still further, in Warren's mind, when he learned that George Meade agreed with it. Twenty years later, and after a court of inquiry essentially said that the relief of Warren was unfounded given the revealed facts and testimony it had reviewed, Grant addressed the matter in his memoirs. After saying he was

General Philip Sheridan commander to the Union force at Five Forks who relieved General Warren after he led the Fifth Corps to victory. (Library of Congress)

"much dissatisfied with Warren's dilatory movements," apparently on March 31 and April 1, Grant notes of Warren:

> He was a man of fine intelligence, great earnestness, quick perception, and could make his dispositions as quickly as any officer, under difficulties where he was forced to act. But I had before discovered a defect which was beyond his control, that was very prejudicial to his usefulness in emergencies like the one just before us. He could see every danger at a glance before he had encountered it. He would not only make preparations to meet the danger which might occur, but he would inform his commanding officer what others should do while he was executing his move.

In deference to the general commanding the armies of the United States, Warren's relief stemmed from a perceived slowness in moving and deploying his troops, not his supposed quibbling over orders and contingencies, that General Grant notes in his memoirs. Grant even says Warren could move and deploy "as quickly as any officer," when forced to act. That Warren had previously been perceived as slow and reluctant to attack had been in instances where assaults had been ordered against enemy positions that later had been deemed impregnable, but in the heat of battle and the tactics employed, particularly by Grant's penchant for headlong charges, he had been seen as a general that questioned orders and thus caused delays. Such an instance had, in particular, been the case at Laurel Hill in May of the previous year. Later, General Andrew Humphreys, Meade's chief of staff, spoke in support of Warren's actions and the matter was put aside but not forgotten.[8] However, there is little in the record to suggest Warren was slow in moving because he was at odds with any order Grant, Meade or Sheridan might have given him on March 31 or April 1. Nevertheless, like George Meade, Gouverneur Warren was an engineer. Taking into consideration all contingencies that may be confronted in a project is, in part, what engineers do as part of their job. General Meade had been accused of planning to retreat from Gettysburg, ordering that some officers familiarize themselves with the roads leading from the battlefield if withdrawal became necessary. The controversy surrounding this logical contingency order—perceived as a retreat order—was argued long after the general had left the scene. But as an engineer, and as the general commanding the army, this contingency planning would have been one of the first things thought of when preparing for battle. So it was in the case of Warren but, unlike Meade, he was a combat leader, not the general commanding and he did not put this deemed negative attribute aside in leading a corps into battle prior to Five Forks to the annoyance of his superiors. On this particular occasion it was not evident in the primary evidence available to us. Sheridan would emerge from the war with a superior reputation as a leader, but as remarked by one historian he was "a better soldier than a man …"[9]

As for the human cost of the fight at Five Forks, Luman Tenney and his brother Theodore rode with the 2nd Ohio Cavalry in the operation. The regiment was fighting dismounted in front of Pickett's division as Sheridan waited for Warren's infantry to attack on the flank and rear of the Rebels. Theodore was killed. In Tenney's diary for April 1 is the following:

> Here brother Thede [Theodore], noble and brave boy was struck through with a piece of shell. Helped him from the field. Suffered awfully. In answer to my question he said: 'Luman, I think my wound is mortal. I can not live. I have tried to do my duty today. Tell mother I only wish I had been a better boy. I hope God will accept me and take me to Heaven.' He had his senses for 30 or 40 minutes when he sank away as we carried him and died before we reached the hospital. I thought that he had fallen asleep. I spoke to him but received no answer. His pulse beat feebly. I knew then that he was going. The Doctor gave him some brandy, but no life appeared. I buried him … beneath a cedar tree in front of the house and across the road and cut the head board with a knife. God sustain mother.[10]

A year later on the anniversary of his brother's death, Tenney wrote again to his mother and sisters.

> I know that you would be sad to feel that the boy should be taken in his youth, the hope of his mother and the joy of his friends, and yet I felt that you would inwardly thank God that his death had brought glory to him and freedom to men … We ought to feel—I do—that we have a living interest in this grand good accomplishment and sealed by the blood of our dearest friends. And we certainly have reason to trust that Theodore's inheritance is in Heaven drawing us thither.[11]

Luman Tenney settled in Minnesota after the war and engaged in farming and business until his death in 1880.

***

General Robert E. Lee and his Army of Northern Virginia could not sustain an offensive or a defensive operation after Five Forks. All he could hope to do was move, an attempt at escaping the ring closing around him. With the victory at Five Forks, Grant ordered a general assault at dawn the next day along the line at Petersburg. The attack forced Lee to abandon his defensive line about Petersburg and Richmond during the night of April 2. During the assault and breakthrough of the Petersburg line an officer, Thomas Hyde of VI Corps, was advancing, and the Rebels retreating, when a battery:

> … opened on our left almost enfilading the line, and several times, as it was forced to change position … we noticed each time a fine-looking old officer, on a gray horse, who seemed to be directing its movements.

Hyde related later in a reminiscence, that after the position was taken:

> I asked a mortally wounded artillery officer who was propped up against a limber what battery it was. 'Captain Williams of Pouge's North Carolina battalion,' said he. And who was that officer on the gray horse, I continued? 'General Robert E. Lee, sir, and he was the last man to leave these guns,' replied he, almost exhausted by the effort.[12]

The march of the Army of Northern Virginia and its pursuit by the Army of the Potomac began and seven days later it would end at Appomattox Court House. For the Potomac Army, the pursuit of Lee's forces once they were out of the Petersburg field works was a sprint, with springtime road conditions and rear-guard firefights marking the movement. The soldiers doing the fighting and marching had caught a glimpse of an end, the end of the war. After it was over, it was noted in the history of the 11th Pennsylvania that the troops were aware of what was happening. "From his place in the ranks," Chaplain William Locke wrote, "each private soldier could see the end of the rebellion …"[13] A clerk in V Corps headquarters, writing home on April 5 with rear echelon bravado, predicted the end of the campaign saying, "There will be precious little left of the Army of Northern Virginia by the time we are done with it."[14] The direction of Lee's retreat would be dictated by the source of supply for his army. Hoping initially to move to Danville, Virginia, and to have supplies forward to him by rail as he moved, Lee found his path blocked by Sheridan's cavalry. He turned toward Lynchburg and ordered up rations from there. The Rebel army, as it marched, was hounded in its rear by both Sheridan's mounted force and Meade's infantry. As he approached the vicinity of Appomattox Court House and Appomattox Station, Lee had to know the end had arrived. The rations for his men ordered from Lynchburg sat on trains at Appomattox Station already captured by George Custer's 3rd Cavalry Division, the troopers emptying the freight cars and helping themselves. Communications with the Confederate army were opened with the Union commander appealing to Lee to see the reality of his situation and stop any further effusion of blood. Early on the morning of April 9, there was one last attempt to break through the Union cordon and escape. It failed. Later that day, the two commanding generals met at a residence at Appomattox Court House and Lee surrendered the Army of Northern Virginia. The war in the east was over.

Among the last of the casualties of this closing campaign was Lieutenant-Colonel Augustus Root of the 15th New York Cavalry. On the night of April 8, for some unexplained reason, Root took some men and rode into Appomattox Court House. There was no indication at that moment that there would be a capitulation the next day. The regiment's history contains the following concerning Root. He "… was shot down by the enemy in the streets of Appomattox in front of the Court House. His body was found the morning after the surrender, lying in the road where he fell, stripped of all outer garments. His remains were temporarily buried near by, and eventually taken up and forwarded to Syracuse, N.Y., where they now repose in that city's beautiful cemetery."[15]

The historian of the 1st Maine Cavalry remembered the Sunday morning of April 9 by saying:

> … men awoke in fine spirits. Never before during the three years or more of service had there been any prospect of the end. All that hard marching and fighting of three summer campaigns, and the long hours on picket and in dull winter quarters, had been with no such encouragement

as they now had ... Richmond was captured ... the goal for which they had marched and fought, and for which so many brave boys had died, was reached—the backbone of the rebellion ... Had now been broken ... and was beyond healing ... It was exciting to even think of the situation, that spring morning.[16]

It was Palm Sunday and about 4pm when the news of Lee's surrender reached the 22nd Massachusetts. Later, it was written into the regiment's history that "the men behaved like children, nothing being extravagant for the expression of their joy. Ordinary discipline was relaxed." And the next day "the soldiers fraternized with their late enemies, and freely dividing rations." An officer in the 118th Pennsylvania, years later remembered:

As I rode through Lee's army and conversed with officers and men, I felt more sympathy than resentment toward these men, and I believe this was the feeling that prevailed throughout our army.[17]

Chaplain Alanson Haines of the 15th New Jersey Infantry recorded the reaction of his regiment upon the announcement of Lee's surrender. Along with the throwing of caps in the air, there was:

... every demonstration of joy imaginable ... men were shaking hands and shedding tears of gladness ... The men of the two armies were ready to fraternize at once. Our boys opened their haversacks to give to the hungry rebels, and soon full rations were distributed to them. Many of them expressed their satisfaction that the fighting was over. One called out, 'Say, Yanks! You're mighty glad the war's over, but ye're hain't half so glad as us are.'"

In the 118th Pennsylvania, it was noted that the hungry Rebel soldiers looked on in amazement, "the sweet aroma of real coffee staggered the Confederates, condensed milk and sugar appalled them, and they stood aghast at just a little butter which one soldier ... happened to have preserved."[18]

Robert Wallace, now a staff officer, was close by as Grant and Lee met in the McLean house at Appomattox Court House as the ceasefire continued around them. All were aware the war was over. Wallace later wrote that after Lee had signed the surrender document:

It was a very interesting sight to see the officers of the two Armies fraternizing as if they had not been fighting each other for four years. I very well remember the meeting between Gen. Custer and a rebel officer who had been his classmate at West Point. Each threw his arm around the other and seemed really glad to meet again as friends.[19]

General Joshua Chamberlain of V Corps took the formal surrender of the Army of Northern Virginia from General John B. Gordon on Wednesday, April 12. During the two days since General Lee's surrender, paroles had been made out and rations distributed, with the men generally resting, recovering from the war's last week of marching and fighting. Then, on that Wednesday, the Confederate force marched past Chamberlain's command and received their salute. They had asked the Union generals in charge not to have to march and then stack their arms, but this was refused, General Chamberlain later recalling it was satisfying after all they had gone through but not of the kind that showed any disrespect towards their now former enemy. The Rebels stacked their arms and laid down their battle flags and marched away in silence. According to Chamberlain, it was a solemn moment.

Looking back upon this day in his remembrance, Robert Wallace tells us how he felt at the time and what the Union soldiers were told to do:

> No one not there can have any idea of how we all felt after the surrender. It was as if a great black cloud had been dispersed and the sun had again come out in all its splendor.

Wallace said, as the ceremony went on:

> ... a Division of Union Infantry was drawn up in line and the Confederates marched up, laid down their arms in front of the line and went their way. Our men were instructed to make no insulting remarks during the passing of the Rebels but to keep a respectful silence, which order was obeyed to the letter as far as I could learn.

In closing his little memoir, Wallace then noted, "So ended the last act of the greatest tragedy of the age." Joshua Chamberlain remembered the marching column saying, "... on our part not a sound of trumpet or drum, not a cheer, nor word nor motion of a man, but awful stillness, as if it were the passing of the dead."[20] The historian of the 1st New York Dragoon remembered the Appomattox surrender 35 years later, saying:

> But now the hour had come; treason had been subdued, armed rebellion overthrown, and the political heresy of States' rights trampled in the dust. The majesty of the law was vindicated. The sovereignty of the nation maintained ...

With the ceremony over, a witness recalled the Confederates signed their paroles and "on the following day scarcely a rebel could be found on that historic field."[21] Chamberlain recalled, using the words he copied from Oliver Norton's reminiscence of the 82nd New York Infantry, that early the next morning, "over all the hillsides in the peaceful sunshine, are clouds of men on foot or horse ... making their way as by the instinct of an ant, each with his own little burden, each for his own little harbor or home."[22] Another soldier standing with a Maine regiment was Theodore Gerrish and almost two decades later remembered seeing Rebels he had been fighting for so long:

> As a rule they were tall, thin, spare men, with long hair and beard of tawny red color. They were all clad in the uniform of Southern gray; nearly all were very ragged and dirty, while their broad-brimmed, slouched gray hats gave them anything but a soldierly appearance.[23]

Like General Lee, George Meade did not attend the surrender at Appomattox, remarking in a letter to his wife that he had been suffering for some days from a malady and was being treated by a doctor. In two letters dated April 10 and 12

Meade speaks to his wife about closing out the war in Virginia and his growing annoyance, possibly approaching bitterness, at the portrayal of his role in it is evident:

> Lee's army was reduced to a force of less than ten thousand effective armed men. We had at least fifty thousand around him, so that nothing but madness would have justified further resistance.

Reading this letter, one gets the impression the commander of the Army of the Potomac is somewhat put out, indeed wounded by things either said or intimated by others that had found their way into the national press. If newspaper reporting is the first draft of history, George Meade seems to feel his record in the war will not be what he thinks it should be. To his wife he said:

> I have seen but few newspapers since this movement commenced, and I don't want to see any more, for they are full of falsehood and of undue and exaggerated praise of certain individuals who take pains to be on the right side of the reporters.

Meade said his conscious was clear and that he did the best of which he was capable; but was particularly annoyed with Sheridan.

> His determination to absorb the credit for everything done is so manifest as to have attracted the attention of the whole army, and the truth will in time be made known. His conduct towards me has been beneath contempt, and will most assuredly react against him in the minds of all just and fair-minded persons.

Nevertheless, frustrated, Meade admits, "I don't believe the truth ever will be known, and I have a great contempt for History."[24]

It is the spring of 1865 and Generals Grant, Sherman and Sheridan, in the pages of history yet to be written, will be spoken of as the great commanders of this war. Some other notable players will get recognition, eventually, be it an approving nod in a sentence buried in the middle of a thick book or some via a revisionist reconsideration from some future historian. Others will not, while still others will be written and spoken of as incompetents, drunkards, frauds and liars, and rightly so. Some will be remembered as fighters, but characters with which one would not care to associate with off the battlefield. George Meade deserves from history something better than he has thus far received.

When Lincoln was shown the Confederate battle flags captured at Five Forks, it is recorded he said, "Here is something material, something I can see, feel, and understand. This means victory. This is victory."[25] Lieutenant H. G. Bonebrake of the 17th Pennsylvania Cavalry who, as part of Thomas Devin's 1st Cavalry Division, was quite active during the first nine days of April. His diary contains the note that all the men that had captured Rebel battle flags at Five Forks were sent to Washington after the surrender to present the flags to the War Department. These men were put on a boat at City Point and got to the capital on April 15. "We arrived at Washington at 7:30 a.m.," noted Bonebrake. Before taking the flags to the War

Department, "I stopped at the St. Charles Hotel … Last night President Lincoln was assassinated at Ford's Theater. An attempt was made to assassinate Secretary Seward at his private home. The greatest excitement prevails in the city. President Lincoln died this morning at 7:22." Three days later the lieutenant noted, "The public is permitted to view the remains of President Lincoln. I saw his body at 12:30 p.m. The crowd to view the remains was immense." Lieutenant Bonebrack was one of 51 Union soldiers sent to Washington with captured Confederate battle flags from the Appomattox Campaign. He received a 30-day furlough and the Medal of Honor.[26]

All the men of the Potomac army wanted to do now was get the money owed them and go home. The war was over, and those tough, ragged, half-starved and courageous Rebels were walking the roads to their homes, all with the respect of the Billy Yanks that had been shooting at them for the past four years. In the mind of at least one Union veteran—and probably many others—those Rebels deserved some respect, but those at home in the North that had urged peace whatever it took, the Copperheads, had better watch themselves as the Potomac soldiers returned. Oliver Norton, once a soldier in V Corps and then an officer in a black regiment, warned those at home about the way he felt soon after the surrender:

> I can listen with a quaint smile to the sad story of a rebel soldier who had fought bravely through the war for a bad cause and acknowledges himself beaten. That is punishment enough for him, but for the villain at home too cowardly to fight for the cause he helped with his tongue and influence, I have only infinite scorn and loathing. I curse him from the bottom of my heart.

This was not an opinion formed in the quiet after the surrender. Oliver Norton, as far back as Gettysburg had written home, "Every man who is not with us is against us, and I would just as soon fight a cursed copperhead as a southern rebel."[27]

During the month of May, the two great armies, Meade's in Virginia and Sherman's in North Carolina, where he had taken the surrender of the Confederate army there, began moving toward Washington. On May 23 and 24, there was planned a Grand Review of these soon-to-be veterans. Years later the Grand Review was written of with obvious reverence and its symbolism:

> At sunrise on May 23, the spectators were gathered. The sky was blue, a soft breeze stirred the roses, and from the capitol to the White House was aflutter with waving flags and handkerchiefs, when at nine o'clock the signal gun was fired, and General Meade rode out on his garlanded horse at the head of the Army of the Potomac.

There was a holiday crowd of the city's citizens, school children and out of town visitors waiting to observe the spectacle. The Cavalry Corps led the way. A trooper remembered, "Pennsylvania Avenue was packed from one end to the other with a dense mass of humanity, and the troops received a perfect ovation at every step."[28] Before the White House was a grandstand and:

The Grand Review of May 1865 in Washington. (Library of Congress)

> As the corps and division commanders went by, the President and General Grant and Mr. Stanton and the rest stood up, and swords were lowered in salute and the colors dipped. General Meade had taken his place on the reviewing stand, as did the corps commanders in their turn ... All day, Meade's spectacled scholar's face looked down on the pageant of the army he had led to victory, with glory overshadowed by Grant.[29]

Indeed, it took all day for the army to pass.

Noah Brooks was a newspaperman who had reported from Washington during most of the war. He witnessed the Grand Review and noted with a reporter's eye in a later memoir that 29 regiments of cavalry passed his reviewing stand that morning, followed by 33 artillery batteries that in turn were followed by 180 infantry regiments. Marching down Pennsylvania Avenue this day was Battery L, Second New York Artillery, a volunteer outfit organized in 1861 in Flushing, New York. It had fought through 1862 in Virginia, in 1863 in the western theater and in 1864 again in Virginia with the Army of the Potomac. When the battery first took the field in 1862 with its six artillery pieces, it mustered 133 men, five officers, 115 horses and one laundress. The commander of the battery, Captain Jacob Roemer, in his reminiscences noted, "the possession of a laundress was a luxury of which few organizations could boast." Roemer explains, "This was the wife of one of the men and had insisted on going with us, and at the final review in Washington in 1865 rode on a limber chest with the men."[30]

Indeed, it had taken all day and then Noah Brooks, knowing an end to the Army of the Potomac was at hand noted:

> The pageant faded. The men-at-arms who had spent their years and lavished their energies in camp or on the fields of battle went from the national capital to their own homes, to take up once more the arts of peace and the cares and joys of sweet domesticity.[31]

The next day, General William Tecumseh Sherman and the president reviewed the army he had led from Tennessee to Atlanta, to Savannah, to North Carolina while the same witnesses looked on:

> They had a gaunt, rough look about them, like frontier soldiers, taller and bonier than Eastern men. There was something bold, aggressive and magnificent in their rolling, cadenced stride … Pioneer corps of huge Negroes, with picks and spade and axes, marched ahead of each division.

Again, it took all day.

> The sun slanted in the west, as Sherman's men dispersed, to get drunk and disturb the peace of Washington, to fight with Eastern soldiers in the saloons, and blast the name Stanton. The grand review was ended.[32]

In the weeks that followed, and continuing through the summer, regiments processed the paperwork necessary for the mustering out of many thousands of men:

> War Department clerks were totting up muster and pay rolls. Day after day, the goodbyes said and hands shaken, the troops departed. The countryside began to wear the aspect of a deserted fairground, and quiet descended on the city's battered streets.[33]

They had turned in their weapons, been paid off and started on individual journeys home. In the coming years, hundreds of regimental associations would be instituted, each with their reunions, with ceremonies of remembrance and renewed camaraderie. Through the remainder of the century, memorials of granite and statues of bronze would be commissioned and put in places of significance for these veterans, places where they had fought and were some had died. Eventually, nearly every regiment that marched down Pennsylvania Avenue in the Grand Review would produce its own history and many individual soldiers, privates to generals, would sit for long evening hours by lamp light handwriting their memories, reminiscences, recollections and memoirs, their, and now our, history of the Civil War.

Many of these published histories recalled the Grand Review in their last pages. A trooper in the 10th New York Cavalry marched passed the Capitol and on to Pennsylvania Avenue:

> … where myriads of Sunday-school children were waiting with flowers, with which they strewed the streets and bedecked the officers and men. One little miss threw a large wreath over the neck of General Avery's horse. General Custer's division presented a striking appearance, every man wearing a red neck-scarf with long, flowing ends.[34]

And so it went.

Promoted to major during the Appomattox Campaign, Robert Wallace marched with his regiment, the 5th Michigan Cavalry, in the Grand Review along with, by his estimate, 200,000 soldiers. It was a sunny day as the Army of the Potomac marched down Pennsylvania Avenue. Wallace later wrote of this army, "They were no Sunday soldiers, but the real stuff, weather beaten, war worn, hardened veterans, nothing bright about them but their arm."[35]

In 1869, Wallace found his way to Montana, eventually starting a successful grocery business. He married, raised a family and lived into the 20th century. At the urging of his children, Wallace, like so many others from this war, penned, *A Few Memories of a Long Life*, "entirely from memory." In a brief introduction, he recommended caution for the pages he wrote "are not intended for the public eye, but should they chance to fall into the hands of any outside the family; don't expect much, and you'll not be disappointed."[36]

Chauncey Norton of the 15th New York Cavalry produced a history of his regiment in 1891, *The Red Neck Ties or History of the Fifteenth New York Volunteer Cavalry*. In closing the chronology apparently based on a diary he had kept he says:

> Comrades, my task in done. The lapse of a quarter of a century since we disbanded and the vast territory over which the survivors of the gallant old 15th are scattered, has made the work a somewhat difficult one, but I hope and trust you will pardon all omissions.[37]

Thomas C. Devin had been in the New York State Militia before the war and was the first colonel of the 6th New York Cavalry. By the end of the war, after serving under John Buford and Phil Sheridan, commanding the 2nd brigade of Buford's 1st Cavalry Division, Devin, now a general, commanded the 1st Cavalry Division through 1865. The division marched and fought with Sheridan in the Shenandoah Valley in the fall of 1864 and then from Five Forks to Appomattox. After leading his division up Pennsylvania Avenue in the Grand Review, Devin was recommended for a permanent commission in the army, serving as lieutenant-colonel of the 8th U.S. Cavalry in Arizona among other assignments. Later, he was promoted to colonel of the 3rd U.S. Cavalry but was forced to return to New York City on sick leave before taking actual command. Tom Devin died at his residence at 219 E 48th Street on April 4, 1879, from what was termed exposure and improper food while on duty in Arizona.[38]

William Wheeler, the New York artillery officer, went in the fall of 1863 with XI Corps to the western theater, fighting with Sherman's army in Georgia. He was killed on June 22, 1864, while positioning his battery to engage the Rebels. His family gathered together and published his letters in 1875.

On June 16, 1865, the 126th New York was discharged. According to its regimental history, nearly three years after it had left Elmira 1,000 strong, it returned 221 strong:

> Where are the missing? The green fields of Pennsylvania, Maryland and Virginia hide the remains of many; the cemeteries of Ontario, Yates and Seneca are the resting places of others. Some, with honorable scars or frames enfeebled ... still linger among us to receive our gratitude and honor.[39]

It was 20 years after Appomattox that S. Millett Thompson made a visit to Virginia, returning to some of the fields his regiment, the 13th New Hampshire, had fought on as part of IX Corps. Three years later, in 1888, this graduate of Phillips Academy would produce a history of his regiment, offering it to the public and to each of the regiment's veterans and families of its fallen for $3.50 each. This former lieutenant based his history on the diary he kept as well as materials gathered from other members of the command. Near the end of his history, Thompson included a chapter detailing his Virginia visit and his interaction with Confederate veterans he encountered. He detailed his views on some of the differences between the war years and the year 1885. His discourse on the experiences he had during this visit is the most interesting portion of the work, the opening of a time capsule from 1885 revealing Thompson's unrealized prejudice, yet contemporary view of a portion of the South during the war era and some 20 years after. Everyone was exceedingly friendly to him during his trip. He observed other visiting Union veterans as well as ex-Confederates, saying the former soldiers, North and South, "nine out of ten ... now ... meet as friends." Reconciliation had taken hold. Thompson, referring to the start of the war, relates that the Southern soldiers, now veterans like himself, differed, back then, from his northern counterparts, "... in training, education and hotness of temperament that a hot climate seems to provoke in English stock." He tells of his speaking with one Confederate veteran, the old soldier comparing the past with the present. Thompson relates the veteran saying:

> ... the South was educated to the States' Rights idea, the North to the National idea; now we are all one, that root of evil, slavery, is gone, and we are all glad of it. Before the war and during it here, the poor white man of the non-slaveholding class had little or no redress for mischiefs, insults or wrongs done by the rich man's negro [sic]—but now any white man is just as good as any nigger.[40]

This truly is a mild rendition of this attitude. We are hearing the white, late 19th century point of view of many, perhaps most, Southerners, pervasive racism laced with relief that now he can have "redress," the form of which was, in its mildest form, the relegation of millions to an ignored underclass. After speaking with veterans and describing battlefields, Thompson summarizes his own view of the differences between the regions that brought on the catastrophic war;

> The differences in and between the peoples of the two sections in 1860–5 can be written in one sentence—the South was more religious and the north was more Christian.[41]

Perhaps. This can only be taken to mean that one was religious but with a blind eye turned toward a core institution and one with a clear eye seeing a wrong. It wasn't that simple. It remains an era in which every facet of human endeavor is entwined in the causes, the events and the consequences of the Civil War. An era of complexities, of which the memoirists might or might not have been aware, that the historians since have listened to and sought to explain.

The spring of 1865 settled over Virginia and four years of fighting were over, the stream of uncounted tears of remembrance just beginning. White paper that would become brittle with age, with faded ink and hard to read handwriting, was being scribbled on by some, early arrivals in what would become the Civil War's archive, its repository of remembrance. General Joshua Chamberlain, after taking the formal surrender of the Army of Northern Virginia at Appomattox in April and marching in the Grand Review in May, waited like all the others to go home and then waited fifty years to put a memoir of these days into print. He spoke in his remembrance of these days of waiting. The order was coming down, he knew it, but admits that when it did it "moved us deeply." He included the beginning of it in his memoir.

> Headquarters, Army of the Potomac
> June 28, 1865
> By virtue of special orders, No. 339, current series, from the Adjutant General's office, this army, as an organization, ceases to exist.[42]

CONCLUSIONS

Again, Remembrance as History

A fierce but short engagement ended in the entire rout of the enemy … Drove them back two or three miles and then returned. The casualties in the regiment were quite heavy, among the killed being … Samuel A Fanshaw.
HILLMAN A. HALL, IN *HISTORY OF THE 6TH NEW YORK CAVALRY*, 1908

Fifty years hence, our grand children will come on pilgrimage and tread, with sacred awe and holy reverence, these places where every sod is a soldier's sepulcher.
REV. A. M. STEWART, 102D PENNSYLVANIA INFANTRY, WRITING IN 1865

We shall never any of us be the same as we have been.
LUCY BUCK, VIRGINIA RESIDENT

I see them now, more than I can number, as once I saw them on this earth.
OLIVER WENDELL HOLMES, JR., FORMER OFFICER, 20TH MASSACHUSETTS[1]

Summers in the Mad River Valley of Vermont are lush, lovely and, most importantly, peaceful. E. F. Palmer and his nine-month volunteer regiment had fought at Gettysburg and then been discharged, their term of service ended. Before the end of July, Palmer was home in Waitsfield, Vermont, and he set to work immediately. Within six months he wrote and published a history of the 2nd Vermont Brigade. This brigade had been assigned to the defenses of Washington but was ordered into I Corps for the campaign resulting in the battle at Gettysburg, with Palmer and his Vermont neighbors playing a significant part in turning back the Rebel infantry assault of July 3. His expectations for the book were not as lofty as the Green Mountain standing above the valley and his hometown, but he had his purpose:

When peace shall have been established, and the young men of the Second Brigade shall have grown venerable in age, possibly a perusal of these hastily written pages may revive some sweet (I hope not sad) memories of the camp and the field.[2]

Many that wrote of their personal experience of the Civil War waited decades before delivering their remembrances to a printer. A captain in the 9th Massachusetts did not, publishing his regimental history in 1867, recalling events only three years in the past. Of the Wilderness, his melancholy is present on the page, as he speaks of the vicious fighting and the regiment's losses while still fresh in memory.

> But history, which is not written for to-day, but for all time, does not allow the exercise of useless regrets or vain sorrowings. It demands a consistent following of the record, even if, to pen it, the wounds reopen, and the old sorrows return afresh.

Martin Haynes of the 2nd New Hampshire waited until 1916 to present his remembrance, saying as he did so, "I feel lonesome when I realize that I am almost the last survivor of those who live and move in the following pages." His purpose, wrote Haynes in a preamble, "Here is recorded the small talk of camp, and many incidents that are too trivial for big histories ... And one can get a very fair idea of what manner of men they were."[3]

In 1890, before publishing his memoir, Alonzo Foster, of the 6th New York Cavalry, made a sentimental journey to Virginia, visiting some of the places where his regiment had camped and fought during the war. Touring the National Cemetery at Arlington, he came upon the headstone of a mass grave, the resting place for 2,107 unknown Union soldiers killed in Virginia. Two years later he recorded in his reminiscences that next to the grave was a large oak tree:

> I took an acorn which lay at my feet and laid it carefully away, that I might plant it; the oak that grows from it I will cherish with the utmost care, for its parent shelters one of the sacred spots on earth.

Later in his journey in Virginia, Foster visited the Bull Run battlefield and gathered seeds from shrubs growing near a Confederate monument. Returning home to Brooklyn, Foster planted the acorn and the seeds next to each other so that, "they shall grow side by side and equal care shall be bestowed on both."[4]

By the time Foster published his reminiscences, the residual animosity—for some a degree of hatred—of the veterans from the two sections that had fought each other had, to a degree, faded. Indeed, in the personal memoirs produced by Union veterans it is extremely rare to note any personal bitterness toward former Confederates. The North and South were reconciling, partly the result of the defeated section's integration into the continental economy and the abandonment by the North of its commitment to civil rights for the region's blacks. For the South, cotton, as well as rice and sugar, was still its major economic underpinning, but now spindles in the hundreds of thousands spun in textile mills, the work of entrepreneurs that may not have had economic diversification and sectional reconciliation as a primary goal. Where there had once been talk of expansion of a now deceased institution into the territories, now there was talk of expansion of all things in all directions. New textile mills were only one example of what was new in the New South. Iron and later steel production came into its own centered around the new city of Birmingham, Alabama. Coal production increased in the southern Appalachian Mountains to feed the growing industrial appetite both North and South.

At all of the Union regimental reunions that were occurring across the North during the years that the South was becoming new, the guest speakers or former unit commanders spoke in reverent tones of the bravery of the men, the battles fought, the campaigns they struggled through, the sacrifices made and the near holiness of the cause for which they fought—the restoration of the American Union. Only occasionally was there mentioned of the freedom the fight brought to millions. Perhaps it was all an oversight caused by the times. But by the time reconciliation was in full bloom among the veterans of both sides, the South had taken the first steps in subverting that freedom the victors had brought to the millions.

***

All the while Alonzo Foster was writing his memoir, many other books about the conflict continued to find their way on to the bookshelves of veterans and articles contributed by them filled every page of each issue of publications like the *National Tribune* and *Confederate Veteran*. It had been the former soldiers that had reconciled first, followed by the public in general in whose wake walked a generation that had no first-hand memory of the war or its causes. Symbolic of this reconciliation was the funeral of Ulysses S. Grant in 1885 where both Union and Confederate generals served as pallbearers. Henry Cribben had been a captain in the 140th New York Infantry and a prisoner of war for nearly 10 months. The editor of his memoirs related in the preface to the book:

> Although he had suffered so terribly at the hand of the rebel government, yet he cherished no vindictive feeling against the Southern people. In the year 1900 a Confederate veteran spoke in Mr. Cribben's church on a Sunday evening. At the conclusion of the service the pastor invited the Union veterans who were present to step forward and shake the hand of the Confederate before the benediction was pronounced. They came promptly, Mr. Cribben leading the way ... Cordially greeting the representative of the Confederacy which had starved him almost to death.[5]

Perhaps reconciliation came because those that had been shooting at each other 15 or 20 years before had grown older, wiser and more open to it than those that hadn't carried a gun. It was May 1885, and the Society of the Army of the Potomac was holding its 16th annual reunion in Baltimore. It had been noticed in some way that a reunion of Confederate veterans was being held in the city at the same time. A motion was put before the society's membership that the "Robert E. Lee Camp of Confederate Veterans, then in the city, be invited to attend the meeting, and take part in the celebration of this society." The motion passed. A quick visit was made to the Confederates, the invitation extended and "The camp responded with the rebel yell, which was greeted with enthusiastic applause." That night there was a meeting in which many ex-Confederates were in attendance and, after a long welcoming speech, one of invited officers responded:

We are ready to meet half-way any one who extends the right hand of fellowship. Let us ex-soldiers, Confederate and G.A.R. men from all parts of the country, let us join hands and conquer peace—we can do it. (Applause.)[6]

As this was spoken, and the applause rippled across the room, the written report of the meeting noted that there were many a gray uniform sprinkled throughout the audience. The next night there was a banquet to which many, if not all, the former Confederates were invited. After the green turtle soup, the spring chicken *a al Cream*, the sweetbreads garnished with green peas and harmony croquettes, there were the toasts. In response to the last of the evening's toasts, Charles Marshall, a former colonel on General Lee's staff spoke in reply, emphasizing reconciliation, but not naming it as such. In his remarks, Marshall spoke of:

… a story went about the camp fire in '63 and '64, which was known as the dream of Gordon's man. There was a soldier of Gordon's division, who dreamed this dream one night, and I will tell you what it was, and then I will tell you the interpretation of it. The man had been thinking about the war and how long it was to last until he fell asleep, and dreamed that he had slept for fifty years; and he awoke and saw a procession going by of very venerable men. There was a sergeant and then ten or twelve men following him, and then a quartermaster and a commissary who carried his stores in his pocket. Gordon's man raised up and said, 'Who are you, sergeant?' And the sergeant replied, 'We are what remains of the Amy of Northern Virginia, and we understand the Army of the Potomac is on the others side of the river and we are going over to attack them, and if we beat them this time, it will put an end to the war.' Now this is the interpretation of the dream: The Army of the Potomac was on the other side, and the Army of Northern Virginia crossed, but in the 'halo of that peace which makes this republic immortal.' (Great applause and three cheers for Col. Marshall).[7]

During the cavalry action at Aldie, Virginia, in June 1863, Major Henry Lee Higginson of the 1st Massachusetts Cavalry received a severe saber cut across the face from a Confederate officer. Higginson later recovered but his fighting days were over. Now it was years later, and a statue of Fighting Joe Hooker was dedicated in Boston and among the invited guests was former Confederate Cavalry general Thomas Rosser. Higginson and his son were dining at the University Club that evening when a gentleman approached their table. Without introducing himself, Thomas Rosser said to Higginson, "'I want to see how good a job I did on your face, that day at Aldie.' The Major gave him both hands, and the two old men fraternized until the small hours of the morning."[8]

Reconciliation, for some ex-Confederates, did not mean their being fully reconstructed, even after the passage of many decades. The Reverend Wayland Fuller Dunaway D. D. published his *Reminiscences of a Rebel* in 1913, close to the end of that period veterans were penning and printing firsthand stories. Dunaway was a former captain in the 40th Virginia Infantry and had become a clergyman after the war. Although in his writing he now vigorously professed his loyalty to the United States, Dunaway states on the book's first page:

Notwithstanding the title of this volume, I do not admit that I was ever in any true sense a rebel, neither do I intend any disrespect when I call the northern soldiers Yankees.

Yankee, he says was merely the name given to the opposing force. Reconciled but only about half reconstructed four decades after Appomattox, the Reverend Dunaway in the closing pages of his memoir noted:

Withdrawal from the Union was the right of the Southern States, as appears from the history of the making and adoption of the federal constitution; and great was the provocation for it.

He admitted secession was a mistake, but nevertheless:

... the war that was waged by the Federal Government was a crime against ... the constitution, humanity, and God.

And as for what came after, the actions of the Congress were "unnecessary, vindictive, and malignant ..." Virginia was treated as a "conquered territory," when all through the war Washington had considered it still a state in the Union but in rebellion. But with the war won by the North, "It was not enough that the South was conquered, it must be humiliated by African domination!" The South had fought "... to make good the inherited belief that 'all just government derives its power from the consent of the Governed.'" Virginians all along were merely asserting their belief in "a God-given right."[9] It may be that Reverend Dunaway was expressing a commonly held view of some Southerners of this period, the number of which cannot be truly calculated.

For the cavalrymen of the Army of the Potomac in 1864, reconciliation was far in the future, a future some of them would not see. Beginning in May, they rode and they fought, they crossed the Rapidan, shot their way through the Wilderness, rode to Yellow Tavern, whipped Jeb Stuart and rode back. Through the end of the month, more fighting with and around Grant's army, before riding to Trevilian Station, an obscure place far to the northwest of where the Army of the Potomac was then fighting. Now spring had become summer and the cavalry divisions that had gone to Trevilian Station were slowly returning. There were shortages of everything except for dust and heat on this first day of a Virginia summer.

It was June 23, 1864, and there was an action at Jones' and Long Bridge on the Chickahominy River. A short time later, Colonel Tom Devin, still commanding the 2nd Brigade of the 1st Cavalry Division, filed a report. He didn't include Samuel Fanshaw's name but briefly described what happened. Colonel Devin reported:

... the Sixth New York on Long Bridge road were attacked by a heavy force of the enemy, who succeeded in flanking their barricades and drove them into within 500 yards of the main road. They were quickly re-enforced [sic] by the other squadrons and the enemy were checked until I came up with the Fourth New York and Seventeenth Pennsylvania. In the meantime, [General] Getty, whose column had haltered near the road, had offered me a colored regiment until I could get my other regiments up. The colored soldiers behaved well enough at first, but their officers could not be found, and they were soon in hopeless confusion. I relieved them with the Seventeenth Pennsylvania, and sending in the Fourth New York on the right, drove the enemy back to a strong position, which he had barricaded, and from which on my again advancing to assail him, he retired with precipitation. I immediately established my pickets 1 mile in advance of my former position and returned to camp. The attacking force was Chambliss' brigade and two guns. Our loss was 6 men killed, 1 officer and 8 men wounded, and 1 man missing, nearly all the killed being from the pickets of 6th New York, and showing the desperate tenacity with which they endeavored to hold their position.[10]

Another version of the events of June 23, written years later, illustrates the difficulties inherent in reconciling descriptions of Civil War actions written close to the time they occurred and those written much later. This account comes from the history of the 13th Ohio Cavalry. Howard Aston was a cavalry lieutenant and published a history of his regiment in 1902. In it he uses less than 80 words—probably notes copied from a diary he might have kept—to describe the action of June 23:

We started at 2 a.m. with the trains, the heat intense during the day. Crossing the Chicahominy river about 3 p.m., boys straggling badly. About 4 p.m. the rebels attacked. The negro [sic] regiment with us charged them and drove them back and out of a line of earthworks, then Sheridan's cavalry came up and went forward, our regiment in line of battle in pine woods, protecting the right flank.[11]

Decades after the event, Gilbert Wood remembered and included in the 6th New York's history:

At 1 p.m. the pickets of the 6th New York … were suddenly attacked by a large force and driven in; the regiment went at once to their support and a sharp action took place, the enemy being much superior in numbers.

Reinforcements came up and together the men of the 6th drove the Rebels back. Wood said the:

… fierce but short engagement ended in the entire rout of the enemy … The casualties in the regiment were quite heavy, among the killed being Corporals Samuel A. Fanshaw and David Phillips of Troop I, and Sergeant Samuel May, wounded.[12]

This, along with what was written to the family by Gilbert Wood, constitutes all the known records relating to the death of Corporal Samuel Fanshaw.

After the war there was a Federal effort to locate and then gather in the soldiers buried on battlefields during the war, often buried close to where they fell. Samuel Fanshaw's remains were eventually re-interred in the Glendale National Cemetery in Richmond and the family was able to locate his grave. The close relationship of Gilbert Wood and the Fanshaw family endured after the war. Gilbert later married Samuel's sister, Emily, the Emma mentioned in Samuel's letter of June 22, 1864. Eventually, they settled in Toms River, New Jersey.[13] Gilbert Wood was an active member of the 6th New York veterans' association. Like so many others from this war, Wood appreciated that the record of his unit should in some fashion be preserved and his effort, and those of the others on the regimental history committee, eventually resulted in a unit history. Without Gilbert Wood and those many others from Civil War regiments, the content of the chronicle of the Civil War would be much thinner. These many men who put their thoughts and experiences on to paper could sense somehow a future, something beyond the horizon of their era. And now we of a different era have their words to ponder and then splice together as we write our history of them and what they accomplished.

As 1864 closed, Lieutenant Henry Howe began thinking of his future. His three-year enlistment was up in January and in a letter dated the 11th he ruminates:

> I consider myself capable of filling any position … I don't care what it might be. I can also bring recommendations from every officer in my regiment concerning my military career. If I remain with the service I could be Quartermaster or Captain right away, but I have made up my mind to retire from the army, the war being virtually over, and follow a business avocation for the remainder of my life. I'll find a good position if I have to go as far as California.

Henry Howe worked in the lumber industry in Waltham, Massachusetts, thereafter, became a member of the Grand Army of the Republic in 1882, elected President of the 13th Massachusetts veterans' association in 1883 and a member of the Military Order of the Loyal Legion of the United States in 1884.[14] Henry Howe left us his letters and diary from the war, publishing them in 1899.

***

James Stone, a veteran from the 21st Massachusetts and writing half a century after the fact, told us in his way why he had picked up a pen. It was:

> … in the hope that it may be an aid in calling to mind fading recollections of pleasant incidents, as well as heroic deeds performed by comrades … In studying the history of the Revolutionary War, I have often wished I could read the diary of a private soldier of that time, that I might form an impression of the life of a soldier in the ranks during that war … If, someday, a student should come along who is interested in the history of the Civil War, and who would like to know something more about it than just the main facts, which is all that histories usually give, it is hoped that these recollections will be of assistance to him in that respect.[15]

The depth of feeling for the men with which he served was evident when a volunteer from Maine was writing his recollections many years later, saying:

> … even now I can see the faces of all … I see them just as they looked then, enthusiastic and boyish, but of those eighty most are now with the silent majority. Four years in the 7th Maine did not prove favorable to longevity.[16]

James Bowen of the 1st New York Dragoons, writing in 1900, said there weren't many left from the regiment, yet of those remaining:

> We are the rear guard, the main body having crossed the dark river and pitched their shining
> tents 'where glory stands with solemn rounds the bivouac of the dead.'[17]

Each of these men preserved for us a sliver of what had happened, had happened to them and to the nation during their time. Since then, their record and memories have been preserved and woven into the fabric that to us is the history of the Civil War. One man, a former general, had more than a sliver of the Civil War to remember. He had commanded thousands and seen many fall. Winfield Scott Hancock, the former commander of II Corps would run for President of the United States on the Democratic ticket in 1880. He lost to another war veteran, James Garfield, by less the 10,000 votes in over nine million cast. Of course, as one of the heroes of Gettysburg, where his corps took the brunt of the July 3 attack and where he was wounded, Hancock attended many reunions after the war. At one encampment of the Grand Army of the Republic, he stood on a reviewing stand as hundreds of veterans marched by. A senator standing nearby inquired of Hancock why it was that so few veterans of II Corps were marching that day. Hancock gave his answer quickly. "The general turned to the senator saying, 'The men of the 2d Corps, Senator, are mostly in heaven.'"[18] Hancock died in 1886.

Those men, the war's survivors, also set aside a day to remember those that had not. It is now called Memorial Day where all the fallen are remembered. But in their day, the survivors, Union veterans, perhaps because of the numbers, gathered at cemeteries with spring flowers and speeches to remember and honor. These survivors felt or believed they owed it to those taken by the war; that they be remembered after the then living had passed. In every town from Mississippi to Maine a bronze statue or stone monument found its way to some public place, its presence there not merely to honor the living veterans that put it there but to honor the "constituency of the slain." The living, the veterans standing before these memorials, had been "sentenced to life." It was they that had to make sense of it all if they could. They, the living, had to remember "the men whose very absence from American life made them a presence that could not be ignored."[19] Oliver Wendell Homes, Jr., a veteran volunteer, wounded three times, and later a justice of the U.S. Supreme Court, in a Memorial Day address, took note of the day and the meaning it had for him:

> I think that, as life is action and passion, it is required of a man that he should share the passion
> and action of his time at peril of being judged not to have lived.

Memorial Day was for Holmes "… the most sacred of the year," and he believed it would continue to be observed with pride and reverence:

> But even if I am wrong, even if those who are to come after us are to forget all that we hold
> dear, and the future is to teach and kindle its children in ways as yet unrevealed, it is enough
> for us that to us this is dear and sacred … For one hour, twice a year at least—at the regimental
> dinner, where the ghosts sit at table more numerous than the living, and on this day when we
> decorate their graves—the dead come back and live with us. I see them now, more than I can

number, as once I saw them on this earth … The generation that carried on the war has been set aside by its experience. Through our great good fortune, in our youth our hearts were touched with fire. It was given to us to learn at the outset that life is a profound and passionate thing. While we are permitted to scorn nothing but indifference, and do not pretend to undervalue the worldly rewards of ambition, we have seen with our own eyes, beyond and above the gold fields, the snowy heights of honor, and it is for us to bear the report to those who come after us.[20]

***

Future Supreme Court Justice Oliver Wendall Holmes as an officer in the Twentieth Massachusetts. (Library of Congress)

It was a different United States after the Civil War. In a country where before the war the average citizen's only contact with the federal government was when he or she went to the post office, now the structure and reach of Washington touched nearly everyone, as had the war touched nearly every family in some manner. The growth and reach of Washington, for better or worse, would continue through the end of the century and beyond. For the Union veterans, their interaction with Washington most likely came with contact with the Pension Bureau and it would extend to the very kind of money they received from the bureau and put in their pockets, dollars backed by gold or silver or faith. Writing in the next century and commenting on the close of the war and after, the author of *Reveille in Washington, g*ave a glimpse of the change not without a hint of nostalgia:

> The old jog trot would not come again in Washington. It had vanished forever with the pleasant provincial society, the grinning slaves and the broad-brimmed hats of the planter-politicians. Not in the battles of Yankee efficiency and the war left its supreme mark on Washington, not in the tumbling contraband huts, or the wreckage of men in the big white hospitals; but in the great centralization of Federal authority which had transformed a country town, reserved for the business of government, into the axis of the Union … Washington was securely established as the capital of a lusty nation; and no one looking on the public buildings, spoke of the ruins of antiquity any longer.[21]

The historians, writing of why the war came, and of the four years of killing, relate, in essence, that the political system of the age had failed. Beyond that,

Reconciliation at work. Two Veterans, a Yankee, and a Johnnie, shake hands. (Library of Congress)

the economic systems of the North and South, one founded on slavery, the other in free labor, had been moving in opposite directions for decades. That one section could only get bigger, stronger, richer and more diverse under a republican government while the other could only grow weaker with its dominant one crop economy, was known, particularly by observant Southerners, if not always explicitly stated. Control of the national government, or at least a significant say in its running, had been slipping slowly from the hands of the South's political leaders for years and they were keenly aware of it; the demographic and economic numbers were all going against them. And now there arose in the North a political party thought by Southerners to be totally against, and determined to destroy, the South's peculiar institution, the foundation of its society, its civilization. The main social, economic, indeed political, currents of the 19th century seemed to be flowing on a course that, if left alone, would doom the conservative world of Southern civilization. National loyalty can only stand for so long if it is thought one's very world is threatened with cultural annihilation and political subjugation as its economy increasingly became a mere appendage of a larger, diverse and overwhelmingly more powerful North populated by those thought to be scornful of Southerners and their way of life. It appeared to many Southerners that a second American Revolution was needed in order to save their world; when in the course of human event, and so on. Probably with some degree of frustration in his voice, Jefferson Davis understood and perhaps said it best. He phrased it simply: all he and his constituents desired was "to be left alone," alone in a world that was moving in a far different direction and one in which for most Southerners there was no desire for accommodation. But was the revolution the election of Abraham Lincoln? The South saw a radical and determined administration about to come to power that was, to Southerners, determined to eliminate their institution, their civilization. They didn't wait; they acted preemptively, seceding to preserve their perceived civilization. A counter-revolution to that of Election Day, November 1860 is one way of looking at it.

***

If they knew then what we know now, what? That the men of the Army of the Potomac, those riding with the cavalry or marching with the infantry in Virginia, knew of the forces at work in their world as they maneuvered against the Rebels is doubtful. If articulated by them it was all about keeping together one continental nation under one government. Everything else, slavery included, could be worked out, somehow, but only under the roof of that one government. As it happened, if slaves had to be set free to accomplish this, fine. They won.

James Little enlisted in the 6th New York Cavalry at age 23 on October 24, 1861, in Franklinville, New York, a small place in the western part of the state. He was a sergeant when discharged on June 27, 1865, and went home with his federal bounty. During the last year of the war, Little had kept a diary, simple jottings of what he did, the weather and, in some cases, what was important at the time. For June 27, 1865, he wrote while at Cloud Mills, Virginia, "Very hot day. Was mustered out." The next day he started home. "Went over to Washington where we were paid. Got our pay and started for New York City." June 29, 1865, "Arrived at New York about daylight." After a side trip up the Hudson River Valley for reasons he did not include in the diary, Little started for Franklinville. July 4, 1865, "Took 6pm express at New York City. Riding all night. Binghamton at daylight. Cool and very pleasant. Arrived at home on stage at 6pm. People at Franklinville very undemonstrative. All quiet." July 7, 1865, "Quite pleasant. Spent the day at home and around town. Wrote some letters." For James Little it was an apparent seamless transition from soldier to civilian. The author of the history of VI Corps also spoke of his transition to the home front:

> The wonder of the war was the sudden absorption of both armies into the body politic again with scarcely a ripple upon its surface.[22]

This testimony, particularly referencing "both armies," must be taken as wishful opinion rather than fact gained by observation.

Of the veterans returning home, there is little mention of it by those writing their recollections. For the majority of veterans, such as James Little, an immediate and seamless transition to civilian status was expected and the veterans, it seems, did their best to comply. There would be no recollections or memoirs penned by this veteran. Former Sergeant James Little lived out the remainder of his life in Minnesota, working and raising a family. Probably only his family knew he was a veteran, had been at Gettysburg, Five Forks and Appomattox. Did he receive a copy of the 6th New York's early history? Did he sit in the evenings turning its pages by the light of a kerosene lamp as his memory of places, events and people were again illuminated by the words put down by Gilbert Wood? James Little did what was expected of him and those like him, but there were uncounted thousands of others, some missing an arm, some hobbling along with the aid of crutches, also doing the expected, or trying to. Then there was the sizeable contingent that got off the train or boat, walked home, hugged the family, and to all outward appearances was fine, but in his dreams that night, and the nights after, he saw the blood that was splattered on his blue jacket when the soldier next to him had his face torn off by a large caliber, low-velocity round from a Rebel rifle.

***

Again, it was pensions, the residuals for the actors in the tragedy produced over four years on the national, indeed world, stage. Lincoln had said it in his second inauguration, the pension program's purpose was "to care for him who shall have borne the battle, and for his widow, and his orphan." To the Civil War veterans, no other issue on the political landscape during the final decades of their century was more personally important than that of pensions. Henry Cobb of the 40th New York Infantry returned home on April 14, 1865, not quite a year after being wounded in the Wilderness, with an established pension of $5.33 per month. Isaac Rathbun, wounded while fighting with the 86th New York at the Second Battle of Bull Run in August 1862, was discharged and got home in January of 1863 without a pension as yet. He noted in the diary he kept:

> I am left with a hole in my side, out of employment, don't know what to do with myself or where to go. A pity indeed![23]

In the decades to come veterans' associations, those of mere regiments or that of the national Grand Army of the Republic (GAR), saw to it that the politicians—many of whom were also veterans—secured the funding in the government's budgets year after year to fulfill its promise. Being a veteran certainly helped if one desired to hold office. Indeed, beginning in 1868, nine of the next 10 Republican Presidential candidates

50th Anniversary of the Gettysburg battle, veterans meet atop Cemetery Ridge. (Library of Congress)

were Union veterans and they and the GAR actively courted the veteran vote. Conversely, during the same period, only one Democratic candidate for president was a Union veteran, Gettysburg hero Major General Winfield Scott Hancock. The Republicans, in many of their campaigns rallied the veterans by waving the "bloody shirt," reminding veterans it was Democrats that led the South into rebellion and the old soldiers of the Union should "vote that way you shot." As one Republican senator commented on the state of the electorate in the post-Civil War years:

> ... the men who saved the country in war and have made it worth living in in peace ... find their place in the Republican party ... The slave-holders ... the saloon-keeper ... the criminal class of the great cities, the men who cannot read or write, commonly and as a rule ... find their congenial place in the Democratic party.[24]

It was during the war, in 1862, that Congress passed legislation aimed at financially helping those that suffered from physical disabilities caused by the war and the widows and children of those taken by it. By 1884, not yet 20 years after Appomattox, there had been close to 900,000 applications for pensions and, of these, 380,000 were subsequently judged invalid by the Pension Bureau in Washington. Subsequently, many of these rejected applications were taken over by a growing cadre of Washington lawyers. They lobbied Congress to enact individual pension bills. What was causing this? According to a near-contemporary history, "The Treasury surplus presented an irresistible temptation to foolish and pauperizing liberality. Greedy pension attorneys loved the 'swag' which the system offered." The war records of individual soldiers were accessible from the War Department and these attorneys used them to solicit clients whether deserving or not. Congress, always mindful of the veteran vote, complied with many of these pleadings by civilian attorneys and presidents signed them. Former cavalry officer Charles Francis Adams was disgusted with such activity in a compliant Congress, writing:

> We had seen every dead-beat, and malingerer, every bummer, bounty-jumper, and suspected deserter … rush to the front as the greedy claimant of public bounty. If there was any man whose army record had been otherwise creditable … we soon heard of him as a claimant of a back pension … or as being in regular receipt of his monthly stipend.[25]

The workload upon Congress was such the House of Representatives needed one "meeting" per week while in session devoted "to the passage of these personal bills, only a handful, far less than a quorum, being present." In the Senate, individual pensions bills faced a streamlined procedure. In one meeting in April 1886, the Senate passed 500 pension bills in two hours. One apparently conscience-stricken senator rose at about this time to complain but only stated the obvious:

> We flatter ourselves that we are great men. We are Senators of the United States who make laws for the people, but behind us there is another power greater than ourselves, controlling our action if not our judgment. The pension agents who sit around the Capitol issue their circulars and decrees, and petitions come up for pensions, and the Senators of the United States, great and mighty as they may be, bow to the behests of the pension agents and vote the money … We all know it, and the country knows it.[26]

But in this same year, 1886, during which this senator lamented over the many pension bills, President Grover Cleveland vetoed 101 individual bills of the 747 passed by Congress. In that the president elected in 1884, Cleveland, was the first Democrat elected to that office since 1856—the party having acquired a besmirched reputation during the Civil War—the Republican press editorialized against him with a passion. Nevertheless, only one of Cleveland's vetoed individual pension bills was passed over his veto.[27]

Not every individual pension bill that went through the Congress was a fraud and some representatives of the people, veterans themselves, saw to it that issues brought to their attention were handled or expedited. In the Wilderness, the casualties among the line officers in the 6th Wisconsin were numerous. A sergeant named Kent was promoted in the field to captain of Company G on May 10, 1864, and the paperwork was duly sent to the governor of Wisconsin so it could be made official. When the authorization was returned approved, it was dated June 18, the same day that Captain Kent was wounded in action. For 14 years Kent had been receiving a disabled veteran's pension as only a sergeant. His former brigade commander, Edward Bragg, 14 years after the war, was a congressman when he was informed of Captain Kent's situation. Congressman Bragg had an individual pension bill passed in 1878 authorizing Kent to receive the monthly allotment of a captain. Also, from the 6th Wisconsin, there is mention of the hand taken by Congressman Rufus Dawes of Ohio, late colonel of the regiment. Former Captain William Remington of the 6th Wisconsin, twice wounded, had applied for a pension in 1879. The application had not included the address of his former commanding officer, now a Representative from Ohio, and not been approved. Congressman Dawes, when informed of the situation, in 1882, contacted the Pension Bureau and saw to it that the papers were processed and approved. Remington, in his original applications for a pension, according to Dawes, apologized for asking but was forced to, he says, because "his boys were all girls." Later, and shortly before Remington's death, Congressman Dawes received a note of thanks that included: "If an Angel from Heaven, had appeared to help me, I could not have been more surprised."[28]

In 1878, payments from the Pension Bureau ran at about $29 million and the next year Congress passed, and President Rutherford B. Hayes signed, the Arrears Pension Bill, paying veterans and widows back to the date of disability for soldiers or the dawn of widowhood for spouses. It was estimated this one piece of legislation cost the government $254 million. Historian James Ford Rhodes, writing early in the 20th century and speaking of this period, called it "the heyday of the pension attorneys" and in passing judgment says, "the desire of pelf... is repugnant to the moralist, especially when he sees it exhibited by the veterans of the Civil War." By 1885, payments to veterans and widows reached $65 million and in 1887 came the Dependent Pension Bill, also known as the Pauper Bill. Eligible veterans, unable to work, regardless of whether the condition was a result of his service, or indigent widows would be provided with pensions. Historian Rhodes concluded this bill was "a scheme engineered in the main by pension attorneys." President Grover Cleveland vetoed the bill as he had other individual pensions bills. In his veto message the president noted that, for 1887, payments totaled $75 million and since payment began, and through July 1, 1886, the Treasury had dispensed over $808 million.[29]

It wasn't until 1888 that one D. A. O'Mara was able to generate enough response from the veterans of the 59th New York Infantry to form a regimental association, and this was only after it became known that the State of New York would "provide" for monuments to be placed on the Gettysburg battlefield for each regiment that had fought there. O'Mara advertised nationally for the regiment's veterans and enough came together to form the Associated Survivors of the 59th New York Veteran Volunteers. The association applied for a charter from the state, which was apparently necessary to secure the funds to purchase the monument and have it transported to the battlefield. On July 2, 1889, members from across the state, and others since re-located to other points in the country, gathered at Gettysburg for their first look at the monument—the design of which they had only seen in drawing—and to duly dedicate it.

The 59th New York had fought at Gettysburg with Hancock's II Corps and was one of the regiments under General John Gibbon that took the assault of July 3 head on. During the battle on July 3, the regiment's commander, Lieutenant-Colonel Max A. Thoman, was killed. It was decided by the association that the monument would be placed at the spot where their commander had fallen. Upon their arrival at Gettysburg, and before doing anything else, the veterans went to see the monument and commented that it "surpassed our expectations." The dedication the next day included a prayer and a poem before the oration by the first colonel of the regiment, William Linn Tidball. This was followed by an afternoon tour of other parts of the battlefield and a gathering at the Eagle Hotel where the reunionists did "what old soldiers usually do when they meet after a long separation." They agreed that they would meet again the following year at the Antietam battlefield, where the regiment had fought in 1862. After all the veterans had returned home, D. A. O'Mara had a pamphlet printed detailing the monument's dedication ceremony and had it sent to all the association's members. To help underwrite the printing and mailing costs of this pamphlet, the last few pages are taken up with advertisements aimed particularly at veterans, an example of which is for a firm located at 1419 F Street NW, Washington, D.C.:

Milo B. Stevens & Co.

Solicitors and Attorneys for Claimants
Claims for pensions, increases in pensions,

Additional pensions, Bounty,
Arrears of pay, etc.,

Will receive special attention.

This firm also specialized in "Lost horses and equipment claims of officers and enlisted men."[30] Pension attorneys continued their activities, advertising and lobbying members of Congress well into the 20th century.

In 1888, Benjamin Harrison was running for president on the Republican ticket and commented on the large surplus in the Treasury before an audience of veterans. Also, the candidate was touting Cleveland's veto of the Dependent Pension Bill to secure the veteran's vote. Harrison, the former colonel of an Indiana regiment, said:

When you lifted your hand and swore to protect and defend the constitution and the flag you didn't even know what your pay was to be … And now peace had come; no hand is lifted against the flag; the Constitution is again supreme and the nation one. My countrymen, it is no time to use an apothecary's scale to weigh the rewards of the men who saved the country.

Among office seekers and incumbents of this era, governmental fiscal conservatism enjoyed a status just below that of the Ten Commandments, but pork was another matter entirely. History concludes that President Harrison, nevertheless, "…saw no harm in dispensing federal pensions lavishly to undeserving veterans," viewing the Pension Bureau and the "goings-on" of the commissioner, as noted by a biographer, "with a simplicity almost childlike."[31] Another factor contributing to Harrison's winning the White House with the help of aging veterans was Cleveland's appointment of former Confederate general Lucius Quintus Cincinnatus Lamar as secretary of the interior and the administration's proposal to return captured Confederate battle flags to their respective states. Cleveland approved the flag return order on June 7, 1887. The protest from individual veterans was so quick and loud that Cleveland had to revoke the order on June 15. President Cleveland, a non-veteran, had previously accepted an invitation to the GAR encampment scheduled for St. Louis, but excused himself from visiting the veterans because of the uproar over the battle flags.[32]

After his election, President Benjamin Harrison, in a "most unfortunate appointment," according to historian James Rhodes, made a former corporal, James Tanner, his new Pension Commissioner. The new commissioner probably meant well, but according to Rhodes, Tanner's time in office and his "conduct of the pension office was not a credit to the Harrison administration." This probably stemmed from statements made by the corporal such as, "For twenty years I have been able to only plead, but now I am thankful that at these finger-tips there rests some power …"[33] James Tanner, a double amputee from the Second Battle of Bull Run, had every intention of disposing of the apothecary's scale. Although many millions were distributed to veterans, some actually received as little as $3.75 per month. Corporal Tanner would recalculate the payment schedules. Justifying his action, Tanner said, "… no man ought to be down on the pension roll of the United States for less than the miserable pittance of one dollar per week, though I may wring from the hearts of some the prayer 'God help the surplus.'"[34]

After an indecently short time in office, Tanner was relieved of his position by the secretary of the interior, whose department included the Pension Bureau. The relief of the veteran Tanner did not end the pension issue because of its significance among a sizable portion of the voting public, the Civil War veterans, and organizations like the Grand Army of the Republic. Former Major General Benjamin Butler, a Massachusetts Democrat, had devoted a large portion of his speech at the reunion of the veterans' association of the 1st Maine Cavalry in September 1889 to the pension issue. Butler told the cavalrymen in his audience:

> Tanner was eager and anxious to do his duty. He worked diligently with that end in view, although he had no legs to stand on to do it. For what was he turned out of office? At the call of the mugwamp press. (To the reporters, 'Put that down, sure'—tremendous applause.) His desire was simply to aid his comrades and their wives and children, and that as fast as he could, as they are now dying off and would not want it much longer. Pensions which have belonged to them have been kept back by the trickery of the officials. The cry was made against him:

'Why, he is robbing the treasury.' Good God! There never would have been any money in the treasury if it had not been for us soldiers. (prolonged applause and laughter, amid cries of 'That is so') … The government must and shall understand that we shall have what we seek. Which is simply honest justice to ourselves, our wives and our children; and, God helping us, we will have that, because our votes can settle that question when we vote together.[35]

In 1890, Congress passed the Dependent Pensions Act, granting pensions to all veterans that had served at least 90 days and who were "unable to perform manual labor, or suffered from a disability 'not the result of their own vicious habits.'" This bill was essentially the bill vetoed by President Cleveland and grew the Pension Bureau's expenditures by 1894 to $141 million. This act provided pensions from $6 to $12 per month to such individuals veterans not a victim of "vicious habits" while widows deemed unable to provide for themselves received $8 and an additional $2 per child, even though children of a father killed in the war would have long since passed into adulthood. Between the passage of the Dependent Pensions Bill in 1880 and 1907, the United States spent $1 billion on pensions. It was after the turn of the century, with pensions accounting for one-third of the Federal budget, that Congress further liberalized the pension scheme, granting payments to all veterans based upon length of service alone.[36]

After James Little returned to Franklinville in the summer of 1865, there was both a forced reunification and a forced and complete reordering of the defeated region's social and economic foundation. Mostly unrepentant for some years as to the war's outcome, the South went about rebuilding and diversifying as its white political leaders sought an end to reconstruction and supervision by Washington. The Democratic Party slowly, but inevitably, regained control of the former Confederate state governments. Reconstruction was allowed to fade away. The result was that the former slaves, the freed men, despite constitutional amendments guaranteeing their rights, were, in succeeding decades, isolated both politically and economically, the drive for a New South speeding ahead within the national framework, but without them.

Years would pass after Appomattox, perhaps 15, perhaps 20, before any conditional reconciliation surfaced among Southern veterans and their Yankee brothers. For Southerners, repentance it was not; merely acknowledgement that they had, together with their Northern comrades, swirled about within the same historical vortex. Everyone had been brave and done their duty as God gave them to see their duty. Residing beneath the growing economic diversity, and the one-party rule in the South, was a form of nostalgia, for a civilization now gone with the wind, that remained for generations. James Little died in 1912 with the South now largely integrated into the industrial nation the United States had become, although some might see integration as mere colonial status. In the former Confederacy, commerce and industry merged with crop production in a New South, with the United States only a few years away from becoming a world power, and as the veterans reconciled in the last decades of the century, aging Johnny Rebs and Billy Yanks gathered in joint reunions. Something was missing or had fallen to the roadside along this road to reunion, though. It was the root cause of why these armies had been raised in the first place. The black American, emancipated, was consigned to near invisibility in the North and to a "separate but equal" status in the South. Although there were some black regimental associations with their gatherings and remembrances during these years, essentially, reconciliation had no significant or viable black component.

**

The cavalry veterans, men like Hillman Hall, Gilbert Wood, and James Little, took their bounty money in the summer of 1865 and went home, each in his own way a contributor to what the United States had become—and would become—after 1865. A hundred or so years would pass, histories and memoirs written, the veterans passing away, battlefields made into historic places of remembrance, and full freedom eventually acquired by the descendants of those contrabands, escapees from an institution that was, deep down, the root of it all, all the fighting and bleeding, all the graves. The nation that had torn at itself in Civil War remained under the roof of that one government.

Rufus Dawes was in Congress representing a district in Ohio. He was one among many veterans that walked the halls of the Capitol during the closing decades of the 19th century. Like many other officers in Civil War regiments, once in the field, Dawes hired a personal servant, typically a contraband paid directly by the man he served. The servant's name was William Jackson and when Dawes left the army at the end of his enlistment, he took William Jackson home with him and found him a job, first as a hotel waiter and then with a railroad. As Dawes remembered, "He needed no more help." After 12 years, Jackson started his own business. Colonel Dawes provided no explanation for why he did this, but one suspects a strong strain of altruism within the makeup of this strong soldier.

Near the close of his reminiscence of his Wisconsin regiment, Rufus Dawes quotes from a letter written to his wife while he was in Congress. "I have to-day worshipped at the shrine of the dead. I went over to the Arlington Cemetery." Dawes visited the graves of all six soldiers from his regiment that were buried there and then wrote to his wife:

> … the shadows of age are rapidly stealing upon us. Our burdens are like the loaded knapsack on the evening of a long and weary march, growing heavier at every pace.

Then turning from the dead to the living, Dawes wrote words aimed not for the ears of the public or his civilian constituents but the veteran:

You have lived to see spring up as the result of your suffering, toil and victory the most powerful nation of history and the most beneficent government ever established.[37]

E. F. Palmer of the 2nd Vermont Brigade had not seen nearly as much of the killing, maiming and marching as had Rufus Dawes. It might be assumed he had a seamless transition from soldier to civilian in the months after Gettysburg. After only nine months of service, he was on his way home, but he had wandered the Gettysburg battlefield on the night of July 3 and again the next day. He spoke in his history and in a letter he wrote home on July 4 of his inability to describe the carnage, the number of bodies and parts of bodies lying twisted and contorted in front of his brigade's position on Cemetery Ridge. His command left the area while many of the bodies were yet to be buried and before the atmosphere had turned completely rank. Not too many days later, as the train he was on rattled along, Palmer recalled in a soothing manner:

> …those white cottages, surrounded by flowers and fruit trees, and near by garden patches filled with vegetables; those green pastures; school-houses and churches—all tell us that we are once more in New England.[38]

It was the individual soldiers, mostly the volunteers, and not the generals who reunited the country. By picking up a pen Lincoln might free slaves, but the private soldier with a rifle in his hands was the agent of change during those four years. It was now a changing continental country that emerged from the conflict, a vastly different entity after the late unpleasantness, and many were not there to see it, Lincoln included. And there were those that might not really understand all that had happened to and around them. While the troops were in the field, fighting and dying, those back in Washington, chiefly Republicans, without the hindrance of southern Democrats, were legislating. The railroad to the Pacific authorized, the Morrell Act, land grant state colleges voted in the affirmative, a national currency and banking system established, the Homestead Act, the populating of the Great Plains and the creation of a nearly bottomless American breadbasket—all authorized with Republican votes, all during wartime.

As the years rolled by and the veterans brought forward their recollections and histories, and as natural as the aging process itself, the men took pride in what they had done while young. It all helped by association with those other veterans, those that were remembering and were aging, and they had every reason to be proud and somehow out of this came a keen awareness that the testimony they would leave behind would form a part, perhaps a significant part, of the nation's collective memory, its history.

Beyond this, the Civil War veterans in the final decades of the 19th century were aware of their distinctiveness or something similar to it. There he was and then there were all the others, the others that hadn't fought, the less cause committed, the women and children. The veteran was a member of a great fraternity. Later, those that he had shot at down in Virginia could become quasi-fraternity fellows, but those residing in the North that came to the cause in 1861, his neighbors or the men he met in the ranks later, were all linked by experiences shared. The successful Gilded Age company president like Colonel Charles Fitzhugh of the 6th New York; the one-legged man seen on the street as the veteran walked to work in the morning; the strange, reclusive old man who lived some distance from town that somehow materialized on Memorial Day dressed in a blue uniform; the fellow who swept out the stable at the edge of town who has never really been right since Fredericksburg; the man like Delevan Miller of the 2nd New York Heavy Artillery who owned the dry goods store on Main Street and had bought dinner for two veterans; the town drunk that did odd jobs for beer money; and the future Supreme Court Justice, Oliver Wendell Holmes who, in the spring of 1861, had his "heart touch with fire,"; all linked by experiences shared. They were all veterans, each in his way recalling, every day of their lives, their small role in the great American historical event. They knew, perhaps subconsciously, they had been set apart, and many wanted others, their children, and those to follow in time, to know, to hear at least an echo of their accomplishment, what it had cost, what had been purchased with so much blood.

We, in our age, can study and, hopefully, learn and then understand. The old soldiers, if they knew what we know and were here, would they understand and appreciate our attempt to know of them and their times? Indeed so. They surely would willingly testify, tell us in some massive oral history what it all had been like. Would they be pleased with what their country has become since they turned in their guns and went back to their lives in the summer of 1865? Perhaps. Possibly. Probably. Living in that one nation, striving for liberty and justice for all, under that continental-sized nation's one government, those veterans might understand and very well appreciate that only in the United States of America could there be a road, one along which they had marched and fought, and along which many of their comrades are buried, Jefferson Davis Highway, Route 1, running south from the Potomac and on through the heart of Virginia, a blacked-topped, sign-posted, speed-limited thoroughfare named for the leader of a failed revolution.

Bibliography

Adams, Charles Francis, *Charles Francis Adams 1836–1915, An Autobiography*, Boston: Houghton Mifflin Company, 1916.

Adams, F. Colburn, *The Story of a Trooper*, Washington: McGill and Whiterow, 1864.

Agassiz, George R., ed, *Meade's Headquarters, 1863–1865: Letters of Colonel Theodore Lyman from Wilderness to Appomattox*, Boston: Massachusetts Historical Society, 1922.

Alberts, Don E., *Brandy Station to Manila Bay*, Austin: Presidial Press, 1980.

Alexander, E. P., *Military Memoirs of a Confederate: A Critical Narrative*, New York: Charles Scribner's Sons, 1907.

Alleman, Tillie Pierce, *At Gettysburg: or What a Girl Saw and Heard of the Battle*, Private, 1888.

Allen, Stanton P., *Down in Dixie: Life in a Cavalry Regiment in the War Days from the Wilderness to Appomattox*, Boston: D. Lothrop and Company, 1893.

Andrews, E. Benjamin, *The History of the Last Quarter-Century in the United States, 1870–1896*, New York: Charles Scribner's Sons, 1895.

Annals of War Written by the Leading Participants North and South, Philadelphia: The Times Publishing Company, 1879.

Annual Report of the Adjutant-General of the State of New York for the Year 1894, Albany: James B. Lyon, 1895.

Aston, Howard, *History and Roster of the Fourth and Fifth Independent Battalions and Thirteenth Regiment Ohio Cavalry Volunteers*, Columbus: Press of Fred J. Heer, 1902.

Badeau, Adam, *Military History of Ulysses S. Grant, from April, 1861, to April, 1865*, New York: 3 Volumes, D. Appleton and Company, 1882.

Banes, Charles H., *History of the Philadelphia Brigade*, Philadelphia: J. B. Lippincott & Co., 1876.

Bates, John Richard, *Soldiers True: The Story of the One Hundred and Eleventh Regiment Pennsylvania Veteran Volunteers, and of its Campaign in the War for the Union, 1861–1865*, New York: Eaton & Mains, 1903.

Bates, Samuel P., *The Battle of Gettysburg*, Philadelphia: T. H. Davis & Co., 1875.

Beach, W. H., "Some Reminiscences of the First New York (Lincoln) Cavalry," *War Papers Read Before the State of Wisconsin Commandery of the Military Order of the Loyal Legion of the United States*, Volume 2, Milwaukee: Burdick & Allen, 1896.

Benedict, George D, Papers, Southern Historical Collection, Louis Round Wilson Special Collections Library, University of North Carolina, Chapel Hill, North Carolina.

Benedict, George G., *Vermont in the Civil War*, 2 volumes, Burlington: Free Press Association, 1888.

————, *Army Life in Virginia*, Burlington: Free Press Association, 1895.

Bennett, Edwin C., *Musket and Sword: The Army of the Potomac*, Boston: Coburn Publishing Co., 1900.

Benton, Charles E., *As Seen from the Ranks: A Boy in the Civil War*, New York: G. P. Putnam's Sons, 1902.

Beveridge, John L., "The First Gun at Gettysburg," in *Military Essays and Recollections: Papers Read Before the Commandery of the State of Illinois, Military Order of the Loyal Legion of the United States.*, Volume 2, Chicago: A. C. McClurg and Company, 1894.

Billington, Ray Allen, *The Far Western Frontier, 1830–1860*, New York: Harper and Row, 1956.

Blackford, William A., *The War Years with Jeb Stuart*, New York: Charles Scribner's Sons, 1945.

Blake, Henry N., *Three Years in the Army of the Potomac*, Boston: Lee and Shepard, 1865.

Blight, David W., *Race and Reunion: The Civil War in American Memory*, Cambridge: Harvard University Press, 2001.

Boatner, Mark M., *The Civil War Dictionary*, New York: David McKay Company, Inc., 1959.

Beaudry, Richard E., *War Journal of Louis N. Boudrye, Fifth New York Cavalry*, Jefferson, N.C.: McFarland and Co., Inc., Publishers, 1996.

Boudrye, Louis N., *Historical Records of the Fifth New York Cavalry*, Albany: J. Munsell, 1868.

Bowen, James R., *Regimental History of the First New York Dragoons*, Published by the Author, 1900.

Brooks, Noah, *Washington in Lincoln's Time*, New York: The Century Co., 1895.

Bruce, George A., *The Twentieth Regiment Massachusetts Volunteer Infantry, 1861–1865*, Boston: Houghton Mifflin and Company, 1906.

Buell, Augustus C., *The Cannoneer: Recollections of Service in the Army of the Potomac*, Washington: The National Tribune, 1890.

Buffum, F. H., *Sheridan's Veterans, No. II*, Boston: W. F. Brown & Company, 1886.

Burns, Vincent L., *The Fifth New York Cavalry in the Civil War*, Jefferson, NC: McFarland and Company, Publishers, 2014.

Carter, Robert Goldthwaite, *Four Brothers in Blue: Sunshine and Shadows of the War of the Rebellion*, Washington: Press of Gibson Bros., Inc., 1913.

Carter III, Samuel, *The Last Cavaliers: Confederate and Union Cavalry in the Civil War*, New York: St Martin's Press, 1979.

Carter, William H., *From Yorktown to Santiago with the Sixth U.S. Cavalry*, Baltimore: The Lord Baltimore Press, 1900.

Catton, Bruce, *This Hallowed Ground: The Story of the Union Side of the Civil War*, New York: Doubleday and Co., 1956.

_____, *Glory Road*, New York: Doubleday and Company, 1952.

_____, *Mr. Lincoln's Army*, New York: Doubleday & Co., 1951.

Chamberlain, Joshua Lawrence, *The Passing of Armies… Personal Reminiscences of the Fifth Army Corps*, New York: reprint, Bantam Books, 1913.

_____, "The Military Operations on the White Oak Road, Virginia, March 31, 1865," in *Papers Read Before the Commandery of the State of Maine, Military Order of the Loyal Legion of the United States*, Volume 1, Portland; The Thurston Print, 1898.

Cheney, Newel., *History of the Ninth Regiment New York Volunteer Cavalry*, Poland Center, New York: private, 1901.

Clarke, Augustus P., "The Sixth New York Cavalry: Its Movements and Service at the Battle of Gettysburg," *United Service*, November 1896.

Clark, George., *A Glance Backward: or Some Events in the Past History of My Life*, Houston: Rein & Sons, nd.

Collis, Septima M., *A Woman's War Record, 1861–1865*, New York: G. P. Putnam's Sons, 1889.

Comte De Paris, *The Battle of Gettysburg: From the History of the Civil War in America*, Philadelphia: Porter & Coates, 1886.

Conyngham, D. P., *The Irish Brigade and its Campaigns*, New York: William McSorley and Company, 1867.

Cook, Benjamin F., *History of the Twelfth Massachusetts Volunteers (Webster Regiment)*, Boston: Twelfth (Webster) Regimental Association, 1882.

Cooke, Sidney G., "The First Day at Gettysburg," in *Walk Talks in Kansas: Papers Read Before the Kansas Commandery of the Military Order of the Loyal Legion of the United States*, Kansas City, MO: Franklin Hudson Publishing Co., 1906.

Corby, William, *Memoirs of Chaplain Life: Three Years Chaplain in the Famous Irish Brigade*, Notre Dame: Scholastic Press, 1894.

Correspondence of John Sedgwick, Major General, 2 Volumes, Private, 1902.

Cribben, Henry, *The Military Memoirs of Captain Henry Cribben of the 140th New York Volunteers*, Chicago, 1911.

Crotty, D. G., *Three Years Campaigning in the Army of the Potomac*, Grand Rapids, MI, Dygert Bros. & Co., 1874.

Crowninshield, Benjamin W., *History of the First Regiment Massachusetts Cavalry Volunteers*, Boston, Houghton, Mifflin and Company, 1891.

Dana, Charles A., *Recollections of the Civil War: With the Leaders in Washington and in the Field in the Sixties*, New York; D. Appleton, 1898.

Davies, Henry E., *General Sheridan*, New York; D. Appleton and Co., 1895.

Davis, Charles E., *Three Years in the Army: The Story of the Thirteenth Massachusetts Volunteers from July 16, 1861, to August 1, 1864*, Boston; Estes and Lauriat, 1894.

Dawes, Rufus, *Service with the Sixth Wisconsin Volunteers*, Marietta, OH; E. R. Alderman & Sons, 1890.

De Trobriand, Regis, *Four Years with the Army of the Potomac*, Boston, Ticknor and Company, 1889.

De Wolfe, Mark, *Touched with Fire: Civil War Letters and Diary of Oliver Wendell Holmes, Jr., 1861–1864*, Cambridge; Harvard University Press, 1946.

Diary of John Inglis, Ninth New York Cavalry, New York State Library.

Doster, William E., *Lincoln and Episodes of the Civil War*, New York; G. P. Putnam, 1915.

Doubleday, Abner, *Chancellorsville and Gettysburg*, New York; Charles Scribner's Sons, 1912.

Dunaway, Wayland F., *Reminiscences of a Rebel*, New York; The Neale Publishing Company, 1913.

Eby, Cecil D., ed., *A Virginia Yankee in the Civil War: The Diaries of David Hunter Strother*, Chapel Hill; University of North Carolina Press, 1961.

Ellis, Thomas, *Leaves from the Diary of an Army Surgeon*, New York; John Bradburn, 1863.

Emory, William H., "Cedar Creek, October 19, 1864: Extract from a Letter to Colonel Benjamin W. Crowninshield," *Papers of the Military Historical Society of Massachusetts*, Vol. 14, Boston; Military Historical Society of Massachusetts, 1918.

Faulkner, Harold U., *Politics, Reform and Expansion, 1890–1900*, New York; Harper and Row, 1959.

Faulkner, William, *Intruder in the Dust*, New York; Random House, 1948.

Faust, Drew Gilpin, *The Republic of Suffering: Death and the American Civil War*, New York; Alfred A. Knopf, 2008.

Favill, Josiah M., *The Diary of a Young Officer*, Chicago; Donnelley & Sons Company, 1909.

Fleming, George Thornton, ed, *Life and Letters of Alexander Hays*, Pittsburg; private, 1919.

Fiske, Samuel, *Mr. Dunn Browne's Experiences in the Army*, Boston; Nichols and Noyes, 1866.

Foner, Eric, *Reconstruction: America's Unfinished Revolution, 1863–1865*, New York; Harper Collins, reprint, 1988.

Ford, Worthington Chauncy, *A Cycle of Adams Letters, 1861–1865*, 2 Volumes, Boston; Houghton, Mifflin Company, 1920.

Forbes, George S., *Leaves from a Trooper's Diary*, Philadelphia, np, 1869.

Foster, Alonzo, *Reminiscences and Record of the 6th New York V. V. Cavalry*, private issue, 1892.

Foote, Shelby, *The Civil War: A Narrative, From Fredericksburg to Meridian*, New York: Random House, 1963.

Fox, William F., *Final Report on the Battle of Gettysburg*, 3 Volumes, Albany; J. B. Lyon, 1092.

Freeman, Douglas Southall, *Lee's Lieutenants: A Study in Command*, Stephen W. Sears, ed., Old Saybrook, CT; Konecky and Konecky, 1998.

Gallagher, Gary W., "Our Hearts are Full of Hope: The Army of Northern Virginia in the Spring of 1864," in *The Wilderness Campaign*, Gary W. Gallagher, ed., Chapel Hill; University of North Carolina Press, 1997.

Gerrish, Theodore, *Army Life: A Private's Reminiscences pf the Civil War*, Portland; Hoyt, Fogg & Donham, 1882.

Gordon, George H., *A War Diary of Events in the War of the Great Rebellion, 1863–1865*, Boston; James R. Osgood and Company, 1882.

Gordon, John B., *Reminiscences of the Civil War*, New York; Charles Scribner's Sons, 1904.

Goss, Warren Lee, *Recollections of a Private: A Story of the Army of the Potomac*, New York; Thomas Y. Cromwell and Company, 1890.

Gracy, S. L., *Annals of the Sixth Pennsylvania Cavalry*, E. H. Butler and Company, 1868.

Graham, Matthew J., *The Ninth Regiment New York Volunteers (Hawkins' Zouaves)*, New York; private, 1900.

Glazier, Willard, *Three Years in the Federal Cavalry*, New York; R. H. Ferguson and Company, 1874.

Grant, Ulysses S., *Personal Memoirs and Selected Letters*, Reprint, New York; Literary Classics of the United States, 1990.

Grimsley, Mark, *The Hard Hand of War: Union Military Policy Toward Southern Civilians, 1861–1865*, Cambridge; Cambridge University Press, 1995.

Guelzo, Allen C., *Gettysburg: The Last Invasion,* New York; Alfred A. Knoff, 2013.

Haines, Alanson A., *History of the Fifteenth Regiment New Jersey Volunteers*, New York; Jenkins & Thomas, Printers, 1883.

Hall, Hillman A., W. B. Besley, Gilbert G. Wood, comp., *History of the Sixth New York Cavalry … 1861–1865.* Worcester, MA; Blanchard Press, 1908.

Halstead, E. P., "The First Day at Gettysburg," in *War Papers*, Papers Read Before the District of Columbia Commandery of the Military Order of the Loyal Legion of the United States, Volume 1, Washington; DC Commandery 1887.

Hamilton, J. G. De Roulhac, ed., 3 Volumes. *The Papers of Randolph Abbott Shotwell*, Raleigh; The North Carolina Historical Commission, 1929.

Hard, Abner, *History of the Eighth Cavalry Regiment Illinois Volunteers During the Great Rebellion*, Aurora, IL; private, 1868.

Harwell, Richard, ed., *Lee: An Abridgement in On Volume of the Four-Volume R. E. Lee* by Douglas Southall Freeman, New York; Charles Scribner's Sons, 1961.

Haskell, Frank, *The Battle of Gettysburg*, Madison, WI; Wisconsin Historical Commission, 1908.

Haynes, Martin A., *A Minor War History Compiled from A Soldier Boy's Letters to the Girl I Left Behind Me*, Lakeport, NH; private, 1916.

Herrmance, William L., "The Cavalry at Gettysburg," *Personal Recollections of the War of Rebellion: Addresses Delivered Before the Commandery of the State of New York of the Military Order of the Loyal Legions of the United States*, Volume 3, New York; G. P. Putnam, 1907.

Heth, Henry, Letter of June 1877, Southern Historical Society Papers, Volume. 4, Richmond; Johns & Goolsby, Printers, 1877

Hitchcock, Frederick L., *War From the Inside or Personal Experiences, Impressions, and Reminiscences of One of the "Boys" in the War of Rebellion*, Philadelphia; J. P. Lippincott Company, 1904.

Hopkins, Luther W., *From Bull Run to Appomattox, A Boy's View*, Baltimore; Fleet— McGinley, 1908.

Howard, Oliver O., *Autobiography of Oliver Otis Howard, Major General United States Army*, 2 Volumes, New York; The Baker and Taylor Company, 1908.

Howe. Henry Warren, *Passages from the Life of Henry Warren Howe Consisting of Diary and Letters written during the Civil War, 1861–1865*, Boston; private, 1899.

Huey, Pennock, *A True History of the Charge of the Eighth Pennsylvania Cavalry at Chancellorsville*, Philadelphia; Porter & Coates, 1888.

Huidekoper, H. S., *A Short Story of the First Day's Fight at Gettysburg*, Philadelphia; Bicking Print, 1906.

Humphreys, Andrew A., *The Virginia Campaigns of '64 and '65*, New York; Charles Scribner's Sons, 1903.

Hyde, Thomas W., *Following the Greek Cross or, memoirs of the Sixth Corps*, Boston; Houghton Mifflin and Company, 1894.

Imboden, John D., "The Confederate Retreat from Gettysburg," In *Battles and Leaders of the Civil War*, Robert Underwood Johnson and Clarence Clough Buell, eds., 4 Volumes, New York; The Century Company 1887.

In Memoriam: The Letters of William Wheeler, Private, 1875.

Isham, Asa B., *An Historical Sketch of the Seventh Regiment Michigan Volunteer Cavalry*, New York; Town Topic Publishing Co., 1893.

_____, "The Cavalry of the Army of the Potomac," in *Sketches of War History, 1861–1865*, Ohio Commendary of the Loyal Legion of the United States, 7 Volumes., Cincinnati; 1888–1910.

Jacobs, M., *Notes on the Rebel Invasion of Maryland and Pennsylvania*, Philadelphia; J. B. Lippincott & C0., 1864.

Johnson, Clifton, *Battlefield Adventures: The Stories of Conflict in Some of the Most Notable Battles of the Civil War*, Boston; Houghton, Mifflin, Co., 1915.

Johnson, Robert Underwood, and Buell, Clarence Clough, comp., *Battle and Leaders of the Civil War*, 4 Volumes, New York; Century Publishing Co., 1887–1888.

Johnson, Clifton, *Battleground Adventures: The Stories of Conflict in Some of the Most Notable Battles of the Civil War*, Boston; Houghton, Mifflin Co., 1915.

Kempster, Walter, "The Early Days of Our Cavalry in the Army of the Potomac," *War Papers Read Before the State of Wisconsin Commandery of the Military Order of the Loyal Legion of the United States*, Volume 3, Milwaukee; Burdick & Allen, 1913.

Kidd, James H., "The Michigan Brigade in the Wilderness," in *War Papers, Read Before the State of Michigan Commandery of the Military Order of the Loyal Legion*, Volume 1, Detroit; Winn & Hammond, Printers, 1893.

_____, *Personal Recollections of a Cavalryman with Custer's Michigan Cavalry Brigade in the Civil War*, Ioinia, MI; private, 1908.

Lee, Robert E., *Recollections and Letters of Robert E. Lee* New York, reprint, Barnes and Noble, 2004.

Letters from Two Brothers Serving in the war for the Union to Their Family at Home, Cambridge; private, 1871.

Letters of Richard Tylden Auchmuty: Fifth Corps, Army *of the Potomac*, Private, nd.

Letters of Calvin Haynes, One Hundred and Twenty-fifth New York Infantry, New York State Library.

Lewis, John H., *Recollections, 1860–1865*, Washington; Peake & Co., 1985.

Life and Letters of Wilder Dwight, Boston, Ticknor and Fields, 1868,

Locke, William Henry, *The Story of a Regiment*, Philadelphia; J. B. Lippincott & Co., 1868.

Long. A. L., *Memoirs of Robert E. Lee*, New York; J. M. Stoddart & Company, 1886.

Longacre, Edward G., *The Cavalry at Gettysburg: A Tactical Study of Mounted Operations during the Civil War's Pivotal Campaign, 9 June–14 July 1863*, Lincoln; University of Nebraska Press, 1986.

_____, Lincoln's Cavalrymen: A History of the Mounted Forces of the *Army of the Potomac*, Mechanicsburg, PA; Stackpole Books, 2000.

_____, *General John Buford: A Military Biography*, Conshohocken, PA; Combined Books, 1995.

Longstreet, James, *From Manassas to Appomattox: Memoirs of the Civil War in America*, Philadelphia; J. B. Lippincott and Company, 1896.

Lyman, Theodore, *Meade's Army: The Private Notebooks of Lt. Col. Theodore Lyman*, Kent, OH; Kent State University Press, 2007.

MacNamara, M. H., *The Irish Ninth in Bivouac and Battle: or Virginia and Maryland Campaigns*, Boston; Leeds and Shepard, 1867.

McClellan, George B., *McClellan's Own Story*, New York; Charles L. Webster & Company, 1887.

McClellan, H. B., *The Life and Campaigns of Major-General J. E. B. Stuart*, Boston; Houghton, Mifflin and Company, 1885.

McDonald, William N., *A History of the Laurel Brigade*, Privately issued, 1907.

McKinney, Edward P., *Life in Tent and Field, 1861–1865*, Boston; Richard G. Badger, 1922.

McKim, Randolph H., *A Soldier's Recollections*, New York; Longmans, Green and Company, 1910.

McPherson, James M., *The Battle Cry of Freedom: The Civil War Era*, New York; Oxford University Press, 1988.

_____, *Drawn with the Sword*, New York; Oxford University Press, 1997.

Meade, George G., *The Life and Letters of George Gordon Meade*, New York; Charles Scribner's Sons, 1913.

Meyer, Henry C., *Civil War Experiences Under Bayard, Gregg, Kilpatrick, Custer, Raulston, and Newberry, 1862, 1863, 1864*, New York, G. P. Putnam's Sons, 1911.

Michie, Peter S., *The Life and Letters of Emory Upton*, New York; D. Appleton and Company, 1885.

Miller, Delavan S., *Drum Taps in Dixie: Memoirs of a Drummer Boy, 1861–1865*, Watertown, N.Y.; Hungerford-Holbrook Co., 1905.

Morison, Samuel Eliot, Henry Steele Commager, William E. Leuchtenbuerg, *The Growth of the American Republic*, Two Volumes, New York; Oxford University Press, 1969.

Moore, Frank, ed., *The Rebellion Record: A Diary of American Events*, Volume 7, New York; D. Van Nostrand, Publisher, 1864.

Morse, F. W., *Personal Experiences in the War of the Great Rebellion from December 1862 to July, 1865*, Albany, NY; private, 1866.

Moyer, H. P., comp., *History of the Seventeenth Regiment Pennsylvania Volunteer Cavalry*, Lebanon, PA; Sowers Printing Company, 1911.

Neese, George M., *Three Years in the Confederate Horse Artillery*, New York; The Neale Publishing Company, 1911.

Nettleton, Bayard, Second Ohio Cavalry, "How the Days Was Saved at the Battle of Cedar Creek," *Papers Read Before the Minnesota Commandery of the Military Order of the Loyal Legion of the United States*, St. Paul; Commandery, 1887.

Nevins, Allen, ed., *A Diary of Battle: The Personal Journal of Colonel Charles S. Wainwright*, New York; Harcourt, Brace and World, 1962.

Newhall, F. C., "The Battle of Beverly Ford," in *Annals of War Written by the Leading Participants North and South*. Philadelphia; The Times Publishing Company, 1879.

Newhall, Walter S., A Memoir, Philadelphia; Sherman, Son & Co., 1864.

Newell, Joseph Keith, *Ours, Annals of 10th Regiment Massachusetts Volunteers in the Rebellion*, Springfield, MA; C. A. Nichols & Co., 1875.

New York Legislature, Report of the Adjutant General's Office, 43 Volumes., Albany; Argus, 1895–1906.

New York Monuments Commission for the Battlefields of Gettysburg and Chattanooga, *Final Report on the Battle of Gettysburg*, Volume 1, Albany; J. B. Lyon, 1900.

New York Monuments Commission for the Battlefields of Gettysburg and Chattanooga, *Final Report on the Battle of Gettysburg*, Volume 2, Albany; J. B. Lyon, 1902.

Nightingale, Henry O., *Diaries*, Special Collections and Archives, University of California, Merced Library.

Norton, Chauncey, *The Red Neck Ties or History of the Fifteenth New York Volunteer Cavalry*, Ithaca, New York; Journal Book and Job Printing House, 1891.

Norton, Henry, *Deeds of Daring, or History of the Eighth New York Volunteer Cavalry*, Ithaca, NY; private, 1889.

Norton, Oliver Willcox, *Letters, 1861–1865*, Chicago; private, 1903.

Norton, Oliver Willcox, *The Attack and Defense of Little Round Top, Gettysburg, July 2, 1863*, New York; The Neale Publishing Company, 1913.

O'Mara, D. A., *Fifty-ninth Reg't, New York Veteran Volunteers: Report of Proceeding, Re-union and Roster of Surviving Members*, New York; private, 1889.

Page, Charles D., *History of the Fourteenth Regiment Connecticut Vol. Infantry*, Meridian, CT; The Horton Printing Co., 1906

Palmer, E. F., *The Second Brigade; or, Camp Life*, Private, 1864.

Parker, John L., *Henry Wilson's Regiment: History of the Twenty-second Massachusetts Infantry*, Boston; Regimental Association, 1887.

Pearson, Henry Greenleaf, *James S. Wadsworth of Geneseo*, London; John Murray, 1913.

Perry, Bliss, *The Life and Letters of Henry Lee Higginson*, Boston; The Atlantic Monthly Press, 1921.

Perry, Martha Derby, *Letters from a Surgeon of the Civil War*, Boston; Little, Brown, and Company, 1906.

Pfanz, Harry W., *Gettysburg-The First Day*, Chapel Hill; University of North CarolinaPress, 2001.

Phisterer, Frederick, *New York in the War of Rebellion*, 3rd ed., Albany; J. B. Lyon Company, 1912.

Pleasonton, Alfred, "The Successes and Failures of Chancellorsvillec," in Robert Underwood Johnson and Clarence Clough Buell, eds., *Battles and Leaders of the Civil War*, 4 Volumes, New York; The Century Company, 1887.

Polley, Joseph Benjamin, *A Soldier's Letters to Charming Nellie*, New York; Neale Publishing Company, 1908.

Porter, Burton B., *One of the People, His Own Story*, Private, 1907.

Preston, Noble, *History of the Tenth Regiment of Cavalry, New York State Volunteers, August 1861 to August 1865*, New York; D. Appleton, 1892.

Pyne, Henry R., *The History of the First New Jersey Cavalry*, Trenton; J. A. Beecher, Publisher, 1871.

Reunion of the Sixth New York Cavalry, Worcester, MA; 1904.

Rhea, Gordon C., *The Battles for Spotsylvania Court House and the Road to Yellow Tavern, May 7–12, 1864*, Baton Rouge; Louisiana State University Press, 1997.

Rhodes, James Ford, *The History of the United States from the Compromise of 1850* New York; Harper and Brothers publishers, 1895.

_____, *History of the United States from Hayes to McKinley, 1877–1895* New York; The MacMillan Company, 1919.

Robertson, Robert S., "From the Wilderness to Spotsylvania," in *Sketches of War: Papers Read Before the Ohio Commandery of the Military Order of the Loyal Legion of the United States*, Volume 1, Cincinnati; Robert Clark & Co., 1888.

Rodenbough, Theodore F. "Sheridan's Richmond Raid," in Robert Underwood Johnson and Clarence Clough Buell, eds., *Battles and Leaders of the Civil War*, 4 Volumes, New York, The Century Co., 1888.

Roemer, Jacob, *Reminiscences of the War of Rebellion, 1861–1865*, Flushing, New York; The Estate of Jacob Roemer, 1897.

Rosengarten, J. G., *William Reynolds, John Fulton Reynolds: A Memoir*, Philadelphia; J. B. Lippincott and Co., 1880.

Rusling, James F., *Men and Things I Saw in Civil War Days*, New York; Eaton & Mains Press, 1899.

Scheibert, Justus, *Seven Months in the Rebel States During the North American War, 1863*, Confederate Publishing Company, Inc., 1958.

Schurz, Carl, *The Reminiscences of Carl Schurz*, Volume 2, New York; The McClure Company, 1907.

Sears, Stephen W., *Gettysburg*. Boston; Houghton, Mifflin Company, 2003.

_____, Stephen W., *Controversies and Commanders: Dispatches from the Army of the Potomac*, Boston; Houghton Mifflin Company, 1999.

_____, Stephen W., *Landscape Turned Red: The Battle of Antietam*, Boston; Houghton Mifflin Company, 1983.

_____, Stephen W., *Lincoln's Lieutenants: The High Command of the Army of the Potomac*, Boston; Houghton Mifflin Harcourt, 2017.

Sheridan, Philip H., *Personal Memoirs of P. H. Sheridan*, reprint, New York; Barnes and Noble, 2006.

Shuricht, Herman, "Jenkins' Brigade in the Gettysburg Campaign—Extracts from the Diary of Lieutenant Herman Shuricht, 14th Virginia Cavalry," *Southern Historical Society Papers*, Volume. 24, Richmond; Published by the Society, 1896.

Simpson, Brooks D., "Great Expectations: Ulysses S. Grant, the Northern Press, and the Opening of the Wilderness Campaign," in *The Wilderness Campaign*, Gary W. Gallagher, ed. Chapel Hill; University of North Carolina Press, 1997.

Smith, John Day, *The History of the Nineteenth Regiment Maine Volunteer Infantry, 1862–1865*, Minneapolis; The Great Western Printing Company, 1909.

Society of the Army of the Potomac, *Report of the Sixteenth Annual Re-Union, at Baltimore, MD, May 6 and 7, 1885*, New York; MacGowan & Slipper, 1885.

Speeches of Oliver Wendell Holmes, Boston; Little, Brown and Company, 1896.

Starr, Stephen Z., *The Union Cavalry in the Civil War: From Fort Sumter to Gettysburg, 1861–1863*, Volume 1, Baton Rouge; Louisiana State University Press, 1979.

_____, *The Union Cavalry in the Civil War: The War in the East from Gettysburg to Appomattox, 1863–1865*, Volume 2, Baton Rouge; Louisiana State University Press, 1981.

Stevens, C. A., *Berdan's Sharpshooters in the Army of the Potomac, 1861–1865*, St Paul; MN, 1892.

Stevens, George T., *Three Years in the Sixth Corps*, 2nd edition, New York; D. Van Nostrand, Publisher, 1870.

Stewart, A. M., *Camp, March and Battlefield or, Three Years and a Half with the Army of the Potomac*, Philadelphia; Jos. B. Rogers, 1865.

Stewart, James, "Battery B, Fourth United States Artillery at Gettysburg," in *Sketches of War History, 1861–1865, Papers Prepared for the Ohio Commandery of the Military Orders of the Loyal Legion of the United States*, Volume 4, Cincinnati; The Robert Clark Company, 1896.

Stone, James Madison, *Personal Recollections of the Civil War*, Boston; private, 1918.

Thirteenth New Jersey Veteran Association, Reunion, 1st—9th, 1887–1894, Newark; private, nd.

Thirty-Fifth Anniversary and Reunion of the Tenth New York Cavalry Veterans Held in Buffalo, New York, Oct. 6, 7 and 8, 1896, Homer, N.Y.; Stevens and Danes, 1896.

Thomas, Emory, *The Confederate Nation, 1861–1865*, New York; Harper and Row, 1979.

Thomas, Hampton S., *Some Personal Reminiscences of Service in the Cavalry of the Army of the Potomac*, Philadelphia; L. H. Hamersley, 1889.

Thompson, S. Millett, *Thirteenth Regiment of New Hampshire Volunteer Infantry in the War of Rebellion, 1861–1865, A Diary Covering Three Years and a Day*, Boston; Houghton, Mifflin and Company, 1888.

Tilney, Robert. *My Life in the Army: Three Years and a Half in the Fifth Army Corps, Army of the Potomac, 1862–1865*, Philadelphia; Ferris & Leach, 1912.

Tobie, Edward P., *Service of the Cavalry of the Army of the Potomac*, Providence; W. Bangs Williams & Co., 1882.

_____, *First Maine Bugle*, Champaign, IL; First Maine Cavalry Association, 1892.

_____, *History of the First Maine Cavalry, 1861–1865*, Boston; Press of Emory and Hughes, 1887.

Trudeau, Noah Andre, *Gettysburg: A Testing of Courage*, New York; Harper Collins, 2002.

Tyler, Mason Whiting, *Recollections of the Civil War*, William S. Tyler, ed., New York; G. P. Putman's Sons, 1912.

U. S. War Department, *War of Rebellion ... Official Records of the Union and Confederate Armies*, 128 Volumes, Washington; Government Printing Office, 1880–1901.

Van Alstyne, Lawrence, *Diary of an Enlisted Man*, New Haven; The Tuttle, Morehouse and Taylor Company, 1910.

Von Borcke, Heros, *Memoirs of the Confederate War for Independence*, Edinburgh; William Blackwood and Sons, 1866.

Veterans Association of the Thirteenth Regiment New Jersey Volunteers, 1861–1865, *Fourth Reunion at Montclair, N. J., September 18, 1889*, Newark; private, 1889.

Walcott, Charles F., *History of the Twenty-first Massachusetts Volunteers in the War For Preservation of the Union, 1861–1865*, Boston; Houghton, Mifflin and Company, 1882.

Walker, Francis A., *History of the Second Army Corps in the Army of the Potomac*, New York; Charles Scribner's Sons, 1886.

Wallace, Robert C., *A Few Memories of a Long Life*, Helena, MT; private, 1916.

Ward, Geoffrey E., *The Civil War: An Illustrated History*, New York; Alfred A. Knopf, Inc., 1990.

Ward, Joseph R. C., *History of the One Hundred and Sixth Regiment, Pennsylvania Volunteers, 2nd Brigade, 2d Division, 2d Corps, 1861–1865*, Philadelphia; F. McManus, Jr. & Co., 1906.

Wert, Jeffry D., *The Sword of Lincoln: The Army of the Potomac*, New York; Simon and Schuster, 2005.

Wheeler, Richard, *Witness to Gettysburg*, New York; Harper and Row, Publishers, 1987.

White, Richard, *The Republic for which it Stands: The United States during Reconstruction and the Gilded Age, 1865–1896*, New York; Oxford University Press, 2017.

Whitman, Walt, *The Complete Prose Works of Walt Whitman*, New York; G. P. Putnam's Sons, 1902.

Whittaker, Frederick, *A Complete Life of General George A. Custer*, New York; Sheldon & Co., 1876.

Wickersham, Charles I., "Personal Recollections of the Cavalry at Chancellorsville," in *War Papers Read Before the Commandery of the State of Wisconsin Military Order of the Loyal Legion of the United States*, Volume 3, Milwaukee; Burdick and Allen, 1903.

Williams, Charles R., ed., *Diary and Letters of Rutherford Birchard Hayes: Nineteenth President of the United States*, 2 Volumes, Columbus; The Ohio State Archaeological and Historical Society, 1922.

Willison, Arabella M., *Disaster, Struggle, Triumph: The Adventure of 1000 Boys in Blue*, Albany; The Historical Committee of the Regiment, 1870.

Wise, Jennings Cooper, *The Long Arm of Lee, or the History of the Artillery of the Army Northern Virginia*, Lynchburg, VA; J. P. Bell Company, Inc., 1915.

Wittenberg, Eric J., Karla Jean Husby, eds., *Under Custer's Command: The Civil War Journal of James Henry Avery*, Washington, D.C.; Brassey's, 2000.

Wittenberg, Eric J., J. David Petruzzi, Michael F. Nugent, *One Continuous Fight: The Retreat from Gettysburg and the Pursuit of Lee's Army of Northern Virginian, July 4–14, 1863*, New York; Savas Beatie, 2008.

Wittenberg, Eric J., *Gettysburg's Forgotten Cavalry Actions: Farnsworth's Charge, South Cavalry Field, and the Battle of Fairfield, July 3, 1863*, New York; Savas Beatie, rev. ed., 2011.

Wormeley, Katharine Prescott, *The Other Side of War with the Army of the Potomac*, Boston; Ticknor and company, 1889.

Young, Louis G., "Pettigrew's Brigade at Gettysburg," in Walter Clark, ed., *Histories of the Several Regiments and Battalions from North Carolina in the Great War, 1861–1865*, Goldsboro, North Carolina; Nash Brothers, 1901.

Internet Sites

New York State Military Museum, www.dmna.state.ny.us/historic
New York State Library, www.NYSL.gov
New York Times, www.New York Times.com

Source Notes

1   New York State Military Museum, 6th Regiment Cavalry, *Samuel Fanshaw Collection*. The Museum's web site is www.dmna.state.ny.us/historic and here will be cited as NYMM.
2   Ibid., NYMM.
3   New York Legislature, *Annual Report of the Adjutant General's Office* Albany, Argus, 1895–1906, p. 345, NYMM.
4   NYMM, 6th Regiment Cavalry, *Fanshaw Collection*.
5   New York, *AGO Report*, p. 653.
6   Ibid., NYMM, 6th Regiment Cavalry, *Fanshaw Collection*.

Chapter One

1   Newel Cheney, *History of the Ninth Regiment New York Volunteer Cavalry*, Poland Springs, NY, private, 1901, p. 5; Thomas W. Hyde, *Following the Greek Cross or, Memoirs of the Sixth Corps*, Boston, Houghton, Mifflin and Company, 1894, Preface, np; Walt Whitman, *The Compete Prose Works of Walt Whitman*, New York, G. P. Putnam' Sons, 1902), p. 140.
2   Edward P. Tobie, *First Maine Bugle*, No. 7, Boston, First Maine Cavalry Association, 1892, pp. 46, 51–54, 63, 82.
3   Ibid., np.
4   Ibid, pp. 44–82.
5   James Marten, *Sing Not War: The Lives of Union and Confederate Veterans in Gilded Age America*, Chapel Hill, University of North Carolina Press, 2011, p. 4.
6   Cheney, *Ninth New York Volunteers*, pp. 7–8; Joseph Keith Newell, *Ours, Annals of the 10th Regiment, Massachusetts Volunteers in the Rebellion*, Springfield, MA, C.A. Nichols, 1875, p. 91.
7   John Day Smith, *The History of the Nineteenth Regiment Maine Volunteer Infantry, 1862–1865*, Minneapolis, The Great Western Printing Company, 1909, p. 77.
8   New York Legislature, *Report, AGO*, NYMM, 6th Regiment Cavalry.
9   Ibid., p. 482; NYMM, 6th Regiment Cavalry.
10 Ibid., p. 392.
11 Ibid., p. 462.
12 Alonzo Foster, *Remembrances and Record of the 6th New York Veteran Volunteer Cavalry*, Brooklyn, private, 1892, p. 5.
13 Lawrence Van Alstyne, *Diary of an Enlisted Man*, New Haven, The Tuttle, Moorehouse & Taylor Company, 1910, p. v.
14 Hillman A. Hall, William H. Besley, Gilbert G. Wood, *History of the Sixth New York Cavalry, 1861–1865*, Worcester, MA, Blanchard Press, 1908, p. 133.
15 Stephen W. Sears, Controversies and Commanders: Dispatches from the Army of the Potomac, Boston, Houghton, Mifflin Company, 1999, p. 175.

16 James H. Kidd, "The Michigan Cavalry Brigade in the Wilderness," in Volume 1, *Papers Read Before the Michigan Commandery of the Loyal Legion of the United States*, Detroit, Winn and Hammond Printers and Binders, 1889, p. 254.

17 Bruce Catton, *Mr. Lincoln's Army*, Garden City, NY, Doubleday & Company, 1951, p. 359; Hall, *Sixth New York Cavalry*. p. 5.

18 Hyde, *Following the Greek Cross*, pp. 1–2.

19 Hall, *Sixth New York Cavalry*, p. 100.

20 F. H. Buffum, *Reunion of Sheridan's Veterans Association, September 15–24, 1885 at Winchester*, Boston, W. F. Brown & Company, 1885, pp. 6, 16–17ff; Drew Gilpin Faust, *The Republic of Suffering: Death and the American Civil War*, New York, Alfred A. Knopf, 2008, p. 241.

21 H. P. Moyer, *History of the Seventeenth Regiment Pennsylvania Volunteer Cavalry*, Lebanon, PA, Sowers Printing Co., 1911, pp. 22–23.

22 Noble Preston, *History of the Tenth Regiment of Cavalry, New York State Volunteers, August 1861 to August 1865*, New York, D. Appleton, 1892, pp. iii, v.

23 Benjamin W. Crowninshield, *A History of the First Regiment Massachusetts Cavalry Volunteers*, Boston, Houghton, Mifflin Company, 1891, p. iii.

24 *Thirty-fifth Anniversary and Reunion of the Tenth New York Cavalry Veterans held in Buffalo, New York, October 6, 7, and 8, 1896*, Homer, NY, Stevens and Dames, Printers, 1896, pp. 3–9.

25 Ibid., p. 15.

26 Ibid., p. 17.

27 Ibid., p. 29.

28 Ibid., p. 31.

29 Ibid., pp. 32–33.

30 Joseph R. C. Ward, *History of the One Hundred and Sixth Regiment Pennsylvania Volunteers, 2nd Brigade, 2nd Division, 2nd Corps*, Philadelphia, F. McManus, Jr., & Co., 1906, pp. iv, i.

31 Francis A. Walker, *History of the Second Army Corps in the Army of the Potomac*, New York, Charles Scribner, 1886, pp. iii–iv.

32 Charles E. Davis, *Three Years in the Army: The Story of the Thirteenth Massachusetts Volunteers from July 16, 1861, to August 1, 1864*, Boston, Estes and Laurat, 1894, pp. vii, 224.

33 Paul H. Buck, *The Road to Reunion, 1865–1900*, Boston, Little, Brown & Company, 1937, p. 259–260; *New York Times*, July 1, 1888; Shelby Foote, *The Civil War: A Narrative, Red River to Appomattox*, New York, Random House, 1974, p. 539.

34 Matthew J. Graham, *The Ninth Regiment New York Volunteers*, New York, private, 1900, pp. 466–481.

35 *Thirteen New Jersey Veteran Association, Reunion, 1st—9th, 1887–1894*, Newark, private, nd, p.12.

36 *New York Monuments Commission for the Battlefields of Gettysburg and Chattanooga: Final Report on the Battle of Gettysburg*, Volume 1, Albany, J. B. Lyon Company, 1902, pp. 197, 200, 236, 237. Dan Sickles served as chairman of the Commission until 1912 when he was relieved for "mishandling funds." Mark Boatner, *The Civil War Dictionary*, New York, David McKay Company, Ins., 1959, p. 760.

37 *Final Report on the Battle of Gettysburg*, v. 1, p. 204.

38 *Thirteenth New Jersey, Reunion,*1888, pp. 3, 6, 16.

39 Ibid., Reunion, 1889, p. 12.

40 Ibid., p. 203.

41 Delvin S. Miller, *Drum Taps in Dixie: Memoirs of a Drummer Boy, 1861–1865*, Watertown, NY, Hungerford Co., 1905, pp. 52–57.

42 John L Parker, *Henry Wilson's Regiment: History of the Twenty-second Massachusetts Infantry*, Boston, Regimental Association, 1887, pp. 537, 543, 544, 548–549.

43   A. D. Rockwell, *Rambling Recollections: A Autobiography*, New York, Paul B. Hoeber, 1920, p. 156.

44   *The Annals of War Written by the Leading Participants North and South*, Philadelphia, Time Time Publishing Co., 1879, p. ii.

45   Buck, *Toad to Reunion*, pp. 247–248.

46   Brian Matthew Jordan, *Marching Home: Union Veterans and Their Unending Civil War*, New York, Liveright Publishing Company, 2014, pp. 83–88.

Chapter Two

1   Jacob Roemer, *Reminiscences of the War of Rebellion, 1861–1865,* Flushing, NY, Estate of Jacob Roemer, 1897, p. 54; George B. McClellan, *McClellan's Own Story*, New York, Charles L. Webster & Company, 1887, pp. 612, 614.

2   James Ford Rhodes, *The History of the United States from the Compromise of 1850*, New York, Harper Brothers Publishers, 1895, vol. 3, p. 455.

3   F. Colburn Adams, *The Story of a Trooper*, New York, Dick & Fitzgerald Publishers, 1865, pp. 99–100.

4   James F. Rusling, *Men and Things I saw in Civil War Days*, New York, Eaton & Mains Press, 1899), p. 210.

5   NYMM, 1st Regiment Cavalry, Newspaper Clippings.

6   Ibid.

7   Ibid.

8   Hall, *Sixth New York Cavalry*, pp. 15–19.

9   Henry R. Pyne, *The History of the First New Jersey Cavalry*, (Trenton, J. A. Becher, Publisher, 1871), p. 17.

10   Edward P. Tobie, *History of the First Maine Cavalry, 1861–1865*, Boston, Press of Emory and Hughes, 1887, pp. 13–14.

11   Edward G. Longacre, *Lincoln's Cavalrymen: A History of the Mounted Forces of the Army of the Potomac*, Mechanicsburg, PA, Stackpole Books, 2000, p. 2; Stephen Z. Starr, *The Union Cavalry in the Civil War: From Fort Sumter to Gettysburg, 1861–1863*, Baton Rouge, Louisiana State University Press, 1978, pp. 54, 67–68, 72, 207.

12   Walter Kempster, "The Early Days of Our Cavalry in the Army of the Potomac," in *War Papers Read Before the Commandery pf the State of Wisconsin, Military Order of the Loyal Legion of the United States*, Vol. 3, Milwaukee, Burdick & Allen, 1903, p. 70.

13   Hall, *Sixth New York Cavalry*, pp. 8, 17; Thomas Ellis, *Leaves From the Diary of an Army Surgeon*, New York, John Bradburn, 1863, p. 17.

14   Tobie, *History of the First Maine Cavalry*, pp. 3, 13.

15   Hall, *Sixth New York Cavalry*, p. 13; W. H. Beach, "Some Reminiscences of the First New York (Lincoln) Cavalry," in *War Papers Read Before the Commandery of the State of Wisconsin, Military Order of the Loyal Legion of the United States*, Milwaukee, Burdick & Allen, 1896, vol. 2, p. 281.

16   Worthingtom Chauncey Ford, ed., *A Cycle of Adams Letters, 1861–1865*, vol. 2, Boston, Houghton Mifflin Company, 1920, p. 269.

17   Edward G. Longacre, *The Cavalry at Gettysburg: A Tactical Study of Mounted Operations During the Civil War's Pivotal Campaign, 9 June–14 July, 1863*, Lincoln, University of Nebraska Press, 1986, pp. 51–52.

18   Ellis, *Leaves from the Diary*, pp. 17–18.

19   Hall, *Sixth New York Cavalry*, pp. 31–32; Ellis, *Leaves from the Diary*, p. 25.

20   Tobie, *History of the First Maine Cavalry*, p. 5.

21 Warren Hopgood Freeman, Eugene Harrison Freeman, *Letters from Two Brothers Serving in the War for the Union*, Cambridge, private, 1871, pp. 4, 8.

22 NYMM, 69th Regiment Infantry Newspaper Clippings.

23 NYMM, 6th Regiment Cavalry Newspaper Clippings.

24 Ellis, *Leaves from the Diary*, p. 26; Hall, *Sixth New York Cavalry*, pp. 31–35.

25 Hall, Ibid., p. 36.

26 NYMM, 8th Regiment Cavalry Newspaper Clippings.

27 Warren Lee Goss, "Going to the Front," in Robert Underwood Johnson, Clarence Buell, eds., *Battles and Leaders of the Civil War*, 4 Volumes, New York, The Century Company, 1887, vol. 1, p. 153.

28 Adams, *Story of a Trooper*, pp. 6, 61.

29 Edward P. Tobie, "Service in the Cavalry of the Army of the Potomac," in *Personal Narratives of Events in the War of Rebellion being Papers Read Before the Rhode Island Soldiers and Sailors Historical Society*, Providence, N. Bangs Williams & Company, 1882, pp. 5–6; Starr, *Union Cavalry in the Civil War*, vol. 1, p. 142; Tobie, *History of the First Maine*, p. 14; Willard Glazier, *Three Years in the Federal Cavalry*, New York, R.H. Ferguson & Company, 1874, p. 35.

30 NYMM, 73rd Regiment Infantry Newspaper Clippings.

31 Stephen Z. Starr, *The Union Cavalry in the Civil War: From Gettysburg to Appomattox, 1863–1865*, Baton Rouge, Louisiana State University Press, 1981, vol. 2, p. 149 note 17; Regimental History Committee, *History of the Third Pennsylvania Cavalry in the Civil War*, Philadelphia, Franklin Printing Company, 1905, pp. 23–27.

32 Starr, *The Union Cavalry in the Civil War*, vol. 2, pp. 82–83, 150–152.

33 NYMM, 1st Regiment Cavalry Newspaper Clippings, NYMM, 8th Regiment Cavalry Newspaper Clippings.

34 George G. Benedict, *Vermont in the Civil War*, vol. 2, 534.

35 Ibid., pp. 534–546.

36 Goss, "Going to the Front," *Battles and Leaders*, vol. 1, pp. 157–158.

37 Charles A. Dana, *Recollections of the Civil War: With Leaders in Washington and in the Field in the Sixties*, New York, D. Appleton, 1898, pp. 4–5.

38 Quoted in Stephen W. Sears, *Landscape Turned Red: The Battle of Antietam*, Boston, Houghton, Mifflin Company, 1981, p. 77.

39 Ibid., p. 157.

40 Carl Schurz, *The Reminiscences of Carl Schurz*, 3 volumes, New York, The McClure Company, 1907, vol. 2, p. 334.

41 Freeman, *Letters from Two Brothers*, p. 35.

42 Katharine Prescott Wormeley, *The Others Side of War with the Army of the Potomac*, Boston, Ticknor and Company, 1889, pp. 190–191.

43 McClellan, *Own Story*, pp. 444–446.

44 Ibid., p. 449.

45 Ibid., pp. 487–489.

46 Ibid., pp. 389, 761.

47 Roemer, *Reminiscences*, p. 54.

48 Ibid., p. 41.

49 James M. McPherson, *The Battle Cry of Freedom: The Civil War Era*, New York, Oxford University Press, 1988, p. 526.

50 NYMM, 86th Regiment Infantry, Isaac Rathbun Collection, Rathbun Diary.

51 Charles F. Walcott, *History of the Twenty-first Massachusetts Volunteers in the War for the Preservation of the Union, 1861–1865*, Boston, Houghton, Mifflin Company, 1882, p. 188; Hall, *Sixth New York Cavalry*, p. 364.

52 Frederick, Hitchcock, *War From the Inside or Personal Experiences, Impressions, and Reminiscences of One of the Boys in the War of Rebellion*, Philadelphia, J. P. Lippincott Company, 1904, p. 44.

53 Charles Richard Williams, *Diary and Letters of Rutherford B. Hayes*, The Ohio State Archeological and Historical Society, vol. 2, pp. 355–357.

54 Quotes in Sears, *Landscape Turned Red*, pp. 131; Stephen W. Sears, *Lincoln's Lieutenants: The High Command of the Army of the Potomac*, Boston, Houghton, Mifflin Company, 2017, pp. 362–363.

55 David L. Thompson, "In the Ranks at Antietam," in *Battles and Leaders*, vol. 2, pp. 558–559.

56 Sears, *Lincoln's Lieutenants*, pp. 366–367.

57 Cecil D. Eby, ed., *A Virginian Yankee in the Civil War: The Diaries of David Hunter Strother*, Chapel Hill: University of North Carolina Press, 1961, p. 108; M. H. MacNamara, *The Irish Ninth in Bivouac, or the Virginia and Maryland Campaigns*, Boston: Lee and Shepard, 1867, pp. 120–121.

58 Benjamin F. Cook, *History of the Twelfth Massachusetts Volunteers (Webster Regiment)*, Boston, Twelfth Regiment Association, 1887, p. 70.

59 Hitchcock, *War from the Inside*, pp. 7, 13, 14.

60 Ibid., pp. 55–56.

61 Ibid., p. 57.

62 Ibid., pp. 60, 62. Hitchcock when writing his recollections identified the young Confederate as Lieutenant Colonel J. M. Newton of the Sixth Georgia Infantry.

63 Rufus Dawes, *Service with the Sixth Wisconsin Volunteers*, Marietta, OH, E. R. Alderman & Sons, 1890, pp. 88, 95; Cook, *Twelfth Massachusetts*, p. 73.

64 *Life and Letters of Wilder Dwight*, Boston, Ticknor and Fields, 1868, p. 293.

65 Eby, *A Virginian Yankee*, pp. 112, 114; MacNamara, *Irish Ninth*, pp. 119–120.

66 Sears, *Lincoln's Lieutenants*, pp. 412, 415; McClellan, *Own Story*, p. 512.

67 McPherson, *The Battle Cry of Freedom*, pp. 544–555; Quoted in Sears, *Lincoln's Lieutenants*, p. 411.

68 McClellan, *Own Story*, p. 612.

69 Eby, *A Virginian Yankee*, p. 113.

70 McClellan, *Own Story*, p. 614.

71 Eby, *A Virginian Yankee*, pp. 116–119.

72 Ibid, pp. 118–119

73 McClellan, *Own Story*, p. 613.

74 Ibid., p. 615.

75 James H. Wilson, *Under the Old Flag*, 2 Volumes, New York, D. Appleton and Company, 1912, vol. 1, pp. 126–127.

76 Mason Whiting Tyler, *Recollections of the Civil War*, William S. Tyler, ed., New York, G. P. Putnam's Sons, 1912, pp. v–ix, 57.

77 William N. Pickerill, *History of the Third Indiana Cavalry*, Indianapolis, private, 1906, pp. 33–34.

78 E. F. Palmer, *The Second Brigade; or, Camp Life*, Private, 1864, pp. 40–41.

79 Comte De Paris, "McClellan Organizing of the Grand Army," in *Battles and Leaders*, vol. 2, p. 122.

80 James Madison Stone, *Personal Recollections of the Civil War*, Boston, private, 1918, pp. 93, 97.

81 McPherson, *Battle Cry of Freedom*, p. 497; Jeffry D. Wert, *Sword of Lincoln: The Army of the Potomac*, New York, Simon and Schuster, 2005, p. 212.

82 Palmer, *Second Brigade*, p. 97; John R. Boyle, *Soldiers True: The Story of the One Hundred and Eleventh Regiment Pennsylvania Veteran Volunteers, and its Campaigns in the War for the Union, 1861–1865*, New York, Eaton and Mains, 1903, p. 80.

83 John Day Smith, *The History of the Nineteenth Regiment Maine Volunteer Infantry, 1862–1865*, Minneapolis, The Great Western Printing Company, 1909, pp. 41–42.

84 George H. Gordon, *A Diary of Events in the War of the Great Rebellion, 1863–1865*, Boston, James R. Osgood and Company, 1882, p. 8.

85 Cook, *Twelfth Massachusetts*, p. 76.

86 Quoted in McPherson, *Battle Cry of Freedom*, p. 528.

87 George G. Meade, *Life and Letters of George Gordon Meade*, 2 Volumes, New York, Charles Scribner's Sons, 1913, vol. 1, p. 320, Sears, *Lincoln's Lieutenants*, p. 430.

88 McClellan, *Own Story*, p. 660; Sears, *Landscape Turned Red*, p. 341.

89 Eby, *A Virginian Yankee*, p. 129.

90 Ford, *Adam Letters*, Vol. 1, p. 198.

Chapter Three

1 Robert E. Lee, *Recollections and Letters*, New York, Barnes & Noble, reprint, 2004, pp. 81–82; Quoted in John Bigelow, *The Campaign of Chancellorsville*, New Haven, Yale University Press, 1910, p. 34.

2 D. P. Conyngham, *The Irish Brigade and Its Campaigns*, New York, William McSorley & Co., 1867, p. 373; St. Ckair Mullholland, *The Story of the 166th Regiment Pennsylvania Infantry*, Philadelphia, F. McManus, Jr. & Co., 1899, pp. 77–78, 91–92.

3 W. Corby, *Memoir of Chaplain Life: Three Years Chaplain in the Famous Irish Brigade*, Notre Dame, Scholastic Press, 1894, pp. 141–142. Father Corby would in later years become president of Notre Dame.

4 Thomas Livermore, *Days and Events*, Boston, Houghton, Mifflin Company, 1920, pp. 186–187; D. G. Crotty, *Four Years Campaigning in the Army of the Potomac*, Grand Rapids, MI, Dygert Bros. & Co., 1874, p. 81; Josiah M. Favill, *The Diary of a Young Officer*, Chicago, R. R. Donnelley and Sons, 1909, p. 225; Corby, *Memoirs of Chaplain Life*, pp. 140–142, 144; Conygham, *The Irish Brigade*, pp. 306, 373–374; Mullholland, *116th Regiment Pennsylvania*, p. 82; Wert, *Sword of Lincoln*, p. 228.

5 Charles Francis Adams, *An Autobiography*, Boston, Houghton Mifflin Company, 1916, p. 161.

6 Bigelow, *Chancellorsville*, p. 5. See also *Appleton's Cyclopaedia of American Biography*, vol. 3, pp. 250–251.

7 Meade, *Life and Letters*, vol. 1, p. 319; D. G. Crotty, *Four Years Campaigning in the Army of the Potomac*, p. 81.

8 Smith, *Nineteenth Maine*, p. 29; Stone, *Recollections*, pp. 116–117; *The Papers of Randolph Abbott Shotwell*, J. G. de Roulhac Hamilton, ed., 3 Vols. Raleigh, The North Carolina Historical Society, 1929, vol. 2, pp. 430–431.

9 Palmer, *Second Brigade*, p. 75.

10 Mullholland, *Story of the 116th Regiment Pennsylvania*, p. 53.

11 Wert, *Sword of Linclon*, pp. 210, 202, 204; Conyngham, *Irish Brigade*, pp. 342–343.

12 Conyngham, *Irish Brigade*, pp. 350, 353, 347.

13 Ibid., p. 357.

14 George S. Forbes, *Leaves from a Troopers Diary*, Philadelphia, np, 1869, p. 67.

15 Bruce Catton, *Mr. Lincoln's Army*, Garden City, NY, Doubleday & Company, 1951, 14.

16 Bruce Catton, *Glory Road*, New York, Doubleday & Company, 1952, p. 81.

17 Dawes, *Service with the Sixth Wisconsin*, p. 115; *War Letters of William Thompson Lusk*, New York: private, 1911, pp. 244–245, 256.

18 Alanson A. Haines, *History of the Fifteenth Regiment New Jersey Volunteers*, New York, Jenkins & Thomas, Printers, 1883, p. 37.

19 Rev. A. M. Stewart, *Camp, March and Battlefield or, Three Years and a Half with the Army of the Potomac*, Philadelphia, Jas B. Rodgers, 1865, p. 308.

20 Stone, *Recollections*, pp. 117–118.

21 Edwin C. Bennett, *Musket and Sword: The Army of the Potomac*, Boston, Coburn Publishing Co., 1900, p. 124; Henry R. Pyne, *The History of the First New Jersey Cavalry*, Trenton, J. A. Beecher, Publisher, 1871, p. 147.

22 Bigelow, *Chancellorsville*, p.6.

23 Hitchcock, *War From the Inside*, pp. 195–197; Willard Glazier, *Three Years in the Federal Cavalry*, New York, R. H. Ferguson & Company, 1874, p. 163; John R. Boyle, *Soldiers True*, p. 81; Bennett, *Musket and Sword*, p. 127.

24 James F. Rusling, *Men and Things I Saw in Civil War Times*, New York, The Neale Publishing Company, 1911, pp. 298–300.

25 Quoted in Wert, *Sword of Lincoln*, 227–228.

26 Joseph Keith Newell, *Ours, Annals of the 10th Regiment Massachusetts Volunteers in the Rebellion*, Springfield, MA, C. A. Nichols & Co., 1875, pp. 199–200.

27 Abner Hard, *History of the Eighth Cavalry Regiment Illinois Volunteers During the Great Rebellion*, Aurora, IL, np, 1868, p. 228.

28 Hitchcock, *War From the Inside*, p. 208.

29 Hall, *Sixth New York*, p. 102.

30 Ibid., pp. 101–102; See also Charles I Wickersham, "Personal Recollections of the Cavalry at Chancellorsville," in *War Papers read Before the Commandery of the State of Wisconsin, Military Order of the Loyal Legion of the United States*, Milwaukee, Burdick & Allen, 1903, vol. 3, p. 455.

31 Alfred Pleasonton, "The Successes and Failures of Chancellorsville," in *Battles and Leaders*, vol. 3, pp. 175–176.

32 *O.R.*, Series I vol. XXV, Part 1, p. 774.

33 Longacre, *Cavalry at Gettysburg*, p. 49; Ford, *Adams Letters*, vol. 1, p. 8.

34 New York *Times*, May 4, 1863.

35 Ibid.

36 Ibid.

37 Foster, *Reminiscences*, pp. 39–40.

38 New York *Times*, May 4, 1863.

39 Foster, *Reminiscences*, pp. 40–41.

40 Hall, *Sixth New York*, pp. 101–106.

41 Stephen W. Sears, *Chancellorsville*, Boston, Houghton Mifflin Company, 1996, pp. 190–191; William L. Herrmance, "The Cavalry at Chancellorsville," *Personal Recollections of the War of the Rebellion, New York Commandery of the Military Order of the Loyal Legion of the United States*, New York, G. P Putnam, 1897, p. 227.

42 Hall, *Sixth New York*, p. 107.

43 Quoted in Foster, *Reminiscences*, pp. 42–43.

44 Herrmance, "Cavalry at Chancellorsville," pp. 223–224; Hall, Sixth New York Cavalry, pp. 433, 439, 440.

45 Bruce Catton, *This Hallowed Ground: The Story of the Union Side of the Civil War*, New York, Doubleday & Co., 1955, p. 241.

46 Shelby Foote, *The Civil War: A Narrative, Fredericksburg to Meridian*, New York, Random House, 1963), pp. 282–287; Douglas Southall Freeman, *Lee's Lieutenants: A Study in Command*, Stephen W. Sears, ed., Old Saybrook, CT, 1998, pp. 471–475.

47 *In Memoriam: The Letters of William Wheeler*, private, 1875, p. 387.

48 Shelby Foote, *The Civil War: A Narrative, Fredericksburg to Meridian*, pp. 292–297.

49 *Letters of Richard Tylden Auchmuty: Fifth Corps, Army of the Potomac*, private, 1875, p. 387.
50 Catton, *Glory Road*, p. 208; Emory M. Thomas, *The Confederate Nation, 1861–1865*, New York, Harper & Roe, 1979, p. 217.
51 Pennock Huey, *A True History of the Charge of the Eighth Pennsylvania Cavalry at Chancellorsville*, Philadelphia: Porter & Coates, 1888, pp. 8, 35–36; Wickersham, *Personal Recollections*, p. 460; Edward G. Longacre, *Lincoln's Cavalrymen: A History of the Mounted Forces of the Army of the Potomac*, Mechanicsburg, PA, Stackpole Books, 2000, p. 148.
52 Longacre, Ibid., pp. 148–149.
53 Jennings Cropper Wise, *The Long Arm of Lee, or the History of the Artillery of the Army of Northern Virginia*, 2 Volumes, Lynchburg, VA, J. P Bell Company Inc., 1915, vol. 2, pp. 593–594; Huey, *A True History*, pp. 40, 57, 55, 59, 66.
54 Quoted in Longacre, *Lincoln's Cavalrymen*, p. 149.
55 Hitchcock, *War From the Inside*, p. 222.
56 *In Memoriam … Wheeler*, pp. 396, 402.
57 Ibid., pp. 399–400.
58 Bennett, *Musket and Sword*, p. 131.
59 Rusling, *Men and Things I Saw*, pp. 302–303.
60 Stephen M. Weld,, *War Diary and Letters of Stephen Minot Weld, 1861–1865*, private, 1912, pp. 194–198; Meade, *Life and Letters*, vol. 1, pp. 272–273.
61 Palmer, *Second Brigade*, p. 127.
62 Boyle, *Soldiers True*, pp. 5–6, 100.
63 New York Monuments Commission, *Final Report… Gettysburg*, vol. 2, p. 513.
64 *O. R.*, Ser. I, vol. XXV, Pt. 1, p. 776

Chapter Four

1 Lee, *Recollections and Letters*, p. 84; William Blackford, *War Years with Jeb Stuart*, New York, Charles Scribner's Sons, 1904, p. 212.
2 Heros von Borcke, *Memoirs of the Confederate War for Independence*, 2 Volumes, London, 1866, vol. 2, p. 264.
3 H. B. McClellan, *The Life and Campaigns of Major-General J. E. B. Stuart*, Boston, Houghton, Mifflin Company, 1885, p. 261; George M. Neese, *Three Years in the Confederate Horse Artillery*, New York, The Neale Publishing Company, 1911, p. 167; Blackford, *War Years*, p. 211; von Borcke, *Memoirs*, p. 266.
4 Blackford, *War Years*, Justus Scheibert, *Seven Months in the Rebel States During the North American War, 1863*, Stanley Hoole, ed., Confederate Publishing Co., 1958, p. 86.
5 Blackford, Ibid., pp. 212–213; von Borcke Ibid., pp. 266–267.
6 Starr, *Union Cavalry*, vol. 1 p. 375, note 28.
7 Edward P. Alexander, *Military Memoirs of a Confederate, A Critical Narrative*, New York, Charles Scribner's Sons, 1907, p. 370.
8 *O. R.* Ser. 1, vol. XXVII, Pt. 3, p. 8
9 *O. R.*, Ser. 1, vol. XXVII, Pt. 1, P. 906; Hampton S. Thomas, *Some Personal Reminiscences of Service in the Cavalry of the Army of the Potomac*, Philadelphia, L. R. Hamersly & Co., 1889, p. 9.
10 Tobie. *First Maine Cavalry*, p. 147; Samuel L. Gracey, *Annals of the Sixth Pennsylvania Cavalry*,
11 Hard, *Eighth Illinois*, p. 243.
12 Burton B, Porter, *One of the People, His Own Story*, private, 1902, p. 139.
13 Hard, *Eighth Illinois*, p. 243.

14 Starr, *Union Cavalry*, vol. l. 1, pp. 378-379; *O.R.*, Ser. 1, Vol. XXVII, Pt. 1, p. 1047.
15 NYMM, 8th Regiment Cavalry Bew Paper Clippings
16 Starr, *Union Cavalry*, vol. 1, pp. 378–379.
17 *O. R.*, Ibid., p. 903.
18 *O. R.*, Ser. 1, vol. XXVII, Pt. 3, p. 38.
19 Ibid., pp. 47–48.
20 Ibid., p. 39.
21 *O. R.*, Ser. 1, vol. XXVII, Pt. 1, p. 903.
22 Starr, *Union Cavalry*, vol. 1, p. 381.
23 Quoted in Wert, *Sword of Lincoln*, p. 261.
24 David M. Gregg, "The Second Cavalry Division of the Army of the Potomac in the Gettysburg Campaign," *Pennsylvania Commandery of the Military Order of the Loyal Legion of the United States*, pp. 6–7.
25 Tobie, *First Maine Cavalry*, pp. 148–149, 156.
26 Walter S. Newhall, *A Memoir*, Philadelphia, Sherman, Son & Co., 1864, pp. 104–105.
27 Gregg, "Second Cavalry Division," p. 7.
28 Henry C. Meter, *Civil War Experiences Under Bayard, Gregg, Kilpatrick, Custer, Raulston and Newberry, 1862, 1863, 1864*, New York, G. P. Putnam's Sons, 1911, p. 31.
29 *O. R.*, Ser. 1, vol. XXVII, Pt. 1, pp. 903–908.
30 Gregg, "Second Cavalry Division," p. 7.
31 *O. R.*, Ser. 1, vol. XXVII, Pt. 1, p. 914.
32 Ibid., Pt. 3, pp. 48–49.
33 Ibid., p. 49.
34 F. C. Newhall, "The Battle of Beverly Ford," in *The Annals of War by the Leading Participants North and South*, Philadelphia, The Time Publishing Company, 1879, pp. 145–146; Weld, *Diary and Letters*, p. 213; Meyer, *Civil War Experiences*, p. 31.
35 *O. R.*, Ser. 1, vol. XXVII, Pt. 3, p. 57.
36 Quoted in Longacre, *Cavalry at Gettysburg*. P. 51.
37 Ibid., pp. 90–91, 161.
38 NYMM, 8th Regiment Cavalry Newspaper Clippings
39 *O. R.*, Ser. 1 vol. XXVII, Pt. 3, p. 70.
40 NYMM, 63rd Regiment Infantry Newspaper Clippings
41 Edward P. Tobie, *First Maine Bugle, Reunion at Boston, September 17, 1889*, Boston, First Maine Cavalry Association, 1892, p. 55.
42 Hard, *Eighth Illinois Cavalry*, p. 249.
43 Palmer, *Second Brigade*, p. 165.
44 Ibid., pp. 171, 173, 176.

Chapter Five

1 Robert E. Lee, *Recollections and Letters*, New York: Barnes and Noble, reprint, 2004, p. 84.
2 Quoted in Henry G. Pearson, *James S. Wadsworth, Brevet Major General*, London, John Murry, 1913, p. 203; Augustus C. Buell, *The Cannoneer: Recollections of Service in the Army of the Potomac*, Washington, The National Tribune, 1890, p. 61.
3 James Kidd, *Personal Recollections of a Cavalryman with Custer's Michigan Cavalry in the Civil War*, Ionia, MI, private, 1908, pp. 120–121; Eric J. Wittenberg, ed., Karla Jean Husby, comp., *Under Custer's Command: The Civil War Journal of James Henry Avery*, Washington, Brasset's, 2000, p. 29.

4 Newel Cheney, *History of the Ninth Regiment New York Volunteer Cavalry*, Poland Springs, NY, private, 1901, p. 101.

5 Quoted in Wittenberg, *Under Custer's Command*, p. 29.

6 Hillman A. Hall, William H. Besley, Gilbert G. Wood, comp., *History of the Sixth New York Cavalry, 1861–1865*, Worcester, MA, Blanchard Press, 1908, p. 133.

7 Cheney, *Ninth New York Cavalry*, Ibid; John L. Beveridge, "The First Gun at Gettysburg," in *Military Essays and recollections: Papers Read Before the Commandery of the State of Illinois, Military Order of the Loyal Legion of the United States*, Chicago, A. C. McClung and Company, 1894, vol. 2, p. 88.

8 H. P. Moyer, comp., *History of the Seventeenth Regiment Pennsylvania Volunteer Cavalry*, Lebanon, PA, Sower Printing Co., 1911, p. 396.

9 Comte de Paris, *The Battle of Gettysburg: From the History of the Civil War in America*, Philadelphia, Porter and Coates, 1886, p. 77.

10 Abner Hard, *History of the Eighth Cavalry Regiment Illinois Volunteers During the Great Rebellion*, Aurora, IL np, 1868, p. 255.

11 Hall, *History of the Sixth New York*, p. 133.

12 Mark M. Boater, *The Civil War Dictionary*, New York, David McKay Company, 1959, p. 97; Edward G. Longacre, *General John Buford: A Military Biography*, Conshohocken, PA, Combined Books, 1995, p. 97; Ray Allen Billlington, *The Far Western Frontier, 1830–1860*, New York, Harper and Row, 1956, p. 214.

13 David Heidler and Jeanne Heidler, eds., *The Encyclopedia of the Civil War*, Santa Barbara, 2000, p. 3101; Boatner, *Civil War Dictionary*, p. 97; Longacre, *John Buford*, p. 214.

14 U.S. War Department, *Official Record of the Union and Confederate Armies in the War of Rebellion*, 128 Volumes, Washington, Government Printing Office, 1888–1901, Series 1, vol. XXVII, Part 1, p. 926. Hereinafter cited as *O. R.* Intelligence report later revised as army headquarters changed this from two regiments to one company of North Carolina infantry. See Edwin C. Fishel, *The Secret War for the Union: The Untold Story of Military Intelligence in the Civil War*, Boston, Houghton Mifflin Company, 1996, p. 506.

15 Allen C. Guelzo, *Gettysburg, The Last Invasion*, New York, Alfred A. Knopf, 2013, p. 124.

16 Buell, *The Cannoneer*, pp. 61–62.

17 James Stewart, "Battery B: Fourth United States Artillery at Gettysburg," in Sketchers of War History, 1861–1865, *Papers Prepared for the Ohio Commandery of the Military Order of the Loyal Legion of the United States*, Cincinnati, The Robert Clark Company, 1895, vol. 4, p. 183.

18 Frank Moore, ed., *The Rebellion Record: A Diary of American Events*, New York, D. Van Nostrand Publisher, 1864, vol. 7, p. 325.

19 Quotes in Samuel Carter III, *The Last Cavaliers: Confederate and Union Cavalry in the Civil War*, New York, St. Martin's Press, 1979, p. 163.

20 Moxley Sorrel, *Recollections of a Confederate Staff Officer*, New York, The Neale Publishing Company, 1905, 179.

21 George M. Neese, *Three Years in the Confederate Horse Artillery*, New York, The Neale Publishing Company, 1911, pp. 186–187.

22 Richard Wheeler, *Witness to Gettysburg*, New York, Harper and Row, 1987, 82.

23 Luther W. Hopkins, *From Bull Run to Appomattox, A Boy's View*. Baltimore, Fleet-McGinley, 1908, p. 109.

24 Herman Shuricht, "Jenkins' Brigade in the Gettysburg Campaign—Extracts from the Diary of Lieutenant Herman Shuricht, 14th Virginia Cavalry," *Southern Historical Society Papers*, vol. 14, Richmond, Published by the Society, 1896, p. 340. At this time the peace party as spoken of here was that wing of the Democratic Party in favor of a negotiated settlement and an end to the fighting.

25 Tillie Pierce Alleman, *At Gettysburg, or What a Girl Saw and Heard of the Battle*, private, 1888, p. 21; M. Jacobs, *Notes on the Rebel Invasion of Maryland and Pennsylvania*, Philadelphia, J. B. Lippincott & Co., 1864, pp. 15–16.

26 Alleman, *At Gettysburg*, p. 22; Samuel P. Bates, *The Battle of Gettysburg*, Philadelphia, T. H. Davis & Co., 1875, pp. 29–30; Jacobs, *Notes on the Rebel Invasion*, p. 71.

27 Walter S. Newhall. *A Memoir*, Philadelphia: Sherman, Son & Co., 1864, p. 106.

28 Moore, *Rebellion Record*, vol. 7, p. 325.

29 *O. R.*, Ser. 1, vol. XXVII, Pt. 3, pp. 370, 377; James H. Kidd, *Personal Recollections*, pp. 120–121; Wittenberg, *Under Custer's Command*, p. 29.

30 John Day Smith, *The History of the Nineteenth Regiment Maine Volunteer Infantry, 1863–1865*, Minneapolis, The Great Western Printing Company, 1909, p. 77.

31 Charles Francis Adams, *Charles Francis Adams, 1836–1915, An Autobiography*, Boston: Houghton Mifflin Company, 1915), p. 157.

32 Ibid., p. 73.

33 Bliss Perry, *The Letters of Henry Lee Higginson*, Boston, The Atlantic Monthly Press, 1921, pp. 194, 201.

34 D. G. Crotty, *Three Years Campaigning with the Army of the Potomac*, Grand Rapids, MI, Dygert & Co., 1874, pp. 88–90,

35 *O. R.*, Ser. 1, vol. XXVII, Pt 2, p. 421.

36 *O. R.*, Ser. 1, vol. XXVII, Pt. 1, p. 992; Vincent L. Burns, *The Fifth New York Cavalry in the Civil War*, Jefferson, NC, McFarland, 2014, pp. 80–81.

37 Louis G. Young, "Pettigrew's Brigade at Gettysburg, July 1–3, 1863," in *Histories of Several Regiments and Battalion from North Carolina in the Civil Warm 1861–1865*, Walter Clark, ed., vol. 5, Goldsboro, NY, Nash Brothers, 1907, 115. The Knights of the Golden Circle was a loose confederation opposed to freeing slaves as a war measure and the supposed suppression of civil liberties under the Lincoln administration. Before the war the Knights had advocated American expansion into Mexico and the Caribbean.

38 Young, Ibid., p. 115.

39 Young, Ibid., p. 116; Noah Andre Trudeau, *Gettysburg: A Testing of Courage*, New York, Harper Collins, 2002, pp. 128–132; Stephen W. Sears, *Gettysburg*, Boston, Houghton, Mifflin Company, 2003, p. 129.

40 William L. Herrmance, "The Cavalry at Gettysburg," in *Personal Recollections of the War of Rebellion: Addresses Delivered Before the Commandery of the State of New York Military Order of the Loyal Legion of the United States*, New York, G. P. Putnam's Sons, 1907, p. 199.

41 Alleman, *At Gettysburg*, p. 28.

42 John L. Beveridge, "First Gun at Gettysburg," in *Military Essays and Recollections: Papers Read Before the Commandery of the State of Illinois, Military Order of the Loyal Legion of the United States*, vol. 2, Chicago, A. C. McClung and Company, 1894, p. 90.

43 *O. R.*, Ser. 1, vol. XXVII, Pt. 1, p. 923.

44 Joseph G. Rosengarten, *William Reynolds, John Fulton Reynolds, A Memoir*, Philadelphia, J. B. Lippincott & Co., 1880), p. 17.

45 Quoted in Edwin B. Coddington, *The Gettysburg Campaign: A Study in Command*, New York, Charles Scribner's Sons, 1968, p. 236.

46 Guelzo, *Gettysburg*, pp. 126–127.

47 Edward G. Longacre, *The Cavalry at Gettysburg: A Tactical Study of Mounted Operations During the Civil War's Pivotal Campaign, 9 June–14 July, 1863*, Lincoln, University of Nebraska Press, 1986, p. 183; Trudeau, *Gettysburg*, pp. 156–160; Rosengarten, *Reynolds*, p. 17.

48 Cheney, *Ninth New York*, pp. 105–106.

49 *O. R.*, Ibid., pp. 923–924.

50 Ibid., pp. 923–924.

51 Quoted in Trudeau, *Gettysburg*, pp. 141, 580–583, 591; Bates, *Gettysburg*, p. 55.

52 Beveridge, "The First Gun at Gettysburg," p. 90.

53 Harry W. Pfanz, *Gettysburg: The First Day*, Chapel Hill, University of North Carolina Press, 2001, p. 70; Pfanz here is citing Allen Nevins, ed., *A Diary of Battle: The Personal Journal of Colonel Charles S. Wainwright*, New York, Harcourt, Brace and World, 1962, p. 1962; Sidney G. Cooke, "The First Day at Gettysburg," in *War Talk in Kansas: Papers read Before the Kansas Commandery of the Military Order of the Loyal Legion of the United States*, Kansas City, Franklin Hudson Publishing Co., 1906, p. 278.

54 *O. R.,* Ibid, p. 922.

55 *O. R.*, Ser. 1, vol. XXVII, Pt. 3, p. 414.

56 Benjamin F. Clark, *History of the Twelfth Massachusetts Volunteers*, Boston, Twelfth Regiment Association, 1882, p. 104; Trudeau, *Gettysburg*, pp. 566–567.

57 Henry Heth, "Letter of 1877," Rev. J. William Jones, ed., *Southern Historical Society Papers*, vol 4, Richmond, 1877, pp. 151ff.

58 Henry G. Pearson, *James S. Wadsworth, Brevet Major-General*, London, John Murry,1913, pp. 200–201.

59 Abner Doubleday, *Chancellorsville and Gettysburg*, New York: Charles Scribner's Sons, 1912, p. 126.

60 *In Memoriam: The Letters of William Wheeler*, private, 1875, p. 364.

61 George A. Bruce, *The Twentieth Regiment Massachusetts Volunteer Infantry, 1861–1865*, Boston, Houghton, Mifflin and Company, 1906, p. 181.

62 James Longstreet, *From Bull Run to Appomattox: Memoirs of the Civil War in America*, Philadelphia, J. B. Lippincott Company, 1896, 291.

63 Robert Tilney, *Life in the Army: Three and a Half Years in the Fifth Corps, Army of the Potomac, 1862–1865*, Philadelphia, Ferris and Leach, 1912, p. 28.

64 Bruce, *The Twentieth Regiment*, p. 161.

65 Quoted in Jeffry D. Wert, *Sword of Lincoln: The Army of the Potomac*, New York, Simon & Schuster, 2005, p. 90.

66 Joseph Keith Newell, *Ours, Annals of the 10th Regiment Massachusetts Volunteers in the Rebellion*, Springfield, MA, C. A. Nichols & Co., 1875, p. 91.

67 Quoted in Chapman Biddle, *The First Day of the Battle of Gettysburg, an Address … Historical Society of Pennsylvania*, Philadelphia, J. B. Lippincott & Co., 1880, p. 2.

68 Heth, "Letter of 1877," *SHSP*, vol. 4, p. 153; Hopkins, *From Bull Run to Appomattox*, p. 110.

69 Douglas Southall Freeman, *Lee: An Abridgement in One Volume of the Four Volume R. E. Lee*, Richard Harwell, ed., New York, Charles Scribner's Sons, 1961, p. 308.

70 Edward P. Alexander, *Military Memoirs of a Confederate: A Critical Narrative*, New York, Charles Scribner's Sons, 1907, p. 322, note 1.

71 Heth, "Letter of 1877," *SHSP*, vol. 4, p. 153.

72 Ibid., p. 157.

73 Young, "Pettigrew's Brigade at Gettysburg," p. 116.

74 Young, Ibid., pp. 116–117; Trudeau, *Gettysburg*, pp. 140–141; Heth, "Letter of 1877," *SHSP*, vol. 4, p. 157.

75 Young, Ibid., p. 117.

76 Clifton Johnson, *Battlefield Adventures: The Stories of the Conflict in Some of the Most Notable Battles of the Civil War*, Boston, Houghton, Mifflin Co., 1915, pp. 193–194.

77 Heth, "Letter of 1877," *SHSP*, Vol. 4, p. 157.

Chapter Six

1 Freeman, *Lee, Abridgement*, p. 322; Edwin C. Bennett, *Musket and Sword: The Army of the Potomac*, Boston, Coburn Publishing Co., 1900, p. 139; John Inglis, Ninth New York Cavalry Diary, July 2, 1863, New York State Library.

2 Quoted in Hall, *Sixth New York*, p. 136; Longacre, *Cavalry at Gettysburg*, p. 184.

3 Freeman, *Lee, Abridged*, pp. 321–322.

4 Ibid., p. 322.

5 Heth, "Letter of 1877," *SHSP*, vol. 4, p. 158.

6 Freeman, *Lee, Abridged*, pp. 322–322.

7 *O. R.*, Ser. 1, vol. XXVII, Pt. 1, p. 934.

8 Longacre, *Cavalry at Gettysburg*, pp. 186–187; Longacre, *John Buford*, p. 170.

9 Quoted in Trudeau, *Gettysburg*, pp. 162–164.

10 H. S. Huidekoper, *A Short Story of the First Day's Fight at Gettysburg*, Philadelphia, Bicker Printing, 1906, pp. 4–5. The author of this short work was lieutenant colonel of the 150th Pennsylvania Infantry and would be wounded later in the day but remained on the field leading the regiment. See Trudeau, *Gettysburg*, pp. 216–217.

11 Samuel P. Bates, *The Battle of Gettysburg*, Philadelphia, T. H. Davis & Co., 1875, p. 55. Here Bayes is quoting Lt. Aaron Jerome, Buford's signal officer stationed in the seminary's capola. This version was originally written into the account by John W. De Peyster in his *Decisive Conflicts of the Late Civil War*, New York, MacDonald & Co., 1867; Stephen M Weld, *War Diary and Letters of Stephen Minot Weld*, private, 1912, p. 229.

12 Beveridge, "The First Gun at Gettysburg," pp. 88–89.

13 Trudeau, *Gettysburg*, p. 172, quoting De Peyster, *Decisive Conflicts*, 153; See also Bates, *Gettysburg*, 60.

14 William L. Herrmance, "The Cavalry at Gettysburg," *Personal Recollections*, New York MOLLUS, vol. 3, p. 201.

15 Weld, *War Diary*. pp. 229–232.

16 Henry Edwin Tremain, *Two Days of War: A Gettysburg Narrative and Other Excursions*, New York, Bonnell, Silver and Bowers, 1905, p. 155; Weld, *War Diary*, pp. 229–232; Comte de Paris, *The Battle of Gettysburg: From the History of the Civil War in America*, 1886. The account gives credit to the fight at Gettysburg to the cavalry general. "It was Buford who selected the battlefield," p. 95; Guelzo, *Gettysburg*, p. 124.

17 Oliver Otis Howard, *Autobiography of Oliver Otis Howard, Major-General United States Army*, New York, The Baker and Taylor Company, 1908, pp. 126–127.

18 *O. R.*, Ser. 1, vol. XXVII, Pt. 1, p. 924; Allenman, *At Gettysburg*, p. 34.

19 Stewart, "Battery B," p. 184.

20 Herrmance, "Cavalry at Gettysburg," p. 200.

21 Stewart, "Battery B," p. 185.

22 *O. R.*, Ser. 1, vol. XXVII, Pt. 1, pp. 924–925.

23 Trudeau, *Gettysburg*, p. 207.

24 Longacre, *Cavalry at Gettysburg*, pp. 191–192.

25 Edward G. Longacre, *Lincoln's Cavalrymen: A History of the Mounted Forces of the Army of the Potomac*, Mechanicsburg, PA, Stackpole Books, 2000, pp. 181–189.

26 *O. R.*, Ser. I, vol. XXVII, Pt. 1, pp. 934–935.

27 Ibid., p. 927.

28 Ibid., p. 938.

29 Hall, *Sixth New York Cavalry*, p. 138.
30 Ibid., p. 139.
31 Ibid., p. 140.
32 Ibid., p. 141.
33 Ibid.
34 Ibid., p. 142.
35 Ibid.
36 Ibid., pp. 939, 1021; NYMM, 8th Regiment Cavalry, Newspaper Clippings.
37 Hall, *Sixth New York Cavalry*, pp. 142–143.
38 Ibid., p. 143.
39 Cheney, *Ninth Regiment New York Volunteers*, p. 115.
40 Quoted in Wert, *Sword of Lincoln*, p. 286.
41 Trudeau, *Gettysburg*, p. 306.
42 Trudeau, Ibid. p. 306; *O. R.*. Ser. 1, vol. XXVII, Pt. 2, p. 490.
43 *O. R.*, Ser. 1, Vol. XXVII, Pt. 1, pp, 1058–1059.
44 William E. Doster, *Lincoln and Episodes of the Civil War*, New York, G. P. Putnam, 1915, pp. 216–217.
45 U.S. Congress, 2nd Session, 38th Congress, *Report of the Joint Committee on the War*, Washington, Government Printing Office, 1865, p. 359; Longacre, *Cavalry at Gettysburg*, pp. 205–206; "The Meade-Sickles Controversy, Reply by Daniel E. Sickles," in Robert Underwood Johnson and Clarence Clough Buell, eds., *Battles and Leaders of the Civil War*, 4 Volumes, New York, The Century Co., 1887, vol. 3, p. 415.
46 Frank Haskell, *The Battle of Gettysburg*, Madison, WI, Wisconsin Historical Commission, 1908, p.154
47 Johnson, *Battleground Adventures*, pp. 195–196.
48 Cheney, *Ninth Regiment New York Volunteers*, p. 115.
49 Haskell, *Gettysburg*, p. 40.
50 Ibid., p. 42.
51 W. Corby, *Memoirs of Chaplin Life: Three Years in the Famous Irish Brigade*, Notre Dame, Scholastic Press, 1894, p. 182.
52 Ibid., p. 187.
53 Ibid., pp. 182–184.
54 George Clark, *A Glance Backward, or Some Events in the Past History of My Life*, Houston, Press of Rein and Sons, nd, pp. 36–37.
55 Arabella M. Williston, *Disaster, Struggle, Triumph: The Adventures of 1000 Boys in Blue*, Albany, Historical Committee of the Regiment, 1870, 178.
56 Bruce Catton, *This Hallowed Ground: The Story of the Union Side of the Civil War*, New York, Doubleday & Co., 1955, pp. 256–257.
57 *The Papers of Randolph Abbott Shotwell*, G. de Roulhac Hamilton, ed., 3 Volumes, Raleigh, The North Carolina Historical Society, 1929, Vol. 1, p. 501, vol. 2, pp. 13–14.

Chapter Seven

1 William Faulkner, *Intruder in the Dust*, New York, Random House, 1948, p. 194.
2 Frank A. Haskell, *The Battle of Gettysburg*, Madison: Wisconsin Historical Commission, 1908, pp. 78–79, 88, 90–92, 94.
3 Ibid., p. 93.
4 Trudeau, *Gettysburg*, pp. 412, 559; Haskell, *Gettysburg*, pp. 90, 183–184.

5   Mullholland, *The Story of the 116th Regiment Pennsylvania Infantry*, pp. 411–412.
6   Haskell, *Gettysburg*, p. 79.
7   Palmer, *Second Brigade*, p. 193.
8   Miller, *Drum Taps*, p. 223.
9   Haskell, Gettysburg, p. 94; Samuel Fiske, *Mr. Dunn Browne's Experiences in the Army*, Boston, Nichols and Noyes, 1866, p. 188; Haskell, *Gettysburg*, pp. 107–108, 111; George Clark, *A Glance Backward, or Some events in the Past History of My Life*, Houston, Press of Rein & Sons, nd, p. 39.
10   Thomas W. Hyde, *Following the Greek Cross or, Memoirs of the Sixth Corps*, Boston, Houghton Mifflin Company, 1894, pp. 155–156.
11   *O. R.*, Series, 1, vol. XXVII, Pt. 1, p. 454; Edmund Rice, "Repelling Lee's Last Blow at Gettysburg," in *Battles and Leaders* vol. 3, pp. 387–388; Smith, *History of the Nineteenth Regiment Massachusetts*, p. 81.
12   Fiske, *Browne's Experiences*, pp. 188–189.
13   Haskell, *Gettysburg*, p. 113.
14   Ibid., pp. 115–116.
15   Clark, *A Glance Backward*, p. 39.
16   Quoted in Stephen W. Sears, *Gettysburg*, Boston, Houghton Mifflin Company, 2003, p. 418.
17   Quoted in Trudeau, *Gettysburg*, pp. 487–488; Franklin Sawyer, *A Military History of the 8th Regiment Ohio Vol. Inf'y*, Cleveland, Fairbanks & Co., Printer, 1881, p. 131; Wayland F. Dunaway, *Reminiscences of a Rebel*, New York, The Neale Publishing Company, 1913, p. 93.
18   Trudeau, *Gettysburg*, p. 591.
19   Palmer, *Second Brigade*, p. 195.
20   Ibid., pp. 196, 205.
21   Report of General Hayes, *O. R.*, Ser. I vol. XXVII, p. 1, p. 454.
22   Palmer, *Second Brigade*, pp. 195–197, 203; Trudeau, *Gettysburg*, p. 584.
23   Quoted in Geoffrey C. Ward, *The Civil War: An Illustrated History*, New York, Alfred A. Knopf, Inc., 1990, p. 263.
24   NYMM, 150th Regiment Infantry Newspapers Clippings.
25   Ibid.
26   Ibid.
27   George G. Benedict, *Army Life in Virginia*, Burlington, Free Press Association, p. 17.
28   McPherson, *Battle Cry*, p. 662; Haskell, *Gettysburg*, p. 148.
29   Davis, *Three Years in the Army*, pp. 237–238.
30   Letters of Calvin A. Haynes, One Hundred and Twenty-fifth New York Infantry. New York State Library.
31   Charles E. Benton, *As Seen from the Ranks: A Boy in the Civil War*, New York: G. R. Putnam's Sons 1902, p. 57; Dawes, *Service with the Sixth Wisconsin*, pp. 161–162.
32   Eric J, Wittenberg, *Gettysburg's Forgotten Cavalry Actions: Farnsworth's Charge South Cavalry Field, and the Battle of Fairfield, July 3, 1863*, New York:,Saves Beatie, Rev. ed., 2011. All the details and sources concerning the cavalry actions of Jul 3 can be found in this work.
33   *O.R.*, Ser. 1, vol. XXVII, Pt. 1, p. 75.
34   Charles E. Davis, *Three Years in the Army: The Story of the Thirteenth Massachusetts Volunteers, July 16, 1861, to August 1, 1864*, Boston, Estes and Laurial, 1894, p. 241; Regis DeTrobriand, *Four Years with the Army of the Potomac*, Boston, Ticknor and Company, 1889, p. 514.
35   New York Monuments Commission for the Battlefields of Gettysburg and Chattanooga, *Final Report on the Battle of Gettysburg*, Albany: J. B. Lyon *In Memoriam: The Letters of William Wheeler*, pp. 417–418.

36 Company, 1902, vol. 1, pp. 206, 236, 239.

37 Ibid, p. 237.

38 Ibid.

Chapter Eight

1   Quoted in Allen C. Guelzo, *Gettysburg: The Last Invasion*, New York, Alfred A. Knopf, 2013, p. 447; *O. R.*, Ser. 1, vol. XXVII, Pt, 1. pp. 92, 93.

2   *Letters of Richard Tylden Auchmuty: Fifth Corps, Army of the Potomac*, private, nd, pp. 94, 96, 102.

3   John D. Imboden, "The Confederate Retreat from Gettysburg," in *Battles and Leaders in the Civil War*, vol. 3, pp. 421–423.

4   Imboden, Ibid., pp. 422–425. See also Henry Norton, *Deeds of Daring, or History of the Eighth New York Volunteer Cavalry*, Ithaca, NY, private, 1889, pp. 70–71 and Newel Cheney, *History of the Ninth Regiment New York Volunteer Cavalry, 1861–1865*, Poland Spring, NY, private, 1901, p. 117.

5   NYMM, 8th Regiment Cavalry Newspaper Clipping.

6   Norton, *Deeds of Daring*, pp. 70–71.

7   Cheney, *History of the Ninth Regiment*, pp. 115–117; Eric J. Wittenberg, J. David Petruzzi, Michael F. Nugent *One Continuous Fight: The Retreat from Gettysburg and the Pursuit of Lee's Army of Northern Virginia, July 4–14, 1863*, New York: Savas Beatie, 2008, pp. 96–97.

8   Quoted in Wittenberg, Ibid., pp. 97–98. See also the *National Tribune*, March 6, 1884, and April 4, 1884, *Final Report on the Battle of Gettysburg*, vol. 3, p. 943.

9   NYMM, 8th Regiment Cavalry Newspapers Clippings.

10 Imboden, "The Confederate Retreat from Gettysburg," p. 429.

11 Wittenberg, *One Continuous Fight*, p. 146.

12 Imboden, "The Confederate Retreat from Gettysburg," pp. 426–427; Joseph Benjamin Polley, *A Soldier's Letters to the Charming Nellie*, New York, The Neale Publishing Company, 1908, pp. 135–136.

13 Cheney, *History of the Ninth Regiment*, p. 118.

14 *O. R.*, Ser. I, vol. XXVII, Pt. 1, pp. 943–944.

15 Ibid., p. 935.

16 Imboden, "The Confederate Retreat from Gettysburg," pp. 427–429.

17 William L. Herrmance, "The Cavalry at Gettysburg," in *Personal Recollections of the War of Rebellion: Address Delivered Before the Commandery of the State of New York, Military Order of the Loyal Legion of the United States*, New York, G. P. Putnam, 1907, vol. 3, p. 198.

18 *O. R.*, Ser. I, vol. XXVII, PT. 1, pp. 81–83.

19 Meade, *Life and Letters*, vol. 2, pp. 133–134; Dawes, *Service with the Sixth Wisconsin*, p. 192.

20 *O. R.*, Ser. 1, vol. XXVII, Pt. 1, p. 84.

21 NYMM, 8th Regiment Cavalry Newspaper Clippings.

22 *O. R.*, Ibld., pp. 91–92.

23 Ibid., pp. 91–92.

24 NYMM, 8th Regiment Cavalry Newspaper Clippings.

25 Guelzo, *Gettysburg*, pp. 438–439; Wittenberg, *One Continuous Fight*, p. 242; Longacre, *The Cavalry at Gettysburg*, p. 255.

26 Luther Hopkins, *From Bull Run to Appomattox: A Boy's View*, Baltimore, Fleet-McGinley Co., 1908, p. 108; Neese, *Three Years in the Confederate Horse Artillery*, p. 198.

27 NYMM, 6th Regiment Cavalry Newspaper Clippings.

28 Buell, Cannoneer, p. 123.
29 Quoted in Sears, *Gettysburg*, p. 495.
30 NYMM. 8th Regiment Cavalry Newspaper Clippings.
31 Fiske, *Mr. Dunn Browne's Experiences*, p. 210.
32 Scheibert, *Seven Months in the Rebel States*, p. 122.
33 *O. R.*, Ser. 1, vol. XXVII, Pt. 1, pp. 91–93.
34 *The Correspondence of John Sedgwick, Major General*, 2 Volumes, private, 1902, vol. 2, p. 135.
35 *O. R.*, Ibid, p. 936.
36 Hard, *Eighth Illinois Cavalry*, p. 265.
37 *O. R.*, Ibis., pp. 936–937; Dunaway, *Reminiscences of a Rebel*, p. 102.
38 Rusling, *Men and Things I Saw*, pp. 12–14.
39 Meade, *Life and Letters*, vol. 2, p. 133.
40 Ibid., p. 135.
41 Randolf H. McKim, *A Soldier's Recollections*, New York, Longman, Green, and Co., 1910, pp. 181–182.

Chapter Nine

1   Meade, *Life and Letters*, vol. 2, p. 141; Lee, *Recollections and Letters*, p. 98.
2   NYMM, 2nd Regiment Cavalry Newspaper Clippings.
3   Meade, *Life and Letters*, vol. 2, p. 141.
4   NYMM, 102nd Regiment Infantry Newspapers Clippings.
5   *In Memoriam: The Letters of William Wheeler*, p. 423.
6   Wert, *Sword of Lincoln*, p. 318; De Trobriand, *Four Years with the Army of the Potomac*, pp. 544–545.
7   Freeman, *Letters from Two Brothers*, pp. 88–89.
8   Ibid., p. 90.
9   Stewart, *Camp, March, and Battlefield*, p. 365; Hyde, *Following the Greek Cross*, p. 176.
10 Dawes, *Service with the Sixth Wisconsin*, pp. 227–230.
11 Robert Goldthwaite Carter, *Four Brothers in Blue: Sunshine and Shadows of the War of the Rebellion*, Washington, Press of Gibson Bros, Inc., 1913, p. 375.
12 Meade, *Life and Letters*, vol. 2, pp. 156, 158–159.
13 Oliver Willcox Norton, *The Attack and Defense of Little Round Top, Gettysburg, July 2, 1863*, New York, The Neale Publishing Company, 1913, p. 328.
14 Livermore, *Days and Events*, p. 178; Pyne, *History of the First New Jersey Cavalry*, pp. 210–211.
15 Tyler, *Recollections*, p. 132.
16 Livermore, *Days and Events*, p. 285.
17 Pyne, *History of the First New Jersey*, pp. 212, 214.
18 Tyler, *Recollections* p. 125.
19 George D. Benedict to Mrs. Sarah Benedict. January 26, 1864, George D, Benedict Papers, Southern Historical Collection, Louis Round Wilson Special Collections Library, University of North Carolina, Wilson Library, Chapel Hill.
20 Livermore, *Days and Events*, p. 182.
21 Robert S. Robertson, "From the Wilderness to Spotsylvania," in *Sketches of War, 1861–1865, Papers Read Before the Ohio Commandery of the Military Order of the Loyal Legion of the United States*, Cincinnati, Robert Clark & Co., 1888, vol. 1, p. 253.

22 Warren Lee Goss, *Recollections of a Private: A Story of the Army of the* Potomac, New York, Thomas Y. Crowell & Co., 1890, p. 256; Porter, *One of the People*, pp. 149–150.

23 Pyne, *History of the First New Jersey*, pp. 311, 212–213.

24 Charles E. Davis, *Three Years in the Army*, p. 303; Wert, *Sword of Lincoln*, p. 323; Quoted in Bruce Catton, *A Stillness at Appomattox*, New York, Doubleday, 1953, pp. 395–396, note 26.

25 Henry N. Blake, *Three Years in the Army of the Potomac*, Boston, Lee and Shepard, 1865, pp. 272, 269; Davis, *Three Years in the Army*, p. 302.

26 *O. R.*, Ser. 1, vol. XXXIII, Pt. 1, p. 553.

27 George R. Agassiz, ed., *Meade's Headquarters, 1863–1864: Letters of Colonel Theodore Lyman From the Wilderness to Appomattox*, Boston, Massachusetts Historical Society, 1922, pp. viii, ix.

28 Ibid., pp. 1–2.

29 Ibis., p. 73.

30 Ibid., pp. 76–77.

31 Kidd, *Personal Recollections*, p. 234.

32 Agassiz, *Meade's Headquarters*, pp. 74–75.

33 Josiah M. Favill, *The Diary of a Young Officer*, Chicago, R. R. Donnelley & Sons, 1909, p. 282.

34 Hamilton Gay Howard, *Civil War Echoes, Character Sketches and States Rights*, Washington, Howard Publishing Co., 1907, p. 214.

35 Ibid., pp. 221–222.

36 Robertson, "From the Wilderness to Spotsylvania," pp. 254–255.

37 Meade, *Life and Letters*, vol. 2, p. 167.

38 Favill, *Diary of a Young Officer*, p. 280.

39 Joseph R. C. Ward, *History of the One Hundred and Sixth Regiment Pennsylvania Volunteers, 2d Brigade, 2d Division, 2d Corps*, Philadelphia, F. McManus, Jr. & Co., 1906, p. 233.

40 Septima M. Collis, *A Woman's War Record, 1861–1865*, New York, G. P. Putnam's Sons, 1889, pp. 34–35.

41 Agassiz, *Meade's Headquarters*, pp. 74–75.

42 Howard, *Civil War Echoes*, p. 214.

43 Fiske, *Mr. Dunn Browne's Experiences*, p. 355.

44 Stephen W. Sears, *Controversies and Commanders: Dispatches from the Army of the Potomac*, Boston, Houghton Mifflin Company, 1999, pp. 246–248.

45 Meade, *Life and Letters*, vol. 2, pp. 190–191 Andrew A. Humphreys, *The Virginia Campaign of '64 and '65*, New York, Charles Scribner's Sons, 1883, p. 75.

46 Samuel H. Merrill, *The Campaigns of the First Mane and First District of Columbia Cavalry*, Portland, Bailey & Noyes, 1866, pp. 176–177; *O. R.*, Series 1, vol. XXX, Pt. 1, p. 185.

47 Quotes in Sears, *Controversies*, p. 244. Here Sears is quoting from the diary of General Marsena Patrick the army's Provost Marshal that was published in 1964.

48 Martin T. McMahon, "From Gettysburg to the Coming of Grant," in *Battles and Leaders of the Civil War*, vol. 4, pp. 91–93.

49 Frederick Whittaker, *A Complete Life of Gen. George A. Custer*, New York, Sheldon and Company, 1876, pp. 220–221; T. J. Stiles, *Custer's Trials, A Life on the Frontier of a New America*, New York, Alfred A. Knopf, 2015, pp. 160–162.

50 Stiles, *Custer's* Trials, Ibid., pp. 160–161.

51 Kidd, *Personal Recollections*, pp. 261, 262, 263–264.

52 Ibid., p. 262.

53 Ibid., p. 263–264.

54 NYMM, 8th Regiment Cavalry, Newspaper Clippings.

55 Ibid.

Chapter Ten

1   Favill, *Diary of a Young Officer*, p. 282; Neese, *Three Years in the Confederate Horse Artillery*, p. 258; Quoted in Tobie, *History of the First Maine Cavalry*, p. 251; Quoted in Wert, *Sword of Lincoln*, p. 332.

2   Favill, *Diary of a Young Officer*, p. 282.

3   Corby, *Memoirs of Chaplin Life*, pp. 223–224.

4   John G. B. Adams, *Reminiscences of the Nineteenth Massachusetts Regiment*, Boston, Wright & Potter Printing, 1899, p. 84.

5   Corby, *Memoirs of Chaplin Life*, pp. 220–221.

6   Ibid., pp. 223–228.

7   Richard E. Beaudry, *War Journal of Louis N. Beaudry, Fifth New York Cavalry: The Diary of a Union Chaplain Commencing February 16, 1863*, Jefferson, NC, McFarland & Company, Publishers, 1996, p. 108. The spelling of the Chaplain's name is consistent with how he spelled it at the time.

8   Ibid., pp. 107, 109.

9   Adams, *Reminiscences of the Nineteenth* Massachusetts, pp. 84–86.

10   Agassiz, *Meade's Headquarters*, p. 84; David W. Lowe, ed., *Meade's Army: The Private Notebooks of Lt. Col. Theodore Lyman*, Kent, OH, Kent State University Press, 2007, p. 115.

11   Frank Wilkeson, *Recollections of a Private Soldier in the Army of the Potomac*, New York, G. P. Putnam's Sons, 1887, p. 42; Morris Schaff, *The Battle of the Wilderness*, Boston, Houghton Mifflin Company, 1910, p. 84.

12   Peter S. Michie, *The Life and Letters of Emory Upton*, private, 1886, p. 89.

13   Quoted in Gordon C. Rhea, *The Battles of Spotsylvania Court House and the Road to Yellow Tavern, May 7–12, 1864*, Baton Rouge, Louisiana State University Press, 1997, p. 163.

14   Michie, *Life and Letters of Emory Upton*, pp. 88–89, 108.

15   Alanson A. Haines, *History of the Fifteenth Regiment New Jersey Volunteers*, New York, Jenkins & Thomas, Printers, 1883, p. 140.

16   Wert, *Sword of Lincoln*, pp. 252, 202, 342.

17   Robert Goldthwaite Carter, *Four Brothers in Blue: Sunshine and Shadows of the War of the Rebellion*, Washington, The Press of Gibson Bros., Inc., 1917, p. 388.

18   Noble Preston, *History of the Tenth Regiment of Cavalry, New York State Volunteers, August 1861 to August, 1865*, New York, D. Appleton, 1892, pp. 169–170.

19   Neese, *Three Years in the Confederate Horse Artillery*, p. 261.

20   Stephen M. Weld, ed., *War Diary and Letters of Stephen Minot Weld*, private, 1912, pp. 285, 287.

21   Neese, *Three Years in the Confederate Horse Artillery*, pp. 261, 262.

22   Tyler, *Recollections*, p. 158.

23   Wilkeson, *Recollections*, p. 37; Buell, *Cannoneer*, p. 156; Favill, *Diary of a Young Officer*, p. 286; Tobie, *History of the First Maine Cavalry*, p. 247; Bennett, *Musket and Sword*, 198–200; Ford, *Adams Letters*, vol. 2, p. 128; Stanton P. Allen, *Down in Dixie: Life in a Cavalry Regiment in the War Days from the Wilderness to Appomattox*, Boston, D. Lathrop Company, 1893, p. 191; Quoted in Brooks D. Simpson, "Great Expectations," in Gary W. Gallagher, ed., *The Wilderness Campaign*, Chapel Hill, University of North Carolina Press, 1997, p. 9.

24   Tyler, *Recollections*, pp. 137–138.

25   Hyde, *Following the Greek Cross*, p.180.

26   Quoted in Gary W. Gallagher, "Our Hearts Are Full of Hope: The Army of Northern Virginia in the Spring of 1864," in Gary W. Gallagher, ed., *This Wilderness Campaign*, Chapel Hill, University of North Carolina Press, 1997, pp. 50–51.

27   Edward P. Alexander, *Military Memoirs of a Confederate*, p. 364.

28 Agassiz, *Meade's Headquarters*, p. 100; S. Millett Thompson, *Thirteenth Regiment of New Hampshire Volunteer Infantry in the War of the Rebellion, 1861–1865, A Diary Covering Three Years and a Day*, Boston, Houghton Mifflin Company, 1888, p. v.

29 Hampton S, Thomas, *Some Personal Reminiscences of Service in the Cavalry of the Army of the Potomac*, Philadelphia, L. R. Hamersly & Co., 1889, p. 9.

30 Meade, *Life and Letters*, vol. 2, p. 176.

31 Agassiz, *Meade's Headquarters*, pp. 81–82.

32 Philip. H. Sheridan, *Person Memoirs of P. H. Sheridan*, New York, Barnes and Noble, Reprint, 2006, p. 174.

33 Quoted in Starr, *Union Cavalry in the Civil War*, vol. 2, p. 77.

34 Morris Schaff, *The Battle of the Wilderness*, Boston, Houghton Mifflin Company, 1910, p. 282.

35 Tobie, *History of the First Maine Cavalry*, p. 248.

36 Starr, *Union Cavalry in the Civil War*, vol. 2, pp. 87, 92–93.

37 Stewart, *Camp, March and Battlefield*. pp. 375–379.

38 Vincent L. Burns, *The Fifth New York Cavalry in the Civil War*, Jefferson, NC, McFarland and Company, Publishers, 2014, pp. 178–182; William Royall, *Some Reminiscences*, New York, The Neale Publishing Company, 1909, p. 28; Louis N. Boudrye, *Historic Records of the Fifth New York Cavalry*, Albany, J. Munsell, 1868, p. 123.

39 A. L. Long, *Memoirs of Robert E. Lee*, New York, J. M. Stoddart & Company, 1886, p. 327.

40 Schaff, *The Battle of the Wilderness*, pp. 58–59; Stewart, *Camp, March and Battlefield*, p. 376; John B. Gordon, *Reminiscences of the Civil War*, New York, Charles Scribner's Sons, 1904, p. 237.

41 Agassiz, *Meade's Headquarters*, p. 90.

42 Wert, *Sword of Lincoln*, p. 342; John Day Smith, *The History of the Nineteenth Regiment Maine Volunteer Infantry, 1862–1865*, Minneapolis, The Great Western Printing company, 1909, pp. 146, 166.

43 Ibid., Smith, pp. 147–148.

44 James Hall to Mrs. Sarah Benedict, May 18, 1864, George D. Benedict Papers, Southern Historical Collection, Louis Round Wilson Library, University of North Carolina, Chapel Hill.

45 Wormeley, *The Other Side of War*, pp. 166, 195.

46 *O. R.*, Series 1, vol. XXXVI, Pt. 1, p. 789.

47 Rhea, *The Battles of Spotsylvania Court House*, pp 45–49.

48 Quoted in Rhea, Ibid., pp. 58–59.

49 Ibid., Rhea, pp. 65–66.

50 Wert, Sword of Lincoln, pp. 350–356.

51 Rhea, *The Battles of Spotsylvania Court House*, pp. 67–68.

52 Horace Porter, *Campaigning with Grant*, New York, D. Appleton, 1897, pp. 83–84.

53 Sheridan, *Memoirs*, p. 189.

54 Agassiz, *Meade's Headquarters*, pp. 105–106.

55 Agassiz, Ibid; Starr, *Union Cavalry in the Civil War*, vol. 2, p. 96; Porter, *Campaigning with Grant*, pp. 83–84.

56 Meade, *Life and Letters*, vol. 2, pp. 195–196.

57 Foster, *Reminiscences*, pp. 51–52; NYMM, 6th Regiment Cavalry, Roster.

58 Foster, Ibid, pp. 51–54.

59 Kidd, *Recollections*, p. 283.

60 Agassiz, *Meade's Headquarters*, p.102.

61 Ford, *A Cycle of Adams Letters*, vol. 2, pp. 131, 135.

62 Weld, *Diary and Letters*, pp. 302, 303, 306.

63 Carter, *Four Brothers*, pp. 389, 397.

64 Ibid., pp. 401–402.

65   Henry O. Nightingale, *Diaries*, Special Collections and Archives, University of California, Merced Library, www.library.ucmerced.edu

66   NYMM, 72nd Regiment Infantry, Peter Ostrye Letters.

Chapter Eleven

1   Mark de Wolfe, *Touched with Fire: Civil War Letters and Diary of Oliver Wendell Holmes, Jr., 1861–1864*, Cambridge, Harvard University Press, 1946, p. 121.

2   Boudrye, *Historic*, p. 127.

3   Beaudry, *War Journal*, p. 114.

4   George T. Stevens, *Three Years with the Sixth Corps*, 2nd Edition, New York, D. Van Nostrand, Publishers, 1870, pp. 333–344.

5   McPherson, *Battle Cry of Freedom*, p. 730, note 18. See also *Battles and Leaders*, vol. 4, pp. 173, 175–176.

6   Ibid., McPherson, pp. 730–731; de Wolfe, *Touches with Fire*, p. 117.

7   Ibid., McPherson, p. 732.

8   De Wolfe, *Touched with Fire*, pp. 121–122.

9   F. W. Morse, *Personal Experiences in the War pf the Great Rebellion from December 1862 to July, 1865*, Albany, private, 1866, pp. 100–102.

10   Michie, *Life and Letters of Emory Upton*, pp. 108–109.

11   Alanson A Haines, *History of the Fifteenth Regiment New Jersey Volunteers*, New York, Jenkins & Thomas, Printers, 1883, p. 208.

12   Ulysses S. Grant, *Personal Memoirs and Selected Letters*, New York, Literary Classics of the United States, 1990, p. 735.

13   McPherson, *Battle Cry of Freedom*, p. 735.

14   Martha Derby Perry, comp., *Letters from a Surgeon of the Civil War*, Boston, Little, Brown, and Company, 1906, p. 187.

15   Mason Whiting Tyler, *Recollection of the Civil War*, William S. Tyler, ed., New York, G. P. Putnam's Sons, 1912, pp. 210, 214.

16   McPherson, *Battle Cry of Freedom*, pp. 733–734.

17   Meade, *Life and Letters*, vol. 2, pp. 205–206.

18   Tyler, *Recollections*, p. 231.

19   McPherson, *Battle Cry of Freedom*, pp. 739–741.

20   Tyler, *Recollections*, p. 233.

21   Benjamin F. Clark, *History of the Twelfth Massachusetts Volunteers (Webster's Regiment)*, Boston, Twelfth (Webster) Regiment Association, 1882, pp. 137–138.

Chapter Twelve

1   Roy P. Basler, *The Collected Works of Abraham Lincoln*, 9 Volumes, Brunswick, NJ, Rutgers University Press, 1953–1955, vol. 7, p. 514.

2   Charles H. Banes, *History of the Philadelphia Brigade*, Philadelphia, J. B. Lippincott & Co., 1876, pp. 218–282; Arabella M. Willson, *Disaster, Struggle, Triumph: The Adventures of 1000 Boys in Blue*, Albany, Historical Committee of the Regiment, 1870, pp. 263–264; Agassix, *Meade's Headquarters*, p. 170.

3   Banes, *Philadelphia Brigade*, pp. 280–281.

4   Tyler, *Recollections*, pp. 277, 229.

5   Agassiz, *Meade's Headquarters*, p. 173.

6 McPherson, *Battle Cry of Freedom*, pp. 740–741.

7 Ibid., p. 742.

8 Ibid., p. 743; Morris Schaff, *Battle of the Wilderness*, p. 38.

9 Ibid., pp. 756–757.

10 Stevens, *Three Years with the Sixth Corps*, pp. 376, 381.

11 Agassiz, *Meade's Headquarters*, pp. 199–201.

12 Ibid., pp. 208–209, 214–215.

13 Ibid., pp. 204, 212.

14 Ibid., p. 226.

15 Henry Warren Howe, *Passages from the Life of Henry Warren Howe Consisting of Diary and Letters Written During the Civil War, 1861–1865*, Lowell, MA, private, 1899, p. 176.

16 Ford, *A Cycle of Adams Letters*, vol. 2, pp. 221–222.

17 Luman Harris Tenney, *War Diary … 1861–1865*, Cleveland, Evangelical Publishing House, 1914, p. 34.

18 Agassiz, *Meade's Headquarters*, p. 259.

19 NYMM, 1st Regiment Dragoons, Green Letters.

20 James R. Bowen, *History of the First New York Dragoons*, Published by the Author, 1900, pp. 264–267, 263–264.

21 Tenney, *War Diary*, p. 136.

22 Bowen, *First Dragoon*, pp. 271–274.

Chapter Thirteen

1 Joshua Lawrence Chamberlain, "Military Operations on White Oak Road, Virginia, March 31, 1865," in *War Papers Read Before the Commandery of the State of Maine, Military Order of the Loyal Legion of the United States*, Portland, The Thurston Print, 1898, p. 248; Frederick Newhall, *With Sheridan in Lee's Last Campaign*, Philadelphia, J. B. Lippincott & Co., 1866, 118; *O. R.*, Series 1, vol. XLVI, Pt. 1, pp. 836–837.

2 Joshua Lawrence Chamberlain, *The Passing of the Armies: Personal Reminiscences of the Fifth Army Corps*, New York, Bantam Books, reprint, 1913, pp. xvii–xviii.

3 Ibid., *O. R.*

4 William Henry Locke, *The Story of a Regiment*, Philadelphia, J. B. Lippincott & Co., 1868, p. 393.

5 John L. Smith, comp., *History of the Corn Exchange Regiment, 118th Pennsylvania Volunteers*, Philadelphia, John L. Smith, Publisher, 1888, pp. 580–581; *O. R.*, Ibid., p. 836.

6 Newhall, *With Sheridan*, pp. iv–v.

7 Chamberlain, *Passing of the Armies*, p. 120.

8 Ulysses S. Grant, *Personal Memoirs and Selected Letters*, New York, Literary Classics of the United States, 1990, pp. 701–702; See Andrew A Humphreys, *The Virginia Campaigns of '64 and 65* New York, Charles Scribner's Sons, 1903, p. 57.

9 Longacre, *Lincoln's Cavalrymen*, p. 334.

10 Luman Harris Tenney, *War Diary of … 1861–1865*, Cleveland, Evangelical Publishing House, 1914, pp. 149, 153.

11 Ibid.

12 Hyde, *Following the Greek Cross*, pp. 256–258.

13 Locke, *The Story of a Regiment*, p. 394.

14 Robert Tilney, *My Life in the Army: Three Years and a Half in the Fifth Corps, Army of the Potomac, 1862–1865*, Philadelphia, Ferris and Leach, 1912, p. 199.

15   Chauncey S. Norton, *The Red Neck Ties, or the History of the Fifteenth New York Volunteer Cavalry*, Ithaca, N.Y., Journal Book and Job Printing House, 1871, p. 73.

16   Starr, *The Union Cavalry*, vol. 2, p. 467; Tobie, *History of the First Maine Cavalry*, p. 413.

17   John L. Parker, *Henry Wilson's Regiment: History of the Twenty-second Massachusetts Infantry*, Boston, Regimental Association, 1887, p. 585; Smith, *History of the Corn Exchange Regiment*, p. 398.

18   Haines, *History of the Fifteenth New Jersey*, p. 309; Smith, *History of the Corn Exchange Regiment*, p. 593.

19   R. C. Wallace, *A Few Memories of a Long Life*, private, nd, p. 41.

20   Wallace, *Memories*, pp. 42, 44; Chamberlain, *Passing of the Armies*, p. 196.

21   James R. Bowen, *Regimental History of the First New York Dragoons*, Published by the Author, 1900, p. 297; Smith, *History of the Corn Exchange* Regiment, p. 596.

22   Norton, *Army Letters*, p. 355; Chamberlain, *Passing of the* Armies, p. 205.

23   Gerrish, *Army Life*, p. 261.

24   Meade, *Life and Letters*, vol. 2, pp. 270–271.

25   Quoted in Foote, *The Civil War*, vol. 3, p. 893.

26   H. P. Moyer, comp., *History of the Seventeenth Regiment Pennsylvania Volunteer Cavalry*, Lebanon, PA, Sowers Printing Co., 1911, pp. 154, 156.

27   Norton, *Army Letters*, pp. 259–260, 173.

28   Margaret Leech, *Reveille in Washington, 1860–1865*, New York, Garden City Publishing, Inc., nd, p. 415; Norton, *The Red Neck Ties*, p. 81.

29   Leech, *Reveille*, 416.

30   Noah Brooks, *Washington in Lincoln's Time*, New York, The Century Co., 1895, p. 317; Roemer, *Reminiscences*, p. 31.

31   Brooks, *Washington*, p. 323.

32   Leech, *Reveille*, p. 417.

33   Ibid., pp. 418–419.

34   Noble Preston, *History of the Tenth Regiment of Cavalry, New York State Volunteers, August 1861 to August, 1865*, New York, D. Appleton, 1892, pp. 263–264.

35   Wallace, *Memories*, pp. 43–44.

36   Ibid., Introduction, np.

37   Norton, *The Red Neck Ties*, p. 86.

38   New York Legislature, *Report of the Adjutant General's Office*, Albany, Argus, 1895; *New York Times*, April 5, 1879.

39   Arabella M. Wilson, *Disaster, Struggle, Triumph: The Adventures of 1000 Boys in Blue*, Albany, Historical Committee of the Regiment, 1870, pp. 293–294.

40   Thompson. *Thirteenth Regiment of New Hampshire*, pp. 634, 631.

41   Ibid., p. 635.

42   Chamberlain, *Passing of Armies*, p. 299.

Conclusion: Again, Remembrance as History

1   Hall, *Sixth New York Cavalry*, p. 202; Stewart, *Camp, March, and Battlefield*, p. 353; Quoted in Faust, *Republic of Suffering*, p. 268; *Speeches of Oliver Wendell Holmes*, Boston, Little, Brown and Company, 1896, p. 5.

2   Palmer, *The Second Brigade*, p. 3.

3   M. H. MacNamara, *The Irish Ninth in Bivouac and Battle: or Virginia and Maryland Campaigns*, Boston, Lee and Shepard, 1867, p. 244; Martin A. Haynes, *A Minor War History: A Soldier Boy's Letters to the Girl I Left Behind Me, 1861–1864*, Lakeport, NH, private, 1916, Preamble.

4   Foster, *Reminiscences*, pp. 15–17.

5   Henry Cribben, *The Military Memoirs of Captain Henry Cribben of the 140th New York Volunteers*, Chicago, 1911, pp. vi–v.

6   The Society of the Army of the Potomac, *Report of the Sixteenth Annual Reunion, at Baltimore, MD, May 6 and 7, 1885*, New York, MacGowan & Slipper, 1885, pp. 10–12.

7   Ibid., pp. 73–74.

8   Bliss Perry, *The Life and Letters of Henry Lee Higginson*, Boston, The Atlantic Monthly Press, 1921, p. 196, Note 1.

9   Dunaway, *Reminiscences of a Rebel*, pp. 5, 127–131, 133.

10   *O. R.*, Series I, vol. XXXVI, Pt. 1, p. 844.

11   Howard Aston, *History and Roster of the Fourth and Fifth Independent Battalions and Thirteenth Regiment Ohio Cavalry Volunteers*, Columbus, Press of Fred J. Heer, 1902, p. 13.

12   Hall, *Sixth New York Cavalry*, p. 202.

13   New York Legislature, *Report of the Adjutant General's Office*, 1895, NYMM, 6th Regiment Cavalry, *Fanshaw Collection*.

14   Henry Warren Howe, *Passages from the Life of Henry Warren Howe Consisting of Diary and Letters Written During the Civil War, 1861–1865*, Lowell, MA, private, 1899, pp. 182, 8.

15   James Madison Stone, *Personal Recollections of the Civil War*, Boston, private, 1918, pp. 6, 192.

16   Hyde, *Following the Greek Cross*, p. 14.

17   Bowen, *Regimental History of the First New York Dragoons*, p. 116.

18   Quoted in Miller, *Drum Taps in Dixie*, p. 116.

19   Faust, *Republic of Suffering*, pp. 249, 267.

20   *Speeches of Oliver Wendell Holmes*, pp. 3–5, 11.

21   Leech, *Reveille*, p. 418.

22   NYMM, 6th Regiment Cavalry, *James Little Diary*; Hyde, *Following the Greek Cross*, p. 269.

23   NYMM, 85th Regiment Infantry, *Rathbun Collection*; 40th Regiment Infantry, *Cobb Collection*.

24   Samuel Eliot Morrison, Henry Steel Commager, William E. Leuchtenberg, *The Growth of the American Republic*, 2 Vols., New York, Oxford University Press, 1969, vol. 2, pp. 148–149.

25   Morison, *Growth of the American Republic*, vol. 2, p. 163; E, Benjamin Andrews, *The History of the Last Quarter Century in the United States, 1870–1895*, 2 vols., New York, Charles Scribner's Sons, 1896, vol. 2, p. 111.

26   Quoted in Morison, *Growth of the American Republic*, vol. 2, p. 164.

27   Andrews, *History of the Last Quarter Century*, vol. 2, p. 112.

28   Dawes, *Service with the Sixth Wisconsin*, pp. 297, 306.

29   James Ford Rhodes, *History of the United States from Hayes to McKinley, 1877–1896*, New York, The MacMillan Company, 1919, pp. 294–300.

30   D. A. O'Mara, comp., *Fifth-ninth Reg't, New York Veteran Volunteers: Report of Proceeding, Reunion and Roster of Surviving Member*, New York, private, 1889, pp. 7, 11, 12, 28, 29, 31, 36.

31   Quoted in John A. Garrity, *The New Commonwealth, 1877–1900*, New York, Harper and Row, Publishers, 1968, pp. 296, 298.

32   Andrews, *History of the Last Quarter Century*, vol. 2, pp. 113–114.

33   Rhodes, *History … from Hayes to McKinley*, p. 332.

34   Quote in Rhodes, Ibid.

35   Tobies, *First Mane Bugle*, pp. 52–53. Mugwumps was the name given to reform minded elements within the Republican Party at this time.

36   Morrison, *Growth of the American Republic*, vol. 2, p. 167; Harold U. Faulkner, *Politics, Reform and Expansion, 1890–1900*, New York, Harper and Row, 1959, p. 97; Andrews, *History of the Last Quarter Century*, vol. 2, p. 174; Rhodes, *History … from Hayes to McKinley*, p. 332; Eric Foner,

Reconstruction: America's Unfinished Revolution, 1863–1877, New York, Harper Collins, 1988, p. 23; Richard White, *The Republic for which it Stands: The United States during Reconstruction and the Gilded Age, 1865–1896,* New York, Oxford University Press, 2017, p. 632.

37   Dawes, *Service with the Sixth Wisconsin*, pp. 314–315, 316–317.

38   Palmer, *Second Brigade*, p. 212.

Index